CW00739507

Rich is
Beautiful

RICHARD D NORTH

Richard D North (born 1946) has written for most of Britain's broadsheets and the *Wall Street Journal, Europe.* He has been a talking head or pundit on many British TV and radio current affairs shows, and has written and presented, or appeared in, several radio and TV documentaries. Much of his recent work is available at www.richarddnorth.com.

Editor, www.direct-action.info, 2004–present
Editor, www.livingissues.com, 2003–present
Media Fellow, Institute of Economic Affairs, 2001–present
Sunday Times: Environment Columnist, 1990–92
Independent: Environment Correspondent, 1986–90
Vole, Editor, 1980–81

BOOKS

Life On a Modern Planet: A manifesto for progress,
Manchester University Press and St Martin's Press, New York, 1995.
Fools For God, Collins, 1987.
Schools for Tomorrow, Green Books, 1987.
Working the Land (with Charlie Pye-Smith), Temple Smith, 1985.
The Real Cost, Chatto & Windus, 1984.
Wild Britain, Century, 1983.
The Animals Report, Penguin, 1982.

PAMPHLETS

Risk: The human adventure, Institute of Economic Affairs, 2000.
GMOs at the Start of the Troubled Biological Century, 2001
(at iea.org.uk).
Fur and Freedom: A defence of the fur trade, Institute of Economic Affairs, 2000.
Hereditary Peers: The case as yet unheard, Social Affairs Unit, 1999.
The Hunt at Bay: A defence of deer hunting, Wildlife Network, 1999.

Rich is Beautiful

A VERY PERSONAL DEFENCE OF MASS AFFLUENCE

Richard D North

THE SOCIAL AFFAIRS UNIT

© The Social Affairs Unit 2005

British Library Cataloguing in Publication Data
A catalogue record of this book is available from the British Library

Book production by Crowley Esmonde Limited
Printed and bound in the United Kingdom

ISBN 1-904863-02-7

Social Affairs Unit
314-322 Regent Street
London W1B 5SA
www.socialaffairsunit.org.uk

DEDICATION

For VB, with much love

CONTENTS

A personal manifesto   11

CHAPTER 1 Introduction   13
CHAPTER 2 Mass affluence and happiness   35
CHAPTER 3 Mass affluence and inequality   64
CHAPTER 4 Mass affluence and globalization   84
CHAPTER 5 Mass affluence and status   108
CHAPTER 6 Mass affluence and society   155
CHAPTER 7 Mass affluence and corruption   184
CHAPTER 8 Mass affluence and spirituality   197
CHAPTER 9 Mass affluence and 'sustainable development'   221
CHAPTER 10 Mass affluence and the real modern malaises   242
CHAPTER 11 Conclusion   261

APPENDICES

I   RDN's prejudices   267
II   RDN's special heroes   284
III A note on spirituality   292
IV   Ivan Illich's Radical Monopoly   295

Index   297

ACKNOWLEDGEMENTS

I am very grateful to Michael Mosbacher of the Social Affairs Unit for suggesting that I write this book, and for finding some funding for it.

SPELLING AND WEBSITES

I have generally used UK English spellings. I cannot bring myself, however, to see 'globalization' without a 'z' and have broken my rule for all the permutations of that word. I have tried to keep quotations in whatever form the original had.

While every effort has been made to verify web addresses, I can obviously offer no guarantee that any given site will remain active, or that its content will remain appropriate.

'LIBERAL', 'NEO-LIBERAL', ETC.

The world 'liberal' is a nightmare. It shifts meanings as it crosses the Atlantic and according to whether it is being said admiringly or sneeringly. I use 'liberal' to mean kindly, left-leaning people who are socially permissive but politically correct, and who would like a larger State Take than I would. I use 'neo-liberal' to imply the drier sort of 'low-taxes' economic liberal most commonly found in the US but imitated elsewhere. I use 'Enlightenment Liberal' to evoke the person who believes that liberties matter and are conflicted. I don't use 'liberal' to mean 'libertarian' (as I might if I were a German).

A PERSONAL MANIFESTO

We live in the best of times. We are applying more knowledge than humans ever have to the business of being the conscious corner of the universe. Wherever we look, education and democracy are spreading, and even where they aren't, the economic logic and the moral spirit of the times is working towards them. Much more deliberately than previous generations, we are working out how to respect each other, while at the same time enjoying ourselves. More and more people are free to live chosen, deliberate, lives. We can see nothing on the horizon that will seriously dent the unfolding of human life. But we are not omniscient (we don't know what will happen next), and we are not saints (virtue is not our big thing). Beyond a certain rather limited point, we can't prepare for every eventuality, and can't or won't care about everyone around us, or the unborn.

The upshot is that we can't and won't be unduly cautious or virtuous. The good we do each other is more personal or unintended than moralists might like. But there is plenty of good being done. Not least, our greed, and the capitalism that flows from it, are forces for good.

It has taken a while for me to understand these things. I want this book to describe the way that I do so: that is, wholeheartedly and (if it is not too pretentious to say so) intellectually, too. A year or so ago, a friend said she thought it was a pity that 'you hold views that only your charm makes acceptable'. She meant, I think, that holding these views amused me, but wasn't sustainable except as a sort of theatre. In 1993, Richard Mabey, the naturalist and writer, came up to me at an exhibition of Walter Sickert's paintings at the Royal Academy and said: 'You don't really hold these views. You're in denial.' (Just logically, that's a hard rap to beat, of course.) This book is intended to show the paths – the evidence and the circumstances – by which I have arrived at these positions. (An appendix expands on the more personal of these paths.)

I have experienced what felt like deep inner peace in a monastic cell, and in a first-class seat on a jumbo jet. Bliss has all but knocked me off my feet a few metres from a speaker-stack at a rock concert, and come upon me lying on my back in a snowdrift in the Arctic. I shouldn't like to say which was the more profound experience.

I have elected to defend Mass Affluence because it is the world of getting and spending that is most, and most widely, criticised by intellectuals at the moment, as it has been increasingly over the centuries. Concentrating on wealth has been criticised as bad for people and societies. These critics are, I believe, blinded by the selfishness and the materialism that lie behind our affluent world. I argue that we need to look through the apparent bleakness of these features of human life, and see the excitement and vigour that Mass Affluence represents.

Modern culture does, of course, have its flaws; but every age has those. The deepest flaw would be to believe that we ought to be above struggle, vulgarity and animal spirit. We would be wrong if we were to say we should disdain stuff and think mostly of spirituality or society. Rather, we should see that stuff, animal spirit, society and spirituality are all of a piece. Of course, reflection and reform are necessary – but so is pressing on. We have to try to take the whole of life's realities and see what is unfolding in them.

Most of my influences are those of any middle-brow person of any age. It is very conventional to say it, but the life of Erasmus (and my rather small reading of his work) set me alight when I was at school. Among 'contemporary' people older than me, at or after school I read H A L Fisher (on European history), A J P Taylor (on modern British history), Paul Johnson (on any of his subjects), Gibbon on Empire, Philip Zeigler (on Melbourne, especially), Isaiah Berlin (on liberty), Antony Flew (on the history of philosophy); of people about my own age, or a little older, there is Roy Strong (on Englishness), the late Roy Porter (on the Enlightenment), Tom Stoppard (on nearly everything).

For more on my prejudices and what has influenced me, see the Appendices.

CHAPTER 1

INTRODUCTION

A handful of propositions sum up this book. Here they are, in note form:
Our manners are not what they might be. What else is new?
Our morals, likewise.
Those who get rich do good.
Mass Affluence has turned us all into aristocrats.
Grace and gratitude are the keys to combining wealth and well-being.
Wealth is good. The more the merrier.
Societies that are good at creating wealth are good at spreading it.
There is less poverty now, and much less inequality than supposed.
'Stuff, space and speed' are not the enemies of spirituality.[1]
People are not often conned by capitalists.
Class is dead, long live class.
Only extreme inequality makes for a bad society.
Modern malaises require a 'rightward' drift in politics.

OUR 'BIG IDEA'
The central proposition of the book is that 'The System' is not failing 'The People'. Rather, they are failing it.

THE CRITICS OF MASS AFFLUENCE IN A NUTSHELL
A year or so ago, Matthew Taylor, a highly intelligent adviser to New Labour, remarked on BBC TV's *Newsnight*, 'You don't have to believe that capitalism's evil to know that it's doing your head in.' It was a classic modern view: not old-hat socialist, and yet laden with disquiet about the state of the modern world and mind.

And then, here is the present Archbishop of Canterbury, a man praised for his intellect, in his *Writing In the Dust* (a reflection on the world after the 9/11 atrocity): 'Every transaction in the developed economies of the West can be interpreted as an act of aggression against the economic losers in the worldwide game.'² This is the classic modern howl against globalization, a process that is seen as imperialism dressed up for an age that uses satellites and consumer goods instead of gunboats.

These are two crucial, popular responses to the modern world that I want to expose as thoughtless, heartless and bereft of spiritual value.

IN A BIT MORE DETAIL

Wealth, lots of it and widely available, is lovely and good. Mass Affluence has been desired for centuries and is desired now, where and when we have it; and even more when and where we don't. Yet it has few defenders. Most right-wingers take it as self-evident that wealth is good, and haven't bothered with the idea that it might be a problem. The left used just to dislike the way wealth was created and spread, but have now out-flanked the right with new charges.

A recent spate of leftish books, and the *Zeitgeist* of liberal opinion, has it that capitalism has invaded our minds, and made us live a life that is driving us half mad. Capitalism is, of course, trying to get us to be avid consumers, but the real harm caused to modern people stems from the Anxiety Industry³ and its new branch office, the Status Anxiety Industry. These industries come from a pseudo-dissident culture, which denigrates nearly everything that is valuable, including Mass Affluence, wealth creation and the political and legal structures that help create wealth and preserve many other important liberties. One of its dislikes is globalization. (I say 'pseudo-dissident' because these critics are at the heart of academia and journalism: they are as much a part of the main-stream, mortgage-holding, pension-owning Mass Affluent as the rest of us.)

The pseudo-dissident culture almost always misses the point. It is, of course, itself a globalizing force (for good or ill) since liberalism of any kind (even bad liberalism) is a universalist creed. In rather the same way, anti-commercialism is condemned by modernity to deploy the tools it affects to hate. Naomi Klein, for instance, wants to be a world influence; she desires to be globalized and probably does not disdain to be affluent, and so has submitted to becoming a brand in herself. But more interestingly, she does not mention that the anti-Establishment crowd has always had brands and has been brilliant at promoting them. It does seem fair to say that self-promoting, or promoted, heroes – especially cult heroes – get discussed and imaged as life-enhancing in the special brand way. It is not merely the merit of their work that gets promoted, but something more luminous, too. Heroes such as Byron, Che Guevara and Dylan are just as iconic as Coca-Cola, and probably more powerful. So, in his day, was my own hero, Erasmus. Note, for instance, how

Madonna – who, many years ago, tired of parodying the Virgin Mary (literally an icon) – was dressed as Che for one of her recent posters. While we're at it, we should note that these images were flyposted around London in the manner of a dissident political message. A middle-aged mother, let alone a millionaire, ought perhaps to know that no message is worth this form of littering. Likewise, George Monbiot ought to have considered whether it was socially aware of him to allow his book to be flyposted around town.

To be sure, elements of the old socialist complaints remain, dressed up in new clothes. Accordingly, modern working methods oppress in modern ways; even now wealth is being spread poorly; the rich are now too grossly rich; a new crass materialism – Trash Affluence – has dumbed us down. But the really modern left has a wholly new, modern complaint of a completely different order. This new beef is that the Mass Affluent have had their brains bent. Like railway companies who blame 'the wrong kind of leaves', or highways managers whose gritters complain of the 'wrong kind of snow', we now have 'the wrong sort' of consciousness about wealth.

This new version of Marxian 'false consciousness' means, one supposes, that the Mass Affluent do not know that they do not like their lives; do not notice that they are bamboozled into consuming; and cannot exercise their democratic power to achieve the leftward drift in society that liberals desire.[4]

These new critics of wealth and of Mass Affluence stress the vulnerability of us all in the face of the very social machinery – the capitalism and industrialisation and the power structures – that has enriched us. Some suggest that we have sacrificed too much to satisfy man's ancient urge to be rich, and that The System has blinded us to its depredations as it half delivers its promise to enrich us, but actually enslaves us. Above all, they say, we are self-enslaved by materialism and ambition. Interestingly, these new critics are making a case that flourished in a tiny ghetto of people who read Ivan Illich in the 1970s.[5]

These new critics bring a fresh vigour to the left's hatred of neo-liberalism, which, they assert, allows capitalism to do its work too brutally. This neo-liberal capitalism (they assert) is vicious and brutal, as it sweeps virtue away in its quest for profit. Above all it is efficient in its own interests, driving prices down and decency out. Very much is made, these days, of the supermarkets and their indifference to the farmer in their pursuit of cheap food. But I counter that this is an important example of a misreading of capitalism's purposes. Capitalism has no interest in cheap food or in miserable producers. Capitalism, in the form of (some) supermarkets, simply recognises that customers care about prices, not farmers. In the form of the boutique organics business, it recognises that some people want something different: and it delivers that too.

The anti-capitalist argument does not castigate all the capitalist economies equally. The new critics of Mass Affluence reserve their severest strictures for the Anglosphere, personified by the hell-for-leather US and the increasingly look-alike UK. They approve rather more of the Franco-German Continentals and the Scandinavians.

THE ENEMIES OF MASS AFFLUENCE

The old socialist left is more or less dead. State ownership of the 'commanding heights of the economy', prices and wages policy, 'picking winners', the rights of unions to impose undemocratic closed shops – all these economic shibboleths are gone.

The big, newish, leftish thesis – articulated most clearly by Will Hutton – is that modern capitalism creates staggering amounts of wealth, but has been hijacked by a neo-liberal mindset that ensures the wealth accumulates in surprisingly few hands, and makes surprisingly few of us happy.[6] This neo-liberalism, it is claimed, has destroyed social – mostly mildly communitarian – values, and thus vindicates a return to a largely leftward way of looking at society, after its apparent defeat in the 'end of history' triumph of democracy and capitalism. Part of this criticism of modern economic life stems from a feeling that modern workers are exploited: overworked, insecure, and instruments of corporate needs, rather than dignified partners in wealth creation. As we shall see, Richard Sennett articulates this view perhaps most clearly, though Madeline Bunting has recently been writing about the overworked culture from a UK perspective.

A softer version of this has been adopted by Adair Turner, the erstwhile director of the Confederation of British Industry (CBI). The line is also reflected by several *Financial Times* writers, and the paper's leader pages.[7] The new leftward view is not anti-capitalist in the way of 'old' socialism. But it quite often renounces the 'Third Way' accommodation between leftish politicians and their capitalist allies. Clinton and Blair were, according to this view (articulated best by Clive Hamilton), suckered by the capitalists into running the economy on free-market principles. This point of view is argued clearly by Robert Reich, one of Clinton's economic policy experts.[8]

The newer charge focuses on the cultural and psychological damage done by consumerism. Martin Jacques wrote in the *Guardian* that consumer culture has hijacked the fabric of our lives and eroded human intimacy. We use technology to communicate more, but our family life is damaged. We are money rich and time poor. We are voyeurs, using the media to consume emotions at one remove. Stripped of meaning, life becomes shopping.[9] Classic stuff, but probably not a good diagnosis of the 'profound malaise at the heart of Western society' (as Jacques has it), nor of its causes.

The standard analysis assumes that we are less happy than we used to be, especially given that we are materially richer now. It develops into an argument that everything we have sacrificed in order to become richer is to be mourned. A major theme of some critics of affluence is that our happiness is essentially relativistic: we can only be happy if we are doing better than someone else, or if we have a 'pack' seniority, which depends on others being poorer, more miserable or weaker than we are. Our being richer can't make any difference to the fact of difference, so we might just as well not sacrifice too much to become wealthier.

These critics can be corralled into two broad camps.

THE FIRST CAMP

One camp bases its criticisms on economic and moral grounds. The core of their argument is that neo-liberal economics has produced a winner-takes-all economics, whose biggest success has been in persuading the majority that they are not losing out. This brand of critic includes:

Will Hutton[10]
Hutton argues that Anglo-Saxon neo-liberal economics leads to extreme inequality and must be reformed in favour of a more internationalist and Continental European model. Critics like Hutton wish that the UK would shift further from, say, the US approach and toward the Continental. Fine, if the electorate can be persuaded – which doesn't seem likely in the immediate future.

John Gray[11]
Gray's view is that the global free market is robbing all institutions – including states and multinational corporations – of power and decency. We see this, he thinks, in the nastiness of right-wing America, and in the economic crises in Asia, Russia and elsewhere in the 1990s. His work has several internal contradictions, however. The big message seems to be that the world's economies are in a crisis, which we insist on not seeing.

Joseph Stiglitz[12]
This academic turned (Clinton) official turned World Bank adviser tells his story of a move from relatively pure to positively wicked worlds (via the conflicted, though good-hearted, Clinton administration) as a sort of morality tale. The message is largely that globalization and markets are good, but that the international institutions of financial and development administration and aid (the WTO, IMF, and World Bank) are under the sway of neo-liberal brutalists, and are in need of large-scale re-visioning and reform. Stiglitz is vastly admired by the more realistic

of the Seattle-style protestors, and their more grown-up gurus (such as Will Hutton).

The difficulty with Stiglitz's account is to know whether his reforms – especially of international finance – would be any kinder than the present situation. Kindly liberal experts do not think so.

Godfrey Hodgson[13]

Hodgson argues that the American Dream has been betrayed by power-ful interests, which produce wealth for a minority, while the poor and middle classes become poorer. Naturally, this is an argument with great resonance in the US, where it forms the basis of the discussion between the Democrats and the Republicans (and even more between Michael Moore and P J O'Rourke). Interestingly, this argument assumes that the Democrats have been forced by the vulgarities of big-dollar electioneer-ing into the maw of the corporates. Thus, in this view, the Democrats of the Third Way are much more neo-liberal than they want to be.

Hodgson implies that the shift is a consequence of the deep conser-vatism of the American people:

In response to national revulsion – it is not too strong a word – against the per-ceived errors and dangers of the Kennedy-Johnson Great Society programmes and of the political turmoil of the 1960s, the American majority accepted a polit-ical culture dominated by corporate business and dedicated to proclaiming the supremacy of free-market capitalism as a value equal to democracy itself.

It is worth noting key features of this analysis: it allows that the shift is a genuinely popular (if populist) one; it asserts that corporations now dominate; and that people now believe capitalism to be a 'value'. The first is true; the second is doubtful; the third seems absurd. It is an analysis shared by Thomas Frank of the US magazine *The Baffler*, whose *What's the Matter With America* discusses the 'Great Backlash', and the genius of the Republicans in getting more people to vote against their economic interests – lured by 'wedge issues' such as abortion and prayer in schools.[14]

George Monbiot[15]

Noticing that western governments have sought to devolve many of their activities and assets to the private sector, Monbiot calls this a 'corporate takeover'. It might, more accurately, have been called a state give-away. Modern governments are deliberately hiving off regulation and provision of public services. Monbiot is not a good guide to the mistakes that are inevitably being made as these reforms progress. For that, one needs journalists who do not especially want the initiatives to fail, as he does (the *FT* and *Economist* give rounder accounts). Monbiot believes that big business subverts democracy and decency. He matters, because he is by far the most popular figure in these arguments: British, populist and radical, he is the new Tony Benn of our age, and has a dash of the green (which Benn never achieved).

Noreena Hertz[16]
The most fashionable of the anti-globalizers, Hertz takes the worldwide privatisation and outsourcing (especially of manufacturing) trends in particular, and blames them for impoverishing people while transferring power from voters and governments, and toward unelected corporations (who buy politicians). Thus, at a meeting in the Royal Geographical Society's Knightsbridge HQ, she remarked: 'Young people aren't interested in politics. They feel excluded, they feel that governments have handed power to the corporates and the markets.' This in spite of the close regulation of multinationals, which remain cultural and legal entities closely tied to their western origins, and, to that extent, among the most disciplined organisations working in the Third World. (We look, in a later chapter, at the problem that modern democrats are over-informed, over-consulted, and perversely discontented.)

Professor Lord Richard Layard
Perhaps the most interesting of these critics is Professor Lord Richard Layard, and I deal with his criticisms in a later chapter on happiness.

THE SECOND CAMP

The other camp bases its criticisms on cultural and psychological grounds. The core of their argument is that we're rich but unhappy. An important subset contains those who believe we are unhappy because, instead of ancient wants that are satisfiable, capitalists have planted needs in us that cannot be satisfied. Critics from this general camp include:

Naomi Klein[17]
Naomi Klein's book is second-rate and really quite important. Though almost all her evidence and insights are second-hand, more even than Hertz's, she brought a leftish and radical set of views to a new, young coffee-table market.

Klein argues against all the old evils exposed by leftist analysis, but makes (actually she only retails) the more novel proposition that corporations and their image makers now sell lifestyle rather than product. I deal with these arguments at some length later.

Alain de Botton[18]
This philosopher argues that western thought has long wrestled with the problem that people want to feel superior to their fellows (especially their immediate fellows) and that they constantly strive for new pleasures,

which pall almost immediately they've been achieved. He advances the case, but rightly doesn't make much of an argument, that Status causes more Anxiety than it used to. I shall argue that there is rather too little Status Anxiety now.

Oliver James[19]

James argues that modern capitalism promises to satisfy people's wants, and fails to deliver because even affluent consumers realise they are still low-ranking in the pecking order – always the crucial determinant of their well-being. In the happy old days, he argues, people compared themselves with people closer to themselves, and thus were able to be large fishes in small pools. In a more leftward future, he suggests, people will have lower expectations and they will be easier to meet. Actually, I shall argue, modern people probably need to raise their expectations, and make higher demands on themselves.

Barry Schwartz[20]

Schwartz argues that people are psychologically swamped by the consumer choices they have, but also that consumers overestimate the pleasure they can have from the choices they make while shopping. 'Unlimited choice, I believe, can produce genuine suffering', he writes. He cites the amount of shirts and jeans he now has to choose between. Celebrating the way he can now get a better fit, he bemoans the strain of picking them out. He doesn't seem to spot that the answer is to pick more or less at random, and thus replicate the haphazardness of old-fashioned shopping. Nor does he spot that the modern range of choice gives one the same effect that was once achieved by the elite with their bespoke tailoring. But that, presumably, was alright because it was a craftsman noting precisely the measurements and requirements of an individual, rather than a question of demographically savvy ranges being offered by computer-controlled stock systems. I can live with the latter and be glad clothes shopping takes so little of my time and budget. You want the old tailoring? It's always been around, and is making a comeback as a feature of Mass Affluence.

Barry Schwartz weighs in with a concern about choice, rather than the things chosen. He is worried about the consumer who is bombarded by choice, and who is all too aware of choices made badly. Such a consumer feels that there may be better choices that he might have made, or that others are making. So there is a kind of opportunity cost to choice. This person is tyrannised by choice. (Naomi Klein, in *No Logo*, argues that we are now defined by desires that advertisers define for us. This is what we might call the tyranny of mindshare.)

Schwartz's book is only partly about the interesting problems that are posed when people have many choices. His subtitle, 'Why more is less' is a double entendre: it applies both to the 'choice' of his main title and to the general 'less is more' thesis, which is covered by our other authors. He spends as much time rehearsing the many problems of the Layard–Hamilton–Easterbrook kind (see below). That's to say, he worries that people are too hung up on material, trivial more-ness to live their lives well.

Clive Hamilton[21]

Hamilton argues that consumer society has produced an answer to 'the economic problem' but has also produced an 'existential depression' and potential environmental destruction that can only be solved by moving to a post-scarcity society – a 'stationary state' – which understands man's deeper relations with nature.

He supposes that modern neo-liberal economics:

excludes the possibility that consumers may prefer to limit the choices available to them…and also the possibility that some consumers may prefer to live in a society free of a vast array of trivially differentiated products, pervasive advertising, and unrelenting attempts to persuade them that their consumption choices can make them happy.

These propositions are extraordinarily different. Western society allows people to limit their choices at will. Of course, however, we live in a society in which people promote their wares to one another. Those few that don't like this would have to take to the woods in a big way to avoid the commercialism most of the rest of us manage not to mind, or even to enjoy.

Hamilton suggests that a kind of emotional poverty is now common and problematic, and that it subsists alongside – is perhaps even caused by – Mass Affluence (as I call it). Spiritual poverty may increase as material poverty is banished, and may even increase because material poverty has been banished.

Hamilton argues that people are bombarded by invitations to consume, and are made all the more aware of the things they cannot choose (because they are too poor). We are on a merry-go-round, drugged or stunned into continued whirling, for fear of the whole thing stopping suddenly and hurling us off. On this account, modern affluence has nonetheless made us into people whose noses are forever pressed against shop windows: we may be better dressed and fed as we envy, but envy we do. We might call this the tyranny of consumerism.

Madeline Bunting[22]

The central paradox for Bunting is that it is not materialism that drives so many successful people to work so hard they have neither the spirit nor time to live properly. 'Money and the consumer goods we can buy with it don't tell the whole story of why some people in the high-skill, high-income, bracket are working harder. They don't explain why being busy is now a status symbol.' She agrees with a commentator who thinks that people have put their very selves on sale. She notes that the answer seems to be for people to get real and assert what they really want, either at their high-powered jobs, or by leaving them.

Richard Sennett[23]

This writer represents the big-boned, check-shirt sort of sociology, long on a mournful, experienced nostalgia for a world of workers and craftsmen rooted in their community and ethnicity. He argues that modern workers are exposed to too much risk and technology: they are simultaneously made to share the ups and downs of their callously entrepreneurial bosses, and robbed of the dignity of craft. In this view, people 'are always starting over': they never get a decent narrative going, never have human capital of their own.

Gregg Easterbrook

Easterbrook is perhaps the most interesting of these critics, and I deal with his arguments later.

THE RIGHT (AND CULTURAL SNOBS) AND MASS AFFLUENCE

Oddly, the identification of a wealth sickness – Affluenza – has created if not an alliance of left and right, at least an unusual confluence of concerns.

The right is capable of worrying about Mass Affluence. They worry about a barren and vulgar consumer materialism that Mass Affluence has created. Digby Anderson, a social conservative, wrote in his *All Oiks Now*[24] about the standards of behaviour in society, and this sort of critic reckons they see now a general diminution of manners. They attribute this, in part, to a new obsession with unbridled consumption. Road rage, binge drinking, rowdy city centres: these are results of affluence (like beer) reaching parts that never knew them before. 'When did people stop looking out for each other? When did they start dropping litter everywhere? Why can't I walk anywhere without dog shit?' asks Superintendent Peter Boyd in BBC TV's *Waking the Dead*, as he confesses to finding modern life depressing. It is a cry that constantly goes up from middle-aged, middle-class Britain.

There are also voices on the right that believe in cultural diversity. When the young rioted over globalization in Seattle, Michael Gove of *The Times* said he rather saw their point, especially as they had chosen the spiritual home of Starbucks in which to do it. He seemed to dislike the cultural smoothing of globalization. Roger Scruton, our foremost conservative philosopher, hates what he believes the supermarket and free trade have imposed on Britain's family farms. For many supporters of the Campaign to Protect Rural England (many of them retired middle-class people) the new wealth threatens older patterns of life, with out-of-town supermarkets, motorways, and a huge demand for houses in the rural landscape.

And then there are voices on the right that believe the old and benign patterns of tradition and class are being threatened by Mass Affluence, and these voices mourn the passing of the traditional relations between people – patterns that are capable of an almost mystical interpretation.

Deep in its lair, ancient British snobbery also growls. Wouldn't it be a turn-up for the conservative books if the masses weren't bright enough, or disciplined enough, to handle affluence and equality? Might they not have been better left quite poor and quite unfree?

There is, of course, snobbery on the left, too. Was not the left – at least the intellectual left – always a middle-class, academic and intellectual phenomenon? As we shall see, it takes an intellectual commentator such as Richard Hoggart to celebrate the old mores of a working class uncontaminated by TV and affluence. He roughs up the gloss by insisting that the working class was not stupidly charming, but more richly edged and vibrant than we suppose, with or without the predations of mass culture.

DEFENDING MASS AFFLUENCE

I prefer an argument that acknowledges that western capitalism is capable of improvement, as every human institution is. But the improvements are boring and minor, compared to the triumphs. The relatively unreconstructed capitalist western societies are very far from brutal, and preserve values that are useful. Those countries which aim to 'soften' capitalism are welcome, of course, to their own view and style, but they pay a price for them; and it's a price not all of us want to pay. If you prefer Germany or Denmark to the Anglosphere, the EU now makes moving between the two as easy as it was centuries ago, when globalization hadn't been named but was – in the form of migration – readily available.

I like an argument that suggests the West is just plain fortunate, and perhaps we in the Anglosphere are especially so, and that we will enjoy ourselves much more when we recognise it and are grateful for it. Lucky people ought to be gracious, and grateful, and if modern society has a failing, it is that we are not yet enjoined to be either. Our intellectuals, artists, our 'role models' tend to line up with the complaint, not the celebration. The 'problem' of wealth – perhaps especially in an age of Mass Affluence – is to remind ourselves that morals and manners matter as much as money.

I am very happy to believe that modern people have to assert a proper balance between getting and spending, and their more private lives. I am even content to believe that many people deceive themselves as to their own real interests. But I assert that these are moral and aesthetic issues for individuals, and that 'The System' will respond perfectly well to them almost wherever they decide to go. We need to stop blaming capitalism for our own failures of character.

MASS AFFLUENCE AND THE RIGHT

Modern Westerners are richer than any people in history, by a long way. Their wealth has produced, and been the product of, extraordinary human advance in nearly every way that any previous generation ever dreamed of, and in some ways they could not have conceived of. There is a problem with this affluence and these advances, and it is not often pointed out. For a couple of generations now, rather few people have faced any sort of moral challenge. Or better: rather few people have been aware that they face a moral challenge.

These reflections matter to right-wingers because it is we who insist that most problems in life are moral, not mechanical. Problems are to do with individuals, not societies. Whether people are rich or poor, what they make of either is a personal matter. It happens that nearly every voice in democratic society clamours for wealth, which the right is rather good at producing. Where the having of wealth produces problems for people, the right is rather able to say – conscience free – 'This is what you asked for, now you must make it work.'

The moral deficit of Mass Affluence arises because we have solved many of the problems that required people to be patient, courageous, forbearing and generous in the face of poverty. Instead, we have a new problem: we need to be patient, courageous, forbearing and generous in the face of affluence. In short, we have not made ourselves into morally worthwhile rich people. Our manners reflect this, of course. We will probably adjust both.

A tranche of recent writing and speaking discusses the moral deficit of the wealth-creating machinery from which we have benefited, and has been inclined to worry about the kind of wealth created. The more interesting difficulty is that we have democratised the old problem of advantage, and magnified it as well. *Noblesse* used to have to *oblige*, and now the masses ought to as well. Nobility was more common in the old aristocrats than is supposed, but – this being a vale of tears – very far from universal. Still, the modern problem is how to make the masses enjoy being aristocrats, and deal beautifully with this new challenge.

We will largely succeed in meeting the challenge. The challenge will be met very variously, and there will be many failures and much excitement. We know this, because the issues we now face are as old as the hills.

In effect, we can forget the history of the working class, and even of the lower reaches of the middle classes. That is all of merely archival curiosity now. All that they achieved and bore is of interest, but not of direct relevance to us now. No, it is to the long tradition of aristocratic advantage – its mores and morality – that we ought to turn. Like Greeks or Romans, we can look around and worry only about the obligations of the great. We need not worry about the well-being of the slaves or the plebs, because in our time these are machines. Measure ourselves against the standards of history's aristocrats, and we see how laughably we often fail. But also, we see plenty of instances of great success. Better still, we know we have templates by which to proceed, if we choose.

Those templates tell us that dealing with advantage can be public and private, hedonistic and moralistic, safe and dangerous. All these possibilities can aspire to and reach properly aristocratic qualities. We are not looking only for do-gooding modesty, for quiet niceness. But we are looking for grace and courage. People's lives may seem very material, or very spiritual, aesthetic or athletic, and they can still meet aristocratic high standards. The point is this: it is the richness of the responses we make to the extraordinary range of choices now before us that will mark us out as civilised or trashy.

The free-market sort of liberal defends people's freedom to do what they like unless it can be found to produce harm to others. We free-market types don't mind if they harm themselves, though there may be some benefit in pointing out the risk to them. Wealth is what happens in free societies, and it's best not to second-guess the vigour of the market which produces this wealth, nor the human instincts by which people queue up to be wealth creators, whatever the cost they personally incur in their ability or failure to achieve their goal.

Actually of course, the right has its moralisers. The traditionalists are authentic right-wingers, and there is much in the world of Mass Affluence that worries them. Even the free-market liberal has a dilemma if what people want seems to be foolish or, if not positively bad, then uninspiring or disappointing. He may hold his nose, as the traditionalist does, but he knows he is committed to wealth creation, whatever its vulgarities. And it is the vulgarity, the carelessness, the joylessness of some aspects of Mass Affluence that is the core of the current writing about modern economic achievement.

The left often argues, of course, as though wealth is bad in itself. It is acquired by abusing the poor, and it is spent as though the poor did not deserve generosity more than the rich deserve extravagance. The greens add to these charges the crime of environmental destruction, or planetary abuse. Both the left and the greens made their charges before Mass Affluence made so many people into villains. Where once it was easy to criticise the rich for being nasty, that is much harder now that there are so many of us. It is bad form, and bad politics, to criticise one's customer or constituents. So now the left's criticism of Mass Affluence is that the people have been duped. In one criticism, we – the affluent masses – have conned ourselves. In a rather commoner criticism, we have been duped by corporate power – and advertising.

In other words, where once one could dislike the rich – and even punish them politically – because they were wicked, or selfish, it is now necessary to see the affluent as being innocent, and perhaps even as victims. What a large change in so short a time: we have come to the point where we pity the affluent. The left is now not so much the scourge of evil, the corrector of wrongs, as the doctor to a sick society. The left is, of course, still doing its old work. It makes criticism, and seeks reform, of the status quo, the normal and the mainstream. Meanwhile, one strand of the right – the Conservative sort – continues its old work: defending the status quo and the mainstream, and wishing it would let go even more. The left sees failings, and suggests (or enforces) policy to address and redress them. The libertarian right suggests that – for good or ill – that's the way the world wags, and it's not half bad anyway.

This is a right-ish account of wealth and Mass Affluence. Since they are here, with us, and have been produced by the mainstream world, the right's old prejudice is to defend them. They are the product of people doing what they like (the libertarian strand) within an orderly society in which the rich flourish (the more traditional dimension). This is even more true now that so many are rich, and many more are likely soon to be so. Yet more than that: it is not implausible to suppose that, within a century or so, the vast majority of people can be lifted out of material want.

The left dislikes Mass Affluence because it is a wickedness made general, and perhaps because it has robbed the left of much of its core support: the resentful poor of yore. There is a strand of right-wing opinion – the traditionalist right – that can find itself disliking Mass Affluence. This strand of thought has a stiff-necked view of society in which the masses (always disliked by many on the right) have proved they are no better at being rich than they were at being poor. This is the view of the traditionalist Digby Anderson.

The 'traditionalist' right is quite different from the libertarian. It likes a view of society in which change is relatively slow, and traditions – even those that seem cruel – are preserved, rather than junked. It is happy with hierarchy, and with the view that societies are at their best when there are few rich and many who are much less rich. The muralist

Roger Scruton expresses this view: he sees something mystical and liberating in the disciplines of the old order of society. The progressive and libertarian right quite often agree. They see the point of liberty, the market, and science. But they are both often at odds with the traditional right, who mourn the decline of old-style religion, ceremony, mystery, class. The progressive and libertarian right sees Mass Affluence as the benign product of an energetic free people working within a market economy, while the traditional right sees it as the Mob getting it wrong again.

Most right-wingers are conflicted, of course. The pleasure of being on the right is that it provides equal licence both for an authoritarian, traditionalist point of view, and for a libertarian, progressive one. In respect of wealth, the traditionalist right-winger has the difficulty that he can hardly propose remedies for the Crass Affluence that worries him, without abandoning core right-ish values like enterprise, wealth creation and going with the flow. I understand and share the dilemma. So it is a particularly ripe pleasure to argue that Mass Affluence is highly defensible.

I can think the mass affluent wrong, and in many matters I do think they are. They are less than admirable, in my view, to find amusement in *Eastenders*, and in wearing Burberry baseball caps.[25] I cannot share their enthusiasm for 4x4 vehicles (one of the few extravagances I have not myself owned). I am pretty sure most school trips overseas are a waste of time and money. I find it very easy to inveigh against these lapses, and I often do. But I am not disposed to ban any of these things, or to deprive people of the new affluence that has made these bits of consumption so easily available to so many. Besides, I recognise that there are intelligent people – better than me – who do not share my disdain for any of them. These habits are – most of them – largely a matter of taste.

Mass Affluence has many attractive features. And it is one of its merits – not a demerit – that it has democratised some very teasing problems about how to behave when one has advantages. Life is a Vanity Fair. As one increases people's opportunities, they become more interesting. Mass Affluence has democratised the range of mistakes that people can make. They can do more good, be more creative, more generous – and they can be the opposite of all that, on a larger scale. My defence is characteristically right wing, in the sense that it does not expect people to be good, or perfectible. It does not altogether give up on the possibility of humans maturing, and ripening – but reformation is perhaps too strong a word for what might happen to them.

So this defence supposes that realism is of immense importance, as one approaches big moral questions. Human beings are wonderful:

various, infuriating, and interesting. The left seeks its satisfactions in producing more policy to put right the faults in human society. The right does not wholly resist these virtuous moves (we have our moralists), but it notes that they go sour – especially when they do not recognise the great merit of human vigour and variety.

This defence does not merely insist that the present is rather good, and that policy to reform it may well backfire. It supposes that life is more interesting when as many people as possible do what they want, get what they want, and have to face the resulting challenges. We assert that the freedom part of that equation tends to produce well-being: so much is traditional to supporters of the free market. The last proposition is the peculiar bit: that the unfolding of challenges – their being met and failed – makes life worth living.

People choose the problems of being rich, and more would do so, given the chance. Very few people choose the problems of being poor.

This business of the voluntary is not a sure guide: it is not a sufficient or a necessary defence of something having virtue and value. And yet it is preferable to compulsion. And when it is proposed that people should be compelled to give up something they freely choose, the proposer had better be very sure of the benefits that will follow. In short, I want to go further down this road to affluence. To retreat seems counterproductive – and cowardly. The critics of this journey – those who want to stop the world and get off, and shove the rest of us off too – seem to me to be humbugs. They are mostly huge beneficiaries of the world about which they complain, and have precious little idea how to improve the lot of those they affect to care about.

The poor were, on the whole, better off without socialists helping them. Socialists and other do-gooders are of little use to the Mass Affluent; they'd be better off mining the deep veins of goodness and usefulness in the traditions of the right.

THIS BOOK IS POLITICS-FREE

This book is a reactionary one: it is responding to the left's complaint that the powers that be and 'The System' are spoiling the life chances of 'The People'. It is a right-wing book: it likes the real world, but thinks it's a tough place. It is a free-market book: it likes the vigour of the modern economy and doesn't propose lots of policy to change it. It is a conservative book: it reminds us of the merits of the old aristocratic order. It is a libertarian book: it believes that people will make good choices – eventually. It is an authoritarian book: it believes people need social structures to thrive.

This is not, however, a political book. It proposes no policy, still less any party policy. I am a little rude about Tony Blair, but more because of his style of government than because of his rightward or leftward drift. And he is the first Chav PM, and that's worth a comment too.

But there is rather little room for political partisanship in our country. One of the issues this book addresses is the 'State Take': my coinage for the share of a country's wealth that is spent by the state. In modern Britain, as Rod Liddle remarked in the *Spectator*,[26] the main political contenders accept that the State Take is now, and will remain, about 40 per cent of GDP. The US has a much smaller tax take; Denmark a much larger one. The citizens of any of these countries are as likely to see themselves as victims of Mass Affluence. So I am not unduly excited about the supposed iniquity of a high or low State Take, and I am even less able to discern a party point to make about it in my own domestic political scene.

Actually, one could make a more general case that it is quite hard to detect a left-right tectonic rift between the parties. Suppose one wanted to see people pay what they can afford for 'public services' such as health and education. Suppose one wanted these to be universally available, even for the indigent and the feckless. Suppose one wanted the services to be provided in facilities owned by the private sector. Suppose one wanted most people – rich and poor – to be treated and educated in the same facilities.

Take these suppositions (they describe my own aspiration), and it is surely the case that they are neither obviously socialist nor conservative, and it will be moot whether it is the Tories or New Labour that will do most to make them happen, or not.

What is more, though they sometimes argue as though it were not the case, most critics of Mass Affluence should, logically, be as angry about Labour (or, in the US, Democrat) policies, as about Tory (or Republican) policies. Some are: no-one is angrier about Blair or Clinton than the people slightly to their left. All mainstream political parties in the West seek to make their peoples rich, and say they have. It was firms that did so, of course, and all politicians could do was try to get the conditions right. From left and right came different approaches to the process, and from left and right alike there were successes and failures in doing so.

THE SPIRIT OF CAPITALISM

I love the competitive spirit in mankind. Thank goodness, in short, for the ambitious, and for those who must be first, best and more than everyone else. They seem to offer the rest of us the immense benefit of their energy and talent, and all in exchange for the promise that there shall be virtually no limit to how influential, famous or rich they become. They are welcome to it. They do us little harm, and much good, when they achieve their ambitions.

THE VIRTUE OF WEALTH

Wealth is not everything people want, but almost all people want it. It is an affectation, almost, to declare oneself immune to the charms of wealth. The desirability of wealth even scoops up in its maw those who do not want it for themselves, but only to disburse it to others.

Wealth's being fungible is very important. It can be spent on philanthropy, display, investment, hoarding, extravagance, vulgarity, aestheticism. These are all faces that wealth wears, and they are very different from one another. But all do the same good, and neither the virtuousness, nor the venality of the person spending the money makes it so.

This sits well, of course, with the free-market argument that stresses, with Adam Smith, that it is not the benevolence of its participants that makes capitalism vigorous and virtuous.

On the one hand, people do not get rich because they are virtuous. Their being rich produces good they don't need to intend. Their being rich does not exonerate them from the need to be virtuous, though their getting rich is likely to have been creative of good just by itself. The rich and successful do not have to adopt the mantra so many of them do adopt: they do not need to do new good works because 'I want to put something back'. They haven't taken anything away: they have added to our happiness.

But, of course, it is right that the rich and famous should feel lucky, and it is lucky that many will go on to be generous. 'You can't take it with you', suggests that one might as well spent the booty in the here and now. Beautifully, it probably doesn't make much difference whether you blow it on extravagances or on philanthropy – both can do good or harm, but good is the likelier outcome.

Interestingly, philanthropy has always most appealed in the most gung-ho society on earth – the US. And it is now appealing to a rather interesting generation of entrepreneurs (Bill Gates is one famous example) who feel that their own children had better start without a vast inheritance (doubtless the Gateses will aim to pass on the richest social inheritances of the class system: educational advantage and a good network).

It is important to note that only in affluent societies can we hope to be comfortable, while not very interested in wealth creation. Capitalism does not destroy leisure, creativity and spirituality; and it creates the wealth that allows these to flourish.

CRASS MATERIALISM

Much wealth (and not only in its Mass Affluence form) is now criticised for its crass materialism. The mega-yacht is not, actually, as disliked as McDonald's. The former is clearly egregious, but is at least amazing. The latter strikes observers as corruptingly trivial.

Old money is seldom prone to crass materialism (it either becomes dignified or is dissipated). This makes an argument that we need only give it time, and Mass Affluence – including extraordinary wealth – will become civilised.

It is important to note that the modern not-very poor do not complain about the modern very rich. Donald Trump and David Beckham are, alike, objects of interest and admiration. Both are stars on populist TV. True, their failures thrill us as much as their success. The 'greasy pole' of great success naturally gives us many opportunities for *Schadenfreude*. I must not overemphasise this source of pleasure: it is too much the mirror image of the Status Anxiety I am suggesting is not very important. Given that I am suggesting we are not made miserable by the success of others, I had better not stress that we are made happy by their failure.

WEALTH: A GEOGRAPHY

The world's rapidly increasing wealth is being spread rather more equally among the planet's human population than we have known in our lifetimes. What is more (and it is not the same thing) the number and proportion of the absolutely poor is also falling. This is going on alongside a picture in which the number and proportion of the rich is also rising.

It is true that some states are 'cowboy' rather than open. Why do some states tend to produce what I have dubbed a 'Barbed Wire Elite', rather than a 'Bossy Middle Class'? Our case is that, for stable and healthy capitalism to work its magic, society must become open and modern, and those elites which resist that insight and development will be damaging their own prospects: they are working against their own interests. Their children will see this, even if they don't.

It is problematic which is the more necessary to wealth creation: capitalism or democracy. We have never seen a closed society with an unresponsive government create wealth, and even China makes this case for us, as it becomes freer as a precursor to becoming richer. Nor have we seen the creation of wealth without a tendency to 'modern' society. The seeming exception – the oil-rich countries of the Middle East – have 'undeserved', or 'unearned' wealth that has come about without the benign interplay of capitalistic and democratic forces.

WEALTH AND INEQUALITY

Is inequality a bad thing? Clearly we need some distinctions: it would make a difference if the richness of the rich created the poverty of the poor. If the rich becoming less rich could help the poor, we might be tempted to recommend it. And it matters whether the rich agree to becoming less rich. After all, globalization makes it easier for them to up sticks, and then where would we be?

By definition, a bad society is one in which suffering is widespread and not ameliorated. But we will argue that few societies get, and stay, wealthy without becoming better societies, even if they start off or stay unequal.

Still, there are examples of bad societies that are quite rich and very unequal. Such societies were characteristic of post-war Latin America. In such societies, the hugeness of the wealth held by a minority was accompanied by extremes of poverty endured by the majority. Even these circumstances don't make an argument against inequality. Had the poor been less poor and the rich even richer, the same degree of inequality might have obtained, but with a happier outcome. Anyway, the situation is improving, and it is not egalitarianism that has improved the societies, so much as economic and political sophistication.

'GOOD' SOCIETIES CREATE WEALTH, AND SPREAD IT, EVEN IF UNEQUALLY

In the West, capitalism, secularism and democracy all arose together and produced benign interrelations. Have we any reason to suppose that similar processes will not happen in the 'less developed' parts of the modern world? Leave aside the possibility that terrorism, or religious fundamentalism, or both will impoverish certain parts of the world, and other cultural features may impoverish parts of Africa: we do seem to see the 'normal' economic and political processes unfolding around the world.

We do not need to suggest that wealth creation is halcyon or utopian. Our argument is that as societies get richer they get freer, and vice versa. Both ends of the equation can be relative.

THE VIRTUE OF WEALTH CREATION

How wealth is created – by individuals or societies – has moral dimensions. Obvious questions are: is exploitation of workers, consumers and the environment necessary to wealth creation? If so, how much of each type of exploitation can be justified by the wealth created? To what extent should the resulting wealth be spread about (voluntarily? involuntarily?) as the justification for the exploitation?

WEALTH: THE NATURAL LIMITS

It is a fallacy that wealth creation must destroy the planet. So far as we know, there is nothing we want – energy, materials – that is not abundantly available to an ingenious species such as ours, and in forms that do not cause worrying pollution. In large measure, economic growth has already been decoupled from many forms of exploitation. The new problems are as much aesthetic as they are ecological; and they are as much about nuisance as about nature.

THE CHALLENGES OF WEALTH

Mass Affluence is indeed throwing down challenges. The exhilaration of modern life lies in addressing these challenges. Being new to them, it is hardly surprising that we have not yet quite grasped their nature, let alone faced up to them properly. We are nouveaux riches: vulgar, dazzled, gauche, uneasy. But to make our wealth and wealth creation into villains is utterly to fail to grasp the fun and demands of our problem. We don't have to agonise about being rich, but about our failure to be rich well. We are failing our wealth, not the other way round.

1 Michael Lind of the New America Foundation coined this handy usage; *Prospect Magazine*, July 2004.

2 Quoted in Peter Mullen, 'The Naivety of Rowan Williams', *The Times*, T2, 7 September 2004.

3 I wrote a short book about this for the European Science and Environment Forum: *Risk: The human adventure*, 2000.

4 For a definition of false consciousness, see: http://en.wikipedia.org/wiki/False_consciousness.

5 Ivan Illich was a hero of mine and this book is in some sense an account of why I have ceased to believe his doctrines.

6 Will Hutton, *The State We're In*, Cape, 1995; *The World We're In*, Little, Brown, 1996.

7 See the *FT*'s view of inequality noted in chapter 3.

8 See www.robertreich.org/reich/biography.asp.

9 Martin Jacques, writing in the *Guardian*, quoted in *The Week*, 25 September 2004.

10 Will Hutton, *The State We're In*, Cape, 1995; *The World We're In*, Little, Brown, 2002.

11 John Gray, *False Dawn: The delusions of global capitalism*, Granta, 1998.

12 Joseph Stiglitz, *Globalization and its Discontents*, Penguin, 2002.

13 Godfrey Hodgson, *More Equal Than Others: America from Nixon to the new century*, Princeton University Press, 2004.

14 Thomas Frank, *What's the Matter with America?*, Secker & Warburg, 2004.

15 George Monbiot, Captive State, *The Corporate Takeover of Britain*, Macmillan, 2002.

16 Noreena Hertz, *The Silent Takeover: Global capitalism and the death of democracy*, Heinemann, 2001.

17 Naomi Klein, *No Logo: Taking aim at the brand bullies*, Flamingo, 2000.

18 Alain de Botton, *Status Anxiety*, Hamish Hamilton, 2004.

19 Oliver James, *Britain on the Couch: Why we're unhappier than we were in 1950s – despite being richer*, Century, 1997.

20 Barry Schwartz, *The Paradox of Choice: Why more is less*, Ecco/Random House, 2004.

21 Clive Hamilton, *Growth Fetish*, Pluto, 2003.

22 Madeline Bunting, *Willing Slaves: How the overwork culture is ruling our lives*, Harper Collins, 2004.

23 Richard Sennett, *The Corrosion of Character: The personal consequences of work in the new capitalism*, W W Norton, 1998.

24 Digby Anderson, *All Oiks Now*, Social Affairs Unit, 2004.

25 When, in 1997, the firm of Burberry got a new American CEO, Rose Marie Bravo, there was a deliberate brand realignment. The firm decided it wanted to be less gun-dog and more gangsta, and to this end started making baseball caps in its famous check. Like all such moves, it risked appealing to some very unattractive types, and taking the brand downmarket. Chavs – the newly labelled breed of pale, gormless, alienated young white males and their laddish female consorts – really took to the cap, as soon as a ripped-off version became available in their local street markets. Apparently, for a while the cap helped the police pick out troublemakers at football matches. Now the trademark check has largely returned to its discreet use as overcoat lining. A Burberry spokesman notes that 'Stealth Wealth' is now the order of the day. Display is passé.

26 Rod Liddle, 'Forty Per Cent of Nothing', *The Spectator*, 3 July 2004.

CHAPTER 2

MASS AFFLUENCE AND HAPPINESS

The October 2004 issue of the *Good Housekeeping* magazine asked the question, 'What do you think would make you happy? A dream house, great job, being fitter, more pampered, single, a better person? Our exclusive survey reveals what really makes women's lives brighter...'[1]

The author of the piece went on: 'Why, when women are wealthier, healthier and have more choices than ever before, has real, lasting happiness become even more of a holy grail – and always just a bit out of reach?'

Quoting a recent Cabinet Office report, the magazine said: 'Despite the huge increases in material wealth, we're no happier than we were in the 1950s.' (This is a standard charge, and we will return to it.)

GH went on: 'The *Good Housekeeping* Happiness survey reveals that almost 50 percent of women would get a huge burst of happiness if they got a pay rise – it would, they say, make them happier than being their ideal weight, or even getting on with their partner.'

There was more materialist news to come: it appears that 40 per cent of women say a dream home would beat a decent pension or a good sex life, and two out of five women would prefer a good pension to a great sex life, and a new pair of shoes cheers them up more than a nice cup of tea or a cuddle with the cat.

That was the data. The author of the piece did not exactly brush it aside, but nonetheless went off on a tour of anecdotal and other expert evidence that proposed a fairly conventional touchy-feely account of what 'really' made people happy. One expert, a famous life coach, Pete Cohen, was quoted as saying that if people put the same effort into personal relationships as they did into their jobs, they'd reap great happiness.

Pete Cohen may be right. But *GH* presumably believes that women know what they want, and what they want is more money, nicer houses and new shoes. Maybe they figure that all the goofy, feel-good, spiritual stuff is in hand, or doesn't matter all that much. If it's a wish list you're after, bring on the cash.

Most of the critics of modern Mass Affluence say that there is something about modern wealth that the wealthy themselves don't like. We have some real problems here. It seems generally to be supposed that the world will go on acquiring material wealth: more opportunities, more leisure, more food, more choices. Do we keep doing this because we don't know we are being made more miserable by it? Have we not noticed our unhappiness? Have we been blinded by achieving the Mass Affluence for which we have yearned? Will we have to learn that the dimly experienced misery we are beginning to feel is actually associated with our wealth?

Intriguingly, the poorer end of the Mass Affluent society does not complain. The old working class, always ready to moan about the state of affairs, is still pretty happy to tell a television reporter that they are 'devastated' or 'stressed' by this or that setback. But in general they are more likely to irritate us as they noisily and flashily (fleshily) barge about the public space having fun.

It is the rich end of the Mass Affluent that complains (and that produces our intellectual critics). They are money rich, time poor. They feel the world is seeking to pollute them, so they buy bottled water. The world is hazardous, so they buy large four-wheel drive vehicles. They're too busy getting and being rich to have children, and so they risk a large unhappiness in pursuit of a small one. They are too busy having their complexes massaged by therapists to consider how tiresome they are.

In my irritation with these quite-rich, am I not complaining about the 'spirit of the times' just as the critics do?

Well, one difference between me and the critics of affluence is that they take the disquiet of the self-enfeebled as a serious criticism of the society in which we live. They say they would mostly like the world to drift leftward, or – something new – to cease its quest for economic growth. By contrast, the reform I would propose is, roughly speaking, of the 'snap out of it and get real' sort. The fact is, the times are great: it's not the times that need changing: it's the people who pretend there's something awful in the air, in the times, in the water, in the Ad Mass.

In the West, we are hugely lucky. All that we need now is for more people to realise it, to live up to the times they're in, and the state we're in.

The manners – and perhaps even the morals – of both ends of the Mass Affluence spectrum are in a state. Part of our bad news is the extraordinary phenomenon of middle-class people seeming to join the worst of the working class in its habits. We can face – with something like patriotic forbearance – the idea of badly behaved English football hooligans from the lower orders. But it is a bit of a shaker to find – as *The Times* did this year – that an archaeology student was among them.

For decades, middle-class young people have aped the ways of the working class, as a sort of rebellion against the bourgeois self-satisfaction of their own backgrounds. They have sought to dress shabbily and indulge in a 'downspeak', so that they could get along in 'classless' comprehensives and universities, and merge with their fellows in pubs. But now they have gone further and given up the gracefulness and charm that used to be the birthright of Englishmen of any class.

So here we are. There are wimpish affluents and hooliganish ones, and there are mockney middle classes, and we can be irritated by them all. But they don't make the case that affluence is immutably bound up with decadence; that we must embrace poverty and give up on economic growth.

These failings of modern society make a case for seeking to address manners and morals – not for weaning ourselves off money.

THE HAPPINESS RESEARCH

First of all, who is measuring what here? Are comparisons not difficult? The young cannot make comparisons between the past and the present: their view of modern life is important to them, but it is not an experienced view. They cannot compare their situation with that of an earlier time: they weren't there for one of the elements of the comparison. 'They don't know they're born', say the old of the young, especially when the young dislike some element of modern life. You should've tried the olden days, say their elders, sagely.

But their elders may be no better than the young at assessing what modern life is like. The old are hideously prone – always have been – to celebrate their childhood privations and adult strains, as somehow something glorious and enjoyable compared to the lives lived by the young they see coming up behind. Golden-ageism afflicts us all once we are nearer the grave than the womb.[2]

We are also comparing different worlds. Nothing in human history has really prepared us for the world of the 1960s onward. There hasn't been much time in which to make adjustments – or measurements. So if people say that modern life is boring, dreadful, worse than the past, we may reasonably inquire who it is making this assertion, and what is being compared to what.

One of the key bits of happiness research is the *Eurobarometer*.[3] Every year it asks Europeans about their level of satisfaction with their lives. It has been doing so since 1973, and it is true that, while wealth has increased since then, self-declared satisfaction with life has not. But so what? The vast majority of Europeans declare themselves to be fairly or very satisfied with their lives, just as they have done, with only slight variations, since the early 1970s. Note that people are being asked whether they are satisfied *now*: they are not asked to compare their present with their past, and yet the older among them must, in fact, be making such a tacit comparison. They are, after all, perfectly free to say that they are not content with the present, given that they find it disappointing compared with their past, and the hopes they nurtured then. Hypothetically, their disappointment with the failure of the present to live up to the promise of the past might have tipped them into responding that they don't much rate the present. But no: asked about what they feel, they declare themselves content with the present, and we can assume that this cheerful view takes account of a comparison of today even with the golden age of their youth and the high hopes it probably nurtured. People's cheerful answers also presumably capture the degree to which they are satisfied with their own lives, even allowing for what they see around them. They see, presumably, large numbers of people getting much richer than they are themselves; they see a society of growing Mass Affluence; they see a society in which they have every reason to suppose that more and more goods and services should be available. They have, in short, been subject to rising and very high expectations, and their answers suggest very strongly that they are fairly or very satisfied that they are getting their share, and that their share produces well-being.

This is surely good news. It implies that Europeans get up every morning and go to work – often to quite hard and demanding work that involves a dreary commute – mostly content that it brings them the good things in life. And it implies that they find those good things to be good. Wouldn't it be an insane situation if they hated their lives, and yet gave as little visible sign of misery as we in fact see? Would they not be hammering on the doors of political parties to campaign for a radically different – less rich – way of life? Would the holiday companies not be bereft of income from fares, as the masses went on camping holidays? Would the hypermarkets not be echoing emptily to the sounds of till-girls chattering among themselves, as people revived the allotments that everywhere we see overgrown with weeds?

What's more, questions about the experience of work reveal that the vast majority of people like their work. Moreover, they expect their feelings about work to improve over the next year. So employment is a pleasure now and is likely to become more so.

This is further good news, and it flies in the face of those who want the merry-go-round to stop.

Among the Europeans, it is the Italians, Spanish, Portuguese and Greeks who show up as marginally less satisfied than northerners.[4] This may be because southern Europeans have old-fashioned lives – lives relatively lacking in modern opportunities – compared with northerners. They see petty (and not-so-petty) corruption, regulatory chaos, lack of economic growth – and they are less than thrilled by these failures. They are rather less satisfied than northerners, and we can wonder whether that is not because they see what northerners' lives are like, and wonder why they may not have such agreeable societies to live in.

This is good news for those on the right who like modern society because it confounds the sort of nostalgia that the critics of affluence adhere to. If such critics want to know the delights of slower, simpler, warmer, less technocratic, more 'human' societies, let them hie southwards and enjoy their dream there. As visitors, retirees, romantics and missionaries spreading the word of the peasant or the pre-industrial life, such northerners are welcome to the South; but the southerners themselves seem not to be as romantic about their nation states.

Suppose, however, that we suggest that the right way to judge what people really want is to see how they vote, live, spend their wealth, freedom and time. We should look at how people behave, not merely how they opine. It might even be that they do indeed suffer from a malaise of some sort or another, but that their wealthiness can still be defended, since, with a few adjustments, it might be redeemed.

We have it on the best evidence that people like their wealthiness. Politicians have a struggle to part them from it. Or rather, while people accept that a certain percentage of their wealth should go into the common pot, it is hard to increase the proportion. And very importantly: it seems easier to impose increases in the 'State Take' from the very rich (the top one per cent, who are not a large voting constituency) than it is to get the vast middle- and upper-range of the Mass Affluent to accept such changes.

If there is a new uneasiness about affluence, we can be glad that there is an attractive argument that the Mass Affluent don't need to give up wealth; rather, they need to acquire some very old-fashioned qualities to enjoy their wealth yet more. What is more, if these old-fashioned values were more visible in society, its wealthiness could become an even greater boon for all parties. This is good news. We are an old species, with long experience, and if some totally new quality were required for us to be content with our lot, we'd be bound to wonder if it might ever come along.

This is a 'morals and manners' defence. Our problem with Mass Affluence is not the money we have newly acquired, but the old virtues we haven't yet properly come to value. This defence claims that our attitude, not our affluence, is making wealthiness problematic for those who have it (and even for those who don't).

GREGG EASTERBROOK

Gregg Easterbrook, a noted 'sceptical environmentalist',[5] writes on this theme in *The Progress Paradox*.[6] He doesn't help the originality or usefulness of his book by mixing up old-fashioned anti-wealth arguments (suggesting, in effect, that the US ought to be more leftish than it is) with a more interesting case.

He clearly wishes that the US was more European in its attitudes to welfare and the Third World. This is an argument that is as old as the hills, and is shared by Will Hutton and Godfrey Hodgson.

Easterbrook writes well about the smooth progress of environmental improvement that we have seen. In the *Progress Paradox* he beefs up his description of how almost everything the greens have decried as bad and getting worse has actually been steadily improving for years and promises to continue to do so. His work is in a useful tradition of accurate, evidence-led 'green' optimism that runs counter to the more famous sort.

As he comes to consider economic and social progress – the story of Mass Affluence in increasingly green and pleasant lands – he does fulsomely accept that, by every possible measure of well-being, most of us are better off than we have ever been: healthier, better educated, more spaciously housed, and so on.

He does accept a little too readily that people report a malaise – a dissatisfaction with their lives – though he suggests that some of this is simply self-indulgent anecdotalism.

He is surely right to discuss the malaise of the modern. He would like to see a little more stoicism and gratitude – graciousness – in the new rich. That fits very well with my thesis.

His list of what is wrong in Mass Affluent America accepts too uncritically the various charges that are made by many of the critics. He accepts that moderns are bewildered by choice (quoting Barry Schwartz approvingly), are made anxious by the speed of progress and scientific change and all the rest of it. Instead of simply condemning their moral weakness in not facing up to the benefits they have and the risks that are associated with, but far outweighed by, them, he seems to want us to blame The System.

Easterbrook nearly faces facts. He notes that Americans could easily choose a secure, pleasant small-town life, and yet by the million they choose the 'sterile' suburb and the frenetic city. He accepts that there are qualities to these ways of life that people like, and that the critics who bemoan the suburb and city should not imagine that they have been imposed on people. He accepts that they have been chosen.

He dislikes quite a few of the choices people make: he loathes, for instance, the SUV. He sees it as a poor choice – reflecting paranoia rather than any transport need or real pleasure – and as selfish, not social. But he lays out his criticisms without distinguishing between them. He says SUVs are dangerous to their users and other drivers, emit too much greenhouse gas, and are, simultaneously, expressions of aggression and signs of paranoia. Any of these factors might be true, and some of them might be remedied in society's wider interest, while others are perhaps worthy of comment but not interference. None of them is an argument against wealth and inequality, or progress, since the money saved on SUVs would be spent somewhere else – perhaps spent better, or perhaps worse.

One great merit in Easterbrook's analysis is that he seems to understand that capitalism is not the only cause of human misery (of course, I am not inclined to assume it is a cause at all). Indeed, he understands some of the ways in which the critics of affluence do more harm than the object of their abuse:

In the Western nations, most things have gotten better, and yet people have become no happier, in the very period that thinkers and educators have proclaimed life meaningless; movies and other forms of popular entertainment advance nihilistic messages; the news media emphasize the most cynical possible interpretation of every event, while discreetly looking away from reporting on human progress or personal virtue.[7]

Best of all, Easterbrook knows that it is left-leaning liberals of one sort or another who have helped create a doom-laden society. The educated elite wraps itself in existential gloom, asserting the secular emptiness of life, and proselytises its misery as the only thoughtful position. The mass media makes a pornography of misery, dysfunction and violence, and knocks down every social institution as 'elitist' and self-interested. Hollywood's left-leaning liberals make the cinema into a vulgar and populist engine of hip disaffection. A generation of Hollywood actors makes this case as much as a slew of films. I enjoy them all, but are not John Cusack, Sean Penn and Edward Norton hand-picked for their capacity to dress nihilism in a grey mac and to slouch down life's existential streets?

But none of this will quite do. A media that 'pornographises' violence, an intellectual elite that proclaims doom, an anti-Establishment, anti-capitalist news media, and a mass media that feasts on the dysfunctional – these are all something like a description of things that are wrong in society. But they don't excuse the moral failure of the Mass Affluent to respond gracefully or gratefully to their circumstances.

We can no more shelter behind the BBC News, or the *Guardian*'s hand-wringing, or Hollywood, than we can behind Saatchi and Saatchi (as was).

Besides, the liberal-left's more dangerous – and very winning – tendency is to make an orthodoxy of dissidence. The young have been educated by generations of teachers to believe that The Establishment, the rich, the elite and the capitalists all rig the world so as to keep voters acquiescent, consumers spending, and the poor numbed. Even the structures of democracy are portrayed as anti-democratic, as left-leaning teachers teach history, politics and literature, as though The Levellers, Tom Paine and Rousseau were still badly needed in our own time, and as though politicians were parasites.

One might argue that so many young people have been indoctrinated by these soft-left biases that it is indeed hard for them to resist the liberal-left bias of the media. But it won't quite do. The young grow out of their teachers in so many ways – not least by going into business – that we ought to be able to assume that they are capable of seeing the world through their own eyes.

Still, I do have some sympathy with young people who can't find their way to anything like contentment in a society that has discarded the way-posts by which they might navigate. But we ought to note some paradoxes here (Easterbrook seems to notice them, though he doesn't stress them). It is likely that Byron and Bob Dylan constitute the real lineage of the nihilism, and therefore of much of the distress, in the West. These anti-heroes are very powerfully influential and are the antithesis of the capitalist, Establishment beast whose power Will Hutton and Godfrey Hodgson criticise as hegemonic. It is the Romantics who kill our chance of feeling warmly about life: now there is a paradox.

There is much in Easterbrook to admire. Yet, ultimately, he is a little too milky to be as useful as his honesty hints he may be. He is also a standard leftist. When it comes to espousing policy, Easterbrook declares himself to be a Christian, and proposes a kindly recipe for a happier world. At home, Medicare for the poor and a doubling of the minimum wage to $10 an hour. Abroad, more aid and more trade.

But he has not teased out the real difficulty with his recipe for greater contentment. To wit, even if we modern affluents were prepared to make some sacrifices for the poor, and even if this did make us feel happier, we would still be left with a great many of the difficulties of modern society. They are the ancient problems of affluence and advantage writ large, and compounded by the kind of negativities Easterbrook does usefully notice.

There is nothing odd in arguing that the US needs to be a little more like Europe. It is even reported that a huge majority of Americans believe that the minimum wage ought to be higher. But do they vote that way in elections? If they don't, is it because they think these measures would harm the poor, or because they are indifferent to the poor?

The Mass Affluent are reluctant to pay more taxes. But Easterbrook doesn't condemn the selfish, paranoid, jumpy modern people he identifies. He won't make that moral judgement. He prefers to see the nervy modern affluent as victims in need of help. He cheerfully assumes that the fatcats of capitalism are to blame for their greed, but not that the consumers are culpable of gullibility and meanness. And even Easterbrook, realist that he sometimes is, assumes that the Mass Affluent are corrupted by advertising. His beloved regular Joes must be feeble indeed.

Still, some of the remedies he picks are well chosen. Easterbrook is a proponent of a 'positive psychology' – the idea that people can educate themselves into a greater happiness by reminding themselves of their good fortune. Indeed, it was the most intellectual optimist of our time, Julian Simon, who makes a good case that a cheerful worldview can heal.[8]

So Easterbrook is in our distinctly modern territory when he addresses the apparent unhappiness of those who have affluence. It is, of course, more apparent than real. But let's accept his case that we ought to be happier than we are, given the progress we've made. Easterbrook wishes very reasonably, and in a way that chimes with my own account, that people were more grateful for their wealth. There is a lot to be said for his positive thinking. But surely he is wrong in emphasising that '[all] this matters not as a moralizing sermon but a matter of self-interest...'. The difficulty is that the problem is moral, and to diagnose it as though it were a matter of sickness or self-interest is only part of the point. It is precisely more outward-looking, upbeat moralising that we need, and less inwardly directed self-interest, however upbeat. We need grace and gratitude for our own sakes, to be sure; but the world also needs us to get going and generate them.

Easterbrook stresses that we ought to be grateful for our wealth. The advantaged must see that their position can only be attractive – people will only feel good about the advantaged, and the advantaged will only feel good about themselves – if they gracefully acknowledge that luck and other people have played a major part in their position. Our wealth is a function of good fortune and the society around us. The 'self-made' man who does not remember this seems to us to have been impoverished. *Noblesse oblige* also acknowledges that there is a great satisfaction about affluence in helping others to enjoy it and benefit from it. It is, of course, one of the many paradoxes of wealth that one cannot very seriously acknowledge the force of *noblesse oblige* and still remain rich enough to indulge it for long. But to acknowledge one's social advantages and obligations is surely a requirement of anything approaching a rich life. This is as true now that the rich are legion, as it was when the rich were rare.

This is not, of course, a plea for collectivism, as the left means it. The left wants the people to relinquish power and income to the state, and then wants to control the state. The right believes that there are masses of alternative forms of cooperation that can avoid most of that centralisation and condescension. The market, contracts, philanthropy and volunteering are part of the picture. So are clever blends of the market and taxation. Presumably, the next hundred years of domestic politics will be about devising new ways of getting those that can pay for 'welfare' services to do so, while providing a safety net for the unfortunate and maybe even the feckless. The right is not even sure whether it has persuaded people that there is more dignity in being a customer for services provided by the market than in being an entitlement-holder for those provided by the state.

Dignity, grace and gratitude cannot be bought in the market. They are moral qualities. But the market is not at odds with them. Indeed, these pages are devoted to the reverse observation: the market is an expression of freedom, and it enriches people. The market allows people to enter a moral universe rich in opportunities. Naturally, the left thinks the new affluence should be used to enrich the state. It is the job of the right to show that civilisation does not need as much state interference as the left supposes. It is perhaps a pity that the argument tends to be about whether the State Take kills affluence. It would be more interesting if we argued the tougher ground: that the State Take should be kept low because the state is a poor spender.

We will see the degree to which there is a continuum from the 'neo-liberalism' of the US through to the 'Eurosclerosis' of the Continental Consensus. Gregg Easterbrook seems to wish that the US was more like, say, the UK, just as most of his kind in the UK wish the UK was more like Germany or Scandinavia (where the happiness levels are much the same anyway). He wants, in other words, to deliver to the US the unsatisfactory levels of happiness that Richard Layard and so many others assert (wrongly) are to be seen in modern Europe.

RICHARD LAYARD'S CASE

Layard matters more than most critics of Mass Affluence because he uses the data more systematically, and because he proposes a direct solution to the problem he identifies. As co-director of the Centre for Economic Performance at the London School of Economics, he brings an economist's clarity to things. If we can get past Layard, the road ahead is clearer.[9]

Layard argues that the *Eurobarometer* research (and more in the same vein) shows that increased wealth does not bring increased happiness. We have looked at one reason why this wouldn't matter, and one reason why it's probably wrong. Firstly, people declare themselves to be happy (and happier at the top end of the income distribution), and, secondly, they do so in spite of rising expectations (so people are satisfied now, even though they expect to be even more satisfied later). Then he notes that people report themselves happy because of their relative affluence. This, says Layard, means that their happiness is predicated on the relative unhappiness of others. (I don't get this, and suggest you read his essay for yourself in order to accept or challenge Layard's point. It's not important to the outcome of the argument.)

Layard then moves on to suggest that the higher echelons of society are imposing unhappiness on the lower echelons, and that this can be regarded as a negative externality, just as we regard pollution. Since we have the (rather poor) 'polluter pays' principle, we could also have one based on the prosperous paying. This novel argument is the route by which Layard gets to a very conventional solution: tax the better-off more heavily.

It is just possible that the better-off in society will allow themselves to be taxed on the principle that this is the way for the whole of society, including themselves, to be happier. But it is hardly likely. (I fail to see how one could avoid the whole comparison thing starting up again, but at lower and narrower levels.) Actually, though, levels of taxation on the rich are already decided on the basis of how that level impacts the rest of us. The Anglosphere has decided that relatively light taxation of the rich is good for improving the prospects of the poor. Raising taxation of the rich has, for decades, been hotly argued over. It is hardly likely that Layard will be successful in foisting this new, improbable case onto the electorate.

A further Layard argument is that we know that people do not, after a certain point, get happier in proportion to their acquisition of new wealth. He assumes, then, that, because large numbers of them continue to acquire wealth, this must be a sign of addiction. They are, according to this picture, continuing with a habit even after it has ceased to do good and in fact does harm. He supposes we ought to tax wealth creation in the same way as we tax any substance that people abuse, like tobacco or alcohol.

All this seems bizarre. Firstly, it forgets that exchequers set taxes with just that lightness of touch that maximises yield without reducing consumption. Secondly, it assumes that wealth creation is bad for society, and that it would have a beneficial overall effect to reduce it. Thirdly, it assumes that the imposition of taxes on wealth creation will not create more unhappiness than it is supposed to alleviate.

Layard also argues that the data shows that people value things like family and security over affluence. He suggests (in common with

most critics of Mass Affluence) that politics does not reflect these preferences. Again, Layard supposes that the solution is to be a bit more leftish in the way we run our economies. Again, one counterargument is
that, unless people are in a 'false consciousness' (they have been stunned
into not knowing what they want) or democracy is radically failing (no
party is offering what they want), then people cannot actually want
these things, or they would be voting for them. The kind of policies and
society Layard wants have been offered to electorates, and largely rejected. The fact is that people have come to the conclusion (at least in the
Anglosphere) that, for instance, policies that focus on job security create
job insecurity. There are societies that have come to much the same conclusion as Layard about what life ought to be like, and people who
agree with him could – at a pinch – go and live in them. France,
Germany, Sweden and Denmark – even Canada – have all gone in that
direction, and are variously open to immigration by discontents from
the Anglosphere.

I have heard Layard argue that government focuses on economic
growth because it is a proxy for happiness, but that we now know
enough about happiness to see that it is a poor proxy. So we should now
focus directly on happiness and, in so doing, we would arrive at different policies. But this is very little use and reminds that Layard has two
mountains to climb. He has first to persuade us that we have mis-
defined happiness. And then that we want to be more socialist. Actually,
one might argue, the problem of much of modern life is that we are too
socialist already. Isn't one of the reasons governments focus on economic growth that we taxpayers are giving so much money toward their
non-economic happiness-creating policies that we need rising pay
packets to cushion us?

The one possibility that Layard and the others have of being right
is this: it is just possible that, when kindly policy was a matter of equity
or social responsibility, voters stayed mean and materialist. But now, a
deeper revolution might be at work. Now, not generosity but self-
interest might make people socialist. By this account, the critics of Mass
Affluence simply have to burst the bubble of self-deception of the Mass
Affluent, our addiction, and we can all march forward, hand in hand,
into the sunset, with a song in our hearts. According to this view, we
might at last understand our natures and interests, and legislate for the
agreeable society that caters to them. To this, I counter that we have
legislated for very much of this agreeable society, and it must cater to
greed, lust and risk or it will inflict greater cruelties.

Perhaps the biggest problem is that Layard looks at the data on
wealth and happiness and does not merely make a cause out of a correlation, but strips out much of the drama of human life. People do not

seek happiness, if they have any sense. Nor do many of them seek mere contentment. They seek drama, risk, inner peace, success, applause, wealth, power, goodness. It is out of the complex realities – the competing dreams of humanity – that we have created capitalism and its wealth creation. One can tamper with this, regulate it, tax it – and we do. But not to see that its pluses and minuses, its benefits and deficits, must be weighed against the vitality of the human spirit that has produced it, seems curiously life-denying.

MOVING ON

One can hardly state these propositions for or against wealth creation without noting that they are, if not trite, at least very ancient. That is to say: the body politic and society have wrestled with these problems for centuries, and Mass Affluence has merely made them more widespread. When the rich were few, they dealt with these issues, and did so in a large variety of ways; so now do the masses.

True, Christianity, Islam and Judaism – to say nothing of myriad secular philosophies – dealt more with the moral obligations of the rich to the poor than they did with the obligations of the rich to themselves. Historically, few people would have complained that their affluence was troubling them, or been taken seriously if they had tried to. But then, no-one, rich or poor, believed he had a right to happiness.

Nowadays, many of us are inclined to expect that happiness is a right and ask ourselves endless questions as to why it has not come about. It seems at least plausible that it is not new misery that we are noticing (though that is what the critics of affluence suppose). What we are noticing is that we are rather happy (bloody well ought to be, given how lucky we are) and are wondering why we can't be even happier.

The critics of affluence spot that we are rich. They admit this has led to well-being, but they aver that well-being has not led to happiness. I am inclined, rather, to say that we are happy, and now want even more of this hitherto scarce commodity.

It would be bizarre if the solution to our current self-questioning were to wind down our affluence. Rather, I suggest, why not 'get real' about happiness; admit that material life is only part of it; accept that happiness is about what we bring to life more than what life brings to us.

And in reasserting these truths we see how old the issues are. We do not have new paradoxes, new dilemmas; we face the same paradoxes and dilemmas that have always challenged the thoughtful. But we have democratised them. The rich were once rare in having opportunities and choices – now many of us do. Our Mass Affluence is fungible, just as aristocratic wealth was: people can now do what they like with their money.

The rich were once unusual in being able to choose extravagance, gourmandising, travel, gambling; or the ascetic, the aesthetic, the self-sufficient, the philanthropic, the prudent. It is obvious that you have to be rich to choose expensive pastimes or missions; it is less clear that one has to be rich to choose poverty. But it is true nevertheless. Some are born poor, while others have poverty thrust upon them – lucky are those who achieve it for as long as they want it. For the rich, temporary and voluntary poverty is as much an option as a travel upgrade.

Historically, it was only a few rich people who got to choose. Some went for materialism, some for spirituality; some were spectacularly selfish, others extraordinarily civic-minded; some were serious, some trivial. Any of these options could prove expensive. Some were ruinous, some very cheap: but as choices, all were luxuries. Few of the rich volunteered deliberately for real, long-term, no-turning-back poverty, though it often came visiting.

Happiness and unhappiness were littered throughout these options. The problem of affluence is that it robs us of the excuse not to consider more properly our failure to be interesting and worthwhile. Of course, people do not become happier in proportion to their wealth, as though there is some iron rule to do with wealth. Their wealth is, or ought to be, a springboard to the more interesting challenges to do with advantage. Indeed, happiness is not the point. I would positively expect modern people to report that they do not feel fulfilled: they ought to be aware that, for the first time in history, the majority of us have switched from being the disadvantaged, who are within their rights to demand more, to becoming the advantaged, who should ask themselves: what have I made of all this?

We all have these opportunities and challenges now, and they make us more interesting than when we were poor.

Among the most important signs that people are seeing their way to this improved worldview is the increasing understanding that positive thinking is at the heart of much of our problem. I agree with Easterbrook and Barry Schwartz in their admiration of the ideas of Martin Seligman and others, which suggest that it is our worldview that causes much of the modern malaise.[10]

Easterbrook and Schwartz stress the moral obligation of fully-fledged people to acknowledge that having advantage places obligations on us as individuals.

Naturally, I see positive thinking not as a strategy for handling Mass Affluence, but as a strategy for dealing with the dreariness of some of the modern culture and our failure to live up to our advantages.

GETTING AND SPENDING

If we were saints or ascetics, or proper hippies, we might all become free of material wants or needs. Of course, that won't happen, though if war or famine or climate catastrophe ensues, doubtless our needs and wants will become radically redefined. Few of us have not toyed with temporary privation: we go camping, or hiking, or play football – and 'suffer' wet and cold and exertion for the fun of it. Perhaps we diet, or 'meditate', as though food were in short supply or we really loved peace and quiet. But we are mostly very busy, and we get and spend like crazy.

But it's no use sneering: there is an enigma in human life and it is that we waste some – or should I say, much? – of what we earn. Some – or is it much? – of what we spend does not bring us the pleasure we thought it might. More discipline, more good sense, more experience might have brought – will bring – some of us greater happiness with less expenditure. And perhaps the most powerful thought some people have is this: less time and effort spent earning might release more time and effort for happiness achieved directly – by doing and being, rather than getting and spending.

We certainly ought to be clear that getting and spending are very unlikely to be all there is to happiness, and may sometimes get in the way of it.

But none of these thoughts is a good argument against wealth and the pleasures it brings.

In an ideal world, those who got the greatest pleasure out of wealth would get the most wealth, and those for whom the leisure part of the wealth–leisure matrix was the better part, would have more of that, with all the grades in between of people who quite liked wealth, and quite liked or didn't mind poverty getting their portions according to their tastes. Of course, there would be very few takers for the full-on poverty option.

But aren't we nearer that situation than is commonly supposed? Plodders choose high-street banking, while high-fliers take on merchant banking. (The plodders may be brave in the Territorial Army or their rugby club; the merchant bankers may whine to their therapists.) People who prize leisure become high school teachers, while the more ambitious become millionaires (who then take off on early retirement). The essential thought is that rich societies produce more opportunities for more varieties of people to shape their lives than do poor ones.

There is a lot to be said for this view. Why bother to work all the hours God sends when a sufficiency of work may provide all the goods and services one wants, and still leave valuable leisure time, or time to bring one's children up well? This sort of line underpinned the thinking of Ivan Illich, and it is seductive.

It is, in theory, an option open to nearly anyone, and yet, in practice, it is open to people who are either quite rich, or prepared to be very poor. It is often a cover for a kind of dependency on the willingness of others to slave very hard. The 'alternativist' in the tepee or the hippy truck who uses the industrialised health services or picks up a dole cheque is infuriating because he or she flaunts the badge of self-sufficiency, but is actually dependent on others to do their materialistic thing and then work some more to pay the taxes which sustain the romantic.

This is not to say that wealth is the only good. Staying put can be better than travel; doing can be better than spending; enjoying what one has can be more pleasurable than getting more. These elementary truths may be as true for societies as they are for individuals. Or rather, societies composed of individuals who prefer poverty to affluence may be happier than those that don't. But we have little evidence for this. That is to say, huge numbers of people presently live, work and vote on the premise that maintaining their existing level of wealth, or getting wealthier than they are, is pretty rational, and emotionally rich too, and they'd like society to be so structured as to produce this desirable outcome for them and for others.

It might be that they come to change their minds. More people may opt for poverty, as they are free to do now (though few do), and they may go on to argue that the whole of society could contribute to happiness by preferring a poverty route to an affluence route. It will remain the case that these are luxuries, which rich societies will find easier to provide than poor ones.

WEALTH AND COMPULSORY AFFLUENCE

The big historical criticism of wealth was that, while the rich had more than they needed, the poor had much less than they did. Now, the critics say our Mass Affluence has made us the victim not of our needs, but of our wants. Our needs really were once our own, but there is an argument now which suggests that our wants have been given to us by capitalists. What's more, they have made it impossible for any of us to have cheap things, cheaply; and simple things, simply. This second proposition touches on a sense that everything has been 'monetised'. It also implies a problem that makes society more unequal: everything in life has become expensive, and so the poor are doubly excluded. Where once they could not have the good things in life, now they can't have many of the ordinary things. They are 'socially excluded'.

In a nutshell: the left complains that most of us consume far too much, and are forced to, and that the poor have a right to share in the same problem.

'A fool and his money are easily parted' and '*caveat emptor*' were once pretty well the only watchwords that were needed as one grew up in the years before Mass Affluence, and when the Consumer Society was in its infancy. No-one thought that people who were spending money were victims. We reserved our sympathy for those who couldn't consume. And we were among their number most of the time.

I say 'we', because most people were short of money, especially when they were young, and so almost the entire world was unified in knowing what it was like to hang about at home or in the street, stony broke. Plenty of young people who were at 'fancy' public schools (almost all of which prided themselves on a routine that was the opposite of fancy) had parents who were also chronically short of cash, usually because of paying for the fancy school. The aristocracy then prided itself on shabbiness, and a good many 'well-born' people were strapped for cash (though they were also said to pride themselves on never paying their bills). (I note elsewhere how this applied in the case of Nancy Mitford.) It goes without saying that the working class were regarded by many as having a decent amount of disposable income, which they disposed of in pubs. Only the upper and lower classes (and the classless bohemians) prided themselves on a degree of fecklessness, which has now spread nearly everywhere.

Of course, affluence was beginning to be nearly commonplace. The 1920s and 1930s had been very tough for very many people (though plenty were doing alright). The Second World War had a similar levelling effect to that noticed in the First World War, too. And then, with the 1950s and 1960s the world began to look recognisably modern. People at every level of society seemed not to be so absorbed with finding money for house and home. They began to be interested in consuming, and in doing so for the pleasure of it.

Naturally, the trend began in the US, as did criticism of the wiles of capitalism for exploiting people's new-found wealth, and for seeking to part them from it. Never mind, for the moment, that capitalism is a merry-go-round: that a mass market of consumers parted from their money produces the very wealth by which they can earn enough replacement readies to be parted from again – and all to everyone's satisfaction.

Vance Packard's *Hidden Persuaders* (1957) was perhaps the first really famous alarm call about the misbehaviour of advertisers: it discussed their use of subliminal messages hidden in images. There was a great fuss about this, and the industry promised to give up the practice, which has never been proven to have any effect anyway. Actually, throughout the post-War period, advertisers and PR people had been deploying 'psyops' techniques developed during the war by both sides to keep their own troops and civilian populations enthusiastic, and to alarm and confuse the enemy.

There have been various attempts to discuss this work. It is a great theme of Noam Chomsky, who believes that money has corrupted politics, and especially because it has allowed the minority to steal the natural dissidence and socialism from the masses.[11] It is possible, one might think, that the great semiologist has been overimpressed by the power of the Word and by the drama of hidden texts.

The most fascinating figure in the manipulation of the American mind was Freud's American nephew, Edward Bernays.

Adam Curtis's BBC2 TV series *The Century of the Self* celebrated this intriguing character through eyes at once uncritical and satirical (and, its critics said, highly partisan). Bernays believed that people's deepest (Freudian) fears and desires could be exploited in such a way as to make them quite biddable. Indeed, he believed this was noble work, since, left to their own devices, the masses could be very flighty and nasty. He used Freud's insights to arrive at this conclusion. Paradoxically, one of the people to be impressed by this work, put together by two Jews, was Goebbels, who (to Bernays' dismay) expressed his indebtedness to the pair for some of the propaganda techniques he used to keep the Germans in a frenzy of hatred of the Jews.[12]

After the war, Bernays parlayed the techniques into campaigns for consumer-goods companies, and developed them for politicians, who had noticed that they could be employed as easily to design policies that would play well with voters.

The most striking observation of Curtis's series was that even an apparently radical rebellion against Freud could be used by mainstream politicians and corporations. In rebelling against Freud, William Reich is regarded as one of the fathers of the 'flower power' rebellion against mainstream America. Good health was found not in conforming to society, which was itself sick. The rational, emotionally valuable response was rejection and rebellion. Radicalism was equivalent to mental health. (How those of us who flirted with this argument devoured our R D Laing, Noam Chomsky and Michel Foucault.)

But here's the odd thing, as noted by Curtis (whom I suspect of over-egging many parts of his case). The mainstream apparently learned from the rebellion: to succeed in the mass market, one must aim to satisfy not merely the innermost desires of consumers, and to play on their fears; one must play to their sense of individuality.

This seems contradictory, and it is. Mass-market individualism cannot happen. Marks and Spencer's slogan (devised in 2003), 'Exclusively for Everyone', is indeed a crass oxymoron. But it is the alchemy and the gold standard advertisers seek. They want products with personality, and products that reinforce personality. They want brands that are like people, in having a nature; and they want us to love their brands, as though they were people.

Bernays hoped his work was 'proper-ganda': that is to say, he thought his work was respectable. Not least because it was deployed in supporting US policy in Guatemala in the 1950s, it naturally upset the left, and perhaps rightly. If his approach was as important as he thought it was, then we would have cause to worry. He was blatant in his belief that he could manipulate the masses. Luckily, we are inclined to think that the wickedness of propaganda – its playing on our weaknesses, on the mania which is so much a feature of mobs – didn't depend on his Freudian or any other deep psychological insights.

The PR Project (an ad-busting 'corporate watch' NGO – Non-Governmental Organisation – in the US) notes that one of the campaigns he was engaged upon was selling cigarette-smoking to women. Apparently, he told the advertisers to pitch the product at women's burgeoning sense of independence. So he is perhaps to blame for causing millions of lung cancer cases by pitching to people's subconscious and making them addicts. Or was he just stating the obvious and playing to what women did indeed find in cigarettes, and had found for themselves during the War, when so many taboos were broken? Or were they, equally voluntarily (unless hypnotised), copying what the plebeian aristocrats of the Silver Screen were doing?

Anyway, advertising of this sort was pointing out the obvious and playing to it. That the obvious might run very deep, or that very deep analysis could reinforce the truth of the trivial observation, does not make the method sinister. Cigarette manufacturers play on the fact that people want to be cool and associate smoking with coolness. How deep is that? How sinister? How much a fact of how people smoke, and how much a consequence of advertising?

How sinister is it now that every sort of psychology and linguistic theory is put to work to build brands? It is worth reading the essays posted at Salon.com on the theme. Whether or not Curtis was right about the path from Freud to Bernays continuing through the counter-Freudian to the focus group, it seems that similar guff is in vogue today. The Jungians, Freudians, the Post Modern structuralists and semiologists are still at it.

The essays posted at Salon.com talk of psycho-engineering firms working with, for instance, oil companies. The oil moguls were told that people's choices – what they like – go back to what they found cosy as children, when they first saw their parents interact with this or that brand. Certainly, and why not?

All my life I have been aware of sticking points and affections, which, I am sure, go back to childhood. If Shell, say, is associated with carefree motoring and wide rural vistas and contented Saturdays, well that is a two-fold connection. In the 1950s I probably had happy experiences in Shell garages on such excursions, but I don't remember them. I do, though, have sharp and happy memories of the travel books, art and ads sponsored by Shell when I was a boy. Shell brilliantly marketed itself through poets and painters and their imaging of the countryside. In the 1970s, I was angry that a firm associated with motoring should have sold me an image of a countryside I thought cars were destroying.[13] But then Jonathan Raban, the man of letters and travel writer, interrupted one of my rants on the subject and told me that motoring in the 50s had indeed given Britain to its people. I didn't buy his argument then; but now that the situation is more extreme, I find that I do, and I extend it to modern motoring, rather than just the motoring of half a century ago. Not that this makes me buy more petrol from Shell rather than from BP or Esso. I am drawn by the unpopularity of oil firms, and by the campaigns against them, to empathise with them all, and I am thus promiscuous in my use of their fuels.

Lyons Teashops had a similar approach to Shell's, and used that firm's artistic director to commission work for them. The Towner Museum in Eastbourne has a lovely series of lithographs displayed and sold in the Lyons cafes. They are work commissioned between 1947 and 1955 by some of the best painters and illustrators of their day: John Nash, Edward Ardizzone, Duncan Grant, Ruskin Spear and many others. J Lyons were, at the same time, pioneering computer stock control. The firm is important in the story of female emancipation: they provided places where working women could go alone and feel comfortable. It was men who, for the first time, were secondary. So we see that what looks merely commercial – or comical or quaint – has often served much grander purposes.

Very often, we refuse to see the value in such things. The modern Starbucks is providing – as Waterstone's the bookstores do – very welcome oases and moments of calm in people's busy days and streets. Starbucks is working out how to have good relations with coffee-growers too. McDonald's, long reviled, have set higher standards of animal welfare than many other butchers, while – unobserved except by Charles Clover – they have set higher standards in getting hold of their fish, too.[14] Are these efforts merely PR? Why would it matter? Firms evolve and understand new things about their customers as they go along.

We can't have it both ways. Do we want firms to patronise us, as though they were missionaries, and we primitive heathen amongst whom they may proselytise? Why is it not better that they should seek to understand what we want, and provide it? We no more want capitalists to assert that they know better than their customers, than we want them to be amoral. (More on this when we come to Corporate Social Responsibility.)

POLITICAL BRANDING

The trajectory of political manipulation followed that of consumer branding. Politicians realised that their parties had to do more than merely make some sort of dull sense (put money in our pockets, lock up criminals); they must touch us, too. We have to like them. One way of pulling off this difficult feat was to ask people what they wanted. But the old opinion poll, in which aggregated preferences could be divined, was not likely to be quite enough. The focus group, which allowed researchers to understand how people felt and wanted to feel about politicians and parties was much more successful. Tony Blair was the apotheosis of this process: he was the first – and may be the last – British politician to take it seriously. He was the first politician to be aware that he had to be, and to articulate, what voters wanted: he had to act it out. He was the voter's avatar. He was the first politician to understand the importance of the tart's answer to her mark's question, and to realise that it applied to politicians. 'What's your name?' the punter asks? 'What do you want it to be, lovey?' she replies.

Luckily, the focus group politician is likely to be a fairly short-lived experiment, especially since Tony Blair realised that he wanted to be a leader (over Iraq) and the voters realise that they need him to be a leader (over nearly everything else).

NAOMI KLEIN'S *NO LOGO*

Naomi Klein does decent service in pulling together the tatterdemalion army of prejudices and arguments of the anti-globalization movement.

We can observe, first of all, that she is not original in any of it, except insofar as she was pretty, intelligent, relaxed and young. Her own bibliography offers a few older sources for almost all she says, but omits all the interesting old ones. She is only really interested in the most recent of the arguments and cases in the area. Like Bjorn Lomborg in another context, she is interesting in part because we are watching a switch of generations and styles in the left (and in Lomborg's case, in the anti-greens). Gone is the downbeat, academic, deadbeat left; enter instead the upbeat Lipstick Radical, glammed-up for television. Lomborg has the honed pecs of a devotee of the gym: he is one of the few intellectuals in these debates who looks good in a T-shirt. These are very good developments: the globalization and environment arguments were, above all, short on glamour and personality. They had seemed dry, and now seem juicy. Now at least we can enjoy the time we spend with these arguments.

Klein was useful because she helped publicise (as a journalist not an activist) a feature of modern campaigning: that it uses the firm's brand against itself. This is little more than an argument that a firm's respectability is its weak point – which campaigners had always known. But it is something more: firms had not noticed that, when they became personable, human, friendly, and when they projected all this through a brand and a slogan, they produced a handy lever, the ideal handle, which campaigners could simply and cheaply invert, subvert, convert into a weapon. In wearing their hearts on their sleeves, firms had placed them where they could be snatched away. The firms had produced a little grenade with which to attack the consumer, and the campaigners realised how easily it could be picked up and lobbed back. Indeed, in using the brand as a weapon, the campaigners forced us all to recognise that firms were using their brands as a weapon, too. It reminded us that firms seem friendly, but can't be. They don't have hearts, they have interests. The campaigners did us a service in reminding people of the fact.

Many people admired the *No Logo* argument, and spotted very little of its weakness: that a firm's brand does still mostly signal its desire for respectability. Thus, firms cannot both be strong and have brands. We need never be frightened of a brand's strength. For as long as a firm makes money out of respectability and affection, it is us – the media, the public – who confer value. We can take away our confidence in a trice, and this ability empowers us.

Oddly, even knowing that a brand is a false friend, I still use the brands pretty much as the firms who promote them intend. As a mark of trust, I find, say, that Sony still works for me. I trust Sony, even though I have bought goods from them that are less good than products I have bought from firms I trust less. I know very well that I should not have kept my credit card debt with the same bank year after year: there have been better deals on offer. But I have an obscure feeling – disproved by my actual experience – that loyalty to my bank will be reciprocated. I am reluctant to switch from BT or even to use the cost-cutting systems that can run in parallel with a BT line. It would be a very good cigarette indeed that made me yearn to smoke, more than the idea – the image – of Camel. My much-loved father owned Vauxhalls, and they did us proud. I own a Vauxhall now, and it does me very proud indeed. But the brand doesn't get to me. My heart sank when I realised that a Vauxhall would suit me: I am not a Vauxhall person. But then, I hadn't been a Lada person, and yet I enjoyed owning one.

So I am not free of brands, nor enslaved by them; neither immune to them nor in their thrall. They are part of a conflicted modern experience, holding out promises that are both true and false. They play games with me and I play games with them. But firms aren't using them for the good of my health, but for the good of theirs. Sometimes – often – these coincide, but not always.

Firms are, of course, far more valuable than campaigners, and do far more good. Their branding and sloganising provide much innocent pleasure, while they sell us little stuff we don't want. But, yes, the campaigners rightly remind us that firms aren't our chums; our chums are. But they are way off beam when they suppose that firms are our enemies.

It is, of course, true that capitalism wants us to spend money in achieving our goals, and it does its best to hype up those goals that it knows we have and that it can satisfy. But it is very doubtful whether it has the power to make idiots of us, unless we are very willing accomplices in its deceptions. It requires very little strength of character to prefer to make an anonymous spaghetti Bolognese at home rather than to buy a branded hamburger in the street. If it turns out to be true that home-cooked food is better than manufactured, then it is hardly likely to be many years before we either opt for the homemade, or the manufacturers better capture the merits of homemade food. Isn't it happening already? Many of us cook for pleasure, just as many people love to buy ready-made food. And very good it is. (And very funny are Crosse and Blackwell when they remind us that Pot Noodle really is not the height of civilisation.) Are we in the maw of capitalism when we opt to buy in rather than cook? Surely not.

Of course, campaigners will say that bad food is in the interest of the capitalists and good food is not. The capitalists are inclined to reply that they have found what works – what sells – and have delivered it. They object to being told they are poisoners – of stomachs, cultures or minds – and point out that the campaigners may not understand the customers as well as food suppliers do.

It is routine now to say that consumers are bamboozled by advertisers into buying goods to satisfy the needs that the advertisers create. It takes a certain disrespect for modern people to say that they are too stupid to know where their preferences lie until advertisers tell them. It is hardly likely that the rich will really buy more Rolls-Royces than they can enjoy, and anyway, who cares about the folly of the advantaged?

The traditional case against ads and brands has been that they have progressed from selling products to selling lifestyle. Firms used to make products that they hoped people would like and would buy again. Then they started to advertise the products, and used brand names to ensure that what they advertised was what we bought. (Not hygiene, or soap, but Sunlight Soap was what Lever Brothers needed us to buy.) But then a subtler move was needed: after Coca-Cola became a branded drink, it became possible for any drink that Coca-Cola might make to confer a pleasurable feeling. Coca-Cola had become, as it were, a Sony or a Ford: a brand that could spread its benign cloak over any version of its product area that the firm chose to enter. Richard Branson takes the thing a stage further: anything that is branded by Virgin has Virginal qualities, and his firm moves into trains, planes, drinks, phones and financial services. Klein usefully notes – I think with disapproval, though its terms are not spelled out – that Body Shop and Virgin are thoroughly modern brands (in the manner of Coca-Cola and Nike), and not least when they are faintly, or even actually, dissident. Indeed, it is hard not to warm to someone who exposes, if rather feebly, how tiresome anti-capitalist capitalists are. (Klein is also capable of the telling phrase, not least when she discusses how a management guru appeals 'to the inner flake' in many a CEO.)

The Adbusters and Klein remind us that Nike and Virgin are alike in being Virtual Firms: Nike doesn't make shoes and Virgin doesn't run a mobile phone network. And the Adbusters and Klein are also right to note that this is very like a brand's real work: to sell us a lifestyle and an idea, at least as much as a physical product. Nike sells us the idea that we can be part of a world of sweaty excellence. Virgin sells us the idea that we can do all the things dreary people do, but do them larkily, edgily, funkily. Never mind that it's still a Nokia or a Boeing that is the guarantor of the reliability and the fact of the experience; it's Virgin that does us the favour of re-visioning the experience for us. This take is a little unfair to Nike and Virgin. Nike does design shoes, and why should it not subcontract their manufacture? Virgin may not make anything or directly provide many services, but it does make its services distinctive, as well as merely spraying a fetching logo over them.

The essence of this newer complaint about brands is that firms have somehow escaped the obligation to make anything, or even to be primarily about the things they appear to be selling us. No, they now sell us dreams about ourselves.

All this sort of thinking is to be found in *No Logo*.

BRANDING OUR ASPIRATIONS

Klein might have gone further, and suggested that there is a kind of false consciousness – a mass delusion – that has been created by modern capitalism. Arguably, it afflicts us all, rich and poor. It is an almost routine charge that individual brands do make our pre-existing appetites all but irresistible; that they mask the realities of the product; that they sell self-image rather than function.

The better charge would be that capitalism has stolen people's aspirations. This would be quite a clever charge. It would suggest that people are no longer capable of perceiving their wants and demands in any terms other than those catered to by capitalists. Capitalism has taken over our desires, which we ought to reclaim. Firms are indeed competing with each other for mind-share, but between them they already own it all. The world of getting and spending has achieved domination of our imaginations. It is not achievement, or being, or doing that defines us, but spending. We don't have selves any more; we have an accumulation of brand choices.

If all this were true, the idea that we were consumers would have attained powerful meaning.

Under this view, it doesn't matter whether one ignores the blandishments of any particular advertisement, or even all of them. There are no other choices to make than among commercial offerings, and these offerings themselves deliver psychological potency well beyond the fact of their pleasing or satisfying our ordinary needs. This is the charge of Ivan Illich, of Noam Chomsky (very lightly touched on by Klein) and many greens.

Klein does a deft feint or two. Her charge is that brand-makers have polluted 'public space, cultural freedom and democracy'. She scorns the traditional critics of advertising who remark on how forceful advertisers are and how weak consumers are. More remarkably, she is equally tough on those who suggest that people feebly volunteer to be branded. Such criticisms of advertising culture are made by people who have already given up the fight. 'What's the point of going through the trouble of trying to knock down the fence? Everyone knows the branded cows will just stand there looking dumb and chewing the cud.'

The problem is that she is keen to impress us with some modernity of insight, and yet at every point her cases are old hat. Klein's admired Adbusters – who sabotage and subvert advertising – can argue that they are useful in pumping up the self-respect and the awareness of consumers, and that this will crush the power of capitalist manipulators. Good: they may be right that consumers have 'lost it' recently. It may be better for the consumer to be better informed and demanding (though plenty of business people are inclined to argue that the consumer is already a stroppy, fickle, demanding, two-faced humbug). The larger point is that when the consumer is more discerning, more demanding, it will signal a yet greater sophistication in capitalism and wealth creation. McDonald's may well become more like a high-class restaurant, and that will be a sign that Trash Affluence has matured. McDonald's customers will have matured into higher-spending connoisseurs, just as tourists will graduate from the mass package toward a holiday at once more demanding and more rewarding – and expensive, and probably more profitable.

The homemade, the artisan-crafted, the organic, the peasant, the unmarketed and unpackaged are all available. As near as makes no difference, we could even now live in a world whose main features predate the world of manufactured aspirations.

Interestingly, to choose this world is to deceive oneself far more even than the brand-buyer does. In the souks of the rich world (those trendy street markets where things are so much more groovy, real, unmediated), rich young people buy the produce of poverty-stricken villages in which handicrafts are carried on with no regard for the pollution caused by dyes or the ill-health caused by high-pressure close handiwork in badly lit yurts, rondavels and huts wherein the occupants gulp down dioxin-laden smoke from dung fires.[15] The hip young children and grandchildren of the Flower Power generation feel themselves to be contributing, not exploiting. Out there, in the villages, the best and the brightest escape this charmed transaction and head for the factories of Nike's subcontractors, where machines do most of the work, where there is light to see by, a dormitory to sleep in and wages to send home.

THE UNBRANDED WORLD

A lot of what matters to us is not branded. Water and electricity and gas and home-owning are not advertised to us in the Klein way. They are not branded. Rather, producers genuinely seek to woo us from others with claims for their own excellence. People don't choose between power utilities as methods of self-expression – but of convenience. People buy houses, but there is little advertising to egg them on into house-buying mode. Houses aren't branded. One can grow one's own food or buy it from like-minded pseudo-peasants in farm shops. It is easy to have unbranded food. I could read only books written and published by pre-modern publishers whose imprimatur is more akin to an old pub shingle than to a brand logo. I could have friends round to make music with me, or only go to 'indie' gigs. I can buy cars so old – but still so good – that they have, so to speak, worn out their brandedness. Insofar as I involve myself in the modern world, it is pretty easy to do so with equipment bought second-hand, and free of marketing.

But this would be to take life to extremes of self-sufficient paranoia. Isn't it probable that most of us enjoy the joke in advertising and brands without being overly influenced by them? Some of the most telling ads of recent times have been for small cars (Renault's Clio; Fiat's Punto; Peugeot's 206). Each is enjoyable, but they are all aimed at the funky, sassy, classy self that young purchasers like to project. Surely this doesn't mean that a person would be made to want to be funky, sassy and classy by the existence of these ads? We know the chicken of people's pleasure in seeming to be those things somewhat predates the egg of the advertisers' production of the images.

We also know, and can handle, a more sinister – more intriguing – component in brand ads. Car firms don't sell us the image they think their vehicle has. Ads are corrective. They sell us an image that the producer fears the public does not have of its vehicle. Volvo's 2004 advertising campaign in print and on TV was called 'Life', and one of its messages was that 'Life is a journey where anything can happen.' The campaign featured a young blonde surf-boarder whose left arm has been bitten off by a shark, and a man who is homeless until a stroke of luck helps him transform himself into a successful Wall Street broker. These are stories of courage, and that's obviously positive stuff. But they are also stories of happenstance and wackiness, and that's far more interesting. Surely Volvo – famously stodgy and sensible, proudly defensive and protective – wanted to be seen as aware of the value of luck and the chance encounter.

There is rather little that is reflexive in advertising; very little that is Post Modern. Firms ask what we would like to be like, and how we see ourselves, and then they deliver it as best they can. And they seek to appeal to different bits – and the same bits – of the demographic, competitively among themselves: VW's Golf takes the chance that there is a po-faced, stolid, demanding, introverted type out there who is seeking expression of a different kind to the Clio-Punto-206 feel. MG had a TV ad which risked appealing to a nihilistic, anti-virtuous, politically incorrect young man, whose disenchantment with self-improvement had led him to seek a full-on, full-fat sports car, and then pulled its punches by noting that at least its car didn't use fur. (Pity.)

Why would car firms not advertise their small-engine hatchbacks by asserting that they are cheekily and unchallengingly chic, given that there is a bottom line of speed, safety, reliability, eco-responsibility that manufacturers must converge on? Of course they have sought to seek a personality for their cars – but it is customer-led, not producer-led. We may be worried when politicians attend to focus groups, but it is only right that firms should.

In short, there is nothing radical in the monopoly that Naomi Klein thinks she has identified.

The difficulty for the *No Logo* argument is that it is best applied to vulgar than to exotic, to cheap rather than expensive, forms of consumption. As we become more the kind of people Naomi Klein seems to wish we were – informed, demanding, free-thinking – we will probably spend more money, not less; we will become more capitalist, not less. Yes, her thinking seems to invite us toward a self-sufficient, educated, post-materialist future, and – yes – some will adopt that. Indeed, when the whole world is home to many more rich people – when Mass Affluence is the norm – it may be that middle-class mores will spread. But it is not likely that this can be achieved before we are more wealthy, generally more capitalist, than we are now. The true home of the ascetic yearning, the downsizing, the home-prepared foodie, is the middle class, and it is always worth remembering that the middle class is richer than the class that doesn't get the hang of such sophisticated, post-materialist ideas.

It would be a nicer world all round if poor people clubbed together, cooperated, bought wholesale, rode bicycles, read books, cooked wholefood – all those simple pleasures that are cheap and wholesome. They, more than the affluent, need to save money and adopt healthy meanness. But they don't. It is the affluent middle class that does these things. When the working class is history, and has been for some time, we will see these skills and disciplines permeate the whole of society. It will be a further evolution if they lead us – as they could – into a cheap, as well as a satisfying, way of life. In the meantime, we should not be surprised if the poor lack middle-class discipline: many of them are poor precisely because they lack discipline in the first place.

Nor should we blame them for seeking cheap, unhealthy, quick thrills, rather than the cheap, healthy, slow delights their betters have urged on them for generations. It took a middle-aged, rotund, ex-chain-smoking Scottish health secretary – John Reid – to point out that the poor sort of deserved such consolations as could be had. He was excoriated for the view: he was at once condoning what should be condemned (the sloppiness of the poor) and condescending to them. Apparently, there is very nearly as much support from the poor for bans on smoking in public places, and many poor people have given up smoking. It's just that fewer poor people, and especially poor women, have given up smoking than the affluent, and Reid felt like expressing some sympathy with them. Given that he was being kindly and accurate, as well as impolitic, it would be hard to condemn him.

It is not so much that such a thing is unimaginable. The privations of war did lead this society to the kind of life that modern downsizers and ascetics affect to find enjoyable. A more stoical generation than ours endured and even thrived during those privations – and threw them off with huge pleasure the moment they were free to.

This is not to say that such privations or exigencies, such emergencies, may not re-emerge. But we simply have no evidence that those who know this way chose it, or prefer it.

As to the poor, there is indeed a compelling case that they opt for cheap-seeming treats today, rather than for the saving and the deferred gratification that will give them richer and greater delights tomorrow. But as they stuff themselves with, say, trashy cake today, rather than saving for a hand-crafted one tomorrow, their choices – and the inadequacy of their choices – seem fairly trivial, and understandable. They are offered trivial choices, and make – arguably – the wrong ones. But they are at least granted the dignity of being included in the world of choice at very low prices of entry. That's part and parcel of their being included in the drama of life, and it is a sort of social inclusion.

Margaret Thatcher wondered why the poor don't buy in bulk. The answer is, in part, that they are poor, for buying in bulk implies larger, not smaller, spending than buying in smaller units. Of course, the poor could cooperatively buy at nearly wholesale prices. But then, one of the reasons modern poor people are poor is that they don't think in those sorts of terms. Like farmers, they value their independence from one another, and suffer for it. But it isn't the capitalists' fault that the poor don't organise themselves better.

Anyway, it is hardly likely that it is because of advertising that the poor smoke more, or eat more junk, than the better-off. It is, rather, that they seek immediate treats.

1 'Surprising ways to raise your HQ (Happiness Quotient)', *Good Housekeeping*, October 2004.

2 Geoffrey Pearson, *Hooligan: A history of respectable fears*, Macmillan, 1983.

3 See *Eurobarometer* 60, Autumn 2003, EU.

4 See *Eurobarometer* 60, Autumn, 2003, EU.

5 Gregg Easterbrook, *A Moment on Earth*, Penguin, 1995.

6 Gregg Easterbrook, *The Progress Paradox: How life gets better while people feel worse*, Random House, 2003.

7 Easterbrook, *The Progress Paradox*, p. 251.

8 See 'My heroes' at www.richarddnorth.com.

9 See www.thersa.org/acrobat/layard_180204.pdf.

10 For a good guide to the big hitters in this argument, see www.warwick.ac.uk/cep/2002_euro_positive.html, an account of an academic conference on the theme. Ralph Waldo Emerson and William James are both interesting on these themes. See: Richard Geldard, *The Vision of Emerson*, Vega, 2001 and R W B Lewis, *The Jameses: A family narrative*, Andre Deutsch, 1991.

11 This story is told in Alex Carey, *Taking the Risk Out of Democracy: Corporate propaganda versus freedom and liberty*, Illinois, 1997.

12 There are many sources on Bernays, including a biography and an autobiography. The web is rich in material. See http://en.wikipedia.org/wiki/Edward_Bernays.

13 This theme is discussed by Stephen Daniels in *Fields of Vision*, Polity, 1993.

14 Charles Clover, *The Spectator*, 3 July 2004.

15 See Richard D North, *Life On a Modern Planet: A manifesto for progress*, Manchester University Press, 1995.

CHAPTER 3

MASS AFFLUENCE AND INEQUALITY

In a nutshell, then: inequality, low taxation of the rich and a low 'State Take' seem rather good for some rich countries: that is to say, they tend to be rather good for everyone in those societies. This implies that at least to some degree the existence of poverty is good for nearly everyone (perhaps including the poor) in rich societies. We look at these curious questions.

INEQUALITY NOW

Our kind of question is: Do the rich need the poor? Do the poor need the rich? Do the rich cause the poverty of the poor? Are the rich obliged to 'solve' the problem of poverty? Do they, in fact, do their bit to alleviate the problem?

In the summer of 2004, IPPR (Institute for Public Policy Research), a left-leaning British think-tank, 'close to New Labour thinking' as the mantra goes, reported that inequality in Britain had risen slightly in recent years (under New Labour), though poverty had fallen somewhat. This was unremarkable news, since it is the continuation of a gradual and perhaps even deliberate trend under the government of the day. However, the *Financial Times* responded with a leader of some interest. Noting what almost everyone thinks is the egregious inequality of earlier decades, and the reduction of inequality since, it said that the recent rise in inequality under the Tories and Labour would perhaps soon falter (because of some complexities which aren't important here).

The leader said the IPPR report

will make for sober reading. While praising progress in reducing child poverty, it highlights many areas where inequalities have persisted or risen...One of the more startling findings is a rise in wealth inequality – the first in more than a century. At the time of Lloyd George's 1909 'people's budget', just one per cent of Britons owned 70 per cent of all wealth. During the following eight decades, asset ownership broadened from a wealthy aristocratic elite to a burgeoning middle class. By the end of the 1980s, that figure was down to 17 per cent. Successive broadening of the asset structure broke the hold of the landed gentry and allowed ordinary Britons to take a real financial stake in their society.

During the 1990s, however, the top one per cent increased its share to 22 per cent. The wealth owned by Britain's richest 10 per cent, meanwhile, rose to over half of all assets...

The leader noted that the rise in inequality had continued unabated under New Labour, and went on: 'Nonetheless, the government could implement some policies to hold wealth inequality back.'[1]

To which the proper response is: why bother? The *FT* had made the characteristic unthinking flinch of the left-leaning liberal from the possibility that the neo-liberal might be getting things right.

Sir Samuel Brittan, in his own column in the paper a few days later, was too polite to point out directly that his leader-writing colleagues were not thinking very clearly. But he pointed out the fallacy of their sort of argument when he discussed how inequality is not an indicator of poverty or iniquity. He said his mantra was 'Redistribution yes, equality no'. One might note that this is, in itself, capable of being a left-wing mantra (if one insisted on a lot of redistribution). But it allows – and this is the important bit – that inequality has nothing whatever to do with poverty, at least in rich societies. That is to say: inequality does not cause poverty, and is not even well correlated with it. One might have a redistribution policy so as to direct resources at the poor, and that could be a good thing. But to have a redistribution policy to reduce inequality would be to assume that it was important to reduce envy, or to bash the rich (since these could be its only real aims).

Even if one gets this sort of thing straight in one's mind (and the *FT* ought to have), the problem of poverty may not necessarily have much to do with the rich or very rich. It might be, for instance, that solutions more properly lie with the middling class of person than the very top end. A possible reason for this counter-intuitive possibility is this: the rich and very rich might be hugely more rich than anyone else in society, but their very richness – the extreme of their richness – might be necessary to improve the lot of the poor. It might, contrariwise, be the case that clobbering the rich might not yield very much advantage to the poor. If the rich were, say, employers in a market such that they could up sticks and do their employing somewhere else, then it might well be worthwhile for the state to pander to them. Actually, the Anglosphere mostly believes the rich yield both jobs and lots of tax, and are doubly to be welcomed.

It is a tense matter to decide how much to 'cane' the rich and very rich, rather than to cane the middle class, to help the poor.

It is also important to consider the degree to which wealth, though 'owned' by this or that sector in society is actually 'tied up', 'controlled' or 'hogged' by them. For instance, we are not owned by the people who own the company that employs us. We don't even work for them. In owning the company that employs us, shareholders own the profits, which their capital and our labour produce. What is more, the opportunities for the Mass Affluent to own wealth are legion: if they choose to spend it rather than save it and put it to work, is that a sign of any sort of inequality that matters?

Very rich people own land, which they mostly cannot monopolise (since there are ancient rights of access to most of it). They own shares, which is a token of the investment by which the rest of us live. They own lots of stuff, which is mostly flaunted, so we can all enjoy it. They own art, which they mostly display. The ebb and flow of life ensures that if the very rich do not give away their wealth, it soon disperses as their children dissipate it. The historical inequality which we all sense to have been egregious probably wasn't, and we make a mistake when we turn its correlation with extremes of poverty into a cause. Our present levels of inequality, even in the Anglosphere, seem positively unexceptional.

Of course, as the *FT* suggests, modern capitalism has been about the rise of a property-owning democracy, in which very many of us have a stake as owners. We show no signs of reducing our keenness on this trend. The present young know perfectly well that they want to own property and have a pension. The supply of the first probably ought to be increased; the supply of the second depends entirely on demand. A small trend toward inequality, or even a large one, might be a sign that the Mass Affluent would rather fritter away their wealth than invest it. It may not be, of course. But even if it is, there is nothing in the inequality trends that makes the Mass Affluent feckless.

This is not to say that inequality is a good thing, either. The very rich seem valuable, and we want them here among us. All the same, the rich are part of an economic system and an organic society, whose health may well require that they make accommodations with the rest of us. If the rich were amenable to being lectured, we could say telling things about their obligations to the rest of society. Some rich people do listen – and even drive – such insights. The more important point, though, is that expediency should make the non-rich understand the great value to the whole of society of the very rich. Imposing equality is more dangerous to us all even than letting inequality rip.

It is normally supposed that an unequal society is necessarily a place where lots of people are relatively (and worryingly) poor, or some (many, perhaps?) are very poor, compared with their fellows. It is often supposed, too, that unequal societies produce poverty, from which it is hard to escape. It is supposed that unequal societies more or less strategically ignore the plight of the poor, or are – to put it more kindly – more inclined to accept it than societies that put a high premium on equality.

It seems sensible enough to make these gloomy assumptions, and we may shrug our shoulders at the inevitability of it all. It might be that the existence of poor people is necessary in some way for the increased or continued happiness of so many of their fellow citizens that their poverty is morally acceptable. There might be a softer version of this scenario which suggests that one should 'tackle' the extremes of poverty, but that a good deal of moderate poverty is more than acceptable, given the well-being of the rest of society that flows from it.

Western societies might indeed have chosen – are usually assumed to have chosen – this sort of view. Reaganomics and Thatcherism were supposed to have turned it into policy. It is true that the Reagan/Thatcher rhetoric, and even their policies, were designed to 'squeeze' the poor and to liberate the rich, and that this was the main distinction between that brand of politics and the politics of the left. But reality seldom follows rhetoric.

Politics is, to a large extent, about this argument. The hard laissez-faire 'right' is indeed prone to the view that the horror of poverty is quite a useful reminder of the costs that fall to those who do not successfully put the aspiration to be better off into effect. If aspiration is the carrot of ambition, dread of poverty is its stick.

More generally, the right does hold that trying to abolish poverty may be a lot more trouble than it's worth: that poverty is remarkably stubborn and many approaches to dealing with it have backfired. That is the story of communism, after all. It is also the story of the modern widespread disenchantment with the welfare state. Large numbers of people have lost sympathy with the poor. Partly, the poor seem to have been featherbedded. Partly, they seem to have rewarded everyone's efforts rather badly.

The evolution of modern politics goes something like this: the post-1945 welfare state flowed from the idea that the poor were deserving, yet by the mid 70s the welfare state had destroyed that widespread belief. In 2004, there is less willingness to pay high taxes for the poor and unemployed in an economy that seems to be short of labour. The middle classes seem to accept that they must build their own pensions. But a big majority of voters resists a shift toward paying for their own education and health services. So the very big political difficulty for the right is that the idea that dignity consists in standing on one's own two feet is endorsed for only part of the welfare state's provisions. And even if the middle classes would endorse a shrivelled welfare state, we are left with the stubborn problem of the poor who won't, or can't, partake in this new generalised self-sufficiency.

So the issue seems, for practical purposes, a matter of how to enlarge the public pot (rather than how to wean the public off it). Economists of the Thatcherite right seem to have persuaded many westerners that apparent indifference to inequality and the advantage of the rich might help the poor. It is accepted that high tax rates on the rich are a greater disincentive to them than might at first seem likely. The maths shows that at very high rates of tax, each percentage point reduction in tax yields a disproportionate increase in real income retained by the taxpayer. The rich really can be encouraged to stay interested in wealth creation if they are not punished for it.

Secondly, lowered taxation rates can yield greater income for the state (for redistribution, for instance) than raised ones: the tax 'take' comes from the larger pot created by increased economic growth, and more people are in work, creating taxpayers out of tax consumers.[2]

This is, naturally, contested territory. In the US, Reaganomics has had its mirror image in the Rubinomics – the creed of Robert E Rubin – that operated under Bill Clinton's presidency. Keen to beat inflation and high deficits, Clinton raised taxes (by a few points overall, with reductions for the poor and increases for the rich, and the middle class left more or less untouched), and growth rose too. It turns out that inflation, the world economy, innovation, the costs of deficits, confidence about the future all have big influences that can appear to confound or confirm both left- and right-leaning strategies.[3]

Yet the US is within its rights to claim that a relatively low State Take, and relatively low tax rates for the rich have been a decent recipe for its economy, and that those countries that adopt its recipe (the UK) seem to benefit too. Clinton's tax 'hike' was within a US model of a relatively low tax take, even if it outraged, and continues to outrage, the right. George W Bush's tax reductions are large enough to outrage the left, but too small to turn the US into a monstrously right-wing economy.

And the US – like the UK – remains a political economy that accepts relatively stingy poverty relief and low minimum wages, even if Clinton, followed by Blair, did somewhat reduce poverty levels. Compared with welfarist politicians, both men were brutalists. The whole of Europe has, with varying degrees of delay, enthusiasm and success, followed their recipe.

UNPICKING POVERTY

We want to know: How much poverty is there in different states? Which societies involve themselves in the problems of the poor, as opposed to pursuing a wealth-creating strategy that tends to ignore them? To what degree do people have upward mobility – out of poverty – and back again?

Measuring poverty is very difficult in itself, and more difficult if one tries to compare its historic trends. It is also hard to compare the condition of poverty and its trends between states. The reasons are simple, even if the answers aren't. One difficulty is that countries do not measure poverty in the same way: the US, for instance, has always posited a particular income that, in any year, ought to be reached (an 'income threshold'). Other countries use a relationship to 'mean' or 'median' income. A further difficulty (implied in both the measures just mentioned) is that the world has been getting richer, and the standards at which people live have been rising too. A working-class person now routinely travels distances, and at speeds, that were once the preserve of aristocrats. A level of health care now exists for almost everyone that could not have been imagined for anyone a few years ago. Items once considered luxuries are now 'necessities' (colour televisions, for instance). But ideas change too: levels of deprivation and its associated suffering that were once considered normal and acceptable are now neither normal nor acceptable. All these are issues that might be thought to constitute changing ideas of absolute poverty – they are about access to goods and services, the absence of which would be taken now to constitute deprivation.

But turn to the idea of *relative* poverty and the problem is yet worse. It is generally accepted – though not, perhaps, by the right – that it is simply unacceptable for people to fall below a certain percentage of the average income of society. This is not about the relationship between the poor and the rich. It is about the relationship between the norm – the mean or median of the nation's income – and those who fall below it. This relationship is not about goods and services at all: it is simply about a sense of poverty that attaches to not being in the right relation to the middling sort of person in society. The right is inclined to say that such matters simply do not constitute poverty, and are a snare and a delusion. The Status Anxiety sort of person is inclined to think that there is indeed a real 'comparison poverty'.

The right would insist that, if comparison poverty exists, it ought to be allowed only for those people who are egregiously more poor than the relatively well off.

The modern left-minded person, liking new forms of jargon, tends to talk of 'social exclusion' as defining the sort of poverty that being poorer than 'normal' people constitutes. The term at its most meaningful encompasses the kind of exclusion that flows from not being able to participate, say, in the labour market because of one's lack of education. But the term easily slops over into implying the kind of exclusion that attaches, say, to someone who can't afford to visit football matches or travel abroad. It implies that there is a norm of consumption and recreation, and that being excluded from it is a form of poverty that matters. Note, of course, that the term also frames the victim as the passive loser in a process: the 'disadvantaged' are actively shut out by some 'other'. It is not their laziness, but society slamming doors in their faces, that is at work.

One problem with measuring trends in poverty is to do with its changing nature. In particular, there is the difficulty of the voluntariness of some poverty. Poverty attaches to certain lifestyles, and these are, to some extent, chosen. More women are now choosing to have children without having the fathers to go with them. Their number is not huge, and they are not a huge proportion of the poor; nor are the numbers of single-parent families hugely more than was ever the case. But there are more women who have chosen this position than there used to be, and to that extent one might ask whether their poverty is as much the state's business as that of previous generations of single mothers who were more likely to have been victims of circumstance. It is a moral question whether it is a woman's right to choose to have children without having a father around; it is an even sharper moral question whether she has the right to take this course if there is a reasonable prospect that it will thrust her and her children into poverty.

A further difficulty is that the kinder a rich society is, the more likely it is to allow immigration that is not economically valuable. Such a society would allow in more people who are likely to start and remain poor. Bangladeshis, Pakistanis and Caribbean black people in Britain are more likely to be poor than their fellow-Britons, whether we compare them with immigrants from India, Asians expelled from Uganda, Orientals, or their white neighbours. We could have had better poverty statistics if we had been more selective – differently selective – in our immigration policies, but we might not have had such good health and public services (which have depended heavily on Caribbean blacks) or been the society we wanted to be.

These remarks make it clear that a state could probably never abolish absolute poverty. The absolute turns out not to be absolute (there is inflation, if you like, even in the absolute). And the comparative becomes more and more of a stick with which to beat society, as comparisons between the only very moderately well-off and the people one rung below them come to seem odious.

None of this is to say that there is not extreme poverty in nearly every society, nor to deny that it is shocking, both because it involves suffering by any definition and because it occurs in the midst of such affluence. Rather, it is intended to note that the poverty data is hard to read and assess. And it is also to note that the degree of poverty that will most concern a right-winger is usually found as a very small, if worrying, component in modern societies.

By almost all measures, there is less old-fashioned poverty in western societies than there used to be. Life expectancy, child mortality, quality of housing, years of education – these are some of the measures by which almost all societies have improved the lot of the poor, and even the very poor, year on year. The US has seen child mortality figures rise, it is true. But they have done so by very little, and it might very well be because of the changing nature of the immigrants who now constitute the very poor, rather than because of a new meanness or carelessness.

POVERTY IN THE US

In the US, according to the US Census Bureau, the percentage of people in poverty declined from around 22 per cent in the late 50s to less than 15 per cent in the early 60s. It continued to fall gently toward 11 per cent until the late 70s, when it started to rise again, reaching 15 per cent again in the mid 80s; it then fell back a few points until the late 80s, when it started to rise back up to reach the 15 per cent level in the mid 90s. Thereafter the rate fell back slightly until the very late 90s, when it started to rise again. In 2002 the poverty level was 12.1 per cent. It is very likely to have fallen since then, because the US economy has been growing well since 2001. There are signs, too, that the growth has recently (2004) started to improve the lot of the workers rather than 'merely' the capitalists it has already enriched. (Will Hutton cites authors who produce higher figures for US poverty; I have not pursued his sources, preferring this official material.) Hutton says that the middle 60 per cent in the US income profile have had stagnant incomes. This is true, except that people in the middle band do, nonetheless, experience rising incomes as their careers progress. People do not experience income stasis. So try this:

Like official government data sources, the PSID (Panel Study of Income Dynamics) data for prime-age, full-time male earners shows relatively flat median earnings and rising dispersion across high earners and low earners between the late 1970s and the early 1990s. The PSID data also indicate a substantial amount of upward mobility over 10-year horizons during the period. There is a moderate amount of downward mobility as well, even though prime-age men typically see their earnings grow as they age.

Overall, these results indicate that upward mobility remains an attainable goal for the majority of working-age individuals. The presence of mobility implies that yearly measures of earnings inequality probably overstate the permanent earnings differences between individuals. That said, the earnings dynamic has changed in recent decades, shifting from one that slightly benefits lower earners to one that slightly benefits higher earners.[4]

The rises in poverty correlate pretty strongly with recessions. But they do not correlate terribly well with the type of politician in power. In our very recent history, poverty declined during the watches of Presidents Reagan and Clinton (and could their rhetorical approaches have been more different?) and rose during the presidencies of Bush, father and son. However, it looks as though it is now declining on Bush Junior's watch (in spite, or because, of his having made every sign of wanting to get back to a Reaganomic approach). Perhaps he will achieve as little real 'cruelty' as the founder of the creed?

Further compounding political cliché, it is worth noting that the left's great hero, John F Kennedy, also cut the top rate of tax dramatically: he took it down from around 90 per cent when he took office to the 70 per cent level, which President Reagan was later to inherit.

Recent analysis of the trends of the tax burden on the poor, the middling sort of person, and the rich shows that the tax cuts of both Reagan and Bush Junior had consequences that the left would not expect. Reagan set in train a reduction in the top rate of tax (from 70 to 50 per cent under him; it is now 39.1 per cent). However, President Reagan did not 'clobber' the state's social spending, and the budget deficit necessarily rose.

As Bruce Bartlett (a neo-liberal commentator) observes:

A convenient starting point is 1984. The Reagan tax cut was then fully phased in (which reduced the top statutory income tax rate from 70 percent to 50 percent) and the 1983 Social Security tax increase had already taken effect (which raised the OASI [Old Age Survivors Insurance] tax rate from a combined 9.5 percent to 10.4 percent). In that year, those in the bottom quintile (20 percent of households) paid an average federal tax rate (individual, payroll, corporate and excise) of 10.2 percent.

Those in the top quintile paid 24.5 percent, the top 10 percent paid 25.2 percent, the top 5 percent paid 26.1 percent, and the top 1 percent paid 28.2 percent. Thus, those at the top paid about two and a half times more than those at the bottom.

Fast forward to 2001 (latest year in the Congressional Budget Office study). The top statutory income tax rate has fallen to 39.1 percent and the total payroll tax rate has risen from 14 percent to 15.3 percent. If one knew these figures in 1984, almost all economists would have projected a sharp decline in taxes paid by the rich and an increase in those paid by the poor.

In fact, the data show that those in the bottom quintile are only paying about half what they did 20 years ago: 5.4 percent. This is down from 6.4 percent just the year before, owing to the Bush tax cut.

Those in the top quintile did pay a little less in 2001 than they did in 2000: 26.8 percent versus 28 percent. But this is still well above the average tax rate they paid in 1984. Interestingly, those at the very top saw virtually no cut at all, even though liberals constantly say that they got the lion's share of the 2001 tax cut. Between 2000 and 2001, those in the top 10 percent of households saw a drop from 29.7 percent to 28.6 percent and those in the top 5 percent saw a decline from 31.1 percent to 30.1 per cent, but those in the top 1 percent saw their effective tax rate virtually unchanged: 33.2 percent versus 33 percent.

All of those in the middle three quintiles paid less in 2001 than they paid in 1984. In other words, between 1984 and 2001 average tax rates for the wealthy substantially increased, while at least 80 percent of households paid considerably less. Progressivity rose as the wealthy now pay about 6 times more than the poor.[5]

The focus now shifts to a matter that is probably more important. The rate of tax (which we have been discussing) is not nearly as important as the yield of whatever tax rate is applied. The left is inclined to think that it is important to 'punish' the rich, and that the degree of punishment is best expressed in the rate of tax. The right is more inclined to think that, insofar as the rich can help the poor, the more rich there are the better, and this will be affected by tax rates. The right argues that lower tax rates produce more rich people, and that means more people able to help the poor. This would be demonstrated by the tax yield from the rich. This is what we seek to optimise, never mind whether it is from a high or low rate.

Bartlett is able to show us that the tax yield from the rich has expanded over the years of relative decline in their tax rate:

Looking at the share of taxes paid shows a similar pattern. From 1984 to 2001, those in the bottom quintile reduced their share of the total tax burden from 2.4 percent to 1.1 percent. Those in the top quintile saw their share rise from 55.6 percent to 65.3 percent. Among the ultra wealthy, the top 10 percent increased their share from 39.3 percent to 50 percent, the top 5 percent raised their share from 28.2 percent to 38.5 percent, and that of those in the top 1 percent went up from 14.7 percent to 22.7 percent.

In short, the poor paid half as much of the federal tax burden in 2001 as they did in 1984, while the rich paid about 50 percent more. Those in the middle paid about a third less.

One would think that those on the left would be happy about this trend. Instead, they constantly demagogue the wealthy as deadbeats unwilling to bear their 'fair share' of the tax burden, and berate the Bush tax cuts for having 'slashed' taxes for the wealthy while the rest of us pay more. As is so often the case, the truth is exactly the opposite of that portrayed in the liberal worldview.[6]

The implication of this work is that the rich have increased the very large help they 'give' the poor, while the middle classes have done rather less. This raises a question as to the likely utility of future policy. If – and it is a big if – the US ought to raise more taxation, it seems reasonable to suggest that the focus ought more to be on raising taxation from middle-income people than from the rich. In any case, we can certainly observe that the myth surrounding rich people (that they pay a very small share of their income in tax and that that share contributes relatively little to the taxation pie) is false. Future policy at the very least would need to take account of the role the rich play in the dynamism of the economy, whose vigour is the biggest determinant of the ability of people to pay taxes.

SOME POVERTY NUMBERS

Here is a fairly characteristic, and probably typical, statement of a western country's poverty. In *Poverty in Canada*, the Fraser Institute says:

While most estimates of the trend in poverty focus on the past 15 or 20 years, Measuring Poverty in Canada [a right-leaning think-tank report] gives an estimate of the rate of poverty in Canada from 1951 to 1996, the most recent data available. This longer term trend reveals that the rate of poverty fell solidly from about 40% in 1951 to about 8% in 1981 where it has more or less stayed. While the decline in the early period is impressive (and is a testament to strong economic growth and a buoyant labour market), the more recent (apparent) stagnation of the rate is a concern. Several hypotheses, including data problems, a different 'character' of poverty, and employment disincentives built into our social programs, are discussed by way of explaining the pattern.[7]

POVERTY IN THE UK

And here, too, is a useful account of dealing with absolute hardship in the UK. A left-leaning poverty specialist writes, of a survey that assessed poverty:

The survey used a comprehensive and careful measure of hardship. It first counted 40 items that families ought to have but went without because they 'cannot afford them' – essential things like hot meals, shoes, coats and family outings, together with modern needs like TVs and washing machines. Then it added problem debts that families say they can do nothing to repay, and signs of overcrowding and poor housing conditions, such as being too cold in winter. Eighty items like these added up to a nine-point summary score. It is not the only valid measure of child poverty but it is a good one.

What were the results? Overall, seven out of 10 British families in 2001 scored zero on the nine-point hardship scale, 23% registered one or two points and only 8% were in 'severe hardship' (three to nine points).

This last figure is the one to watch because it was deliberately designed to divide the poorest from the poor. And the first job of the welfare system is to keep low-income families and their children out of severe hardship. This is especially true of out-of-work families, who have about 2 million children between them. In 1999, 41% of out-of-work families were in severe hardship – a teeth-grindingly high figure after two years of Labour government. By 2001 this figure had dropped to 28% among lone parents and to 22% among out-of-work couples.

These improvements were in direct response to the chancellor's 2000–1 increases in out-of-work benefits for families with children. These improvements ought to continue as the new money starts to affect the less responsive items that make up the hardship scale, such as being able to afford family outings and consumer durables.[8]

I have left in the author's remarks supporting Labour's policy, because it reminds us that people being in work is good for their levels of poverty, which goes toward a conservative case that economic growth and job creation matters. And it speaks of positive benefits from the social efficacy of the current government's policies.

Less controversially, though, we can see that on current measures, 'only 8% were in "severe hardship"'. That is the sort of figure suggested in the Canadian numbers, as well.

By comparison, the Joseph Rowntree Trust has research that relies on a relative number, and it is rather gloomier:

Across Britain, figures for 2001/02 show the number of individuals in homes with incomes below the poverty line (defined as 60 per cent of the median household income after deducting housing costs) fell to 12.5 million, or 22 per cent of the population. Of these, 3.8 million were children, 2.2 million were pensioners and 6.6 million were working-age adults.

The figures compare with a peak of 13.4 million people in low-income households in the mid-1990s and are lower than at any time during the 1990s. There are signs that Britain may have started to move away from the bottom of the European Union 'poverty league' which it shared four years ago with Portugal, Greece, Spain, Italy and Ireland.

Lower poverty levels have been largely due to falls in unemployment. But the report records a lack of equivalent progress in the number of out-of-work adults who are not classed as 'unemployed'. The 1.6 million people aged 25 to retirement who are 'economically inactive but want work' (long-term sick, disabled and others) now outnumber the 'unemployed' by a ratio of two to one.

It also highlights the continuing problem of the high number of low income households where someone is in paid work: an average 3.5 million people were experiencing 'in-work poverty' between 1999 and 2002 compared with three million between 1994 and 1997.[9]

This reinforces the general phenomenon that it is rather easy to 'see' high levels of poverty if one uses comparisons with the median income: it legitimises anxiety over the social condition of 22 per cent of the population, which may seem to many to set rather high the proportion of modern Britons experiencing worrying poverty.

It is also worth noting that the degree of inequality in Britain has slightly lessened under the present Labour government. But it still remains comfortably in touch with the relatively high levels achieved from the mid 1980s onwards.[10]

THE STATE TAKE

Modern states are regarded as 'mean' and 'cruel' if taxation claims around 30 per cent of the nation's wealth, especially if it is also falling, as in the case of the USA. They are regarded as nicely generous if they claim well over 40 per cent, as they do for the EU as a whole (where taxation is falling in general). Britons are inclined to think their country is in the midst of a dynamic, anti-state counter-revolution as its politicians struggle to hold the State Take at a tad over 40 per cent (and rising). The European political argument used to be about whether the State Take should be 50 per cent or 30 per cent. Now it unlikely that a politician would go very far if he strayed much from the 40 per cent mark.[11]

It is hard to imagine the modern electorate accepting that they are too rich, are not enjoying it, and would be happier being less rich and paying more tax. Those that are prone to that line of thought were offered the (old) Labour party, but its supporters were not numerous enough to make it an electoral winner. (Old) Labour only won when – in the hands of Harold Wilson, in particular – it positively renounced socialism. The critics of Anglosphere capitalism have always been able to hold up the Continental and Nordic alternatives, and have done so to little effect. The British probably think that it would be nice to be as nice as the Norwegians, and quite seriously wonder if they shouldn't be as industriously serious as the Germans, and then they fall back, and do a more privately entrepreneurial thing, or go fishing.

The usual measure of the state's preparedness to get involved with the poor is to look at the state's share of the national income. This might not be a perfect proxy for interest in the poor, since the money might be disproportionately spent on, say, the military as opposed to, say, income benefit. And then there is the problem of 'churn': to a large extent, taxation of the middle-income middle classes is accepted by them not least because they get a high percentage of what they pay back again. The process of churn matters to modern politics: the argument goes – and it seems reasonable – that the middle classes accept a high-taxation state because they are themselves consumers and beneficiaries of state provision of, say, education and health services. Indeed, part of the problem for the right wing and for 'conservative' politicians as they argue against a large state is that the most important constituency for their arguments does not yet accept that the risk of 'going private' is worthwhile, even if it meant lower taxes. In short, the middle classes accept that high taxes are a relatively inexpensive way of paying for health and education. It may not be cheap, they think, but it is safe.

Moreover, while the idea of 'Eurosclerosis' (that European states have lousy growth rates, stagnant economies and high unemployment rates because of their relatively high tax takes) is attractive, there is no fixed relationship between low taxes and economic growth. That would be too simple a connection for the real world.

The Holy Grail is vigorous economic growth (which high taxes might indeed tend to stifle), with a highly educated labour force (which high taxes might help produce), with a willing labour force for all the jobs currently on offer (which might be encouraged by low taxes), along with social stability (which high taxes might help to maintain). Ideally, everyone able to work would be willing to work; ideally everyone in work could earn a wage that would support him or her.

The West has generally been pursuing a policy of reducing taxation rates (and the State Take) a little, at the same time as either decreasing social spending by rather less, or actually increasing it.

MINIMUM WAGES

A further feature of domestic policy is the degree to which low wages are tolerated. Most western countries now have a minimum wage, but in all cases it is set too low to provide a modern standard of living for families that try to live on one wage, and quite often even two minimum wage earners won't lift a family out of poverty.

Indeed, every society, and especially rich ones, faces a peculiar conundrum. There is almost always a pool of people who are not qualified for high-wage work. What is more, there are many jobs that society needs to be done but that no-one is willing to pay very much for. Care of the elderly, digging roads, baggage handling, semi-skilled teaching, child care, crop harvesting: these are all jobs which few people in rich countries are willing to do, and which seem 'naturally' to attract low wages. To get these jobs done, a society needs poor people, for whom accepting this work is the best option they have.

States face a decision. One approach is to allow immigrants to come in to take the work, knowing they will accept western poverty in preference to the worse sort they knew at home. Another approach is to set a more 'humane' minimum wage, to tempt domestic workers to take these jobs. A third approach is to bolster the incomes of the working poor.

Each of these strategies risks alienating important, usually quite poor, sections of society and – what may matter more – their professional advocates. To banish the extremes of poverty requires state action, which upsets the not-very-rich, who are fairly content to find quite severe poverty in social strata below their own. So, the ordinary mass of people seem to accept pretty easily that the poor are necessary to society. But are they more important to the rich than to anyone else? Rather the reverse, probably. The poor do indeed keep the price of labour in unpleasant jobs lower than it would have been. What is less clear is whether a society could operate by paying more for these jobs, or by subsidising the low-waged more, or by paying high rates of unemployment benefit, or by allowing these jobs to go undone. Finding answers to these questions has troubled politicians for generations and will continue to do so. But while it is easy to suppose that the rich are in the forefront of pressing for mean policies toward the poor waged and unwaged, it is as much the whole of society – including many who are not rich – who benefit from the job creation, the affordable public services and the cheap food which a low-wage economy creates.

Though the populism of Reagan and Thatcher included the rhetoric of being tough on the poor (or at any rate that was the way it was taken), in fact the rhetoric was much tougher than the reality. It was the middle and lower orders of society that adopted their creed with greater gusto than the better-off and the patrician elements, who had – many of them – long ago come to find a corporatist, high-tax society pretty tolerable.[12] Frank Johnson notes that (Governor) Ronald Reagan only half understood the upper echelons of British business. In 1969 Reagan addressed the Institute of Directors at the Albert Hall. 'Magnificently, he assured the assembled directors that they were entrepreneurs yearning to breathe free if only government would throw off their shackles of regulation and punitive taxation. [Actually, writes Johnson, the leaders quite liked the shackles.] Most of them were doing perfectly well out of the Wilsonian, soon to be Heathian, corporate state, in league with the unions.'[13] That was, incidentally, the Reagan speech that sent Dennis Thatcher back to Margaret with the news that a new sort of political creed was at last in the air.

SHARE OF THE NATIONAL 'CAKE' TAKEN BY THE STATE
(percentage share of GDP for 1990 and 2001)

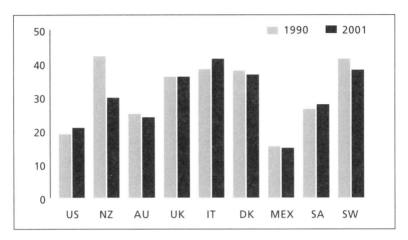

US: United States; NZ: New Zealand; AU: Australia; UK: United Kingdom;
IT: Italy; DK: Denmark; MEX: Mexico; SA: South Africa; SW: Sweden.
Different measures produce slightly different percentages. However, the
comparisons between countries tend to hold good whatever measure is used.
Source: www.worldbank.org/data/wdi2004/pdfs/Table4_11.pdf

THE STATE'S DUTY

All these complicating factors make the State Take a hotly contested
political issue in all western countries. All have tended to try to reduce
the State Take, and most have succeeded to the point of infuriating the
left. But few have succeeded in doing so to the extent of really pleasing
the right. That is to say, the most remarkable feature of modern politics
is the stubbornness of the State Take. Among rich western countries, the
US has been exceptional in holding the percentage of State Take fairly
steady (and lowish). Japan's State Take has risen steadily from a very
low level (compared with western countries), while European countries
have varied rather, but have seen an average of a handful of per cent
higher than the US's, rising to a mid 90s peak more like 10 points ahead
of the US's.

Wealth may be a moral and practical problem in itself. Perhaps,
for instance, rich people do unacceptable environmental damage.
Perhaps being rich is bad for people. However, the absence of wealth –
poverty – is more often seen as a curse. The nastiness of poverty has
usually been taken as being pretty self-evident. This latter thought is, of
course, vitiated by some evidence that poor people are happy. And we
will look at that idea. It is, indeed, a distinctly modern idea that poverty
is quite pleasant, and we will come to that too.

Irrespective of the merits of either wealth or poverty, the disjunction between wealth and poverty – inequality – is very often seen as a crying shame in need of redress. Being rich when one is surrounded by poverty is widely seen as sinful.

BUT IS IT?

There are two large and irreconcilable camps battling over the issue. The first, from the left, emphasises the moral obligation of the rich to the poor. Common humanity dictates that the rich should spare something – perhaps a lot – for the less fortunate. The poor in society, it is often argued, actually create the wealth the rich manage and spend. Where would the rich be without the poor? If the economic system – capitalism – won't even things up, that shows its moral bankruptcy, and politics will have to do its virtuous work. The flow of gratitude ought to be from rich to poor.

A crucial feature of this view is the mental image of a national 'pie' that can be carved up and served in different portions. This is a hangover from the ancient 'mercantilist' view, which could not imagine that trade and commerce could be a 'win-win' game. In trade, mercantilists wanted to sell, but not to buy. The world's wealth was set, and a nation's job was to haul in all it could, while letting go of as little as possible. (Now, we seek to export because we need to pay for imports, which is not the same thing.) In our more modern, more domestic equivalent of mercantilism, what the rich 'hog' (steal, coopt, appropriate, according to taste) is not available to the poor. The 'pie' is static and it belongs to the nation. Again, politics is required to redress the wickedness, as capitalists take more than their share.

Opposing this view, from the right, is an argument that suggests that the poor would be in a much worse mess if they did not have access to the wealth provided by the rich. The poor, in this argument, are more or less useless when it comes to initiating anything. They passively take the work that the entrepreneurial class energetically creates. They passively enjoy the increased wages that the creation of wealth by the rich allows. The flow of gratitude ought to be from poor to rich. In this view, while there is a national 'pie', and while it is shared out, the pie can and does contract and expand, according to economic circumstance. Wealth is created by individuals and firms. It is created – conjured up – out of possibilities that include stasis, and that extend to a distant horizon of limitless, unimagined opportunities.

The greens, as we shall see, assert that there are physical boundaries to this process, and they do so from a point of view that is in tune with an economically mercantilist, rather than an expansionist, point of view. Their economic view informs their ecological one.

In the real world, of course, we are discussing not merely moral arguments but practical ones. The world's societies have to formulate policy. Leave aside the theoretical rights and wrongs of wealth; societies have to decide whether to encourage inequality or to dampen it. Rightly or wrongly, politicians have to weigh the demands and rights of the poor and their advocates against the demands and rights of the rich. They do so against a background of cultural prejudices, political exigencies and economic necessities.

The Anglosphere believes that a wide range of wages and job types, including low-wage, low-skill jobs, is necessary to have people employed (rather than on welfare) and to have an economy that can survive recession without huge state outgoings. It believes in dynamism.

The Continental belief is that the workers ought to be organised and that their pressure to keep wages high is a feature of civilised societies, even if it carries with it a higher systematic level of unemployment. It believes in the dialectic of worker and boss, and tries to mitigate the tension with negotiation.

The Nordic belief is that society is a coherent whole, and that people will pull together without the need for high-powered union–boss conflicts. The welfare state, on this view, is not likely to corrupt people. It believes that there is no special tension between worker and boss.

This ranking is clearly reflected in the social investment made by the different spheres. The UNDP's annual Human Development Report's Human Development Index esteems most highly the Nordic countries (from Sweden through to Denmark), and then moves through the Continental countries – Germany through Belgium (with Japan an honorary Continental country) – and on down to the Anglosphere, Australia through the US, with the US bringing up the rear.[14]

This is, as it were, the 'deliberate kindness' ranking: the ranking by which states invest in kindness. Ranking by nearly every other measure – income, life expectancy, years in schooling – is different. It is interesting the degree to which it is culture and aesthetics that would most likely make a person opt for the Anglosphere or the Nordic or Continental way of life. The ways of life are plainly different, and yet each produces affluence, satisfaction and despair.

In poor countries, levels of taxation are almost always low, and levels of inequality vary substantially. But inequality is not a good guide to the likelihood that a country will achieve economic growth or reduce absolute poverty.

Other factors are at work, and they might best be called cultural. There are two options: to make one's country more like another, or to move to the country that best suits own preferences.

Westerners have a choice, and they have been making it in a big way for about a century, and especially in the last 50 years. Should one's country become more like America, more like Norway, or more like Germany? In any of these, there is affluence – but it is seen differently, spread differently, and treated differently.

THE MORALITY OF MODERN POVERTY

Suppose, for instance, that the biggest cause of poverty is laziness – why encourage it by making poverty easy to bear, or by abolishing it? Suppose, in an even bleaker case, that poverty is more or less genetic, and that alleviating it is to fly very expensively in the face of nature? This sort of thinking is likely to become more relevant as we face a distinctly modern poverty.

We have had 150 years of good free education and tolerable housing for most people. If there remains a stubborn minority who don't take advantage of these to climb out of poverty, it might not be the case so much that they 'won't' progress, but that they really, really, can't. Such people may have to be managed in their poverty, rather than given the means to lift themselves out of it. It may not be worth giving these people the tools to improve themselves; it may be better directly to provide them with the goods and services, or the money, they need not to be an embarrassment or a nuisance to the rest of us. (The existing welfare state does a bit of both.) One might also need to ensure that there were jobs for the stupid to enjoy and flourish in.

Much modern thinking continues to be directed at the poverty problem, to which there is the additional difficulty that modern societies can indeed find a role for such people: the caring and security industries are both large in modern societies, and both need kindly people who do not need to be bright or well-read. Indeed, the preservation or creation of such jobs may have the effect of ennobling those stupid or lazy people who can't or won't take the opportunity to join the technically skilled. They may turn them from dangerously disaffected people, prone to loutishness or despair, and help them become instead highly valued workers.

Western societies seem to have lost the knack of rewarding valuable elites with status, which motivates them even more than money. Our politicians, teachers and judges will never be paid what they are worth – an enormous amount. We will almost certainly have to re-learn the art of respecting them – and showing that we respect them. That is the cheapest, as well as the most rewarding, approach. Perhaps something similar will happen with the poor. Our salad-pickers, care-home workers, nurses and security guards may never be paid much, but they can be valued all the same. You may say that such an approach will afford them scant comfort, to which one can reasonably reply that it is better to be low paid and respected, than merely to be low paid.

1 *Financial Times*, 3 August 2004.

2 See www.heritage.org/Research/Taxes/bg1765.cfm.

3 'Reaganomics vs. Rubinomics: Two decades of economic results favor neither approach – it's a draw,' *BusinessWeek*, 21 June 2004.

4 See www.frbsf.org/publications/economics/letter/2003/el2003-28.html.

5 See www.ncpa.org/edo/bb/2004/20040407bb.htm.

6 See www.ncpa.org/edo/bb/2004/20040407bb.htm.

7 www.fraserinstitute.ca/shared/readmore.asp?sNav=pb&id=216.

8 http://society.guardian.co.uk/socialexclusion/comment/0,11499,1012231,00.html.

9 www.jrf.org.uk/pressroom/releases/091203.asp.

10 www.statistics.gov.uk/cci/nugget.asp?id=332.

11 *The Economist*, quoting the OECD and Institute for Fiscal Studies, 25 September 2004; and www.worldbank.org/data/wdi2004/pdfs/Table4_11.pdf.

12 Simon Heffer, 'The Heroes Who Won the War – and Lost the Peace,' *The Spectator*, 5 June 2004.

13 Frank Johnson, 'Shared Opinion,' *The Spectator*, 12 June 2004.

14 See http://hdr.undp.org/reports/global/2004/.

CHAPTER 4

MASS AFFLUENCE AND GLOBALIZATION

The figures are so gorgeous they take your breath away. Between 1500 and 1992 the world's population increased roughly tenfold. In the same period, its economic wealth increased a hundredfold. Poor old Malthus. By the late twentieth century most countries had achieved 'intensive growth': that is, the kind of growth that outstrips even the vast increase in population size and that is required to lift people out of extreme poverty.

Bring the comparisons a little more up to date and we see some striking things. The regions of the world that were rich in 1820 are much richer. The poorer regions are much richer, too. Only Africa was still, in 1992, poorer than Europe had been in 1820. Asia and Latin America had attained wealth such as no-one had even begun to imagine in 1820. Even Africa had, in the 1980s, been steadily improving its lot for decades (before it then faltered helplessly). The regional rankings of wealth remained the same in 1992 as they had been in 1820, but the gaps between each of the regions had mostly grown. That is to say, it was not merely the gap between the richest and the poorest that had grown, but so too had the gaps between each of the other regions. But growth was all but universal.

The news for poor regions will probably get better even if we become no more capitalist, no better governed and no more generous (all good things if you want a good society; and none inevitable even in our improving world). Some time ago, we entered a period when almost all couples wanted to have fewer children than they had siblings, and almost all had the savvy and kit to achieve the aim. Modern couples bury and educate fewer children. This process should increase the per capita income of states: other things being equal, a given national income will be spread among fewer people. (It may produce 'greying' societies, with too few workers to pay for the old, but we can't have everything and the effects of such demographic shifts are temporary and tough to chart.)

The whole rich world has been trying to keep up with the United States for about 150 years. The US was always a rich country and it just went on getting much richer. Between 1820 and 1992, its per capita wealth grew twentyfold. Switzerland could match that record, pretty well year for year. But no other rich country came close to that explosive growth. Arguably, not all countries tried very hard to: the path to growth of some countries was deliberately nearly socialist, and they may have known that this route was not economically very efficient.[1]

GLOBALIZATION

Much of this progress toward Mass Affluence can be described as globalization.[2] Trade has usually grown in importance to countries as they have grown in wealth. Few have grown rich behind closed doors. Innovation in myriad matters has usually helped bring about growth (and growth has spurred innovation). Countries that have achieved growth have generally acquired certain basic characteristics that might as well be called 'western'. Trade is the getting and spending bit of globalization, which is something much wider. It is not solely a process of westernisation, but that is an important dominant strand that cannot be fudged. The enemies of globalization are right in this, at least: to be successful and modern, a country will pretty well have to accept some developments that were invented in Europe about half way through the last millennium.

Globalization – like William Cobbett's early nineteenth-century Wen (what we might call the City or Wall Street) – is usually hated on the grounds that it is supposed to represent the immoral, anti-social, economic hegemony of western capitalism and its clients, servants and near-slaves around the world. This hegemony, often identified with the 'world's only super-power', the US, is brutally financial; it smashes cultural and biological diversity, wrecks the environment, undermines democracy, slashes wages and abuses human rights. It is assumed to be a Virtual Empire of enormous power, and occasionally deploys real force to protect its interests (so almost all wars are oil wars to some degree). It is a Virtual Empire (RDN's coinage) in having no centre (though one version posits America as something like the directing power); no capital (unless Washington and New York share that role); no vision (unless free trade between solvent nations is its rule book).

Against this gloomy take on globalization one might say that globalization is old, progressive, decent, efficient and voluntary. Our modern anxiety about it might have surprised the eighteenth-century mind. As noted by Tom G Palmer, in 1711 the playwright and controversialist Joseph Addison wrote in the *Spectator*:

Factors [trading agents] in the Trading World are what Ambassadors are in the Politick World; they negotiate Affairs, conclude treaties, and maintain a good Correspondence between those wealthy Societies of Men that are divided from one another by Sea and Oceans, or live in the different Extremities of a Continent. I have often been pleased to hear Disputes adjusted between an Inhabitant of Japan and an Alderman of London, or to see a Subject of the Great Mogul entering in a League with one of the Czar of Muscovy. I am infinitely delighted in mixing with these several Ministers of Commerce, as they are distinguished by their different Walks and different Languages: Sometimes I am jostled among a Body of Armenians: Sometimes I am lost in a Crowd of Jews; and sometimes in a Group of Dutch-men. I am a Dane, Swede or Frenchman at different times, or rather fancy myself like the old Philosopher, who upon being asked what Countryman he was, replied, That he was a Citizen of the World.[3]

Globalization is a Virtual Empire of ideas, habits, deals and agreements which no-one has to sign up to. The World Trade Organization, the IMF, and the World Bank may all be less than perfect (may be too strong, too weak, too ruthlessly capitalist or not ruthless enough), but they are all bodies that have supplicants: there is a queue at their door for their good offices or their money. They are all bodies whose policies are controlled by the states that comprise them. They are all democratic in the degree to which their member states are democratic; all legitimate in so far as their member states are legitimate. Indeed, though not more democratic than the UN, they are less corrupted by its 'Buggin's Turn' system of appointment to top jobs. They are all voluntary: no state is made to join.

To be part of globalization need not be a conscious decision by a state. At a primitive level, to be alive in the modern world is to be subject to globalization. Communications alone ensure that: every ship, airplane, Internet cafe, fax, satellite, pop and football star is a globalizing force. A school may not be globalizing (though most in the Third World teach English); a university pretty certainly is. It is fair to say that all further education is globalizing; and when it isn't, we are watching indoctrination. Globalization is the Enlightenment unfolding, and the Enlightenment – as has been usefully defined by Henry F May – 'consists of all those who believe…that we understand nature and man best through the use of our natural faculties'. This has ineluctably produced the effect that there is a body of evidence that sensible people work with, and where it conflicts with tradition or authority, then it has to prevail. This is reinforced by – and reinforces – the second of May's definitions of the Enlightenment belief: 'that the present age is more enlightened than the past'.[4] That was the eighteenth century's sense of itself, and it can be ours, too. Add to these ideas the liberal sense that each person matters, and you have the triumvirate that constitutes progress, and that educated people share across the world. Only people and nations held in ignorance by remoteness, poverty or the tyranny of rulers or religions are likely to be immune to these forces.

The people who dislike globalization dislike the world becoming a billboard for capitalism. They don't notice that the proliferation of Coca-Cola is the most obvious bit of the process, but is the least of globalization's real effects. Imposing limits on the power of tyrants – domestic and governmental – is a more important effect. So is the gradual assertion of the power of reasonableness over that of bigotry.

Most countries do actively seek globalization. And to globalize is to aim to be efficient and decent. Countries that join the capitalist hegemony – that seek to be economically efficient – have to prove they are tolerably well governed and are making efforts to become more so. The reasons are simple: investment by western countries in poor countries is dependent on an acceptable record. Elementary decency is a requirement for membership of the WTO; and where membership is given before decency is in place, membership will provide leverage for all those who argue for reform.

Almost all the countries that can play this game get richer, and those who don't play seem to suffer lower growth. If there are elements of this process that are worth changing, then these are just further reforms of a reform. They are proposals to tweak the progressive. The first thing a kindly, wrong-headed liberal ought to say about globalization is that it is, of course, great, but in need of subtle change. At their best, Stiglitz and Hutton are probably in this school. If they were very honest, they would say that efforts to refine globalization risk neutering its great qualities: its vigour and rigour. Noreena Hertz is one of many who seem to loathe any hint of these qualities. It is true that she is at pains to stress that 'My argument is not intended to be anti-capitalist. Capitalism is clearly the best system for generating wealth, and free trade and open capital markets have brought unprecedented economic growth to most if not all the world.' And she goes on to say that she is not anti-corporate, for she acknowledges that firms can take their social and environmental responsibilities very seriously. Rather, she thinks, she is 'pro-people, pro-democracy and pro-justice'. But she dislikes the realities of the capitalism we have, as she sees them. 'I mean to question the moral justification for a brand of capitalism that encourages governments to sell their citizens for a song; to challenge the legitimacy of a world in which many lose and few win...' and so on. Her case that the world is becoming less good (less free, less fair), and that capitalism is behind these changes, is at least a modern one: capitalism (not even globalization) is at fault because of its very nature. Governments are so desperate to get capitalism to come to their bit of the world that they sell their people's freedoms and dignity to entice it. Even if it were true that this demeaning process is at work, one could easily counter that such depredations were worth it: the arrival of capitalism and its benign work would soon undo the initial damage. In fact, her book is a litany of thin charges against capitalism's behaviour: in case after case she seems simply to be peddling wilful half-truths, or inflating small wrongs into capital indictments.[5]

But there are many critics of globalization who viscerally, emotionally flinch from it. The people who dislike globalization most are inclined to argue that it is the spread of very bad western habits (habits which have damaged the West) to weaker states abroad. These are the heirs, one might say, of Ivan Illich. A model that has triumphed at home is now taking on the rest of the world. Even those who acknowledge that the West has many good features are inclined to think that globalization consists in the export of its bad features. They figure that the meanest of its capitalist exploiters, the most vulgar of its marketers, the most corrupt of its *hegemons* find a soft target in countries that are too poor to be scrupulous.

One can argue – it is easy and right to do so – that multinationals are probably the most respectable institutions in many countries. One can argue that multinationals press for decency wherever they go: it is their default mode, and they invest only where they see a modicum of it. One could grade the decency of countries pretty much in the order of how successful they are as hosts to multinationals. Oil and mining companies are a complicated exception, since they go where there are physical resources, rather than human ones. And even then, it is worth considering which group will operate more scrupulously, or pay its taxes more diligently: the multinational companies, so reviled by campaigners, or the local cowboys? Of course it matters whether the receiving state has merit, and there are surprises there, too (as I have argued at www.richarddnorth.com). It matters, too, whether the foreign multinational will build indigenous intellectual capital. I have argued that the value of Shell to Nigeria is mostly in its determination over many decades that local people should progress: globalization is a force for the empowerment of a worldwide middle-class professional elite of every colour, religion and location.[6]

It is important to note the initial, visceral flinch of the liberal anti-globalizers. It is the anti-commercial snobbery of the intellectual left. For as long as there has been progress, there have been these malcontents. Occasionally, they held up a purifying light to the process. More often, though, they have hugged their moral superiority to themselves, and while the vulgar world of appetites and aspirations pushed on they nursed their scruples and were enriched.

To hate globalization, it is first necessary to misread it. Take the role of the worldwide brand. It is assumed to represent the cruel imposition of an expensive uniform product by heartless commercial corporations. In truth, corporations have found that very few products, let alone brands, can be marketed worldwide. It seems truer to say that some corporations are trusted at a meta-brand level. Unilever and Procter & Gamble have names that are known around the world, and have different products in each of their markets. They are developing products for poor people, which will not have a global sale. P&G, for instance, have developed a water purification product for poor markets in Latin America. Insofar as it becomes a worldwide sub-brand, it will work, because capitalists have identified a worldwide market of poor people. What is more, well-known global corporations are under huge pressure to behave more ethically than any other economic players.[7] 'The playing field is not level', write Douglas B Holt and other academics. 'People may turn a blind eye when local companies take advantage of employees, but they will not stand for transnational businesses such as Nike and ExxonMobil adopting similar practices.' Furthermore, these authors found, anti-Americanism (which is common) does not translate into a dislike of American brands. Western liberals may be surprised at this: they think they have a neat theory that combines politics and commerce. But they can't, luckily, export this conflation.[8]

Corporations are having to learn new tricks. Some firms seem to have given up the unequal attempt to challenge the NGO (Non-Governmental Organisation) sort of case. Whatever their private feelings, firms find there is more mileage in accommodating as much as possible of the NGO rhetoric. In the case of pharmaceuticals, there has been a largely sterile confrontation between development NGOs and the corporations. The firms can't develop and give away medicines, and especially not those that treat diseases only poor people have. (The NGOs don't realise that such 'charity' would be an act of kindness by shareholders, not by managers, and that shareholders have shown no sign of being interested in making it.) But middle ground has emerged: the Gates Foundation has put billions of dollars into the pot, and GlaxoSmithKline is foremost among the firms in developing ways of harnessing its skills to produce drugs – vaccines especially – for poor markets.[9] Incidentally, it may not be right for large firms to sign up for these developments, and to gain the kudos for them. It may be that small, hungry firms can make more money out of philanthropic donations, and build more imaginative and flexible approaches, as well as profit bases. (This is analogous to the argument that oil firms may not make the best developers of renewable technologies.)

THE STORY OF GLOBALIZATION

To help people like globalization, it may help if they knew a bit of history. Unfortunately, they are inclined to think that they are free to dislike globalization because it is very like the spread of Empire, which they already both misread and dislike. It will be the work of several generations of popular historians to take a fresh look at Empire: it is not fresh research that is needed, though, but a willingness to re-gloss existing knowledge. After years in which this work was done in a ghetto and barely dared to speak its name, the elementary demand that we face facts has begun to win through, as the work of Niall Ferguson shows. I look at this a little later.

Globalization is disliked in its own right, too. And it, too, needs to be seen in its historical context. First up: globalization is a word much more modern than the process it describes. The process predates Empire, suffuses it, and goes on where there is no Empire. Empire is an example of globalization, not the other way round. Globalization needs its own chroniclers and defenders.

The contributors to the pioneering *Globalization In World History*[10] might not like to be thought of as performing both these functions, but they are. While the book (a collection of essays given at a conference at Cambridge University at the turn of the millennium) stresses that the West achieved Empire through power, it also – and more originally – shows that other forms of globalization had been at work for centuries. We find it hard to believe, but modern capitalism, driven by Europe and Empire, worked much more with the cooperation of the non-European than by force. 'Non-European societies were active as well as passive agents in [the] new capitalist globalization', says one contributor about the late eighteenth century.

One of the most important essays, by T N Harper, is fresh because it carves out the way that people and ideas, not power or exploitation alone, were an important part of the process. He (or she) writes, of the late nineteenth century:

Migration…lies at the core of globalization in world history – the migration of funds, of people, technology, of commodities and ideas. For both 'old' and 'new' globalization, the agents of this global sensibility were migrant groups: traders, scholars, agents, advisers. It is the study of these sojourners that is perhaps a key to writing a truly global, as opposed to 'international' or 'world' history.

The essay goes on to say that much of this movement of people, money and ideas was 'voluntary' rather than forced, and that it established patterns of inter-connectedness which Empire cannibalised, but also 're-energised' and 'revitalised' and 'deepened with a downward spread in society'.

The cumulative effect of this collection is to convey the way globalization is made up of many forces. Some of these are voluntary; some of them predate European Empire; some hitch a ride on capitalism, trade and empire, but are to do with ideas and aspirations. Above all – this is where I am, perhaps, going further than most of these authors would go, but it is the message I take from them anyway – globalization is almost always progressive. It has been progressive in the sense that we would wish to undo very few of its effects.

The picture is a complicated one, but since we westerners view it with an embarrassed cringe, it is hardly likely that we see globalization clearly. The forces of political correctness naturally institutionalise the misperceptions. Visit the National Maritime Museum and one sees an exhibition called 'Trade and Empire'. The first third of the space (and, very likely, the visitor's time) is spent on slavery. The next third is on Caribbean immigration to Britain. The final third is a desultory account of trade.

It would have been bold and interesting of the museum to have investigated globalization. Then one, at least, of its subjects – an example of migration – could have been seen in a sharper and more positive light. The presence of blacks in America and the UK is one instance of the myriad forms that globalization takes, and is – for the present generations of those blacks – one of its benign effects. It is a smallish part of the story of Trade and Empire, but it has its place – still not fully unfolded – in the globalization story. We have yet to see whether a new generation of young black men will renounce rap's anti-social mantras and drug-dealing. Too many of them, so far, have chosen the ghetto over globalization.[11]

An emphasis on globalization as the migration of people and ideas would have allowed us to see that the presence throughout the world of Chinese and Jewish people is also important. Diaspora is part of the world's story, and it is tense, conflicted, sometimes violent, but often also tremendously positive. If we concentrate on making migrants into victims, not only do they too often fall for the idea, but the rest of us don't spot the hybrid vigour of the immigrant, and we overlook the way some of the most talented people on earth have done all of us good by transplanting themselves, or being transplanted.

Worried about Empire, we stress the iniquity of slavery because we are obsessed with atoning for the coercion behind it. A focus on globalization would show us that slavery liberated generations of African immigrants. Perhaps the problem is that we concentrate on the obviously human side of the story: on depredations and exploitations. The spread of language, of mutual understanding, of shared science, of laws and rights – these are harder to picture and empathise with.

They are benign, and undramatic, and part of why we are now well off. To build the modern economy, one must first develop a sophisticated society. Our present observation reinforces our historical understanding that this is so. A sophisticated society is one in which powerful elites allow power to ebb away, to become dispersed in other classes. It is one in which citizens are allowed to develop. The erudite David Landes explores almost every element of wealth creation and is brilliant on the vigour and forcefulness of many non-European civilisations. They nearly made it, and often had more promising features – cultural and geographical – than Europe, where modernity was, in fact, born. Wondering how it was that innovation flourished in the West, he pursues several possibilities. 'In the last analysis, however, I would stress the market. Enterprise was free in Europe. Innovation worked and paid, and rulers and vested interests were limited in their ability to prevent or discourage innovation. Success bred imitation and emulation...'[12] Note that, while he stresses it was the market that mattered, it was good government that allowed the market. The market is the expression and offspring of a sound society.

In fact, the birth of capitalism and its development through trade and empire – through globalization – was mightily encouraged by European states. Monarchs sponsored exploration and the privateers who developed not merely the plunder of enemy ships, but also the idea of protecting trade routes. The use of British power in trade was as much – more – to do with keeping the noses of our fellow Europeans out of the foreign trough, or getting the English snout in, as it was about subjugating the native. (A Briton is mercifully free of having to defend the tougher methods of Hispanic or Belgian colonisation.)

The Marxist historian Christopher Hill writes:

England's road was blocked by Spain, on whose empire, in [Francis] Bacon's phrase, 'the sun never sets'. Spain closed the whole American continent to English settlers, English goods, and English religion. So this policy...involved war with Spain. Colonization was thus strategically vital. Occupation of North America could command the Newfoundland fishing banks and the Spanish homeward route from the Indies. 'Traffic followeth conquest' [wrote one contemporary].[13]

Trade, patriotism, faith all flowed together to legitimise the use of force.

Hill's is a study of the role of Francis Bacon, Edward Coke and Walter Raleigh in the invention of what would become parliamentary rule. They might, in our context, be taken to stand, respectively, for the roles of scientific curiosity, the rule of law, and trade (and adventure) in the birth of globalization. The book is a (half-unintended) account of the birth of the modern economy, of trade, empire and globalization. Raleigh, for instance, brilliantly spotted that the Dutch had shown that a country needed trade, not agricultural self-sufficiency. It was a lesson – an argument – that was to dominate politics from the nineteenth century onwards, and still does. He argued that the Dutch enjoyed a regulatory framework that encouraged trade: low customs duties, the absence of monopolies, ports open to all comers. (And encouragement of home manufacturers, something that might have been an embarrassment to a free-trader such as Raleigh, and remains a sticking point among free-traders as they debate how Japan did so well after the Second World War.)

It is a theme that is very well dealt with by Eric Jones, one of the small sub-group of economists who track the progress of globalization. In his *The Record of Global Economic Development*[14] he is concerned at one point to get – like Hill – to the history of his theme prior to the obvious late seventeenth-century Enlightenment. He notes that Adam Smith was right to look to developments of the fifteenth century. 'Much of Europe', writes Jones,

was already capable of utilizing overseas resources without merely squandering them. Moreover, the institutions gradually accumulating in Europe, especially in Britain, were significant for the market economy that in the nineteenth and twentieth centuries was to raise incomes so very much higher. Clearly, many of the institutions were originally designed to benefit elites. The opening sentence of David Gress's *From Plato to Nato* proclaims that 'liberty grew because it served the interests of power. Magna Carta (1215) [and other later Acts] are cases in point, but it is even more to the point that the gradual removal of restrictions on royal and arbitrary power, of limitations on the independence of the law, together with the slow lifting of press censorship and so forth was all generalizable.'

We know of no case where Mass Affluence has flourished that did not follow this very ancient, very well-trodden path. How extraordinary that one can read Walter Raleigh and see a very direct understanding of the process, or see in Magna Carta one of its surest progenitors. A modern dictator would only have to consider Elizabethan history to see what the proper relations of a ruler to his or her subjects might be. That is, if he sought the well-being of the majority, the security of the state, and a place in the history books.

So, two complex and apparently competing elements are necessary for a state to modernise its economy and achieve Mass Affluence. It must, on the one hand, allow the brutalities of capitalism, and it must, on the other, promote a civil society, a comity, a polity. It has to work out how to be both hard and soft.

This was the point of the British Empire: it was surprisingly unforceful, and the cosmopolitan centre exported more liberalism than soldiers. But we have refused to see this for decades.

Thank goodness, then, for Niall Ferguson's book (and 2003 TV show) *Empire: How Britain made the modern world*. Its frontispiece is a world map of shipping routes, done by MacDonald Gill in 1927, which is an important part of the Maritime Museum's trade exhibition. Lots of it is coloured pink; it places Great Britain at the centre of its projection. It is the very image of the world as generations of Britons saw it. That was before the apologetic cringe we have adopted, and from which Ferguson's work suggests we straighten our backs. He says: 'In short, what the British Empire proved is that empire is a form of international government that can work – and not just for the benefit of the ruling power. It sought to globalise not just an economic but a legal and ultimately a political system too.'[15] That political system, by the way, was not intended to be tyranny from the cosmopolitan centre. It was almost always intended to be a benign rule of law. Where white settlement predominated, it quite quickly moved to democracy. Where it never did become democratic, there was at the time an argument (and subsequent events in those places have usually demonstrated the truth of the proposition) that the countries were not yet 'ready' for democracy.

The point is that globalization, of which empire is a form, was much more about the spread of liberal values and of learning – and of affluence – than it was about power. The power comes and goes, but the progress stays.

GLOBALIZING POOR COUNTRIES

It is easy to make an intuitive case that the rich ought to help the poor in 'poor' countries. It is also hard to make them do so. In the Third World, the poor are poorer and the rich more selfish than in other, nicer, parts of the world.

Since every country in the world once knew poverty on the scale now common only in tropical countries, it is reasonable to suppose that contemporary poor countries ought to concentrate on the kinds of changes that transformed the rich world. Many of the poor countries have vast resources, educated citizens, and some very rich people. Shouldn't their development have been a cinch?

Their problem may in part be that geography is against them. Africa is a tough place. But is it much tougher than Singapore, or South Korea, or Malaysia? Isn't it likely that it is something cultural – rather than something in the water – that holds places back? There may be some very deep cultural habits, convenient to the rich of poor countries, and perhaps even necessary to the poor in them, which hold their countries back. Africans are inclined to say that their ability to survive immense hardship amounts to a kind of toleration of it. 'You take it, so you'll never make it': that was the judgement of one northern European to his African friend, as they discussed the get-up-and-go of the North and compared it with the stoical lassitude of the South. Anyone who knows Africa has wrestled with its intractability. Its people are world class: their humour, courage, generosity, intermittent ferocity, and frustration know no bounds. It is possible that one day, should the planet endure some cataclysm, it is Africans who alone will remember how to live alongside the resulting extremes. Africans claim that they have a dreadful history: that colonisation first robbed them and then set up the circumstances where warfare rather than prosperity would follow. It is more likely that their history gave them terrible indigenous leadership.

The single worst problem in poor countries is that, in many of them, the rich, and even the middle class, feel no connection with – no obligation toward – the poor. In some cultures, this appears to be mitigated by the way powerful people and parties look after their own: but this particularised generosity – common in Africa in extreme form, but a feature of the Hispanic world too – merely ensures that the acquiescence of a bare sufficiency of people is bought, while the rest can be forgotten. The more general problem in poor countries is a very severe dislocation between the interests of the advantaged and those of the poor.

One of the paradoxes of the rich world's attitude to such countries is that poor people in rich countries show concern for, and spend their taxes on, poor people in 'poor' countries, while the rich in those poor countries look on indifferently. Not that aid does some countries much good. Indeed, the greater the need for help, the less aid seems to deliver it. (There is a body of evidence that suggests that, beyond famine relief, and sometimes even including it, aid may be counterproductive. Among other harmful effects, it may encourage a kleptocracy that is even more enabled and emboldened to impoverish the poor.)[16] So, in the 'Third World' we see huge inequalities and very low tax rates. These often go hand in hand with low proportions of taxes being used for social purposes.

One way of gauging whether a poor country is likely to have a decent future is to see whether it has a 'Barbed Wire' elite or a 'Bossy' middle class. In some countries and cultures a 'Barbed Wire' elite sees its interests as being furthered by having the poor remain poor. They think social improvement will worsen their own position, and so retreat into a ghetto of affluence. Their wealth allows them to buy a way of life unsurpassed anywhere in the world: beautiful houses, wide-open private (more or less) spaces, and attentive staff. But they are not remotely like the aristocrats of the European eighteenth century (let alone of any previous century), nor like the affluent entrepreneurs of the European nineteenth century. These people are the antithesis of the civic-minded upper class of much of Europe, which has been a feature (in very different forms) of all its centuries. They are also vulnerable to the violent resentment of the poor: they risk being overthrown, just as the French and Russian aristocracies were. They would be wise to consider whether they should not move some way toward the concessions made by the British and American rich of the eighteenth and nineteenth centuries.

In resisting the European model, poor-world elites are postponing the day when their societies must make the thoroughgoing modern transition toward an economy that thrives on a prosperous working class, which increasingly behaves like a middle class and eventually merges with it. Such an effect is achieved by countries where education and modest health provision improves, where local affluence is reinvested locally, or where investment from overseas is reliably rewarded. It is broadly consistent with the kind of thinking known as the Washington Consensus, but it doesn't depend on democracy, a laissez-faire economy or any other doctrine.

This transition is one that was historically made in all western societies, and it was as much self-interest as virtue that brought it about.

It would be nice to show that there is a particular level of inequality, of State Take, or openness to free trade that will ensure growth; but there doesn't seem to be. What seems to matter is that there is a parcel of features (state direction, state ownership, high taxes on profits, import controls, lack of social spending) which, when taken together and to extremes, constitute a dangerous cocktail; and there is a parcel of attributes (rule of law, limited corruption, moderate taxes, a free media, a degree of social spending, openness to the world economy, a shift to manufacturing away from resource-exploitation) which tend to help states do well.

One of the biggest issues in whether a poor country will achieve economic growth is whether or not its ruling elite wants a modern economy. That seems to depend on whether the ruling elite believes its own economic and social well-being will be enhanced by rising general affluence. We know that the overall well-being of a country is enhanced by economic growth, but that may not be of much concern to the rich and powerful in a society. In lucky European countries four or five hundred years ago, the powers that be let go. They let the wider society create and benefit from growth. The elites took the chance that the wider benefit would suit their own rather narrow interests. This amounted to a historical trend that saw the upper classes allowing the middle classes more power.

We can see these processes at work – and often disastrously not at work – in the Third World. Indeed, the most important thing one can do for the poor of poor countries is to improve the chances of the middle class as it struggles to build businesses and politics. Capitalist investment from outside a country, and a flourishing middle class within it, are likely to be more important to the medium and long-term prospects of the poor than any belief that the peasant or urban poor can themselves be the locus of the entrepreneurship that will lift them out of poverty. That is to say, rather than seeking to expand the peasant agricultural sector, it may be better to rely on the medium and large-scale farmers to provide the jobs and cheap food that the poor need.

Yet the role of the Third World middle class – its size, varieties and well-being – is hardly discussed. Interestingly, a rash of modern film-makers let us see the middle class in poor hot countries, and see the world through their eyes. They have a constant struggle for respectability, as they wrestle with their dread of poverty, the expense of pensions and health care, and the indignities of corruption. *Monsoon Wedding* (2001) took us to the prosperous and nearly prosperous middle class of India. These are the kinds of people who are flying India's booming private airlines, with successful children operating as moderns on every continent, and at home. The Brazilian *Central Station* (1999), the Argentinian *Nine Queens* (2002), the Mexican *Y Tu Mama Tambien* (2001) all bring Latin America to life. They do so not least by showing respectable urban living, rather than the criminally picaresque scene of *City of Angels* (1998), or the magic realism of man's confrontation with the rainforest, as seen in *Fitzcarraldo* (1982). *Central Station*, in particular, takes us to housing developments of the kind that are transforming parts of Mexico: 500,000 homes – an entire satellite city – at Tecámac, near Mexico City are being built for sale, mostly for under $25,000.[17]

We have already mentioned the 'Barbed Wire' elite that is to be found in some Third World countries. They take their wealth and retreat behind security fences. If either the elite or the surrounding society is sufficiently nasty, this sort of retreat is all but inevitable. However, if either the elite or the surrounding society is a bit pleasanter, then a critical mass of decency may arise. It is a feature of nearly every large middle class that it cannot afford to retreat from the poverty around it. It cannot defend itself against armed or aggressive burglary and robbery; it cannot afford to make itself private compounds; it cannot avoid the squalor of badly planned waste facilities; it cannot afford corruption. In all these areas the middle class may have enough money to be able to buy a half-decent lifestyle, but only if the public sphere is in a half-decent shape. Such middle-class people do not have to be public-spirited saints. Rather, local politics and support for sensible NGOs will strike such people as a useful investment in time and energy. With luck a 'Bossy' middle class will grow up, such as constituted the best of the European middle class. They have a huge vested interest in professionalism and probity, but most interestingly they seek to spread these.

The virtuous middle classes do not need to be solidly well off or greatly empowered to achieve a good deal of their good work. In the Third World we see consumerism and capitalism in a rather modern way spreading important middle-class habits to people only a little above the poverty line. Let's call these the Micro-Middle Class.

THE MICRO-MIDDLE CLASS AND ENTREPRENEURSHIP

There is evidence that helping poor countries develop financial services (banking, credit and so on) does indeed help reduce poverty: a World Bank paper argues that the quality of financial services correlates well with lower inequality and improved social services – in short with improvements for the poor. The study aimed to go beyond existing work, which has proved well enough that rising general wealth benefits the poor. It wanted to find out whether improved financial services (which fairly obviously improve general wealth) were also specifically good for the poor. The answer is 'yes'. But the paper admits it does not know whether the poor access the financial services themselves, or benefit from others doing so. It cites some evidence that certain poor people do indeed benefit (for instance in borrowing money in lean times to maintain their children's education) but it doesn't try to assess that sort of impact in detail.[18]

Similarly, Hernando de Soto famously suggests that there are millions of business people in the Third World – people already in business – who could be helped to become thoroughly middle class, if only they had more secure legal rights to their plots of land, shops and offices. They need the formal right so as to prove their creditworthiness, and so to grow into larger-scale employers. Paradoxically, one of the advantages of being given title to their land might be that they could sell it, and move on into the modern economy, while freeing their plot to become part of a modern farm. Some of these people are indeed poor, but few would be the poorest of the poor, and many hover above poverty but short of the affluence they could make for themselves.[19]

Technology is helping the Micro-Middle Class to get going. Computer terminals are now bringing to peasants in Bangalore a print-out confirming their claim to their land – at a tenth of the cost of the clerk-driven system it has replaced. 'The old village accountant was corrupt. He'd delay making changes, and he made mistakes too', a farmer called Muniratnama told *BusinessWeek*.[20] The system records 20 million deeds in 30,000 villages. Solar-powered computer kiosks allow farmers to buy materials online, instead of having to trek to market, while doctors can provide online consultations to the remotest places.

It is likely that Third World countries will develop sophisticated and affluent societies without going through the standard European welfare-dependent stage. In this they may be more like the US than Europe, and may well out-US the Americans in their distrust of the welfare state. There is already evidence that poor countries are developing capitalistic and private not-for-profit delivery of education at every level, and to nearly every level of income. It is a chastening surprise to most rich-world visitors to poor countries to find that nearly everyone has to pay something toward their children's education. It is not that alone which makes dirt-poor schools so poignant to visitors: it is obvious to almost all the pupils that they are in the most desirable place on earth.

It is a surprise to find that in Indonesia over half (54 per cent) of secondary schooling is provided by private companies, and that the figure is high in Colombia (40 per cent), India (42 per cent), Argentina (30 per cent) and São Paolo, Brazil (19 per cent). In India, it seems that at the secondary level there is a fairly small gap between the cost to parents of publicly provided schools and private ones. The customers for private schools may not easily be able to pay the difference, but are determined to do so. In rather the same way, forty years ago there were plenty of children at British public schools whose parents made real sacrifices to send them there.[21]

There is a good deal of evidence to suggest that a new worldwide Micro-Middle Class of enormous size and vigour is longing to do its good work and is being held back by legal and political constraints. Later, we look at the role of 'classic' corruption in this process. But one important constraint is office-holding, whether or not it is abused. There is an enormous worldwide clerkdom with its backside firmly and repressively parked on the Micro-Middle Class. Along with an account of ordinary corruption, the Indian businessman Gurcharan Das, gave us an account of bureaucracy gone wrong: 'In the 1950s, the idealistic Jawaharlal Nehru, India's first prime minister, wanted a regulatory framework for his "mixed economy", but instead in the holy name of socialism, the bureaucrats created a thousand controls and killed our industrial revolution at birth. In my 30 years in business [he was formerly CEO of Procter & Gamble India] I did not meet a single bureaucrat who understood my business, yet each had the power to ruin it.'[22]

Doing something, cheaply and quickly, about bad regulation would, argues *The Economist*, be hugely beneficial:

Pointless regulations foster graft. The more irksome the rule, the greater the incentive to bribe officials not to enforce it. An excellent new study by the World Bank, 'Doing Business in 2005', shows that red tape is one of the chief obstacles to growth in almost all poor countries.

In Haiti, for example, it takes 203 days to register a new company, which is 201 days longer than in Australia. In Sierra Leone, it costs 1,268% of average annual income per person, compared with nothing in Denmark. To register in Ethiopia, a would-be entrepreneur must deposit the equivalent of 18 years' average income in a bank account, which is then frozen. That such capital requirements are unnecessary has been amply proven in the 42 mostly rich countries that have abolished them...

Overall, businesses in poor countries shoulder three times the administrative costs and have to struggle through twice as many bureaucratic procedures as their counterparts in rich countries. A popular myth holds that this does not matter, because the rules in poor countries are rarely enforced. Not so. Because it is so hard to obey all the rules, businesses in poor countries tend to remain informal. That is, they remain outside the law and pay no taxes. They stay small to avoid detection. They cannot raise credit from the formal banking system in any case...

The World Bank estimates that if a country in the worst-regulated quartile were to join the best quartile, it would boost its annual growth rate by 2.2 percentage points. In other words, there is probably much more to gain from slashing red tape than from begging for more aid.[23]

John Blundell, the Director General of the Institute of Economic Affairs in London, has been returning to South Africa about once a decade for thirty years. His latest trip, he reported in *Reason*, a US libertarian magazine, had shown him a country that was bursting with entrepreneurship. One black businessman had been a union activist under apartheid, and was forced to become a market trader when he was fired. Now well established, he has just employed his first white working-class employee (his black customers believe whites do certain skilled jobs better than blacks). Still, the bureaucrats are there, harassing traders. But now that these things can be talked about, they stand a chance of being reformed. What's more, another small trader noted, as he brought goods between Zimbabwe and South Africa, he pays a legal duty, not a bribe, at the border.[24]

Just as good societies need policemen, so they need bureaucrats. Not all rules, and not all their enforcers, are bad by any means. I have seen uniformed officials checking logging vehicles as they come out of Malaysia's rainforest, and their honesty and diligence is crucial in preserving the forest even as it is exploited. Often, it comes down to having regulations that make sense to people, and of course the officials need to be trustworthy (paying them decently helps). Indeed, the Micro-Middle Class are people who every day live the passion to make money, to do so legally, and to see order growing around them as they do so.

FREE TRADE AND GLOBALIZATION

Curiously, almost everyone now espouses free trade. Even development

NGOs, which routinely argue that western capitalists want to trade only for their own benefit, now also chorus that farm subsidies in the West scupper the chances for Third World farmers to grow and trade their way out of poverty.[25] This may seem a bizarre switch in view, and it is certainly only a partial one. The NGOs cut their teeth by contesting world trade, back in the 1970s, arguing that countries needed agricultural self-sufficiency. They needed peasants, not plantations. To sense their muddle on the topic, one need only visit the Christian Aid website, which stridently condemns free trade as a form of mugging, and yet seems actually to propose that there should be much more of it. (At least when I read it last on 10 October 2004.)

Even if one accepts that, in general and overall, freer trade equates to more affluence for the Third World, it is not always and everywhere a benefit. Nor is it anywhere a benefit that can be had without social disruption. Arvind Panagariya, a professor of economics at Columbia University, notes that free trade will depress prices, including the prices achieved by producers in poor countries. What is more, the current trade distortions – tariffs, quotas and so on – include some that favour poor countries and their exporters. Under free trade, these would go.[26] It is also sometimes argued that agricultural prices may rise in some cases, and that many poor countries are big importers. The Panagariya case was contested by William Cline, of the Center for Global Development and the Institute for International Economics, in a letter to the *FT*. He wrote, 'The majority of the nearly 500 million people in Less Developed Countries living on $2 a day or less are in countries that have a comparative advantage in food production and trade.' That is to say: it is more profitable for them to sell food overseas than to keep it at home. This doesn't mean that they won't be self-sufficient in food, though that is very seldom the way to get lots of good food cheaply.[27]

No state has produced Mass Affluence, or got anywhere near it, without allowing people to become rich. There is a decent argument that those countries that worried least about the extremes of wealthiness were also those that went on to create Mass Affluence. Allowing inequality is not a sufficient factor for the creation of Mass Affluence, but it does seem to be a necessary one. Both Russia and China tried the Other Thing, and have given it up. They were under no pressure from the IMF or G8 or the World Trade Organization to become more conventionally capitalist – but they have. Globalization did not force them to abandon socialism: socialism's nastiness forced them at last to accept that globalization was infinitely kinder.

The difficulty is that it might be a good move for a country to acquire a fast-growing economy, even if doing so involves ignoring the plight of the very poor, at least temporarily. It is almost certainly unwise for a country to organise its policies as if the present state of the poor was all that matters.

The left is inclined to believe that economic development can all too easily leave the poor behind. David Dollar notes this melancholy facet of left-wing thought, more in sorrow than in anger. And then he demolishes it. Here is the abstract of his paper:

One of the most contentious issues of globalization is the effect of global economic integration on inequality and poverty. This paper documents five trends in the modern era of globalization, starting around 1980.

TREND 1 Poor country growth rates have accelerated and are higher than rich country growth rates – for the first time in modern history. The developing world economy grew at more than 3.5 percent per capita in the 1990s.

TREND 2 The number of poor people in the world has declined significantly – by 375 million people since 1981 – the first such decline in history. The share of the developing world population living on less than $1 per day was cut in half since 1981.

TREND 3 Global inequality (among citizens of the world) has declined – modestly – reversing a 200-year-old trend toward higher inequality.

TREND 4 There is no general trend toward higher inequality within countries.

TREND 5 Wage inequality is rising worldwide (which may seem to contradict Trend 4, but it does not because wages are a small part of household income in developing countries, which make up the bulk of the world in terms of countries and population). Furthermore, the trends toward faster growth and poverty reduction are strongest in the developing countries in which there has been the most rapid integration with the global economy, supporting the view that integration has been a positive force for improving people's lives in the developing world.[28]

This is good news. Still, the world's poor are not to be envied: as the number of people living on less than $1 a day has shrunk, the number of those living on under $2 has increased, as they have been joined by the upwardly mobile.[29]

We can flesh out the inequality and poverty problem of the Third World. The best evidence is that the world is much less unequal than is generally supposed. That is to say, the inequality between rich and poor countries, and between the rich and poor people within 'poor' countries, is less than supposed. It is true that the richest countries are surging ahead in wealth creation and that the poorest are falling behind. Luckily, though, for the people of the world, the numbers of people in Africa's failing countries are very small compared with the numbers either in the rich countries or in the Third World countries that are doing much better. In general, then, it is a mistake to compare countries as though they were equally important (that is, in this context, equally populous) just because they are equally sovereign. David Henderson encapsulates the argument best, and uses some telling cases: 'In 1978, when the first decisive steps towards economic reform were taken in China, the ratio of US to Chinese GDP per head was nearly 19 to 1. By the year 2000 it had fallen almost to 8 to 1.'

He goes on to note that in 2000 nine Asian countries then comprising 2.5 billion people had spectacularly grown their economies by 170 per cent over twenty years, while the rich OECD countries with around 850 million people had grown by only 50 per cent.

Henderson then reviews the evidence of, as it were, personal inequality and poverty in the Third World. He emphasises that it is populations and people that matter, not nations. The stark inequality to be found in one small country should not be seen as capable of outweighing the lessening inequality within another, larger, country. The latter 'matters' more, because the headcount is much greater. It is also important to weight money wealth for its actual purchasing power in the individual countries, not for some notional basket of internationally priced goods.

Weighing this evidence, Henderson quotes a Turkish treasury official, Melih Nemli, who argued that 'as long as we agree that we should use purchasing power parity, weight countries by population and... include China and India in the analysis, the empirical evidence, despite all the data problems, is overwhelming that poverty rates and the poverty headcount have declined... and that world inequality has fallen over the past two decades.'[30]

Keeping people alive and improving their prospects is tough in any age. In primitive times, subsistence farming kept the human population low and perilous. Our improved methods ensure a vastly increasing population, which brings its own problems. However, the large population brings innovations of its own (Julian Simon's luminous argument), and the extraordinary progress we are making also ensures that the size of families is shrinking, which will eventually (perhaps quite soon) lessen the pressure. Most estimates suggest that, after generations of spectacular increase, we are within sight of a human population of around 10 billion, which will likely plateau and gradually fall. The new pressures are likely to come from the greater demands of a steady large population, rather than the historical problem of the minimal demands of a vastly increasing multitude. This is the 'footprint' argument we meet in a later chapter.

The issue, as described by Eric Jones in particular, is to discern the recipe for 'intensive growth'. That is, a growth that can keep ahead of the increasing population and the demands which it creates.[31]

Western aid specialists have spent about a decade and a half insisting that the poor must come first, and that help ought to be directed at the 'poorest of the poor'. Luckily, this was mostly a rhetorical emphasis. In fact, it is very hard for aid to be directed at the 'poorest of the poor', and it is not clear anyway that it should be. While it is pretty easy to get food aid to the starving poor (in-country government willing), it is very hard – and probably counterproductive – to imagine that economic aid will turn them quickly into the engines of economic growth. That is not how the West developed, and it isn't what anyone would do now to revive a flagging rich-world economy.

Capitalism is a prime generator of the middle class. It requires armies of talented, educated, respectable people prepared to work within disciplined structures. In fact, for every red-in-tooth-and-claw entrepreneur, capitalism needs many more quietly respectable people. Capitalism is, in fact, a cooperation between entrepreneurs and professionals – that is to say, between risk-takers and the risk-averse.

The synergy between capitalism and sound societies is not merely a case of capitalism's dependence on decency, but also of capitalism's creation of decency, and not least through its generation of a middle class that has a profound interest in, and ability to affect, the public sphere.

But the elites holding power have to be willing to allow this seepage of power away from the top of society, and down to the next tier. They will often be reluctant. In general, it is harder work to make and maintain great wealth in the modern economy than in old-fashioned economies. Owning and exploiting natural resources – the normal occupation of the rich in simple economies – is a pretty straightforward business compared with building industrial business and professions. In the first case, the exploiter needs secure possession of a resource. In the second, he must put capital at risk, employ hundreds of people, and understand – and employ people who understand – very complicated matters. No wonder the already-rich hope that owning land, fossil fuel reserves, forests and so on will keep its allure. Chemical plants, publishing houses, low-cost airlines – these are all far chancier and more demanding by their very nature. Resource exploitation can take place in the midst of simple, brutal societies. Industrial development can't.

It is also crucial to stress that poor countries, and indeed capitalism anywhere, need strong government. Only liberals and their mirror image, libertarians, disparage the state. In Johannesburg, I have been forcefully reminded by poor people that their lives would be much enhanced by the presence of more policemen on the street. The problem, of course, is that too many states are the enemy of order and decency. In Russia, it is all but impossible for the people to believe that the state could ever be a force for good. In Nigeria, as in many African countries, the state has been a capricious kleptocracy. In Colombia, a huge amount of brave effort is going into producing a formal, well-behaved, constructive government of the sort westerners take for granted. Martin Wolf notes in the *Financial Times* that there is increasing awareness that malevolence is only the most obvious problem with bad states: incompetence can be almost as cruel. Globalization will be a triumph if it spreads certain minimum standards of government, and a few core understandings as to what it's about. This approach might make 'nation-building' a core function of modern 'ethical diplomacy', for all that it takes us toward the controversial interfere-ism of the 'neo-conservatives'.[32]

GLOBALIZATION AND RICH COUNTRIES

Globalization has been largely driven by entrepreneurial and bold figures who have pressed home some advantage, or sought to better themselves as they moved ideas, capital, labour or themselves around the world. Empire, immigration, slavery and trade have all played their part, and some continue to do so.

Interestingly, modern technology is producing a new phenomenon, in which talent does not need to migrate to its place of employment. People who once might have immigrated to the rich world for a living can stay at home and undercut the rich-world labour market from home. But they have some of the advantages of travel: their 'virtual' environment, and most of their customers, are in the rich world, as they man call centres, mark exam papers, write software and do all the dozens of other jobs that might, in previous centuries, have required them to move countries. The effect for their relatives is probably, in financial terms, negligible. But their private lives will be enhanced by family stability. Arguably, too, their 'home' culture and politics will be enhanced, as a middle class burgeons there instead of taking flight.

Naturally, the left in the rich West complains about the 'export of jobs'. But they are not keen on the alternatives either. They are right that rich-world workers are being undercut by cheaper foreigners. We could allow the cheap labour to migrate here, and live on the minimum wage and even so manage to send money home. Or we could let the jobs, rather than the labour, migrate. If we seek to avoid both these difficult choices, we condemn the wider world to poverty – and probably ourselves as well.

1 Data from Angus Maddison, *Monitoring the World Economy*, 1820–1992, Development Centre Studies, OECD, Paris, 1995.

2 The best simple account of the process is to be found in Johan Norberg's little *In Defence of Global Capitalism*, Timbro, 2001; a widely praised and nuanced account is to be found in Martin Wolf's *Why Globalization Works: The case for the global market economy*, Yale University Press, 2004.

3 Tom G Palmer, *Globalization and Culture: Homogeneity, diversity, identity, liberty*, Occasional paper 2, Liberales Institut, 2004; www.libinst.de.

4 Henry F May, *The Enlightenment in America*, Oxford University Press, New York, 1976.

5 Noreena Hertz, *The Silent Takeover: Global capitalism and the death of democracy*, Heinemann, 2001.

6 RDN's work on Shell and BP is posted at www.richarddnorth.com; there is quite a good account of the firm's work in Nigeria in Karl Maier, *This House Has Fallen: Nigeria in crisis*, Allen Lane/Penguin, 2000. A much less convincing one is to be found in Daniel Litvin, *Empires of Profit: Commerce, conquest and corporate responsibility*, Texere, 2003.

7 I have sometimes worried that my *The Real Cost*, Chatto & Windus, 1984 was a little too 'green'. It is a comfort to note that even then I spotted that Brooke Bond ran tea plantations that were hugely favoured by locals as places of work.

8 Douglas B Holt, John A Quelch, and Earl Taylor, 'How Model Behaviour Brings Market Power', *Financial Times*, 23 August 2004.

9 Kerry Capell, 'Vaccinating the World's Poor: Glaxo is betting it can combat Third World scourges – and still make money', *BusinessWeek*, 26 April 2004.

10 *Globalization In World History*, ed A G Hopkins, Pimlico, 2002.

11 At least now there are clear and useful black voices for them to listen to, and it is hardly likely that they will for much longer insist on the studiedly anti-social rather than on integration; David Matthews, *The Trouble With Black Men*, BBC3 TV, August 2004 and David Matthews, 'Why Black Men Like Me Have Run Out of Excuses', *Sunday Times*, 1 August 2004.

12 David Landes, *The Wealth of Nations*, Abacus, 1998.

13 Christopher Hill, *The Intellectual Origins of the English Revolution*, Oxford University Press, 1965.

14 Eric Jones, *The Record of Global Economic Development*, Edward Elgar, 2002.

15 Niall Ferguson, *Empire: How Britain made the modern world*, Penguin, 2003.

16 A useful account of this argument is put in Fredrik Erixon, 'Poverty and Recovery: The history of aid and development in East Africa', in *Aid Trade and Economic Development*, a themed issue of the *Journal of Economic Affairs*, volume 23, number 4, December 2003, IEA, London 2003.

17 'Housing in Mexico: An overlooked revolution', *The Economist*, 28 August 2004.

18 It is worth noting that new financial instruments are emerging, which allow large financial markets to back the market in small loans to the Micro-Middle Class – see 'Tiny Loans, High Finance', *BusinessWeek*, 27 September 2004.

19 Hernando de Soto, *The Mystery of Capital*, Bantam, 2000.

20 'The Digital Village: How new technologies could help alleviate chronic poverty in India', *BusinessWeek*, 28 June 2004.

21 James Tooley, *The Global Education Industry: Lessons from private education in developing countries*, IEA, 2001.

22 Gurcharan Das, 'The Bureaucracy Crippling India', *Financial Times*, 17 August 2004.

23 *The Economist*, 9 September 2004.

24 John Blundell, 'Try, Beloved Country', *Reason*, 8 August 2004.

25 Kevin Watkins [Head of Research, Oxfam], 'The Rich Wreckers of the World Trade Round', *Financial Times*, 5 August 2004.

26 Arvind Panagariya, 'The Tide of Free Trade Will Not Float All Boats,' *Financial Times*, 3 August 2004.

27 See William R Cline, 'Global Agricultural Free Trade Would Benefit, Not Harm, LDC', Letters, *Financial Times*, 9 August 2004.

28 David Dollar, 'Globalization, Poverty, and Inequality since 1980,' World Bank. http://econ.worldbank.org/files/36107_wps3333.pdf

29 See http://econ.worldbank.org/files/36297_wps3341.pdf

30 David Henderson, *The Role of Business in the Modern World: Progress, pressures and prospects for the market economy*, IEA, 2004; *The Economist* magazine tracks this argument closely, and largely concurs with the optimistic view; *The Economist*, 13 March 2004, provides a very useful overview of the competing arguments, and closely parallels Henderson's.

See also: Angus Maddison, a leading scholar in this minefield.

31 Eric Jones, *The Record of Global Economic Development*.

32 Martin Wolf, 'Failing States Are a Danger We Cannot Afford to Ignore', *Financial Times*, 9 June 2004, in which he cites 'On the Brink: weak states and US national security', www.cgdev.org.

CHAPTER 5

MASS AFFLUENCE AND STATUS

The left is currently keen to stress that after the social mobility they half-celebrate as having half-happened in the 1960s, there is a new social stratification, a plethora of glass ceilings, which hold the lower classes in poverty or as unskilled labour. UK data suggests that mobility remains quite high, and that it is generally upward. This is the biggest single fact we have to understand: 'Around half the individuals in the bottom quintile of the income distribution in 1991 spent all or the majority of years in that quintile from 1991–2000. Around 40–50% of those disadvantaged at age 23 (as measured by social class, income, housing tenure etc) remain so at age 33.'[1]

This is to say that, if you were very poor in 1991, there is about a 50/50 chance that you stayed very poor throughout the decade, or most of it. On the other hand, there is a 50/50 chance that you didn't. Getting on for half of the twenty-three year olds who were poor-ish in 1991 remained poor-ish for the decade – and about half didn't.

This research says that in recent years, however, there has been slightly less mobility than had been the case in recent, really very mobile, decades. It is interesting to note that the old, best way out of poverty – education – has lost its unique role. The (New Labour) government think-tank that produced this work by mining official census data speculates that, in the modern economy, there are some skills – people handling, for instance – that are valued, but that are not necessarily acquired through education. One might add that being savvy rather than *simpatico* may matter more than possessing a degree: again, it is an insight that is frequently reported, and taken to mean that being overeducated may not make a person useful, and (which is very different) that people are coming out of modern universities less than half-educated.

It is also possible that in the modern counter-snobbery, being middle class may itself be something of a drawback. It would make it less likely, for instance, that one would be employed as an on-screen news reporter, unless one was black or Asian (when sounding posh is forgiven; something that is – perhaps surprisingly – much commoner than among those with a multi-generation British genealogy).

WEALTH AND MOBILITY IN THE WEST AND THE US

The western world in general has seen similar versions of the post-war experience. The US is typical, and archetypal: wealth and equality and social mobility all increased dramatically in the 60s. Thereafter, equality declined somewhat, while social mobility continued to ensure that young people usually did better than their parents (but still not as well as they might have hoped, since there were spells of recession). The rising tide was raising all the boats, but people weren't anchored to their position in the order of things. Conversely, a society that was not mobile would find it hard to reward innovation, and there is an assumption that mobility is good for growth. As usual, the picture is a bit complicated: Switzerland is socially relatively immobile and yet is rich. The UK and Finland are strikingly mobile, but neither is as rich as either the (relatively mobile) US or (relatively immobile) Switzerland.[2]

Critics such as Will Hutton quote literature that is gloomy about US social mobility. I have not pursued their sources, preferring to cite material from the Urban Institute, a well-established US think tank, which seems well founded, and quite gloomy enough. Try these remarks, the final passage of a series of briefing notes on mobility in the US:

Conclusions

The bottom line? It is clear that there is substantial mobility – both short-term and long-term – over an average life-cycle in the United States. The studies reviewed [earlier in the study] suggest that approximately one-quarter to one-third of the population moves into a new income quintile in any given year. Given a longer time horizon, an even greater percentage of individuals switch income quintiles – perhaps slightly less than one-half over a five-year period, and about 60 percent over a ten-year period.

At the same time, however, there is little evidence that this mobility has changed substantially over time. This indicates that the recent increases in inequality have not been offset by any increase in mobility. Thus, the disparity in economic rewards is increasing, while there has been no positive change in the openness or availability of those rewards to everyone in the population. There is also no evidence that mobility is significantly different in the United States than it is in other countries. This suggests that the United States has not only the highest year-to-year inequality in the industrialized world, but also likely has the highest lifetime inequality among similar countries.[3]

And try this:

> Like official government data sources, the PSID [an academic study of a cohort of Americans] data for prime-age, full-time male earners show relatively flat median earnings and rising dispersion across high earners and low earners between the late 1970s and early 1990s. The PSID data also indicate a substantial amount of upward mobility over 10-year horizons during the period. There is a moderate amount of downward mobility as well, even though prime-age men typically see their earnings grow as they age.
>
> Overall, these results indicate that upward mobility remains an attainable goal for the majority of working-age individuals. The presence of mobility implies that yearly measures of earnings inequality likely overstate the permanent earnings differences between individuals. That said, the earnings dynamic has changed in recent decades, shifting from one that slightly benefits lower earners to one that slightly benefits higher earners.[4]

So, here is a mobile society that is becoming less equal, but no more socially mobile. The 'poor' are getting – or are taking – no more opportunity to escape poverty than their forerunners in poverty. But no less either. And their forebears took – as do their successors in poverty – ready routes out of poverty. Besides, conditions for the lower strata in society are less awful than they used to be.

The general assumption about social mobility is that it arises when there is 'room at the top'. That's to say, not merely do there have to be opportunities for self-improvement, but society must make space in its upper echelons for the newly improved. Sometimes the two are indistinguishable: university places are both 'upper-end' niches and methods of self-improvement. In socially mobile societies, there is every encouragement for people to move upwards. But we need to remember that even though a society may offer high, and even increasing, social mobility, social mobility may slow. Diminishing returns may set in: after centuries of high social mobility, there may be less demand for it from below.

And then there is the problem that some of the remaining indigenous working class may indeed be stupid, lazy or unwilling. In the literature, this problem tends to be discussed as a matter of the 'genetic' inheritability of disadvantage. This does not so much disprove the decades of belief in the inherent improvability of the majority of the working class, as admit to the possibility that the cream of it has probably mostly floated free by now.

MOBILITY AFTER 150 YEARS OF SOCIAL ADVANCEMENT

They say this after 150 years of compulsory and free education. And they say it in spite of deliberate policy to make universities accessible to half the population, even if this would destroy the seriousness – and devalue the worth – of higher education.

A right-winger would be free to say – this one often does – that the state could not reasonably be expected to do more to lift people out of poverty. It is surely fair to say the rungs are there, and those who find them too arduous may just not be very good climbers. Though there have always been several characteristics that distinguish the middle class from the working class, in essence they boil down to three. To be, or to become, middle class requires a modicum of talent, self-discipline and the desire to move upwards.

It may be that nowadays there are fewer working-class people who make it into the middle class simply because they are stupid, lazy or don't see the point. The first two may be genetic. But the third is interesting, too: to be working class is pleasant, in a witless and idle sort of way. A junk lifestyle of immediate pleasures is readily available at low cost and less effort. By contrast, the small steps needed to become middle class are positively arduous. And what awaits one? A requirement to be sober, decent, diligent, and to pay high taxes. No wonder plenty of people can't be bothered.

Or put all this in a nicer way. In the modern world, there are delights and skills to be enjoyed and displayed at every level of society. Farm labourers and plumbers alike have and need interesting skills, deployed in a more pleasant environment – though also a more demanding one – than was ever the case historically. There is less need now for the mildly ambitious person to leave his class and broad categorisation as 'skilled' or 'semi-skilled': an interesting way of life can be found at social 'levels' that would once have provided only arduous and under-rewarded labour.

Indeed, we can be pleased and proud that we have now achieved a way of life so pleasant that, at each level of society, people who know it, cling to it.

That we may have produced a rump of the inept and unpleasant – the underclass – is surely a possibility, and it gnaws at us. And suppose they were to breed disproportionately, while the civilised majority opted for lifestyle over fertility? A nightmare scenario, mitigated only by the likelihood that even the stupid and unambitious poor contain a fair quotient of nice and useful people.

Immigration is important here. One way of increasing social mobility is to import new people who are hungry for it. This is, on some counts, very handy economically (and may even be a form of Third World development). But it produces a need to ensure that there is an ability to 'float' people up the ladder as best one may. Having poor people around may be useful, but keeping them stuck in poverty might seem cruel.[5]

IS IT TRUE THAT WE HAVE SLOWED DOWN SOCIAL MOBILITY?

We need a decent word for the 'stickiness' that holds people to their social stratum. Class remains a rather good one. Money, mores and mobility – these are, importantly, combined in class. Even more so is the idea of inheritance.

The old, classic, kind of class very importantly thinks of heritability as accounting for the stickiness of an immobile society. This stickiness attaches to parents and children. That is to say, a striking feature of a socially immobile society is that the circumstances of one's parents determine one's own position, for good or ill. Heritability – of wealth, learning, diet, sport, whatever – can be very important. It doesn't take a moment to see that our society is less class-ridden than it used to be, but it takes rather a leap to understand the simple fact that the British have never been very class-ridden.

Some societies have made it virtually impossible to overcome the advantages and disadvantages of one's birth. Blood, not capability or luck, determined people's status. In the extreme, aristocrats remained aristocrats, however poor they became, while the lower orders remained 'common' however rich they became. Foreigners such as Voltaire noted one of the striking features of British life (and it accounts, in part, for our invention of new economic methods, such as capitalism and industrialisation): each new generation of wealth creators has been welcomed into the aristocracy within a lifetime or so.[6] Similarly, people rattled up and down between the rather permeable classes, according to their economic circumstances.

This idea is worth bearing in mind when one considers whether class defines people and their circumstances, merely influences them, or is correlated with them. You'll quickly get the hang of this idea if you consider how, in Britain, many people insist they are working class when actually their parents were, but they themselves have a degree, a profession, a high income, and mainly middle-class tastes. Class has not defined them, or influenced their circumstances, and their lives are evidence of mobility and a rather low correlation between parent-status and offspring-status. But they insist on defining themselves as working class.

A rising tide lifts all the boats, but is not evidence of social mobility. Material circumstances for most people are constantly improving, because society is getting richer. Take, for example, a working-class man. If he and all his 'mates' have been lifted out of poverty, or illiteracy, but he has stayed in the same stratum of society, then he has witnessed social improvement, but not social mobility. Class has clung to him – for good or ill.

We are not just interested in, say, wage mobility. We might say that we are interested in mobility in and out of the bottom ten per cent of wages, or out of poverty. But we might also – and differently – be interested in the ability of people to move from skilled labouring to professional work, which could involve a decline in income, as would be the case if one moved, perhaps, from a plumber's to a nurse's wages, or from a crane-driver's wages to a university lecturer's salary.

It seems obvious that there is plenty of social mobility in modern Britain, and that there could be more. That is to say, there is now nothing to stop anyone acquiring core middle-class skills: hardly anyone may not upgrade their reading ability, become numerate, or get a diploma. These are all things that were once rather strongly correlated with heredity, and now are not. Well, they are; but they needn't be. There is something voluntary now about remaining illiterate and powerless, where once such things were hereditary.

It is a refrain of the left that it is now expensive to get a good education. Most people who progress to further education and a degree course will end up with debt. This is deplored by the left, for they say the idea of debt appals working-class people. But actually, the left also laments the indebtedness of nearly everyone in society. It seems not so much that the working class is fearful of debt, but that they are more willing to contemplate debt for a better car, than they are for a better education. It is open to dispute whether someone who is fearful of small levels of debt, which will only be repaid once they have acquired quite a decent income, has fully grasped the value of such an education. In which case, it may be that they haven't yet acquired the frame of mind that could reward the effort of educating them.

The left have probably been tripped up by their dislike of entrepreneurship and their preference for welfare. The modern state is in the peculiar position of offering higher education to nearly everyone, but with the innovative twist that it makes explicit the fact that it cannot afford to do so, and doesn't even want to. It has cut a deal with the electorate, by which the taxpayer invests in a proportion of a person's self-improvement, provided the student makes a matching investment. Of course, it is an investment that involves the minimum of entrepreneurial risk: if the student doesn't make it to a decent job, he doesn't pay the money back.

Still, we ought probably to want to see the working class abolished, or rather abandoned. Noble as its history once was, when it was populated as much by genuinely disadvantaged people of talent and merit as by wantons, wastrels or dullards, there is now no point to it, except – just possibly – as a reserve of cheap labour.

And it is fair to say that the modern class system represents much more a voluntary than an involuntary inheritance of characteristics.

That is why it is reasonable to say now that the class system is dead. Where once there were serious difficulties to be faced by someone seeking to break the bonds of his class, now there are very few. Where once one could fairly blame the 'system' for someone's inability to get ahead, now one may more fairly blame the person himself. Only the very stupid have a good excuse for staying working class.

INCOME MOBILITY

Heritability is not the only measure of social immobility. There are other measures of mobility, or the lack of it. One is whether people move upward or downward through the income or class bands, irrespective of where they started out. That is to say, some societies condemn people to low chances of self-improvement, not so much because of heritability of parental origin at the start of life, as simple lack of opportunity during it. The best way to picture this may be to imagine a working-class boy who breaks free of his parental origins, but once in the middle class is as condemned as everyone else in that class to stay there. One of the reasons people accept their lot in society is that year on year their lot improves. Partly, they will tend to get better salaries as the country's wealth increases. Partly, as their careers progress, they earn better money.

There is also the matter of being able to 'jump tracks' once one is in work. It is often said that one of the anxieties of the Mass Affluent is that they will slide down the income scale. It does happen, but not as often as they slide up. In any case, people are (notwithstanding the commentary to the contrary) surprisingly sanguine about their work prospects. This matters. There are countries in which people do indeed feel rather more gloomy about their prospects – and they are on the 'oh-so-sensible' Continent (France and Germany, for instance).

So we Brits seem to want dynamism, including mobility – lots of it upwards if possible, sometimes downwards if necessary. Luckily, we still have a fair share of both.

MASS AFFLUENCE AND RELATIVE DISADVANTAGE

For people who want to complain about western society, it is something of an embarrassment that the oldest complaint – that many people were poor – has been consigned to history. It was, perhaps, inevitable that new complaints would have to be invented.

To have traction, the new complaints cannot be tied to absolute hardship, deprivation or poverty, since all these have been declining. The obvious move, common to many of the new complaints, is, therefore, to discuss relative disadvantage. We are invited to have, we may say, the Comparison Blues. An interesting feature of this complaint is that it sets the media against itself. While the advertisements, which pay for the media, egg us on, much of the editorial copy bought by the media condemns this new materialism. But remember, of course, it is not the physical stuff that is being condemned, but the yearning we bring to it, and the status we seek as we yearn and spend. We are supposed to suffer the affliction of never being able to have enough. My wealth is not much compared with the wealth I aspire to. It is paltry compared to the wealth advertisers invite me to compare mine with. It is paltry compared with that of others. All around me, I see the rewards of being a winner, but I am condemned, as most people are, to being an also-ran. Sure, old-fashioned class may not blight us any longer, but celebrity, stylishness, thinness, possessions, these all do. Status may not be a matter of dyed-in-the-wool class issues, but it has taken on new guises and cripples us just as well.

The heart of the matter is that we are said not to judge ourselves according to some proper independent assessment of our worth, or according to the dictates of our religion or other code of values. No, it is supposed that we simply assess ourselves according to our ranking, and it is always – of course – too low. In fact, we all know that we occupy some place or another in myriad pyramids. Whether it's excellence, education, affluence or admiration, we sense (not altogether accurately) that all but the lowliest in society look down at the more numerous lower orders beneath their own.

Of course there is a ring of truth to the criticism. People have always wanted status, and those who had it always wanted to keep it for themselves. People have always sought to distance themselves from those beneath them in the social sphere, and to make impermeable barriers between the lower order and their own. They have aspired to enter the social sphere above them, and have sought to weaken the impermeability of the barriers between themselves and the sphere above. That much is history, and it is a story that de Botton's Anxiety Status tells rather well.

In the 1950s, a new argument – born of Mass Affluence – imagined that westerners had fetishised consumer goods. This is an argument that Vance Packard made famous, and which Naomi Klein and Clive Hamilton have now taken up. In the 1960s, in keeping with modern understanding about human biology (some of it quite half-baked), some writers assumed that man's social orders bear comparison with the disciplines of the pack (as in dogs, wolves and apes) or of the flock (as in hens, for instance). It was probably the Austrian Konrad Lorenz who made this argument first in his *On Aggression*, or at least he was the first to be very clear about it. His was an arguably rather gloomy thesis, which suggested that an individual's default instinct was aggression, and

115

this was only mitigated in a few relationships by the self-interested need to breed and operate self-defence communities. It is said that Lorenz was some sort of fascist, and at the very least that he was the wrong sort of Darwinian. By this I mean that he was over-impressed by the crude selfishness at the core of animal and human instincts, over which socialisation provided a rather thin veneer.

One senses in Lorenz's work the origin of comparisons between animals and man, which continued in work on the similarity between non-humans and humans as researchers looked at the hormones at work in flight and fight mechanisms, and in stress, activity and repression. I first saw this properly discussed in Sapolsky's *Why Zebras Don't Get Ulcers.*[7] Later work of this kind surfaced around the deer-hunting debate, as both sides discussed research that had tried to assess how animals responded to being hunted and – very differently – caged. There was also Danish and Dutch work looking at the hormonal status of caged mink (which was surprisingly supportive of the mink farmers).[8] Add this animal work to findings on how humans react to anti-depressants (some of which work on this family of hormones) and it makes sense to suppose that we can use our burgeoning understanding about the chemistry of the brain to see how people's social circumstance relates to their psychological well-being.

This sort of thinking suggested that the way people perceive their social ranking, whether they are giving or taking orders, and enjoying it, might have something to do with stress, depression and heart attacks. This is the strand that brings us to Oliver James's writing in *Britain on the Couch*, and to other modern work even more hotly disputed. But let's first go back half a century, for a little more detail on how thinking about 'Status Anxiety' has evolved.

In its modern form – as applied to consumer society – Status Anxiety goes back to Vance Packard and his view that Americans in the 1950s were obsessed with 'keeping up with the Jones's'. Back in 1957 Packard asserted that 'The Hidden Persuaders' knew better how to sell to us than we knew how to resist their subterfuge. Pop psychology fairly poured out of the US, as indeed it continues to. Hollywood satirised the worker-bee commuter and the consumer society in countless sophisticated movies like *That Touch of Mink* (1962). There was pop sociology too: William H Whyte's *The Organization Man* (1956) fretted that middle-ranking middle-class people were selling their souls and civilisation for status in the corporation. They were giving up a decent place in society for a bureaucratic pigeonhole. Then, in his *The Status Seekers* (1959) Packard ventured that:

Many people are badly distressed, and scared, by the anxieties, inferiority feelings, and straining generated by this unending process of rating and status striving. The status seekers, as I use the term, are people who are continually straining to surround themselves with visible evidence of the superior rank they are claiming. The preoccupation of millions of Americans with status is intensifying social stratification in the United States. Those who need to worry least about how they are going to come out in the ratings are those who, in the words of Louis Kronenberger, are 'Protestant, well-fixed, college-bred.'[9]

This passage holds the clue as to what was being mourned. It was small-town America and its religious and cultural certainties and aspirations, the passing of which was worrying people. The nation felt that rural, stubborn, virtuous America was being bureaucratised and industrialised.

MOVIES AND THE POWER OF THE POWERLESS

These themes are beautifully on display in America's movies, whether from Hollywood or the independents. At least from the 1940s on, they portrayed the mystical old Manifest Destiny of the virtuous American being sold down the river. It was being monetised and commoditised. James Stewart was, in real life, a senior officer in the military, but he was cast as Everyman. And his type was losing out to the Hearsts and the Fords. This is key to understanding American sensibilities. Hollywood does not have an agenda; it is too diverse and opportunistic for that. And yet the right is right to think that it is profoundly anti-American, in the sense that it refuses to see virtue in the progressive that America has been built on.

American cinema is built on the luminous, imaginative, transforming individual, who is judged by whether he is against the powers that be, the corporate, the industrial, the modern. Even gangsters are not despised, because they are against 'the system'. In the most remarkable study of movies I know – Ray Carney's *American Vision: The films of Frank Capra* – one meets this in stark form.[10] It is a book about the movies' fascination with the sheer power of personal virtue and vigour (the vigour of virtue). It is magical, transcendental and redemptive. In Hollywood movies, one looks out for the power of a heroic person and his rebellious imagination. One looks out for the power of nature, of the western frontier (any cowboy film), of Everyman heroics (*The Pledge*, 2001), of the working class (*Mystic River*, 2003; *Unbreakable*, 2000), the blacks (*Far from Heaven*, 2002), the child (*Gloria* 1980, 1999; *Stepmom*, 1998; *Sixth Sense*, 1999), and woodworking (*The Notebook*, 2004; *Message in a Bottle*, 1999). Usually, the audience identifies with the anguished, stressed city slicker as he or she faces the challenge these more virtuous and whole characters represent. Once one realises that this is what Hollywood does (and we love it), then we have the key to the power of this medium, which does not have a real equivalent in European culture, still less in its film-making.

The redemptive person in movies always represents the valuable, neglected, historic, low-status person who holds the key for high-status people, if the latter could but see it. Renounce materialism and society's false values – Hollywood is saying – and you and society can be whole. Down with the rat race.

Europeans can find the visionary part of this trying and trite: we watch a perfectly good film from Hollywood and then flinch as it has its 'American Moment' (am I alone in so naming them?). We Europeans know a Hollywood director is sophisticated (that is, European) when he or she eschews American Moments.

Hollywood's drift is leftward and dissident, but it is much more a matter of redemption than of social reform. As Carney notes, it is the transcendentalism of nineteenth-century America living on. There is a good deal of Ralph Waldo Emerson and William (and Henry) James here. Carney rightly also digresses to discuss the painters Thomas Eakins and Singer Sargent, both of whom are very important in showing the inner rebel in conventionally respectable people.

It happens that Capra's work irritates many people on the right for its ingrained dislike of capitalism, and its longing for the uncorrupted soul of an Everyman saviour. It infuriates, because several of his films – most famously *It's a Wonderful Life* (1946) – suppose that the capitalistic norm is heartless and requires a special community-oriented, redeemed form, which only a special hero can bring forth. Never mind that the hero is a banker: he's the small-town hero variety. In *Moonlight Mile* (2002) writer-director Brad Silberling has Dustin Hoffman as a small-town realtor who tries to sell out to big-time capitalism. His grief for his murdered daughter and contact with her erstwhile lover put him in touch with his real, community-based virtuous self and he gives up the big-time dream. Denim and the down-home once again beat the Suits and the progressive.

Part of the right's horror in the political phenomenon that was Bill Clinton was the feeling that he had broken through an invisible barrier. He had become a star, in the manner of one of Hollywood's creations on and off screen, not Washington's. The last politician to do this was J F Kennedy, who had managed to be loved as only a movie star can be; to project (to have projected on himself) an image that was not true to nature; and to persuade people that he was a kindly, down-to-earth, rebellious sort of liberal, when he was much more what we would now think of as a Republican. Kennedy was, it is true, cast as the right sort of officer and gentleman. Bill Clinton modernised the scenario: he managed to combine the faulty and the heroic, which was just the trick for the New Age, believing as it did in the flawed creature of a flawed society and his struggle for personal and social transformation. He was a virtual Blue Shirt and it is sometimes remarked that he was the first black president. But both men were believed to be capable of the sort of redemptive acts that movie heroes perform.

Interestingly, when Ronald Reagan became the first film star to become a serious politician and then president, it was as a genuinely ordinary guy – not a film star at all – that he triumphed. When he was eventually followed by Arnold Schwarzenegger, the initial disdain, and even disgust, of the chattering classes was replaced by the realisation that this muscle-bound, populist Republican was actually rather a thoughtful, tough-dealing social liberal. It may rather quickly be forgotten that he was an actor.

Both the Kennedy and the Clinton stories were movie scripts; and the success of both came from a place which ordinary politicians can only dream of: the Hollywood in everyone. George Bush Senior once said that he lacked the 'vision thing', and he probably meant that he did not have a Big Idea to tell. He was, in modern terms, short on narrative. He might have said as truly that he did not propose to present himself as a magic-lantern figure.

It was Clinton who pulled off the most remarkable feat: he seemed to be Everyman, poised against the American system that populism has always hated. He set the social aspiration of the politicians who succeeded him, or who seek to. They must race for the bottom, and identify with the folksy as do Bush and Kerry (covert Ivy League men both).

To see Hollywood's dislike of America, one might cite its delight in, and misreading of, corporate malfeasance. *The Insider* is perhaps the clearest example here, but *A Civil Action* (1998), *Erin Brockovich* (2000), *Silkwood* (1983) and many others will do. And then there is the easy assumption that corporations cripple people (*American Beauty*, 1999), that capitalism is beastly (*Wall Street*, 1987; *The Devil's Advocate*, 1997), that consumerism requires a response of deep subversion (*Fight Club*, 1999).[11]

Against modern capitalism, Hollywood deploys the Everyman hero and the innocent. Its Westerns also employ the Frontier as the epic struggle between the Everyman, innocent and inarticulate visionary cowboy with his Colt and colts, versus the grasping, industrialised farmer with his barbed wire and railway trains. (The schoolmistress and the whore are the only bits of civilisation to confuse the picture, by appealing to both cowboy and farmer.) To see how the western Frontier remains crucial, one can note that horses now symbolise the primitive and the pure. The cowboy has become rather a tricky theme, so the courage of the lone man in denim, and his love affair with the primitive, has been transferred to latter-day Wranglers, rodeo has-beens and jockeys (*The Horse Whisperer* (1998), *Seabiscuit* (2003), *The Misfits* (1960), *Junior Bonner* (1972)).

The Frontier has become America's great myth, the bit of history whose conflicted nature it is hard to discuss. The Empire is Britain's equivalent (and similarly, it is the part of our history that we ought to learn to admire). America's real frontier is a permanent, yet virtual one: the nation presses on into the modern in a way that leaves us tired old Europeans a little breathless. Britain explored and colonised less-modern societies; America explores and colonises its own future.

Of course, Hollywood is lying. Or rather, we put on very special glasses when we see modernity through its eyes. Just as gangster films of any sort, and very much drama and poetry, glory in and feed off the world of squalor and deprivation, puffing it up as more real, large and significant than it really is, so Hollywood must traduce the modern and industrialised in order to be able to demonise it.

In short, America is not in the crisis Hollywood loves to pick at.

MODERN SOCIAL STATUS

Plenty of people are thriving in the modern world, but are generally made out to be finding it tough. Vance Packard was among the first to suppose we were too feeble to manage it well. But people found they had only to cultivate the civilised in being middle class (or any class you like), and ignore – or denigrate – the trivially materialist part of life. In a chapter on class I look at how – contrary to these anxieties – most people's views of class did not get very tangled up with possessions, and did stay civilised. As Alistair Cooke put it when he described the passing of cowboy America: it was replaced by men who had the mortgage, but also the PTA, to consider. De Tocqueville's America of community-minded people was not dead.[12] Americans were not yet Bowling Alone, as Robert Putnam's 2000 book title had it, and probably aren't now.

For now, it's worth saying that people, actually, were more likely to be interested in social status than in consumer status, and probably less interested in either than sociologists, Hollywood and novelists liked to imagine. Some modern descriptions of American suburbia maintain the tradition of sneering, assuming that people are mind-stunned by their desire not to be outdone in the display of goods. Actually, though, it is rather likely that people seek suburban life and use the malls for their own sake: because they are pleasant. Similarly, it is likely that people aspire to possessions because they believe that pleasure will flow from them, rather than because of the status that they convey. Sure, it is fun to swank and flaunt – but what evidence is there, really, that the rest of us feel crushed by the affluence of others? And remember, the complaint here is not that people have things and like them; it is that not having them drives the rest of us to distraction.

It is more likely that people realise that there are plenty of other attributes to aspire to, or to envy. The BoHo lifestyle, indeed, is only the latest manifestation of a long-running game played by the authentic against the merely affluent. The beautiful young woman in Oxfam discards is brilliantly self-advertising: in effect, she says to the well dressed, the affluent, the fashionable: 'Now, which of us will stop the traffic?'

Fashion has always eyed the peasant, the savage and the working class with an envious awareness that the style's out there, not in the arty studio. The latest nod is in the direction of the simple life of the camper. Just as the Bright Young Things have continued their annual trek to Glastonbury's 'hippy' festival, it seems that camping is now cool. In response to sightings of models at campsites, 'designer labels have started providing everything these classy new campers might need: Marc Jacobs wellies (£65); a pastel rain poncho from Macintosh (£400); a chinchilla-lined sleeping bag from Prada (£6,000); or a Hermes gas stove (price on application).' The young – especially young parents – have noticed that for sheer sociability and the priceless lesson of roughing it, which cannot be banished from camping, nor easily replicated elsewhere, the outdoors is unbeatable.[13]

How to out-shabby someone else's studied scruffiness, or out-distress his second-hand sofa? Michael Jopling, a Tory MP and farmer, once sneered at the arriviste millionaire Michael Heseltine with the remark that the latter had had to buy his own furniture. The jibe achieved fame when retailed by the arch-snob Alan Clark in his diaries and was about the classiness – status – that could only be inherited. But in an age when few people care about status, and delight in inverting and subverting it, one is as likely to be admired for having done up a junked piece of furniture or a vehicle, or to be sporting Oxfam-chic on one's back.

Still, we seem to be enjoying the idea that the chic and the minimalist and the cheap really can make a lifestyle. It is the plain and affordable that is admired – that is a mark of status – over the extravagant. The top echelon of earners aspire to spend vast sums on trinkets and exquisite gee-gaws. But it is IKEA's car parks that are full of the Mass Affluent. Minimalism is cheaper and more chic than Elton John Versailles-ism. Most of us adore Elton's campery, and he adds to the gaiety of the nation, but his style is more mocked than emulated. Besides, the ostentation that Elton John evinces has its own larky and cut-price imitation. Kitsch can be horrendously expensive, or – in ironic or ignorant form – can be ripped off for very little. A gold Rolex, a gilded cornice, a baroque angel – these can all be had at full price, or ripped off.

Interestingly, the Third World is now a large market for luxury brands and stores. This is good: rich people from poor countries are increasingly making their purchases at home, instead of travelling to swell the coffers of rich countries with their tourism. What is more, noted one luxury retailer in Brazil, the presence of rip-off products in the nearby slums does not deter the rich from buying at full price.[14] The old Jewish joke has it that Gentiles are needed because someone's got to buy retail. Now we see also that the real brand connoisseur simply knows that he has bought full-price and feels the better for it. In our ironic age, from the studio of Jeff Koon, one can even acquire kitsch that is both ripped off and high price.

The delicious thing is that no-one cares very much about whether any of this stuff – minimalist, ostentatious, distressed, branded – confers status. In short, wealth does not confer status, and few of us are troubled with materially keeping up with the Beckhams or the Elton Johns. Their spending amuses and pleases us, and does so far more than it would have a generation ago, when people not merely ached to be better off than they were (some still do that), but smarted under the injustice of their status.

We are all supposed to be shopaholics and to shop till we drop, and maybe some people do. Some people gamble to excess. But one meets few people who enjoy shopping enough to make it a hobby or an obsession, and most of us seem grateful that we have a supermarket (and, yes, a farmers' market) and an IKEA (or whatever) to be able to buy, as near as possible, what it is we want. Few of us wholly enjoy our IKEA excursions: they can be bewildering, tedious, tiring, and end in disappointment (when we stand in front of the empty warehouse shelf and find ourselves thwarted at the very last step of the self-service process). But we know the process is infinitely preferable to not being offered the stuff we want, not being able to afford it, or having to traipse from store to store to find it. In a way, the less affluent, with their Argos catalogue stores, have an easier process. It was ever thus, and they pay for it by having less attractive homes.

The tottering mansion of exploitation and resentment we are supposed to feel as exploited consumers does not tally with our pleasure in the food and furniture and fashion we buy on our trawls. Sure, we're glad to be home and to have that restorative drink, but we know we haven't remotely been abused.

One might argue that a highly unequal society will produce some very rich people, whose presence will always, therefore, raise the aspirations – and, this argument goes, the sense of failure – of all those who are poorer. The critics of affluence argue that we should curtail the affluence of the very affluent, the better to avoid this unfulfilled greediness and its attendant misery. But it is an argument with few takers. For every newspaper article about fatcat pay, there are others celebrating the affluence of, arguably, much less deserving rich people. Elton John and Victoria Beckham are not criticised for their wealth. Their extravagance is enjoyed by those who stand not the slightest chance of imitating it. Roman Abramovich took two mega-yachts to Lisbon for the 2004 football finals, only to be outdone by the three vast yachts one of Microsoft's billionaire founders took to Piraeus for the 2004 Olympics. We sense that the future may lie with yet another inter-net millionaire whose own very large yacht has sails, and that seems satisfactorily both more green and somehow classier. But we guess it's got huge engines in reserve, and that these will get plenty of use.

The mega-yachtsmen at Lisbon and Piraeus were admired much more than criticised. Their love of football or athletics was instantly democratising. They would probably have taken more flak if their extravagance had been associated somehow with their love of opera, a state-subsidised art, rather than with the profitable but corporatised sports world. Go figure.

We know that a rich sportsman is a hero (for as long as he is a winner). If people understood capitalism better, they'd be more inclined to celebrate the wealth of a wealth-creating CEO than of a footballer. They might even suggest that well-paid CEOs do firms good, while overpaid football stars may not have been good for the sporting or eco-nomic health of 'The Beautiful Game'. (I must not labour this point: the market can sort out the value of executives and athletes very well for itself, in the end, given a sufficient flow of information and events from which to gain insight.)

Isn't the remarkable feature of modern life the way the poor vicari-ously share in the almost obscene expenditure of the few? Wealth was once something enjoyed by the remote and the superior, and was wrapped in mystique. It was used to create barriers between 'us' and 'them'. The poor stood at the gates of the rich; they pressed their noses against the shop windowpanes. Now television takes us behind the 'red rope' of the most 'exclusive' showbiz spots. We may even one day fully appreciate that 'exclusive' is usually the silly word dreamed up to cover 'expensive' in glory. Except, of course, in the case of the genuinely exclusive, when excellence is often required. We go into the homes of the rich ('Who lives in a house like this?' asks Lloyd Grossman, as David Frost's stooge in a TV through-the-keyhole show). We poke about in their successes and failures. They give interviews, surrounded by the appurtenances of their moneyed way of life. We don't feel alien-ation; we feel empathy. Indeed, the extremes of wealth we see – the see-ing of the wealth – doesn't seem to put us down; rather, we share in it, vicariously, without cost and without risk. We, the Mass Affluent but not mega-rich, are the lucky ones.

It was probably always so. As Simon Thurley of English Nature told us in his search for vanished buildings, English monarchs were always open to scrutiny by anyone dressed well enough to pass muster at Hampton Court or Whitehall (when it was a palace).[15] Nancy Mitford tells us the same story from the French kings at Versailles.[16] From Jane Austen (among plenty of other sources) we have many examples of the very rich of the eighteenth and nineteenth centuries opening their homes to anyone half-way respectable. The middle and upper classes made free with their gawping (and in doing so provided an important perk for the butler). These rubbernecks and tourists were hardly maddened by seeing the more advantaged close up. Even when hierarchy, snobbery and class really mattered they went, they marvelled, and only the very stupid were enraged with envy. Now, it is the visitors to National Trust buildings who most appreciate it when there is an aristocrat about (one sometimes feels that the conservators themselves could do without the eccentric meddling of some of the resident families).

EXPECTATIONS AND STATUS

Any discussion about the lack of satisfaction supposedly felt by modern people usually centres on the way their new affluence has not made them happier. Looking for explanations, writers have wondered if the Mass Affluent have, for the first time in history, been able to, and been made to, compare themselves with the most privileged in society. By these new, impossible standards they feel low-ranking, whether in spending power or social status.

The critics of Mass Affluence seek to persuade us of one of the apparent merits of the old order: people compared themselves with a far narrower band – their own social sphere – and could negotiate a good deal of self-esteem out of it. People could, in short, be fairly large fishes in small ponds. The complacent among them hardly bothered with a comparison between themselves and the 'Quality', their 'betters', still less with Royalty, which was all but divine. The price of not complying with the system could be very high.

Throughout history, rank mattered because it ordered things; but it also crushed one's life chances. For most of history, the People have struggled to weaken the bonds of rank, since they naturally perceived that they might gain through increased egalitarianism.

Our defence of the modern does not have to trash the past. So, to be sure, we note that people do indeed seem to have been amazingly cheerful, given that they were stuck well down in the pecking order. But don't we have good evidence in novels and history books that Status

Anxiety was greater when rank was more immutable, less negotiable and shiftable than it is now? Indeed, isn't the class-consciousness of the past testimony to the fact that, yes, Anxiety Status was once a very serious factor in people's lives? They longed to change their position in life, and were very frustrated when they found they could do little about it.

People historically did not feel that they were cheerfully rooted in deliciously supportive little communities, happily locked in their micro-rank. To pretend they were is a typical piece of reverse myth-making, on a par with the idealising of the Noble Savage. People of spirit have always felt that 'community' was a matter of a small number of people living too closely together and hating it. For most of history, people of any energy took huge risks to get to a city. This is the story now, world-wide, of people with any gumption about them. Only now that technology has banished geographical distance is the trend seriously being reversed.

CLASS IN BRITAIN

It is fair to say that the frustrations and the Social Anxiety that once afflicted large numbers of people of all classes seem markedly to have eased. The curtain-twitching, Keeping Up Appearances of the Mrs Buckets of the lower middle class, the grinding quest for respectability in much of the working class, the constant attempt to lever oneself up a notch in the upper middle class – these were all real and caused their share of misery.[17] But there was good in it all, too. There was a moral component to 'bettering oneself'. People sought self-improvement through education. To be 'better off' was to have advantage, but also to be a better person – not just better as against other people (doubtless a factor) but also just plain morally better.

Nowadays, by comparison, it seems very few people care about their rank in society, and most probably have no real concept of such a thing. For good or ill – and there is ill about it – social status seems to matter less today than at any time in history. But for Oliver James, problems with status lie at the heart of what he and many others take to be a modern epidemic of depression and stress. His argument is simply put. Advanced capitalism holds out limitless prospects, both of wealth and of consumption. He might have added that it offers access to anybody, in any echelon in society, if only he works hard enough and gets lucky. But he prefers to suggest that people's experience of this process is that they fail its dazzling opportunities. This is to say, their expectations are raised stratospherically, and their real achievements diminish proportionately. 'With the traditional shackles of class, gender, race and even geography removed, and the notion that 'anyone can be President (or Prime Minister)' oft-repeated, although the real world opportunities often do not match up, the aspirations are limitless.'[18]

The upshot, says James, is that people sense themselves to be of low status, and thus – in common with animals stuck with low social status – their levels of serotonin fall. Martin Seligman coined the idea of 'Learned Helplessness' in the late 1960s, following animal studies into the pitiable state of animals that learned to submit to repression or frustration. (Seligman famously went on to discuss 'Learned Optimism', or positive psychology.) James cites work suggesting that, in similar circumstances, people with low serotonin become gloomy, stressed and aggressive (and prone to violence). And yet people with the approved high serotonin levels are, he also notes, 'hard-charging, competitive, impatient, aggressive, distrustful and confident'.[19]

Oliver James then opines that, 'We shall not reverse the epidemic of social comparison and relative deprivation without doing something about advanced capitalism's need to make individualist, consumption-obsessed wannabes of us all.'

He suggests, among other things, that we take a leaf from Will Hutton's book, *The State We're In*, and have friendly, communard (bureaucratic, rule-ridden, Franco-German) capitalism with its stake-holder ethics and so on. It is open to speculation whether the British would really be happier if they were more like the Germans. Less stressed? Less depressed? More employed? It's a tough sell.

ARE OUR EXPECTATIONS REALLY TOO HIGH?

Leave aside the debate about how depressed and stressed we actually are; we can surely be sceptical that our expectations of ourselves are too high. I am not worried that too many people aspire to be multi-millionaires. But I do worry that people are not sufficiently hardened – toughened up – to the inevitability of pain and failure as they pursue success. People should be encouraged to have great ambitions for worldly success, and be told that disappointment only crushes the inadequate. If you can't stand losing, don't play. This is important to the moral quality of capitalism: we allow the winners to take so much because we can't be bothered to worry about the failures.

Success and failure are both impostors, and de Botton rightly points out the comfort to be had from elevating that mantra to the front of one's mind (it is most appealing in the rough patches, but is morally useful in the good times). The ordinary expectation of adults used to be that they understood that the risks they took to be successful were their own risks; that ambition was not the same as well-being; that no-one said life would be fair or easy. It is not the blandishments of capitalism that make people unhappy. It is their failure to understand that life is not a doddle, and that maturity consists in understanding this. The adjustment needed is not great. It is true that anyone might now reasonably aspire to be Prime Minister. But it cannot be too much to ask of people that they remember that the maths hasn't really changed: only a handful of people will be. We really ought to be able to understand that.

We would be happier if we understood that bitter disappointment will come to all. Oliver James wants us to soften the world, to make it a less tough place. (He doesn't propose, but he might have, that we have lots of prime ministers, perhaps in even quicker rotation. Or run the country by committees of prime ministers.) But we have already made it about as gentle as we want it to be, and now it's our job to ensure we are tough enough to handle it. That's the expectation we need, don't have, and which leaves us a bit prone to unhappiness.

Not high, but low, expectations may be causing our unhappiness. (That and, as I argue elsewhere, the absence of those shackles that Oliver James mentions, but whose loss I don't think he understands terribly well.) Oliver James suggests – along with plenty of others – that people need status and stable relationships if they are to be happy. He believes, of course, that advanced capitalism has robbed us of these. But again, it is hard to see how capitalism has done this. And anyway, is it not low rather than high expectations that are at fault? People could rapidly achieve status if they were to involve themselves in voluntary or political work, locally or nationally. They could take more care with their relationships, and work harder at them. These possibilities exist, have always existed, and are not threatened by capitalism.

Society is not failing people by imposing too high expectations on them; rather people are failing society by not having high enough expectations of themselves. As Mrs Thatcher said: there is no such thing as society. It isn't just there, to be discovered, relied on, blamed. Society is what each of us contributes (or fails to contribute) every day. That many of us fail in our obligation to society, and, by that failure, ourselves lose out, is the result of society having too low an expectation of us, not of its somehow imposing on us expectations we cannot meet.

But even this is to concede too much to Oliver James. There are some very odd kinks in his argument. One is that aggressive, thrusting, impatient, high-achievers apparently have high levels of serotonin. But it is this aggression that he finds wanting in low-serotonin people. One could argue, perhaps, that low-serotonin depressives are violent, while high-serotonin people turn their aggression into achievement. Yet the latter are people who live by their nerves, cannot bear to be second in any race, and are prone to (albeit temporary) despair at any setback.

They do indeed seem to be happier than low-achievers, and to live longer. But they are famously stressed and nerved-up and tense. Of course they know great highs; and great lows, too. Certainly, one could see how taking their risks would be satisfactory – and healthy – in contrast with being a low-risk, but put-upon, impotent, frustrated drudge. That bit of James's thesis seems real. And yet his argument seems confused. It suggests that stress – drama and risk – can put one in the high-serotonin band.

But many people are not inclined to take those risks, and it's hard to see that this necessarily makes them candidates for misery. Many people choose a quiet life and opt for relatively low status. They want precisely the balanced sort of life that is widely prescribed by those who suggest that the work-life balance is important. Plenty of people see the rat race and decide not to join it. They don't become poverty-stricken as a result and don't – or shouldn't – feel like low-status monkeys. One imagines that they might indeed be happier than if they had opted to join the rat race.

That's their choice, and it may be a wise one – for them. But who in the rat race really is repressed and put upon now? Advanced capitalism is achieving much of its productivity by allowing more people more control over their work, not less. Surely, more responsibility is shoved down the system than used to be the case? Thomas W Malone, of the Massachusetts Institute of Technology, writes that '[we] are in the early stages of a profound increase in human freedom that might, in the long run, be as important for business as the change to democracies was for governments. The key enabler for this remarkable change is information technology.' He believes that technology will inform the lower echelons of businesses in such a way that they can be empowered. Micromanagement may become history.[20] This possibility seems real enough: one of the ways that outsourcing companies make money is by allowing middle management to wither away, while ensuring that 'low ranking' people in call centres can handle most cases, mostly by themselves. This is more like Illich's 'Tools for Conviviality' than Illich himself would have liked. But we may indeed be entering a period – at last – when home working can be made agreeable and commonplace. And we seem already to be seeing work patterns that allow employees to get the shifts that fit their private life rather better than the old 9–5 office routine did. For all that it is fashionable to complain about the 'McJobs' in call centres, surely there are fewer jobs of mind-numbing stultification, and less pen-pushing, form-filling, time-serving frustration than our grandparents endured? Yes, there are demanding targets and pressure; but one might as easily call these challenges.

We would run new risks if we took Oliver James's medicine and banished some of the tooth and claw from capitalism. One obvious effect would be that the people at the top, who currently have brilliant serotonin levels, would perhaps sacrifice them. They would, after all, be operating in a system that does not offer so much encouragement to thrusting high-achievers. But why suppose this 'capitalism lite' will produce a happier band of lower-order low-achievers? Might they not feel as much second-raters as James supposes they do now? We might all end up with low serotonin levels, and where would that get us?

One much-quoted piece of work suggests that senior civil servants live longer than junior civil servants. So the argument goes that bossy high-achieving/high-serotonin types are less prone to heart attacks, while subordinate low-achieving/low-serotonin types keel over rather younger.[21] One difficulty here is that it seems odd to place much reliance on the experience of civil servants, whose middle ranks may well be more prone to ill-health simply on account of the labyrinthine structures they must use to place prohibitions on their fellow citizens. Bored and boring, these people may, indeed, be healthier if they got out and worked in business, or in the fields. Maybe, too, after years of turmoil, during which many reforms of Whitehall have been attempted, middle-rankers feel themselves to be at the beck and call of rather whimsical masters. Who knows? Civil servants presumably reap the other rewards of being middle class: longevity among them. If there is a difference within these echelons, it will be small indeed. Anyway, what is very interesting here is that we seem to see a situation in which taking on challenges, and really stretching ourselves, is good for our health. Can that really sit well with diminishing our expectations, as James wants?

Another bit of research claims that Hollywood stars who get an Oscar live longer than those who don't.[22] What of the Oscar Effect? I could easily imagine that the horrendously insecure ultra-high achievers who constitute the upper echelons of the acting profession would indeed suffer agonies of frustration and fear when – year after year – they don't make it to the Oscar stage. To sit in that audience annually, hoisting a rictus of approval while one's peers go up those magic steps to spout heartfelt tosh and grab the life-giving statuette – it's a wonder the also-rans don't have seizures there and then. The difficulty is that it is hard to imagine a more status-conscious, socially dominated bunch of people than Hollywood actors. They are a sort of microcosm of the kind of society Oliver James and others posit as being modern: and these archetypal moderns thrive well enough, with their share of troubles, like the rest of us. Is their life really a good model for ours?

I do not say that Hollywood actors and British civil servants are very alike or very unlike each other or the rest of us. I accept, for working purposes, that these bits of research tell us that the very top of the tree is nice, and that very healthy people get there. I even accept that the top of the tree is good for one's life expectancy. I cannot see that any of this proves, or that Oliver James has proved, that not being on the top perch constitutes suffering of any sort, except to people who refuse to be adult.

WE ARE HAPPIER NOW

It is, of course, true that capitalism pours forth blandishments on every side. But even here, there seems to be less aspiration misery than at any time. Partly, consumption has been detached from status (because status no longer matters), and that takes the sting out of it. Partly, more and more people get things that were once denied them (that's obvious), but also get things that were once the preserve of a few (which is less obvious).

Ordinarily poor people now have a car and holidays abroad. It is odd of commentators to suggest that people do not enjoy having goods and services that were once the preserve of the rich, when we can see people actively enjoying what they have.

Unless the cheerful pleasure-taking of the Mass Affluent in all walks of life is a feint or a blind, we have to accept that these people are actually enjoying themselves.

On snobbish grounds, the middle class (that diminishing band who think of themselves in that separate way) may wish the masses weren't in their airports or cafes or traffic jams; but they are, and there is no sign of the masses having much anxiety about it.

People at every level of society seem to be buying what they can afford, and enjoying it on its own terms. People are buying the pleasure things give them, not the status they display.

Part of the genius of Mass Affluence is that it has not only put goods and services into the People's hands, but it has removed much of the status-advantage of being very wealthy. It has taken away what one might think a pernicious and empty drive to affluence – the desire to have what someone else has – but not for its own sake.

And we have robbed the expensive of the status-value it once had. A Rolls-Royce or a Ferrari is now as likely to be thought flashy as it is to be thought desirable. A second-hand Mini is as likely to be thought chic as it is to be thought cheap. Only a very few now buy a Rover because it is somehow more gentlemanly – more suitable for cavalry twill and cravats – than a Ford.

It is probable that the British are beginning to be more like Americans in this. That is: the American is relatively unconcerned about the status of others, since he (or she) believes that more effort could produce the same for himself. We need some such explanation for the way that Americans do not vote to bring the rich down to their level: more than the British used to, they empathise with the rich, because they believe they can join the wealthy, and because their not joining the wealthy is their own problem. (I look elsewhere at the realities of economic and class mobility.)

One of the defining oddities of the age is the desire to wear brand-label clothing, and to wear the brand's distinctive logos for all to see. Where, once, the possession of a Chanel suit was announced by the garment's distinctively Chanel look – a beautiful fabric, beautifully cut – now anyone can wear a ripped-off D&G or Versace or Nike or Rolex for a fraction of the price, replete with logos. Someone wearing the original has the inner peace of knowing theirs is original – everyone else has the pleasure of convincing pretence (as we note elsewhere). Everyone, it seems, is happy.

Of course, we aren't in Paradise, but I am inclined to think that people are rather happier than they used to be. They are a lot less hung up on keeping up with the Joneses.

MUDDLING UP THE CLASSES

Picture a fat woman with cheap jewellery – bling, not costume, certainly not pearls – bursting out of her sports-gear top, complete with logos and go-faster stripes. She is stabbing her podgy hand and its cigarette at some kids (pale, noisy, sneering), as they descend from a school bus in the local supermarket car park. 'Yeah, you tell your mum and dad to come round my house later, if they're brave enough – you tell 'em that and welcome', she roars, and waves her dewlaps in the direction of her own brood of sharp youngsters, who posse off toward the high street. A routine spectacle in modern Britain. How unlike the respectable working class of the past.

A youngish office worker 'does' mobile and laptop with his boat-like shoes on the train seat opposite him; a notice nearby requests people not to put their feet on the seats. Hell, surely he can read – otherwise why the laptop? Surely, he knows what it's like to provide a service? He must know that, for the thing to work, a basic level of cooperation is required of the customer? After all, he's obviously in business or the public sector.

There is a general dumbed-down loutishness, and it may be that we are concerned that it is spreading to the middle class, rather than remaining confined to the prole-ish rump of the working class.

But it won't quite do. This trap ought to be familiar to the middle-aged commentator. We are prone to romanticising the working class of yore. In his mostly elegiac account of the ways of south London before its patchy gentrification, Michael Collins writes:

The day we moved in a woman poked her head through the front-room window. She was typecast, and wouldn't have been out of place alongside Peggy Mount:

a dishevelled nest of hair badly underpinned by kirby grips, and an apron worn like armour. She announced to my mum: 'I'm telling you, before you start, if any of your kids lay a finger on mine, I'll be over here. Mark my words.'[23]

A fair tumble of muddle opens up. Collins notes that, for social commentators such as the ex-working class college lecturer Richard Hoggart, the beginnings of Mass Affluence produced the mass media, which 'had corrupted working class culture, even though much of its oral tradition and "habit, aphorism and ritual" [Hoggart's words] still survived'. Collins goes on to say that affluence may have produced fridges, but didn't make working-class people middle class. Street market and pub, he says, remained their milieu and their essential outlook did not change.

Picking up Hoggart's *The Uses of Literacy*,[24] we enter a world in which Northern England might as well be the rainforest or the arctic, with their splendid primitives threatened with corruption by the superficialities of western capitalism. The front page blurb says it's '[a] vivid and detached analysis of the assumptions, attitudes and morals of working-class people in Northern England and the way in which magazines, films, and other mass media are likely to influence them.'

Hoggart writes of a new-fangled 1950s milk bar:

Compared even with the pub around the corner, this is all a peculiarly thin and pallid form of dissipation, a sort of spiritual dry-rot amid the odour of boiled milk...[The customers] form a depressing group and one by no means typical of working-class people; perhaps most of them are rather less intelligent than the average, and are therefore even more exposed than others to the debilitating mass-trends of the day. They have no aim, no ambition, no protection, no belief. They are the modern equivalents of Samuel Butler's mid-nineteenth century ploughboys, and in as unhappy a position as theirs: 'The row of stolid, dull, vacant plough-boys, ungainly in build, uncomely in face, lifeless, apathetic, a race a good deal more like the pre-revolution French peasant as described by Carlyle than is pleasant to reflect upon – a race now supplanted...'

So we see two centuries of lumpenproletariat, and not even the best of the sort. What is so odd is that Hoggart doesn't discuss the way the working class is, in some sense, simply being got rid of, or getting rid of themselves: they are moving on. He seems to like the good old toughness of the old working class, and notes the infinitely happier circumstance of the modern working class. But he thinks they are being corrupted by mass entertainment, without noticing that many are not only hoovering up junk, but losing family members to universities and diploma courses. The working class is no more a given, a pre-existing fact, than the peasant before him.

Richard Hoggart may be one of the few people left who admire the working class. Class warfare – the war to defend the working class and perpetuate it – is, and always was, largely a middle- and upper-class adventure. The late and very English Paul Foot, newly arrived as a local journalist in Scotland from public school and Oxford, wondered angrily in print how a local constituency could possibly send (the very Scottish) Tam Dalyell – public school and Oxford – to Parliament as its Labour MP.[25]

What's more, notes Collins in an important insight, the obsession with the working class in the 1960s was largely a middle-class phenomenon. The intense interest in working-class life shown by intelligent TV (whether in the BBC's *Play for Today* or dozens of documentaries and panel discussions) was generated not least by university-educated middle-class types, and promoted by positively patrician figures at the BBC and in the media. This was the period when the revival of a 'well-constructed play' of a J B Priestly or a Harley Granville Barker was sneered at by most critics – though they pulled huge viewing figures and have gone on (in the age of *Big Brother*) to fill West End theatres. This was the period when a conventional play 'provided a blessed relief from the stark, realistic, working-class drama that was allegedly the hallmark of *Play for Today*', wrote one of the series' producers, Irene Shubik, wryly registering that not all her offerings in the slot were kitchen sink dramas, while distancing herself from those who thought too many were.[26]

It was the working class who paid for the development of this stuff (and the champagne drunk by its authors), by comprising over 70 per cent of the TV licence fee payers in the early days. Which is to say that the working classes did not have the mass media foisted on them: they created the demand for it. But did they watch the socially aware homage to the sufferings of the poor and the excesses of the rich, which a parade of angry young playwrights put before them? Not, one surmises, when it was a choice between the heavyweight fare and Val Parnell's *Sunday Night at the London Palladium*, in whose neo-music hall variety format The Beatles (in 1963) and the arch-rebels The Rolling Stones (in 1965) both played to an ecstatic nation. Curiously (one might think), when the mass-oriented mass media got going, with ITV aiming at the working class, it produced a soap opera, *Coronation Street*, in which there was not a television in sight. In other words, as Collins again points out, the first real portrait of the modern working class, aimed at the working class, missed out the most important new thing in their lives. We had to wait for the *Royle Family* for TV to get the joke right: TV was a big part of working-class life. But working-class life was, thank goodness, under threat. Plenty of people lived it. Unfortunately, many middle-class people chose bits of it. But it had lost its hegemony. People were freer than ever to abandon it, and many did.

Collins quotes Hoggart as believing that commentators almost always patronised the working class, not least by seeing them as amiable, good stock. In the face of what was a very various working-class experience, generalisations were bound to fail. Commentators tended to plump either for sentimentality or vilification, and each was inaccurate, both by generalising and being a tad extreme. (Hoggart has recently made the rather startling observation that he was surprised in the 1950s, when one of his working-class relatives voiced his dislike of being portrayed as a drunk: does one quite trust a commentator who knows so little of people's pride?)

The difficulty is that if the working-class condition was one that was admirable, then it might be thought a pity that so many people sought to leave it behind; but if it were not admirable, then it could seem rude to point it out. Actually, Hoggart's work did point out the unpleasantness of working-class life. Much more than he can have liked, his celebration of old working-class life gave us arguments that reinforce our pleasure in abolishing his beloved cloth caps.

Reading Hoggart, one is reading anthropology. His writing and that of Hugh Brody, the historian and sociologist of the Canadian arctic, are eerily similar. Brody makes the same mistakes, but offers the same opportunities. In *Maps and Dreams*,[27] we have Brody's account of the hunter's mentality. In tune with nature and cooperative, it is the antithesis of the modern, which is defined by its technology and its individualism. The 'native' way seems feckless to the westerner: it is concerned with arriving at consensus without leadership, and with pooling as much instinctive knowledge as possible. Displaced and dislocated, the ancient order has scant usefulness in the modern age. Indeed, it becomes a nuisance to those who possess it. The difficulty is that Brody's pleasure in the prelapsarian misses the real unpleasantness that it contained, and provides no guide as to how Indians and Inuit are to make sense of the world in which they are – perhaps unfortunately – condemned to exist. Brody's work is like Hoggart's: full of useless yearning. Just as one begins to share these authors' concern for their tribes, one notes instead that the tribes are history, and the sooner everyone accepts it, the better.

Oddly, the modern charge about the whole of British society is that it has fallen prey to the chaotic end of working-class habits. Feckless, overspent, sport-obsessed, inebriated, shameless: the whole nation has descended into the picaresque wing of the working class. On this account Mass Affluence has fuelled the worst of working-class habits and – unaccountably – lured the middle class into sharing them.

This is a giddy triumph of the infantile and the vulgar. Simon Kuper in the *FT* Magazine noted that 24 million Britons watched the June 2004 quarter-final penalty shoot-out, in which England lost to

Portugal, at home. Another eight million saw it in pubs. Kuper cited David Winner, author of a forthcoming book, *Those Feet*, as saying: 'Football is the national game in a way it never was before', and went on to describe a broadsheet-reading, middle-class English type, who contributed mightily to the British purchase of a fifth of all tickets to the Euro 2004 matches. 'Football mania is a symptom of dumbing-down', he writes. He is, however, optimistic: the British male has found a communal experience that is peaceably nationalistic. Sure, we can be glad of that.[28] Still, it seems reasonable to hope that the British male will graduate to more challenging interests.

A CORRECTIVE: THE UPWARDLY MOBILE BRITISH

While it is true that too many middle-class people seem not to understand the best of the mores which go with their inherited or acquired status and stratum, it is hardly true that working-class and ex-working class people do not now aspire to and acquire habits of mind and behaviour that were once more likely to be the preserve of the middle class.

Richard Hoggart seems not to have noticed this, as he changes his focus from the working class to the whole of 'Mass Culture'. His latest book, according to its *FT* reviewer, is about the 'health of the public mind'.[29] He sees, apparently, a degree of 'under-education', and a 'divided, coarsened, consumption-besotted' society corrupted by a profit-driven mass media. This all compounds the old British dislike of intellectuals, who return the favour these days by not engaging with the public. So the critic of the vulgarisation of the working class has moved on to the vulgarisation of the whole of society. Hoggart is doubtless cross that no-one is now queuing up to learn left-wing history, except as a curiosity (just as he was mourning it in the 1950s). But are we divided when tens of millions watch the same football match? Are we coarsened when we have all to sign up to political correctness? And are we short of intellectuals when more lecture halls stage debates between intellectuals, and when more populist brainboxes have TV and radio shows, and get more newspaper space, than ever before?

The shows at the National Theatre or the Royal Shakespeare Company are as good as ever they were. And they are busy, too. Jane Austen is a staple of girls sporting tattoos and studs. Are we really to disdain Classic FM because it plays the catchier bits of old music to a huge audience, which once only knew the delights of the Light Programme or Radio 2? Are Ferguson, Roberts and Starkey a disgrace to Froude, Taylor and Neale? Which is the more taxing: Bragg's panel discussions of intellectual ideas or the old *Brains Trust*?

We should also see and celebrate the huge expansion in the

modern middle class. Many people who declare themselves to be working class are probably middle class. They work with mind and computer, rather than with hand and tool. They are owner-occupiers of their homes. But they feel, perhaps, that their tastes in entertainment, food and sports mark them out as working class, a status that they cling to out of a sort of honesty, and also perhaps out of loyalty to their parents and grandparents. They perhaps like the closeness of family life they ascribe, perhaps rightly, to the working-class origins of their parents. They may want their children to be technically competent, and to get ahead, but they do not aspire to 'poshness' or 'snobbiness' in social or cultural life.

The modern ex-working class do not see their relative affluence as marking them out from their poorer neighbours or forebears. Perhaps they still live in an area of town that was working class, and still predominantly is, so their lives would be awkward if they set themselves apart, as their economic position may enable them to do. They may, for instance, be owner-occupiers in an estate of houses and flats still largely publicly owned and predominantly tenanted. Their children may go to 'sink' or 'bog-standard' comprehensives, and be under considerable pressure to conform to the low expectations around them.

Such recently ex-working class people may be in starter-home estates, surrounded by their fellows with more or less proudly working-class origins. Being la-di-dah on a Bovis Box estate might seem quite a bold and even a ludicrous step. This is a pity, of course. It crushes the aspirational, and does nothing for the cultural or political spheres.

In Moscow, there is a remarkable media club, perhaps the equivalent of our Groucho, or Home House. Club Petrovich is themed as a homage to the homes of Soviet society. It is unabashed in its nostalgia for the domestic scene of the time. It takes only a moment's reflection to see why this would be so: not only did the Soviet period have many positive features, it was the period – for good or ill – that middle-aged Russians look back to. They see not only Stalin, but their parents. They don't see social or historical processes, but their childhoods. It will not do to say that Club Petrovich is ironic in its genuflection. The past is always our home.

But these lines of argument are too gloomy. They see explanations for a certain 'stickiness' – a persistence – in working-class habits that is everywhere belied by many people.

MODERN SOCIAL MOBILITY
The success of IKEA is a good example. Its Scandinavian good taste (a bit folksy, a bit minimalist, a bit ethnic) is partly successful because it comes without any class aspiration. Its customers have got beyond –

or not got into – any thought that they are expressing class status in shopping there. Even the manner of shopping – self-service – makes for an easy experience for people who might not want to appear ignorant in front of the stylish young assistants in Pier. It is easier to be a first-time aesthete in IKEA than in Habitat or Heal's.

Habitat in the 1960s was democratic, in its way: it sought to swing more than to be social discriminating. But the customers who flocked to it knew from the *Sunday Times* and the *Observer* colour supplements that this was their new aspiration. Its social accessibility was nothing to IKEA's, whose charms are obvious from dozens of mass-market TV shows. Bel Mooney writes about this tellingly,[30] when she describes how, as a university-educated ex-working class wife, she was racing ahead of her own parents, who had become lower middle class, with a small semi and small mortgage. With probably a much larger mortgage, she was having a man in to sand the floors and paint the walls with primary colours; and she was using the red-check tablecloths that 'glorious Habitat' had made the thing. Habitat was perfect for her, being both middle class and bohemian. 'I wanted to mimic what people did in my new social class – which was both middle class and déclassé "media" ', she writes.

Young people in the 1960s were putting back the Victorian fireplaces that their parents had removed, as they followed the dictates of pre- and post-War modernity, and hugely popularised by the mid 50s TV DIY shows of Barry Bucknell. Similarly, they were taking off the Bucknell plywood panels that had modernised Victorian doors.

But note a couple of things. The ex-working class middle-aged people the social revolutionaries were leaving behind were actually very modern in being pretty class free. The 1950s had built on long-standing trends in producing a huge middle class. Even before the Second World War, some very 'common' people living in terraced houses had a maid. After it, they wanted a nice car and a modern home, because they were modern and classless. Their children went to university and learned to be rather superior, not so much in class terms but in terms of style and education. But note this: the young, university-educated people of the 1960s were reintroducing a snobbery and superiority that their parents had abandoned. The new young thought themselves 'educated', 'radical', 'liberated' and cultured. They did not want to think themselves middle class, and perhaps they weren't. They were too determined to be 'free' for that. They were too anti-American and anti-Establishment for it, too. But 'superior' they certainly were.

'Bohemian' would have done as a word for what they were after, though I don't remember it being in common parlance then. 'Swinging', 'trendy', 'liberated' were the more likely, rather pathetic, adjectives.

It is good that we are now much more nearly classless than we were in the 1960s. I mean that we are less inclined to feel superior to those who are a bit older, stuffier, less well educated, less stylish, less 'with it' than we are.

The veterans of the Second World War were sneered at for most of the post-war period. The annual Cenotaph parade at the eleventh hour of the eleventh day of the eleventh month (Armistice Day) reminded the young that these middle-aged men in blazers with regimental badges were not like them. But it was not, then, their heroism we recalled, but their tedious stories, their drunken outbursts, their resentment and – above all – their resolute dislike of us. It has taken another generation, of grandsons and daughters and great-grandsons and daughters, to bring these old boys out of the shade. Now that the last of them are soon to die (and now, perhaps, that in old age they are so vividly able to recall their youth) we are moved by them. We have Tom Hanks and Steven Spielberg to thank for that, in part, but we would probably have got there without their wonderful work in *Saving Private Ryan*.

Divorce, abortion, and the other social reforms of the 60s will not fall out of use, but they have fallen out of fashion. Traditional mores will not, probably, stage a comeback – but they are no longer sneered at either. The post-war liberal elite have constituted something very like a class, and may even be the last class the country sees. The floor-sanding, abortion-propagandising, anti-American, liberal elite were, and are, the last club to try to maintain a uniformity of mores and attitudes and to do so with a self-conscious sense of superiority. Luckily, their children are showing rather more independence and variety than was expected of them.

CLASSLESS BRITAIN

IKEA is not an aspirational taste. And modern young people are not being guided toward aspirational tastes.

Conran's Habitat was seen as liberating and fresh. But it was also quite prescriptive. The aesthetic it chose was that of a Provencal farmhouse, and the idea was that 'people' (as Bel Mooney called them) wanted a farmhouse in southwestern France because that's what trendy people were getting, and one could get a slice of that action as well. The nod toward the peasant – as so often – had come to represent the un-bourgeois (and being bourgeois was what the new middle classes were desperate to avoid).

When we come to modern style gurus, we see something quite different at work. Laurence Llewelyn-Bowen is a much more Wildean figure: he is trying to describe for his viewers not one but several sorts of good taste. But it is taste he is after, not message. He wants us to be aesthetes, not make a statement. If he were telling us about clothes, he would want us to be Hip Fops. He is after the aesthetic, not the aspirational. Of course, he's a fright: bossy, camp and a bit absurd. But he is not laying down the law in anything like the way that Habitat did.

Of course, Habitat was genuinely exciting in design terms. And Llewelyn-Bowen would bully us if he could.

One couldn't sell a look to people now on status terms. Customers aren't imitating a narrow type of 'trendy' person. We've said that IKEA, say, is much less demanding – much less intimidating, if that is quite the word – than Habitat was and remains. And in part that's because you don't go to IKEA to launder yourself from one bit of the social spectrum to another. You go there because you'll find something attractive, functional and cheap. But buying it won't tell anyone anything about you, except what you think is nice to have around. There is no mission or statement in IKEA, for all that their ads sometimes hope to persuade you there is one. Actually, 'Out with the Chintz' (one of their advertising themes) was almost exactly the social revolution – the battle cry – that Habitat implied. When IKEA sing that song, they are being comic and, of course, ironic. No-one has any chintz to throw out. Rather, they are chiding us for sitting on our backsides among whatever it is we've had for ages and are fed up with in a lazy sort of way. They are saying they'd like us to spend our money, please, rather than be complacent. They are selling us a sort of perpetual revolution, a perpetual upgrade, while reminding us that they are funny and funky (as they hope their gear will too). Good luck to them.

It has been obvious for years that Indian and Chinese food could be aimed at every market in the UK. Continental food remained elitist for much longer. Pizza Hut is closer to a Soho trattoria than it is to a McDonald's. Yet it requires no social training to be a customer there. There are now no supermarkets – not even the Co-op – which cater only for narrow, traditional working-class tastes. That is to say, where once spaghetti came only in tins, and cheeses were British or Danish Blue, now even low-end supermarkets offer a range that would once have been regarded as classy or posh, not to say exotic and outlandish. What's more interesting is that Tesco – whose creed was once 'Pile 'em high and sell 'em cheap' – not merely caters to middle-class tastes too, but helps make it more likely that all sorts of people can easily venture into all types of food.

Modern television is rightly accused of dumbing down: but only if one means that it has fewer modern and classic 'plays', and has acquired an evenness of style which makes one wonder why the BBC thinks it is superior to the commercial offering. I have argued elsewhere that the BBC should be scrapped: it is doing nothing special these days.

Or rather, when one is watching something special nowadays, it could be on any channel, commercial or not. What's more, the BBC no longer provides a sanctuary for the well spoken. But it is a mistake to claim that television has lost quality. Classic novels are now screened with more vigour and talent than has ever been the case. There are better and more interesting – more demanding – documentaries on all themes. Even *Big Brother* can't be quite as stupid as it looks to a generation that is appalled by it. Too many bright young people find pleasure in it for that to be true. But more interesting is the way that television is in the taste-upgrade business. Cooking, house maintenance, and gardening programmes are all subtly extending the aesthetic range of the masses of people who watch them. They may be common (in the old language of snobbery) and in your face, but they are empowering and improving.

Similarly, there is a wide range of programmes that are doing the outreach work of the Department of Trade and Industry and of further education. Ruby Wax, for instance, takes us behind the scenes to highly successful one-man bands, as they wrestle with the problems involved with growing really large, and with finding a successor to their founders. A plethora of shows takes us behind the scenes of start-ups, be they a hairdresser's in Southampton, a spa in Bath, a pig farm in Essex, or an olive grove in Italy. They are presented as 'reality TV' game shows, in which the winner takes all, and exposes all – but this time it's business, not being banged up (*Big Brother*) or styled up (*Queer Eye for the Straight Guy*), or traded in (*Wife Swap*). The 'Place in the Sun' sort of programme are manuals in how to start businesses and how to emigrate.

The message of all these shows is that self-improvement is within reach, but sometimes risky.

These programmes are, in their way, very serious, very liberating and very instructive. It isn't given to all of us to take the risks with our lives that entrepreneurship demands. But instead of merely dreaming of owning a business, and instead (contrariwise) of taking a punt on doing so, but with too little information, these programmes show us how businesses, and business abroad, work. There could hardly be a better way of getting to grips with becoming an entrepreneur or – just as usefully – realising that one is a born employee or subcontractor. Such shows are about diminishing the barriers to social and economic advancement. They are about helping people see beyond the social and class barriers they might have believed would hold them back.

There is much talk now that we have good things paraded before us, and sense ourselves to be failures if we are unable to achieve it all. But these lifestyle shows have a much more benign effect. They show success in the Big Time for what it is: attainable by the lucky, skilled and energetic, but not easy and not for everyone. They show stylishness for what it is: attainable quite cheaply and by all, but requiring a bit of discipline, experience and guidance. It seems fair to say that, after the social engineering and the pseudo-radicalism of television's 'golden age' in the 1960s, we now have television that is genuinely classless, but quite ambitious. It just dare not say that its game is educational; and too many of us have been deceived into believing it has lost its mission.

Modern multi-screen cinemas show a wide range of movies – from blockbusters to arthouse films – but going through the front entrance is the same (very easy) for everyone. One could easily imagine that the range of movies young people might go to is more easily extended by this plethora of screens in a socially neutral building than could be achieved by opening a self-consciously and separate arty cinema nearby. Similarly, an afternoon show such as *Richard and Judy* can transform the sale of middle-brow novels by reaching an audience that is not obviously middle class.

Out of doors, the armies of people who go round stately homes, heritage sites and nature reserves has for years been free of class distinction. It's a cliché that the credit card squirearchy of the National Trust is middle class. The young families who visit Trust properties may mostly be middle class – and even that's by no means universally true – but among the older visitors, you hear every kind of accent.

Attitudes, too, are much less easy to stratify than used to be the case. While once there was a sort of louche-ness scale, by which aristocrats had very flexible and hedonistic sexual standards, and bigotry tended to increase the further down the scale one went, now – for good or ill – there is a much more permissive attitude anywhere in society one looks. Naturally, this is not all good, and many of us are suspicious of the 60s sexual revolution and its fallout. Still, it is worth noting that attitudes which were once the preserve of the middle and upper classes are now much more likely to be found anywhere.

Furniture, food, culture, leisure, social attitudes – in all of these the barriers seem to have fallen, and people at the lower end of the income scale, and even self-declared as working class, are quite likely to have habits that look distinctly middle class.

These are all signs that Mass Affluence is a genuine social leveller, and a leveller upwards. The scene is deceptive, because many people seek the style but not the status of the middle class – which is, of course, the very nature of the process. They want the pleasure of sophistication for its own sake, not to show off. People have lost interest in social climbing. This is good, not bad.

But it also belies and denies the Status Anxiety that de Botton worries about. He is surely right to say that Jane Austen's characters worry about class and status – about getting it, and, even more gnawingly essential, not losing it. But we moderns surely do not. In any case, he does not point out that Austen's novels satirised snobbery for a willing, new, mass middle-class audience. He writes, 'In almost every great novel of the nineteenth and twentieth centuries we find an assault on, or scepticism towards, the standard social hierarchy, and a redefinition of precedence according to moral qualities rather than financial assets of bloodlines.' This is to say, which de Botton does not, that a middlebrow readership was sloughing off class, materialism and status as core values.

CELEBRITY, NOT STATUS

Indeed, one of the greatest oddities of modern life is that it is not status, and maybe not even wealth, but celebrity that is now sought. One might think that celebrity is no more achievable than status used to be, and so people are condemned to rate themselves second and third rate.

But modern celebrity is amazingly haphazard. Celebrity has been democratised, dumbed down and made 'inclusive'. It isn't beauty or talent that makes Victoria Beckham, or Ozzie Osbourne's daughter, Kelly, famous. No-one believes that Victoria Beckham is 'better' than them; they enjoy her because they find it so easy to empathise with how she responds to her wealth and her having the delicious David to go home to. And they love the troubles in the Beckham marriage. What woman has not known some such betrayal? What woman might not enjoy fantasising that Beckham might stray with her? Not distance, but closeness, is what they like in Victoria and David. Victoria could only be called 'Posh' in an ironic way, or by people who have no conception of what class and classiness meant when the words had real meaning. (True, it is one of the last remaining working-class habits of mind to misunderstand poshness.) Ozzie's daughter is even more the girl one might meet in the chip-shop queue: the neighbourhood overweight, twitchy Goth. Neither of these girls is difficult to emulate or imitate. One can be plain, overly thin or the opposite, undisciplined and undeserving (one might say) – and be famous. The women (it is mostly women, surely) who flick through celebrity magazines are mostly looking at people who could be them.

Again, this surely confounds the de Botton anxiety about status. Modern celebrity is not about the unattainable; far from it. It is not, in that sense, aspirational at all. Chavs have made Burberry their own, and have taken only a handful of years to achieve this extraordinary hijack. (A simple web search will probably reveal the present whereabouts of Chavscum, a site devoted to the phenomenon.) Who nowadays could be sure that this boy is a football hero and that boy is not? They all look alike.

Curiously, there is now a demand for 'role models'. Celebrities are invited to behave themselves, so that the rest of us have a template for human behaviour. This is quite new. For centuries, we have had celebrities whom we worshipped because what they had achieved was quite beyond our reach. Very few people believed they could (or even should) behave like Nelson, or could be as beautiful as a film star. Certainly, these were goals to aim for, but the difficulty of attainment was part of the allure. Now that we have read Oliver James and identified the problem, it is clear that this, far more than anything we now see, encapsulates the problem of high aspirations.

SNOBBERY AND POSHNESS

Anything remotely like self-improvement or attainment is branded as 'snobby'. But after generations of diligent snobbery, it is now a curse word for the British.

In the age of the cocky Chav, the cheerfully assertive semi-naked High Street trollop and the defiantly down-speak footballer and his middle-class academic apologist, isn't this snobbery more a feature of the past than of the present? Wasn't Mrs Bucket in *Keeping Up Appearances* (the TV sitcom) an absurd figure as she sweated – perspired, glowed – over her social status in the 1990s TV show? Absurd, and – more to the point – anachronistic, as she worried over being lower middle class. The nation roared its approval at her defiantly, scruffily, inebriate working-class relatives, and sneered at her desire for self-improvement. Social anxiety was being satirised, not because it is the norm, but because it had become funny – endearing even – in its scarcity.

Perhaps her critics had a point. Wasn't Mrs Bucket comical because her view of self-improvement was all status and class and not education or achievement? She had aspiration, but no style (at least no style of her own). But weren't her unreconstructed relatives even worse, really? Why should we not have a sneaky affection for someone who does, at least vaguely, seek something better? Isn't that preferable to lolling indolently in underachievement, as her relatives do?

The two families in *The Good Life* present an even sharper example. Tom and Barbara (the self-sufficiency types) are a clever blend of the bohemian and the suburban (not many self-sufficiency types were, actually). The snobby neighbour Margo, though, is your perfect stereotype of the middle-class woman – and at the lower end of the type, too. She has little taste, probably little education, few 'smarts'. She aches for status, in a way we all know how to sneer at. She obscurely longs for the unfussy strengths of the Goods. She takes an interest in classical music, but only because it is posh and only in the social side of the activity. She has redeeming features (this being a clever and even kindly show). She knows she has no sense of humour, and wishes she had one. Perhaps she wishes she was actually musical. She is generous to the Goods, and quite often surprises them by the scale and thoughtfulness – the canniness – of her gifts. Tom – the self-sufficiency pioneer – probably quite fancies her, in a random sort of way. Nor is all the virtue with his bohemianism: he is a cheerful sponger, and not sufficiently self-aware to know that he often fails to be half as self-sufficient as he prides himself on being. Gerry – Margo's husband – is the uncelebrated lynch-pin of the show. He is the modern world: he's not snobbish, but pays for Margo's status-seeking without much complaint. Similarly, he pays for Margo's gifts to the Goods, and is always open to a 'touch' from Tom. He is Mr Everyman, with whom most of us sympathise. We hope we would have his forbearance.

Perhaps the important feature here is that no-one watching the show has any doubt that snobbery is comical and absurd. Only Margo is prone to it, and everyone else in the show shares the audience's amusement that she should so wholly not get the point.

The Royle family of course don't know how awful they are. They have too little energy to be cheerful or productive; they simply mulch in front of the telly. Goodness knows what people who live in that way make of the programme. The rest of us presumably feel a nervy kinship with them, in the sense that we, too, spend hours parked in front of the telly, and it is doubly absurd that we find ourselves using some of that parked time to stare at a family staring at a television.

So the satire bites the viewer, as it should. It is the viewer's sense of superiority that is the real joke. But actually, most of us really are pretty busy – and busy at pleasure, as well as work. We are not slobbing out, but painting and decorating, and having friends round, and a million other human activities that the Royles can't be fussed to do. What is remarkable about the Royles is not that they are 'genuinely' 'working class', but that they have no aspirations. They are untroubled, and seem pretty content. But we don't envy them. To be sure, they aren't crippled by expectations – but they make the point that we aren't either. We are, rather, glad we are more driven than they.

The Office does something similar: after a hard day in the office, people come home and watch people going through the rituals they have just escaped from. The silliness of the fictional office is funny because it is realistic. But people also know that people in offices are trying to work out how to manage human relations, and to formalise them so that anyone can become a manager and know how to be managed, too. We can satirise office life, of course, but not many would prefer to go back (or down) to the working-class life of grimy, sweaty labour. In any case, the feature of all these shows is that few people in them have social pretensions, and those that do are the butt of the joke. It is right to satirise management-speak: but it is right, too, to work out how to manage.

So these shows all satirise snobbery and the peculiarity of people's aspirations, or lack of them. And now, contrary to the worry that people are crippled by a plethora of expectations, many of us mourn the passing of the aspirational.

Many of the older people in society, and perhaps especially the children of the 1960s, are now becoming nostalgic for a period when civilisation, restraint and order were among the merits of a more class-conscious society.

When I was a van driver in London in the late 1960s, some of my older colleagues and my immediate bosses (my garage manager, for instance) thought that it was a pity I was wasting my talent and education. I do not say that my garage manager was like Andy Capp,[31] but I never saw him out of his flat cap, or without a roll-up spittle-glued to his lower lip. And I am pretty sure his father would have looked just the same, but with a white scarf round his neck. He drove a Morris Minor. (People one rung up preferred an American look: the warehouse manager, for instance, drove a large Ford. The boss drove a BMW: you see, this was the modern world, and neither class loyalty nor patriotism would drive even the boss to buy a Rover in those union-heavy days.) My garage manager was the only quaintly working-class man around. He lived in a smart, small, dark-painted terraced house of the kind that would now be worth £350,000. It was more likely rented than owned.

My garage manager's disappointment with me was not a question of my not earning what I should, or that I was betraying my class. It was more that I had been given the privilege of being useful in more valuable ways than driving his firm's groceries around London.

It is now forgotten, but when there were much larger apparent divides than there are now, there was much more unity of understanding. The working class accepted that they were less cultured than their 'betters' and very many of them wished that they were more cultured. My failing was not one of status, but of value and usefulness. I fear that his assessment of what I should be doing was more right than my own. He valued what was good in what class had given me, and I didn't.

CLASS IN AMERICA

America is a rather more divided country than Britain. This is not exactly a matter of class, as it might be in Britain. Nor do the Americans have a bourgeoisie, as the continentals do. But there is a real sense of division between the decent, property-owning classes and the tenement and trailer-trash underclass that is shifting, shiftless and threatening. This is partly, but only partly, a racial matter, of WASPs (white Anglo-Saxon Protestants) looking around their country and seeing other races as a problem. Much more, it is a case of people who want and respect order fearing that there are hopeless cases across the tracks, out in the projects, shacks and caravan parks, who do not want to join in the productive, civilised American enterprise. With a nihilistic and disturbed element among young middle-class kids – the *Bowling for Columbine* generation – there is even a fear that the rot may be within their own ranks.

The troublesome underclass is not huge, but its influence is much greater than its numbers. It is a visible problem if one goes to the wrong part of any city. It is much more in people's minds than it is present in their lives. Indeed, it may be the lack of everyday acquaintance with the underclass that makes it all the more threatening.

It's a little like terrorism. The British have lived with it for thirty years. It hasn't touched many of us very directly, but we have always known that it might, and have always seen evidence of it out of the corner of our eye, as it were. We are, to that extent, ready for it when it comes much closer. Similarly, the British have always lived pretty hugger-mugger with their poor. We have employed them, stepped over them in the street, bumped into them in the pub.

The American middle class mostly insulates itself pretty successfully from its worrying 'Other'. Cars, suburbs and shopping malls are, in part, responses to the issue. But this successful insulation only creates more of a sense of threat. What might have been familiar and pretty ordinary becomes much more threatening.

And then there's Hollywood, which has always pumped up the volume, exaggerating every threat. For Hollywood, the bizarrely unhinged drugged-up petty criminal and waster was, and is, a crucial standby. Gangsters and no-hopers, ever ready with violence, are a staple of the American thriller. The American film noir consists in little else. While British and American thriller writers have sought murderous villainy in every class, the American pulp fiction confection often saw respectability under attack by a gangster 'Other'.

Take the thriller *Blank Wall* (filmed first by Max Ophuls as *Reckless Moment* in the 1940s, with Joan Bennett and James Mason, and then as *The Deep End* in 2003). The original novel was written by a woman, Elisabeth Sanxay Holding, and the scene is a middle-class idyll being invaded by a dangerous, lower, 'Other'. A middle-class girl has dared flirt with the underworld, and it pursues her into her mother's middle-class terrain. Stanley Kubrik's *Killer's Kiss* (1956) is a wonderful example of the genre, as two people with respectable backgrounds (he in farming, she in ballet) face the results of their descent into the shady worlds of boxing and dance halls.

The thriller genres – American and British – have become much more alike, as writers such as Iain Banks do a Carl Hiaasen or an Elmore Leonard, bringing something of Miami to these damper shores. But that is Britain imitating American habits of thought. In the form of *Lock, Stock and Two Smoking Barrels* (1998), *Shallow Grave* (1994), or *Sexy Beast* (2000) and a dozen others, the result is a tongue-in-cheek caper movie with edge, rather than genuine noir. The Briton can't take the idea of a serious 'Other' very seriously.

In the US the liberal response to a divided and threatened country is to agonise about inequality and the unruly underclass. The right-wing response is to assume that the issue is at heart a moral one. Republicans stress that a revival of manners should do the trick. Democrat politics discusses the poor as though they were all respectable and abused by the rich. And all parties dissemble as their leaders affect simplicity, rusticity, and, if possible, even poverty.

The truth is that America is, of course, a very decent country, and the most remarkable thing for a Briton arriving there is to find that nearly everyone is stoutly proud of the work they do (whether waiting on table, fixing the lift or running a business). They are also, to British eyes and ears, amazingly polite, in a way that seems almost courtly after British directness. The young defer to the old in a way not seen in Britain for thirty years, at least not outside the English public school.

All the same, America is not a class society in the way that Britain was.

To achieve, for good or ill, the British situation, you need to have a long enough history to believe – to fantasise – that there is something enduring and immutable in the strata of society. One needs to be capable of believing in 'blue blood', that mysterious phenomenon that must – logically – have been invented by robber barons about a millennium ago. One needs at least half a belief in the idea of 'divine right' (implying as it does, the heavenly endorsement of kingship). Class at its best is all wrapped up in ideas about chivalry and its orders (at school, my letters were addressed to R North, Esquire). Almost everyone in Britain believed in this guff, at some level, fifty years ago. Now only a very few die-hards (me, for instance) can get close to it.

Such beliefs could not conceivably hold in a society in which almost everyone arrived in only the last hundred years or so, and whose every founding belief is about denying such preposterous nonsense. Those whose origins go further back – the east coast grandees – do indeed affect a degree of proper, old-fashioned snobbery. But even they could only claim plebeian blood, and a rather ruthless Protestant egalitarianism ought to make snobbery hard for them.

So America is not in any serious way a class society, and it is not obviously worried by status. American sitcoms tell us this story. *Friends* was truly about the modern type: class-free people conducting intensely personal lives. They are interested only in their acquaintances and love affairs. They all want a high standard of living, and some of them want fame. They admire good looks and – marginally – celebrity. Doubtless, few New Yorkers are quite as free of culture and politics – class – as this team are, but you get the point.

Frasier is, of course, right on the money when it comes to discussing class and status. Here the refrain is a two-fold disdain for the brothers' snobbery. Not merely is class dead and absurd on, as it were, historical terms (an abandoned feature of life anywhere in the world), but it is also deeply un-American. Martin Crane, their ex-policeman Dad, camped out in Frasier's apartment, represents the real spirit of the country. That is to say, he likes beer, his old mates, all-you-can-eat buffets, a certain emotional reticence and a pronounced anti-intellectualism.

This is a sophisticated show, though. We laugh at the Crane boys, but we are secretly on their side. Affluent, snobby and camp as they are, they are also genuinely trying to improve themselves. They don't read much (that's always a stretch in sitcom), and their opera-going has its uses in social-climbing – but they love the music, and Frasier actually makes it as well. Frasier can't get happy himself, but he really loves his son and is a good father; he dispenses rather good advice on his radio show. These people are civilised, and we like them for it. There are many middle-class Americans who daily wrestle with the social divides in their country, and they are not by any means all of them sure that the proper response is guilt at their own intellectual and cultural habits. They know that class-consciousness can easily be taken too far, and have no airs and graces. They love America, including its egalitarianism, but they love civilisation too.

Actually, the slew of shows in which homosexuals educate heterosexuals in the ways of taste are an attempt to reassert aristocratic values. While there have been some shows in which 'well bred' people ('toffs') initiate the lower orders into, say, the etiquette of dinner parties, the queers do so with much greater élan and full-on snobbery. When they shriek that something is 'so last year', or 'impossible' one can hear the same giddy certainty with which, say, the Mitford girls speak. Dandyism, the exquisitely grand, always was effeminate, and thus next door to homosexual, but now, in US and UK television 'queer eye' make-over shows, the queers have claimed aristocratic superiority, and given it back to us in the only form we would allow.

There is a confusion between affluence and respectability lurking in Hollywood's take on the 1950s and 1960s, and in the reworking of these themes in homage movies in this new century. It is an element –

for instance – in *Far From Heaven* (2002) and *The Hours* (2002). In these films, we see a suburban way of life rigidly imposing both a certain standard of life and a strict social code on 'belonging' and being respectable. This is not rampant consumerism in quite the 'keeping up with the Joneses' way. To be sure, one needed to have a smart and well-kept home on the right side of town. But life was not a vulgar hunt for the next speedboat, or a ceaseless trading up of speedboat lengths. Nor was it in *Everything Heaven Allows* (1955) (on which *Far From Heaven* is based) in which the nurseryman Rock Hudson teaches the suburban widow Jane Wyman that Thoreau has more wisdom than the harridans of the country club. But it is respectability rather than mere affluence that drives the suburban restraint. The movie is like a foretelling of the 'liberation' that the 60s would bring. It is a fierce critique of the lifelessness and conformity which television and capitalism had ushered in, blinding Americans to frontier, small-town values.

CLASS AND THE BRITS: A SHORT HISTORY LESSON

Britain is famous for its ossified class system, which – along with its sexual repression and reserve – are epitomised in the mono-sexed clubland stuffiness of its ruling Establishment and in the uptight curtain-twitching of everybody else. Quite how this fits with the image of a licentious and libertine aristocracy and a hooligan working class – both happy clichés at home and abroad (beloved both of Thackeray and Hollywood) – is, of course, unclear. Anyway, all bets are supposed to have been off since the 1960s, when we overthrew our class-consciousness and social immobility. But were they ever serious factors?

The fact is that upward mobility has been around for ages. Capitalism was crucially born in Britain precisely because a nobody could become a somebody. In Elizabethan England, those who achieved it often went on to fund educational establishments, aware that this could help others up the same ladder. W K Jordan described the process as having to do with a stable monarchy, the Reformation and

…the emergence of a powerful and responsible gentry, and the swift rise of a principally Puritan urban aristocracy – the merchants – to the seats of economic power…The focus of their attack was on the ancient evil of poverty. But they were prescient enough to sense that poverty could never be destroyed unless the ignorance in which it spawns was relieved. Such men scorned and discarded alms, the mechanism of medieval charity, since they were profoundly persuaded that casual, undisciplined charity was as ineffective as it was wasteful.[32]

They invented the charitable trust instead.

As Britain became quite rich in the mid eighteenth century, a merchant and trading class continued to do well. 'With property', writes

J H Plumb, 'came standing in the society and a future for one's children, for in the early part of the century it was relatively easy to pass from one social class to another – a fact which amazed Voltaire and others.' Then, as now, affluence helped assuage some of the envy. The lesser country gentlemen turned to the Tory party, as they saw their power being eroded by the newly enriched above and below them: 'But the general prosperity which they shared with all classes took away some of the bitterness which a class, losing power, must feel.'[33]

Snobbery is often about a class feeling that its privilege – large or small – is being eroded. Sixty-odd years ago, the grandest aristocrats were alarmed by the new wealth among the middle classes, and by their confidence. Lady Bolden, the local grandee in William Wyler's 1942 film *Mrs Miniver*, remarks of the next rung down: 'Shopping's absolutely impossible nowadays…I've spent the whole afternoon being pushed around by middle-class females buying things they can't possibly afford. I don't know what the country's coming to. Everyone trying to be better than their betters. New minks, but no manners. No wonder Germany's arming.' It's a movie with a Hollywood take on the deeply English. The women are too well dressed, for a start, especially during that war. The scruffiness of the well bred has always surprised the foreigner. And the aristocratic widow has a Rolls and a baronial castle: not many of either among the real aristocracy, whom the Americans Henry James and Edith Wharton very differently, but more accurately, captured half a century earlier. Anyway, Lady Bolden's remarks struck exactly the note that plenty of middle-class people have always felt. A modern generation of fifty-something middle-class people, many of them ex-hippies, are appalled at the tide of informality (which we ushered in). It is bling, tattoos and studs that alarm us now, and we do not so much look down at a stratum beneath us and wonder what's happened, as look out on a sea of class-free loutishness.

The deepest comfort remains the timelessness in these complaints. In a yet earlier war, it is said that one First World War cavalry officer returned early from leave to the horrors of the trenches. Asked why, he replied that London had become impossible: '"But, my dear", he said, "the *noise* and the *people*".'[34]

The great thing about England is that everything has come around before. The famously staid Queen Mary, in the first half of the last century, very much enjoyed her husband King George V's luridly patriotic tattoos. Erotic, authentic and edgy, British men have enjoyed tattoos ever since Captain Cook and Lieutenant Bligh's voyages to the Pacific introduced naval officers and ratings to the exotic, as they sought (among much else) cheaper ways to feed slaves in the Caribbean, and thus to raise the profits from plantations. (And it was the exotic that made the greater impact on the English, even than the English on the exotic.) And nice, steady George V, with his stamps and his demanding, rather populist, routine, paid a courtesan the equivalent of £3 million to hush up his father's passionate affair with her.[35] Kiss-and-tell has become more routine, more public, more democratic, in our age of Mass Affluence. But it is hardly new. Neither are the kiss-and-tell women who flock to the beds of stars of every kind, and then move on to Max Clifford and the tabloids, garnering notoriety and money as they go. Such women in previous times may have been more talented and elegant, and have pleasured aristocrats and power brokers, but as the careers of Harriette Wilson and many, many others show, the basic moves were the same then as now.[36]

We can take comfort that bad behaviour runs very deep. In the early nineteenth century, Plumb observes, 'the most eagerly awaited news of the day for most people was the results of the horse races and the prize fights'. Aristocrats busily found prizefighters to sponsor and to be seen with, sharing their carriages with the protagonists (one of the most famous was a black man) at fights for which a crowd of 20,000 was quite common.

We see an absence of sportsmanship now, when football, say, is taken to be a life-and-death business. A generation of old men who remember being fighter pilots wonders if any sport should be taken so seriously as cricket is now, as Henry Blofeld once remarked to Sue Lawley on *Desert Island Discs*. A game is just a game. But ours is not the first generation of Englishmen to have passionate and violent adherence to this or that team, or to produce sporadic violence between individuals, gangs and teams. Geoffrey Pearson notes several centuries of interdictions against unruly games-playing, and says that the early seventeenth century saw regulations stipulating that young men should not 'weare their haire long nor locks at their ears like ruffians'.[37] He says that, while London was famous for its violence, in 1816 a police commissioner was able to say that crimes were 'much less atrocious than formerly'. Crime was less tolerated, but not more common, than before (a picture we recognise today).

We enjoy, too, the idea that poverty was unrelieved in the eighteenth and nineteenth centuries, while, actually, as M D George remarked, '[f]oreigners generally comment on the sturdy, well-dressed appearance of working people. There was much poverty, but it was being more comprehensively dealt with by the poor laws and by charities than ever before. The death rate for London, as for the whole country continued to decline'.[38] It is part of the problem of modern life that anything our British forebears did must have been awful: Empire, poor law relief and class, are all filtered to us through the lens of disapproval.

We plunder the records of parliamentary commissions of the period, for instance, and devour their gloomy news, much as the media plunders modern research. We would do well to read George (again as quoted by Thomson):

...hardships begin to be talked about only when they are no longer taken for granted: and it is the increased attention paid to them that is perhaps the main feature of the period which opens in 1815. Sweated labour and cellar dwellings were not invented by the men who made the industrial revolution: they were discovered by them, discussed by them, and in the end partially remedied by them.

It is also useful to remember that it was middle-class politicians who invented the municipal politics that transformed the streets and sewers of industrial England. It was parliamentary commissions, some national law, and a huge amount of local activity that made the difference in living conditions. (It took the national Parliament to weigh in to improve factory conditions.) It was manufacturing magnates, as well as radicals, who sought parliamentary reform in the 1800s, the better to bring power to people (the working man was not included then) who shared their interests, rather than leave it with the rural upper classes who did not. Add a dash of quite widespread aristocratic concern (Lord Shaftesbury is the most famous example[39]) and one begins to see English modern history as including a noble working-class struggle, and something much more too.

So prosperity was producing mobility, and was, in turn, produced by it. There was violence and poverty and an appetite for risk. But there was philanthropy, too. As F K Prochaska writes: 'A study of middle-class expenditure in the 1890s established that on average they spent a larger share of their income on charity than on any item in their budget except food.' In the same period, half of working class and artisan families subscribed to charities. *The Times* claimed that Londoners donated more than the whole of the budget of some European states. Private expenditure on public welfare far exceeded the state's.[40]

As Steen Eiler Rasmussen noted in his famous love letter to London,[41] the British are rumbustious as a people, much more given to games-playing and light hooliganism than to business or philosophy. From Chaucer, through Shakespeare, and on to the Beatles, the Rolling Stones or Oasis, it is hard to suggest that Britons have prized reserve over self-expression. We don't do the vision thing, and angst is frowned on. We could not produce a Beethoven, and that may be why we could not produce a Hitler. We prefer our heroes to be magnificent in failure, not success (Scott of the Antarctic is a case in point). We like our successful heroes to be lovers and defenders, not monomaniacal conquerors (we love Nelson most). We are not deep, but quite witty. Dissent is our game, not orthodoxy. Small insights by the thousand matter more to us than large dogmas.

These obvious features of our lives – shared across the classes – in part explain why we were very important in the birth of capitalism and Enlightenment philosophy. We would be wise to tear up the half-baked, uninformed or plain prejudiced stereotypes of the tourist board and the left-wing commentator, with which Britons have been beaten up – and have beaten themselves up – over the years.

1 Research material at www.ippr.org.uk/research/files/team23/project159/LIFECHANCESIPPRPRES2_ppt1.PDF.

2 See www.ksg.harvard.edu/inequality/Seminar/Papers/Jencks.pdf and www.urban.org/Template.cfm?NavMenuID=24&template=/TaggedContent/ViewPublication.cfm&PublicationID=5888.

3 www.urban.org/Template.cfm?NavMenuID=24&template=/TaggedContent/ViewPublication.cfm&PublicationID=6170.

4 See www.frbsf.org/publications/economics/letter/2003/el2003-28.html.

5 See www.ksg.harvard.edu/inequality/Seminar/Papers/Jencks.pdf.

6 Ian Buruma, *Voltaire's Coconuts: Or Anglomania in Europe*, Phoenix, 2000.

7 Robert M Sapolsky, *Why Zebras Don't Get Ulcers*, W H Freeman, 1998.

8 Richard D North, *Fur and Freedom: A defence of the fur trade*, IEA, 2000.

9 www.english.upenn.edu/~afilreis/50s/packard-ch1.html; Vance Packard, *The Status Seekers: An exploration of class behavior in America and the hidden barriers that affect you, your community, your future*, David McKay, 1959.

10 Ray Carney, *American Vision: The films of Frank Capra*, Wesleyan University Press/University Press of New England, 1986.

11 Some of these themes are a subset of the attack on the pornography of violence discussed by Michael Medved in *Hollywood vs America: Popular culture and the war on traditional values*, HarperCollins, 1993.

12 Alistair Cooke, *Alistair Cooke's America*, 1972, available on DVD October, 2004.

13 Giles Hattersley, 'The Smart Set Camp It Up', *Sunday Times*, 25 July 2004.

14 'Brazil's Wealthy Discover How to Spend it', *Financial Times*, 10 August 2004.

15 A series and book: Simon Thurley, *Lost Buildings of Britain*, Channel 4, 2004.

16 Nancy Mitford, *The Sun King*, innumerable editions from 1966.

17 *Keeping Up Appearances*, BBC TV, 1990.

18 Oliver James, *Britain On the Couch*, Century, 1997.

19 *Ibid.*

20 Thomas W Malone, 'Pioneeers That Cultivate a New Model of Work', *Financial Times*, 12 August 2004.

21 Michael Marmot is most associated with this work, www.workhealth.org/projects/pwhiteabs.html.

22 Jonathan Leake, 'Sweet Smell of Success Makes You Live Longer', *Sunday Times*, 30 May 2004.

23 Michael Collins, *The Likes of Us: A biography of the white working class*, Granta, 2004. Peggy Mount, a bassoon-voiced actress, was a staple of British cinema in the 1950s, and most famous on stage for starring in *Sailor Beware!* a huge (middle class) West End hit in 1955.

24 Richard Hoggart, *The Uses of Literacy*, Chatto & Windus, 1957 and Pelican editions from 1958.

25 *The Week*, 24 July 2004, quoting Tam Dalyell's obituary of Foot in the Independent.

26 Irene Shubik, *Play for Today: The evolution of television drama*, Davis-Poynter, 1975.

27 Hugh Brody, *Maps and Dreams*, Penguin, 1983, Faber and Faber, 1986.

28 Simon Kuper, 'Won For All', FT Magazine, 18 September 2004.

29 A C Grayling in the *FT* Magazine, 17 April 2004, reviewing Richard Hoggart, *Mass Media in a Mass Society*, Continuum, 2004.

30 *The Times* Magazine, 3 July 2004.

31 A cartoon character invented by Reg Smythe in 1958 for the *Daily Mirror*.

32 W K Jordan, *Philanthropy in England, 1480–1660: A study of the changing pattern of English social aspirations*, Allen and Unwin, c1960?

33 J H Plumb, *England in the Eighteenth Century: A study of the development of English society*, Pelican, 1950 and many editions since.

34 Quoted by Alan Judd, 'Chips With Everything', *The Spectator*, 24 July 2004.

35 *The Diaries of King George V*, extracts broadcast on BBC Radio 4, July 2004.

36 Francis Wilson, *The Courtesan's Revenge: Harriette Wilson, the woman who blackmailed the king*, Faber and Faber, 2003.

37 Geoffrey Pearson, *Hooligan: A history of respectable fears*, Macmillan, 1983.

38 M D George, *London in the XVIIIth Century*, quoted by David Thomson in *England in the Nineteenth Century: From Waterloo to the First World War*, Pelican, 1950 and many editions since.

39 J L and Barbara Hammond, *Lord Shaftesbury*, Pelican, 1923.

40 F K Prochaska in 'Philanthropy', an essay in *The Cambridge Social History of Britain, 1750–1950*, Volume 3, Cambridge University Press, 1990.

41 Steen Eiler Rasmussen, *London: The unique city*, Pelican, 1934 and 1960; see also Peter Akroyd, *London: The biography*, Chatto & Windus, 2001.

CHAPTER 6

MASS AFFLUENCE AND SOCIETY

The critics of capitalism are very inclined to believe that one must leave morality and thoughtfulness at the kitchen table as one leaves home. At home, one moralises about the world, cares about the planet, and values the family. At work, one stills the quiet voice of conscience, and gets on with exploitation. At best, this gloomy view goes, one can say that funding the good public and private things of one's leisure can only be done by being a success in the less attractive, less valuable, less worthwhile world of work.

It is perhaps a feature of growing affluence, and now of Mass Affluence, that we can afford to sneer at wealth creation. Perhaps – and this must surely be right – we feel we are rich enough not to ignore our scruples.

Perhaps the critics fear what is true. Capitalism is a field in which ambition and aggression – the human appetite for risk – is given full rein. Like war, creativity, science and sport, it is not for the faint-hearted. And yes, in part its value is in providing an outlet for instincts that many feel we should tame, rather than express.

Dislike of capitalism is as old as the beast itself. It is paradoxical, then, that it should have been the northern European Protestant tradition (including its New World spin-offs) that pioneered many of the facets of modern wealth creation. Banking and trading were developed to a high degree in many cultures, and appeared in different forms, centuries before northern Europe's own seventeenth- and eighteenth-century capitalist flourishing. But putting markets, banking, corporate organisation, property protection and mechanisation in harness with one another – and allowing them considerable freedom – does seem to have been a Protestant trick. It was Protestantism which most agonised about the excesses of wealth, while providing the key to creating it: it may have missed the birth of money and merchanting, but it was just in time to put its stamp on manufacturing. As Tawney tells us (and is mirrored in Max Weber and Christopher Hill):

In their emphasis on untiring activity, on work as an end in itself, on the evils of luxury and extravagance, on foresight and thrift, on moderation and self-discipline and rational calculation, they had created an ideal of Christian conduct, which canonized as an ethical principle the efficiency which economic theorists were preaching as a specific for social disorders...Not sufficiency to the needs of daily life, but limitless increase and expansion, became the goal of the Christian's efforts. Not consumption, on which the eyes of earlier sages had been turned, but production, became the pivot of his argument.[1]

No right-wing zealot, Tawney clearly disliked the brutalities that flowed from the early Industrial Revolution. They are more easily defended than he supposed, but in any case they cannot obliterate the fact that it was free societies that produced these advances, not the traditional, elitist autocracies, which were the global norm of the time. They had no future, and capitalism did. They couldn't reform, and capitalism did.

The same worthiness of northern European cultures made capitalism successful and criticised there. It may be that societies that are ambivalent about wealth are best at creating it. The reason is simple: capitalism requires a society capable of engendering order and trust on the one hand, and risk and adventure on the other. A society without virtue could not create the framework in which financial risk flourishes.

Capitalism exists because some people choose to risk a great deal in attempting the new. Its miracle is that it does not require more risk-taking than people want. It allows individuals to choose a level of risk. It allows one to invest in low-risk, low-profit funds, or in high-risk, high-profit funds. It is, by the way, no argument against this range of possibilities that Enron's employees lost their pensions in that famous collapse – rather they ignored the old scepticism about having all one's eggs in one basket, especially the basket that employs you. Nor will it do to say that, in recent years, pension managers have failed their investors. True, the managers did not invest enough in the safe, as opposed to the risky, sort of fund. But both were on offer.

It is, in fact, one of the greatest virtues of capitalism that it allows people who despise it to profit from it. One can dislike risk, and disapprove of it; one can think gambling the opposite of prudent; and still the risk-takers will go forth with a judiciously small portion of the risk-averse person's savings and return them as profits, without demanding that you applaud their ingenuity and courage.

In catering to the richness of humanity – to its moral aspirations and its various temperaments – capitalism is, of course, capable of being moral. As such, it is also capable of being satisfying to people who seek a spiritual dimension to their lives.

Capitalism is forever inviting people to innovate. It rewards people who discover ways of making new goods and services, or new ways of making old goods and services. In this, it is inherently creative. Its critics say that it is unstable; that it is forever charging ahead into the uncharted; that it destroys old and traditional ways and promotes new and useless goods. We might as truly say that people demand progress, which is code for change. Capitalism enjoys that urge, but is not dependent on it. It would be the most efficient way of delivering an unchanging set of goods and services, just as it is the most efficient way of delivering a changing one. If we wanted a stable society that celebrated sufficiency (as Barry Schwartz says we should), it would be capitalists that got there with the minimum of waste. They might be competing in the matter of wastelessness – but compete and profit they would.

But why be so negative? Capitalism is creative, and it rewards creators. Entrepreneurs are inventing our tomorrow, no less than painters and poets, as they relentlessly seek fresh ways of expressing the human spirit.

'UNEARNED' WEALTH

Getting money is not necessarily the same thing as creating it. Almost all investment is good, because it helps create wealth. But it doesn't have to have virtuous intention. Often it will seem very much like gambling, and it is. Oddly, we admire the gambler, who seeks to get something for nothing, but we despise the stockbroker. The one is a spiritual pirate, the other is a rip-off merchant. What is forgotten is that pirates are less productive than merchants.

We are ready enough to see the drama and the poetry in a casino's crap tables, and do so, in countless filmed and written accounts, such as Mike Hodges' 1999 movie, *The Croupier*. The hero is a croupier and a writer. It is obvious to him and his girlfriend that being a writer is the nobler path, if he can pull it off. But it is his casino work that provides the subject which makes him a successful writer: that's where the excitement is. A person betting his shirt at a gaming table obviously has theatre. Philip Seymour Hoffman, in *Owning Mahowny*, plays a banker, modelled on a real-life character, for whom the excitements of legal risk-taking in his banking job don't compare with the thrill of betting, whether at the track or casino. He is quite a good banker, but a useless gambler. The film, for dramatic purposes, has him – late in the game, and close to the end of his tether – win enough money to pay the bank back the money he has stolen to fund his betting failures. In real life, the gambling failures are relentless. Of course, anyway, in the film the gambler goes on one mad punt, and he loses it all. The point is that there is no need for the casino to lavish big rooms and whores on him:

he doesn't choose to gamble, or the place to gamble, on those grounds. He doesn't gamble to get rich. He's not a Walter Mitty type, such as Leonardo DiCaprio plays in *Flying High*: our banker doesn't take his risks so as to look good. He vaguely loves his girl, but nowhere near as much as he loves gambling. He is presented as physically squalid, and morally lost. His is a cautionary tale. But it would be of no interest to us if there were not something magically exciting about risk, and if risk were not central to our lives. We dimly sense that he is fully alive, even as he descends deeper into his private hell.

In *American Sucker*, David Denby, an upper-crust, upper West Side film critic for the *New Yorker* describes his failed attempt to make a million in a hurry during 2002.[2] It seems (this is written before I had the chance to read the book, but I have seen reviews of it) that Denby thinks his country has gone mad for money and credit. He is said to blame his advisers for misleading him, and presents himself as a 'victim of business sharks'.[3] What is amazing is that anyone could have thought that dealing in stocks is easy: that one could leave off some real profession and, in a few months, learn how to beat the market. Why should one believe that to be possible, and any more likely than that one could learn how to be a professional gambler?

The poetry in money, the drama and the risk in a business venture, the talents of entrepreneurs and investors: these are the things we ought to appreciate more than we do. We ought to see that a man betting his shirt to open a sandwich bar, or to buy shares he believes have growth in them, is at least as interesting as one who takes a punt against the known odds in a casino.

Oddly, we may be closer to appreciating this than ever before. When Ruby Wax does her TV profiles of business people, she is after the human drama of the entrepreneurial type. When, in a dozen lifestyle programmes, we watch people build a business from scratch, we are on the edge of our seats as they make mistakes, with unintended consequences wreaking havoc and creating opportunities with wildcard haphazardness.

We watch these shows because they are about people having a go – we half want them to succeed and half want them to fail. At one moment we identify with them; at another, resent them; at another, feel superior. We watch them as we watch circus trapeze acts or grand prix laps: and that's the point. Where once we watched exotic eastern European gypsies do things we could only imagine doing, or watched vanishingly rare daredevil drivers, now we see the drama in the relatively everyday. What is more, we see that in the everyday world – the world near us, in which there are few poets, celebrities or stars – there are people spotting possibilities, exploiting them, being shafted by fate, taking chances, seeking safety, and in all these shifts being creative and poetic. The mundane world of small business and chip shops and salesmanship is seen to have its share of creativity, dignity and worth. This is good. And yet we are reluctant properly to see that we can admire the rich for the skills and courage they've shown, rather than for the luck or nastiness to which we are still inclined to attribute their wealth. So there appear to be – as one might expect – competing trends at work. On the one hand, entrepreneurship is becoming an exciting option that is appealing to more and more people. It is being democratised by Mass Affluence. And, on the other, big business is being described as a cowboy rip-off. The first tendency is very real, and the second something of a chimera.

WEALTH CREATION AND WORK

The obvious thought is that capitalists create work and opportunity, and this is the perfectly reasonable line of almost all politicians as they pursue economic wealth. Promoting wealth creation by firms and their owners is the only known way of getting people into employment, and turning them into taxpayers.

But we can go much further. The modern economy is a far better place to work than any economy before it. An increasing proportion of people work in pleasant environments, and gain mental satisfaction rather than physical exhaustion from their work. More people now exercise interesting choices in their work. Fewer people are engaged in frustrating routine than has ever been the case before.

How do we square this with the far commoner claims that burger-flipping and call-centre pseudo-human relations are all many people can expect? That part-time, catch-as-catch-can insecurity is the norm, as people chase commissions not salaries? That employees must put together a forlorn portfolio to try to prove that they will be loyal and committed, while being ever ready to move on uncomplainingly, as employers pursue a just-enough employment policy?

As we look at the positive, it is perhaps worth reiterating the degree to which old-fashioned work was unpleasant. Peasant agriculture was, and remains, brutally hard work, and tedious with it. Craftsmanship was often achieved at the expense of 'stress positions' (to borrow a phrase from modern discussion of torture methods) and aches and pains specific to various trades. Arthritis and blindness attended the close trades of tailoring and weaving, while deafness attended the butch trade of blacksmithing. There are many people now who are romantic about the old ways of earning a living, and the best rebuttal of their view is to remind ourselves that peasant agriculture and craftsmanship now attract a premium, but few takers.

Very few people adopt peasant agriculture or craft labour, except those who have never known them, or have never known anything else. True, some of the drawbacks of peasant agriculture and craft trades can be mitigated by modern machinery and by the technologies that allow one to live simultaneously in a village or workshop and in the wider world. Many a craftsman now listens to the radio all day, and surfs the Internet and emails extensively at night. That is all to the good, but it is a feature of modern wealth and modern technology. These are perhaps Ivan Illich's 'tools for conviviality', and Kropotkin's liberating small tools: but not quite as these visionaries imagined them.

A job in Burger King or McDonald's is the first chance many youngsters have of seeing how excellence and success works. I have heard testimony on radio from at least two young people who say that this was the case in their own lives. McDonald's is, of course, in large part a series of small firms – it is a franchise operation, and in that sense it provides opportunities for entrepreneurs rather than for 'jobsworths'. (Though this in part is true of the UK, we are unusual in the McDonald's empire, which in other countries is more nearly a wholly franchise deal.)

The food in a McDonald's is made of much better ingredients than is commonly acknowledged, but our point here is that it attempts to show employees that being part of a team and serving customers is something worth doing well, and that hygiene and efficiency matter. It is fairly easy to defend McJobs on the basis that they provide easy entry points to the service economy, and that anyone with ambition could build on them to progress within McDonald's or in the rest of the service economy, whether catering or otherwise.

But there is something more to an easy-come, easy-go job market than that. There are some very important professions – writing, music, acting, and entrepreneurship – which are far easier to pursue if one knows that alternative survival is always available. A socially mobile society is one in which social flexibility – employment flexibility – is available. The idea that we can create unionised, solid, permanent jobs, and that no other kind is needed or desirable, is only tenable if we accept as a corollary a sclerotic situation, in which much that is interesting must remain a hobby to be pursued by amateurs.

It's often been remarked how creatively liberating a good system of dole is, and certainly plenty of musicians and others – including full-time protestors – have depended on it. McJobs are even more useful.

Job security is not a good guarantee of economic security. One of the few unkindnesses big firms routinely visit on their employees is the tacit promise of a job for life. The only honest thing for a caring employer to say is that, as soon as their economic interests dictate, workers will be thrown out of work. Around the edges, employers can try to maintain jobs, and some firms have tried to make a positive virtue of this habit. Volkswagen, for instance, has been praised for its efforts in some of its German factories in this direction. But the attempt has come at the price of increased costs, and therefore prices, and it may be that VW has done more harm than good, even to its own workers, by trying to be kind to them. This is not to say that firms cannot elevate to the front of their minds the idea of employee-friendly policies. But we do need to remember that such policies may well backfire, and apparent brutality might have done better.

Interestingly, there is some evidence to support this anecdotal and intuitive point of view. It seems that countries that legislate for job security fail to achieve it. That suggests that the likelihood of maintaining security of income flows not from job security, but from a vibrant job market.

The main price of trying to achieve long-term loyalty to one's workers is that the employer reduces the employee's sense that the portability of his skills and abilities – and his reputation – is very important. If, say, one worked for IBM in the 1970s and 1980s, one might have believed one ought to develop the skills and approaches that worked well within that firm. One might have so concentrated on IBM that one didn't bother to develop skills potentially useful to another employer, or to cultivate a wider acquaintance than one's IBM colleagues. When, contrary to its own expectations and hopes, IBM downsized, there were undoubtedly employees who were less useful than they might have been. I don't make this a detailed case history, or a certain outcome in all instances. I merely stress the fact that firms cannot deliver job security, and may do harm if they create the expectation that they can.

Business life is provisional, and it can be very useful to remember it. No-one is so securely employed that they can afford not to be a skills-entrepreneur.

That said, the modern Anglosphere economy has not produced a huge amount of self-employment, and the proportion has not risen dramatically in recent years. In the UK, around 60 per cent of employment is in the full-time, permanent job sector. Part-timing and self-employment make up 40 per cent of the earnings of households, and the former has indeed risen quite fast. What's odd here is that it is often argued that there is something inherently wrong about this situation – that's to say, that most people would prefer full time to part time. It turns out that knowledgeable assessments do conclude that many people, especially women, choose part-time work because they want to combine work with child-rearing, say. It is hard to see how we can make a complaint out of this.

It is likely that many couples could easily thrive on the main breadwinner's income. Let's not mince words: most couples could survive on the husband's salary, but most women, including mothers, would rather be out at work. They want independence, and they want a higher household income. Would we rather have a world in which there were fewer part-time slots for them to duck and weave into? It is true, of course, that the picture is much tougher for single mothers: but then, no-one ever said – or rather, few people have seriously argued – that a mother on her own could easily make a household for her children.

A conservative may argue that too many women go out to work for too many hours, and do so for unnecessary material benefit and at the expense of their families and perhaps even of themselves. Whatever the merits of that case, it certainly seems to suit the choices made by many real and self-determining people that they want there to be jobs at every sort of level in a part-time format.

Similarly, self-employment is sometimes forced on people (say, when they lose their jobs in middle age). But probably more often it is a choice made by those who reckon that their skills set and experience has reached the point where they can risk fending for themselves in the market. They do so because they would prefer to have many customers rather than one employer. Sure, they are swapping apparent security for apparent insecurity. The swap may be less pinching than they or others suppose, for all that any self-employed person will have stories to tell of sleepless nights.

The developing practice of people working for themselves is said to produce a greater sense of insecurity than being employed, but there is no reason why this should be true, and it certainly doesn't seem to be. Around a tenth of the workforce is self-employed (a figure that is surprisingly low, given how much modern insecurity is supposed to flow from its being so large). People who are employed full time are at risk of losing their jobs. People with a portfolio of jobs – with many customers for their labour – are less likely to lose everything at once.

Commentators are also keen to stress how much more part-time work there is now, and to make that a matter of complaint. But flexibility of work is one of the prized features of an economy in which more people are doing what they want. Thus, it seems that people do part-time work because it fits their way of life. Agreed that 'choice' may be a funny word to use of, say, a working mother who opts for shiftwork: but the availability of such shifts is a relative luxury, compared with not being able to work at all.

The upshot of the two trends is that full-time permanent employees make up less than 60 per cent of the workforce (again a figure that one might say is surprisingly large).[4]

Anyway, the British are not frightened, so far as one can see.

Having told the *Eurobarometer* that they like their lives, more than half say they expect things to stay about the same for them, a third say they'll get better, and only 11 per cent expect a worsening financial situation.[5]

But remember how concerned we are now about stress. Stress is said to be most serious in people and animals who discover themselves to be powerless. It is underlings, not bosses, who suffer 'learned helplessness'. It is people and animals trapped in non-negotiable hierarchies whose stress we are invited to worry about by Professor Seligman, whose research gets many admiring pages in Barry Schwartz's work. Fine: these are arguments that lead us to think that self-employment, like other forms of entrepreneurship, is likely to be tough and exciting, but not to produce the hierarchy-driven stress that the critics of Mass Affluence often point to. For that, look to a 'safe' job.

We are said to be in the midst of a stress epidemic. 'In Britain, days lost to stress, depression and anxiety increased from 6.5m in 1995 to 13.4m in 2001–02', reported *The Economist*. But it was in an unusually brisk mood (for a paper that, if anything, errs toward the humane):

[The] explanations of increased stress bear little scrutiny. The first of these is that working longer hours increases stress. But hours worked have been in long-term decline – in the mid 19th Century the average was 60 hours a week; they have also dropped recently. Long hours mostly affect British men: four out of five of those working 48 hours or more per week were male. Yet between 1997 and 2002, the percentage of men doing this dropped from 35 per cent to 30.7 per cent.

The magazine dismissed the anxieties about intrusiveness of 24/7 technologies as old hat; a cry as old as the advent of the steam train. As an explanation, it preferred the willingness of people to report distress; their raised expectation of well-being; and fashion. 'Stress can almost become a badge of honour', Eric Teasdale, chief medical officer of the enlightened pharmaceutical firm AstraZeneca, told the periodical. Besides, it noted, people are reluctant to report that they are inadequate, or mismanage their lives: reporting stress is allowed, and – it might have added – shunts blame onto the outside world.[6]

Myrna Blyth argues that women's magazines compound the problem. 'For twenty years, as a US magazine editor, she peddled the notion that modern women have impossibly complicated, stressful lives. Now she has written a book, Spin Sisters, denouncing such dishonesty', wrote Janice Turner in *The Times*.[7] Women's magazines have, for forty years, pushed the idea that feminism properly consists in self-regard and orgasms: motherhood and professionalism have seemed – in their very different ways – a sort of imposition by society. Blyth argues that the prevailing myth was that going to work or looking after children did not constitute the real 'You'; that comes only in pampering oneself. Blyth's about face is attractive to the anti-capitalists, in the sense that self-pampering is profitable to the firms who advertise in the very women's magazines that propagate it. But Blyth's new case is also attractive to those of us who disparage the social revolution of the 60s.

It has, for many years, been fashionable to complain that success in the modern world is attended by an obsessive, stressed, non-stop culture. Most recently, Madeline Bunting has made this case. She admits one major difficulty in her own title: 'Willing Slaves'. She implies that people have a 'false consciousness' about their lives.

It is true that Britons put in longer hours than their Continental neighbours. But it is not a given that this means they are doing more work. It is possible – I don't say it is the case – that Britons have more fun at work, or spend more of their work hours socialising than their neighbours. Clocking up hours is not by itself a sign of anything very much. Nor does it make much sense to suppose that Britons would trade their longer-hours culture for the EU norm of shorter hours, when the latter seems to have higher unemployment as a corollary. A rather similar problem arises with productivity comparisons. There are generally supposed to be more robots in Continental factories than in British ones. If there had to be a trade-off, which would workers prefer? Longer hours and a good chance of employment, or short hours and the chance to sit at home on generous dole and watch programmes about highly mechanised factories?

High productivity in a full-employment economy: that is the ideal. But neither is it, in itself, a guarantor of economic or social good health.

In any case, it is the hours-culture of British high-achievers that most worries Madeline Bunting and others. Many people who can choose to have less demanding jobs, now opt for demanding ones. They want the money, and why not? But they also recognise that they are in a non-stop competition for the eye of their bosses, and of bosses in competing firms. It's worth remembering that people only seem to be working for one exploiting boss. They are always also working to increase the strength of the CV they will be showing the boss they would next like to have, in their current business or elsewhere. High-achievers are always seeking to enrich their chances within their business and within their specialism. They seek high earnings, and quite often they are increasing their portability, too. The willing slave on the M25 is reckoning on Florida or Tuscany as the next employment or entrepreneurship possibility. He is building a stake, or a CV, for higher or different things.

The 'slave' is always thinking of trading masters, or having none. Jobs are not just treadmills, but also springboards. These factors may explain why so many of our most intelligent and energetic people sign up for what, to outsiders, looks like a slave galley. Where Madeline Bunting sees a galley oar, they see an option.

Many people in the full-time, full-commitment economy do dream of giving it all up, getting into the country, and downsizing.

Micky and Alison Griffith seem like very modern people as they approach middle age. 'I cannot imagine stopping work altogether, as long as it is something that I enjoy', Micky told Alison Gibson of *The Times* 'Money section'. He's taking a holiday from work to do the sorts of self-improving things a person might wait until retirement to indulge in. The couple have cut their outgoings, and he cycles everywhere. He's living on his wife's earnings for now. They've worked in Africa as VSO volunteers, and taken time out to take degrees. So they are a bit hippy, caring, and keen on education. She works for a Third World development NGO (Non-Governmental Organisation), and he's a commercial exhibition organiser. They are prudent and careful financially, and even actively savvy. They are childless, and so it is not perhaps fair to take their case as typical. And yet this mixture of capitalistic canniness and moral aspiration seems not so much an exception, as exactly the sort of thing that modern Mass Affluence is allowing and encouraging.[8]

Interestingly, if the innumerable and enlightening television shows devoted to this trend are to be believed, many of these people do not want a peasant way of life at all. Rather, they want to swap employment for entrepreneurship, and to trade managerial work in a wide variety of businesses for being bosses in the leisure and tourism industries. Many of them, when they go into rural entrepreneurship, are aiming at very high-end, high-value organic and niche rural products. Again, no harm in that, but they are in a distinctively glossy, globalized, modern trade. They are living in areas which were once home to peasants, and working what were peasant fields and groves, but they are doing so in a way – and with economic expectations – unrecognisable to the forebears they seek to emulate, and whose image they are exploiting.

Similarly, many people who leave the rat race don't really downsize, and certainly don't drop out. Faith Glasgow took three cases for a *Financial Times* piece. Her first example was of a man in the printing business in Soho, who took off for the Scilly Isles. He began as a fisherman and hotel worker, before starting what is now a nationally known high-tone organic bakery. Her second case was of a central London IT worker who now runs a web-design business (working for UK firms) from Barcelona. Her third case was of a London PR couple who split for Yorkshire, where one works from home and the other commutes to Leeds. These were all business people, and remain so. They are more, not less, capitalistic now. They are dependent on the modern technology that liberated them.[9]

WEALTH CREATION AND CUSTOMERS

To create wealth, one must satisfy customers. It is a common assumption, surely wrong, that modern capitalism exploits its customers. In one obvious way, this is rendered all but impossible by competition rules. There are very few situations in which modern consumers do not have many choices of firm, and very many choices of product, to satisfy their needs and wants. They can go up and down market, they can choose completed or half-completed products, or begin with the very parts themselves. Indeed, as we have seen, the modern complaint is that people suffer too much, not too little, choice.

Naomi Klein did do good with her work on brands. Though her book was a pretty standard compilation of environmental and leftish complaints about capitalism, it did have some originality, and she knew it. She believed that she was exposing the brand businesses, and she was certainly helpful in showing us how that world operated. But she was more useful in showing us how modern campaigners were working.

She realised that brands were the protective shells of companies. The brand-owning firms are unwittingly providing the grab-points with which they can be flipped onto their backs. The more a company is identified with and as a brand, the easier it is to deploy the brand against the firm. The brand becomes a badge of honour and respectability which can be all the more deadly when it is used by campaigners to advertise a fall from virtue – real or imagined.

She was among the first to describe in a systematic way the brand-led tactics of NGOs. For many years, environmental campaigners had targeted large firms, not least because they suspected – rightly – that extractive firms like RTZ and Shell put a high price on their respectability. Especially if one sought to influence events overseas, it was often a useful strategy to aim one's criticism at these multinationals. After all, though they were almost always behaving better than anyone else in some poor countries, and much better than the indigenous politicians and officials, they were also far more biddable. But Shell and RTZ are much more than their advertisements: they are operators with huge technical skill and muscle, with which they wrestle, in the real world, with the earth's crust.

In the 1990s, human rights campaigners borrowed the tactic to shame sportswear firms into disciplining their subcontractors in the Far East. The campaigners were able to say that the sportswear firms were 'virtual', Post Modern firms, owning and managing only a consumer-manipulating brand and none of the physical capital that produced the vehicle of this image-making, the shoe or shirt itself. The real good and harm the firm might do was done by contractors; and little good was done. This claim was substantially off beam: the workers in the subcontractors' workshops were ex-peasants who were glad of a machinist's job. Still, their position was no doubt improvable, though raised standards and higher wages risked job losses, as capital and contracts sought cheaper and more compliant labour among poor societies whose memories of peasant tedium and poverty were sharper.

What was new in these campaigns was that they appeared to be attacking firms that really were little more than their brands. The campaigners were exposing the folly of consumers in buying their goods, whose price mostly consisted of branding and sponsorship.

What was new in these campaigns was that they appeared to be attacking firms that really were little more than their brands. The campaigners seemed to be exposing the folly of consumers in buying their goods, whose price mostly consisted of branding and sponsorship. And yet there are very few sure ways of doing good in the Third World. One is to help it produce good government, and the other is to trade with it. The reviled sportswear firms were doing the latter, and it is not at all certain that the No Logo campaigners did more good than harm in attacking this work.

BRANDING, FASHION AND SPORT

Fashion is one of the most remarkable industries. It seeks to enrich itself by satisfying, to the ultimate degree, our desire for novelty. I am of a generation and mindset that finds it hard to understand why men and women want to pay over the odds for trashy clothes, whose distinguishing feature is that they function as a billboard for the designer's logo. I don't quite get why it is that women want to pay lots of money to look like hookers, nor why they want to be branded. I am pretty sure that up close and personal, some of these clothes are very remarkable, and that in the deliberate outrage there is probably also subtlety – if one only gets close enough. So it may be that the trashiness is ironic, and that it is more obviously so if one sees the clothes in the glamorous settings in which they are actually worn, rather than in a battered *Hello* magazine at the dentist's. But this may be too generous an assessment.

In any case, the follies of fashion have been with us for centuries, and men of my generation and outlook have doubtless been bemoaning much the same decline in standards for as long as, and wherever, women and men have dolled themselves up. Men and women of quality, discernment and education have queued up perennially to make the same fashionable mistake, and it may well be that it turns out not to have been a mistake at all. It certainly isn't a new one, or one generated by high capitalism or advertising.

Besides, high fashion and high fashion brands are adored by people who seem at first glance to represent their antithesis. Tracey Emin is a wonderfully strange creature: squinty, leery and grinning, she has made a name for herself by baring an untidy, but quite large, soul and an even less obviously attractive personal milieu. She is, you might think, counter-culture on legs, yet – like Audrey Hepburn, for instance – she swears by YSL and its jackets, 'which are comfortable and versatile'.[10]

The fashion game – what its brands confer and who will be attracted to them – is not easily predicted. And that is part of its joyful absurdity.

It happens that I think it is a bit creepy that Nike seeks to persuade us that its gear somehow personifies the very world of struggle, aspiration and discipline that the men and women it sponsors actually do personify. But then I remember to get a life. Nike's ads, like any other, catch one's attention and do generally say quite interesting things about achievement. So perhaps this is another good thing they do: though many of their customers are the antithesis of the world of achievement portrayed in the ads, at least sportswear firms can't be faulted for suggesting that getting off one's backside is a very good thing to do.

Sports I admire for other reasons – tennis and rugby – are also admirable in keeping the visible signs of commercial sponsorship under rather better control than football, which I don't admire. In short, sports and sportsmen, like customers, can and do make choices about what they will allow advertisers to do and get away with. That a considerable proportion of Nike's aspirational gear is sold to couch potatoes, and very much of it appears on pasty-faced low-achievers who hang around town centres getting drunk is ironic, but hardly sinful.

Pale Chavs won't sport go-faster stripes forever. Indeed, they won't do so because they will have succeeded in rendering the clothes so unfashionable that even they won't be seen dead in them. It'll be back to paisley and frills, or sharp little mod suits, or cowboy denim, or floral print, or punk, or Goth, or something. And the middle-aged will complain about that, too.

But none of this will have been driven by manufacturers. They will be struggling to keep up with their consumers, not the other way round.

WEALTH CREATION AND COMMUNITY

The most biting charge against modern capitalism is that it is driven by selfish greed, which is pitted against the community. That is to say, it licenses the anti-social individual against the supportive society.

It is less noticed that capitalism is a triumph of cooperation. It can flourish only when society volunteers to produce laws that produce order, contracts and complex markets. Dictatorships have been able to produce a degree of capitalist development, but have never quite permitted their citizens the level of autonomous cooperation that is necessary for capitalism really to develop. That is a function of free societies, and it is the clearest measure of them.

It is obvious that capitalists compete among each other for labour and customers, and, right from the start, that tended to benefit both labour and customers. Poor people flocked to factories begging for work, because the old agricultural economy had developed to the point where it could feed far, far more people than it could employ. At the start, the inequality of the societies in which capitalism flourished did, of course, allow what, even then, was called exploitation – but the societies capable of producing capitalism were also precisely the societies that were capable of legislating against its worst excesses. They could achieve the former and the latter for the same reason: an appreciation of modernity, a sense of progress. In time, the affluence that capitalism uniquely produced uniquely dispelled the need for much of that legislation.

That there were periods when this smooth progress did not seem very evident, and when tens of thousands of people endured decades in which industrialised development was a mixed blessing is, of course, true. But the statistics do not lie: more and more children survived into adulthood in the nineteenth century, in an explosive acceleration of a historic trend. Certainly, it took decades for wealth creation to catch up to the extent that each member of this vastly increased army of young could be given a rising expectation of life. But Malthus was proven wrong. Life expectation did not dip during the years of industrialisation's tough birth. Birth survival rates did rocket. People did get more education. Political life did catch up with the facts of economic modernity. The working class did discover nature, at least those that wanted to. Socialism did become a mass movement, and nearly scuppered the whole thing – but that's another story.

The more modern accusation against capitalists is that the greedy, exploitative nasty individual plays to his worst features, and that's what success consists in.

Actually, however, there are rather few capitalists who can survive in socially dysfunctional isolation. Such a character might thrive in an anonymous market place, equipped with little more than a broadband connection and astuteness. But the myriad firms from which an investor chooses are all conglomerates of people who are working together. The distrust among them – their fallings-out and rows and bust-ups – are legendary and amusing. But what the media cannot so easily portray – what is less visible – is the reverse of this coin. In business, people are all the time making up their minds whether the person they are dealing with can be trusted. It is quite wrong to pick up on this and then make the cynical case that the whole game is one in which people are bluffing and conning each other. Of course, there's an element of that. But it is more remarkable how the good judgement of people, and the qualities they see in other people, is what really builds businesses. Like marriages, there are successes and failures. Like good marriages, these relationships do not always consist in good people picking good qualities in other good people. But reliability and trust are at the root of it all, and admirable qualities are at least as valued as unpleasant ones.

And how could it be otherwise? To get most business started, at least two people must agree that they can get on and have complementary skills or assets. They must persuade people, who usually have plenty of other choices, that they are going to be a decent bet as employers. They have to convince other people – most of them positively dazzled by the choices before them – that they will be reliable suppliers of goods or services. They have to persuade the money market – which usually has much safer bets to make – that they will be reliable borrowers. Bad times toughen these circumstances, of course, but they provide more opportunities for sheer quality of personality to shine through.

The dysfunctional anti-social nerd can function in this economic society, but will be in back-office functions. He will be useless, unless a personable capitalist can see him as an asset and get his talent to market.

Two small stories illustrate some of this. Amy Sacco was the daughter of a New Jersey trucking family (and an amateur trucker for fun as a youngster) when she went into the restaurant business as a hostess. Drinking an after-hours bottle of champagne with a colleague, they agreed that

whoever struck it big first would help the other. When Force, her best friend to this day, hit pay dirt in the international art world, she introduced Sacco to would-be investors so that she could pursue her own dream of opening a club, and she raised the necessary $1.2 million to open Lot 61 [a highly fashionable New York night club] in 1998...'I'm no Park Avenue Princess', Sacco proudly asserts. 'I'm totally self-made. It's not where you're from, it's who you are.' [11]

But Sacco isn't quite right, is she? She sprung from entrepreneurial loins. She made a trusted friend. She impressed investors with what might have been a madcap idea in someone else's mouth. She is in a business where her living depends on high-dollar, volatile, scandal-prone people trusting both her sense of fun and her discretion. So, yes, she's self-made if you like. She is not Ivy League. Her silver spoon may have been a bit greasy. But her parents made her, and her friends, and those who invested in her, and her customers who rely on her.

The truth is, to be self-made is to make connections, even if it doesn't mean starting well connected. Every business deal involves a leap of faith, and the bigger the leap, the larger the profit may be – or the loss. And it is the faith – the trust – in the system that its critics least understand.

Or take the story of Sheeraz Hasan, who got bored making sandwiches in his family's sandwich and burger bar in central London. Two and a half years later, he runs a business that sends interviews with Hollywood's stars to the Asian market. No-one had thought of it before, and a market had gone untapped. His idea came to him while he was channel-hopping in LA, a place he had gone to because it seemed full of the kind of opportunities he vaguely sought. Once he had his idea, he persuaded an Asian TV channel that they should run his interviews. But how to produce the goods? He had no way of getting to the stars.

Every Friday I'd go to the Hollywood sign to pray. It's so peaceful up there and it's an inspiration just to be near it. I was walking down the hill afterwards one Friday in low spirits when this guy out walking his dog stopped me. He told me he'd been in Hollywood 30 years but never seen anyone bowing to the sign.[12]

This stranger obviously took to Hasan, and took to his idea, and he made the necessary connections for the tyro TV producer, who now has a giant success on his hands.

Did the stranger like the young man's spirituality? Did he like the convergence of the spiritual and the commercial? Did he just like the young man's commitment? Did he like the idea, never mind how it came into his life? I have no idea, but the powerful stranger, a major Hollywood producer, must surely have met every kind of chancer and ne'er-do-well in his time and decided that Hasan could be trusted. A powerful person does not hook you up with other powerful people if there's very much chance that you'll damage his reputation for picking winners. That would be very bad for his credibility.

The mystery of these zillions of human relations – these moments when the answer is 'yes', and small and large steps of trust are taken – informs some very lofty accounts of why capitalism works. F A Hayek is perhaps the man who has done most to describe how it is the interactions of millions of people that produce capitalism.[13] He takes Adam Smith's insights and makes them work on a truly industrial scale. But his real insight is often missed: the competitive market place brings forth extraordinary amounts of peaceable, undirected, cooperation.

Very recently, Paul Seabright has tried to repaint the picture for us, in his *The Company of Strangers: A natural history of economic life.*[14] His case is that no-one dictates the means by which millions of people cooperate to produce the hundreds of thousands of sorts of shirts (to take his most quoted example) for billions of consumers. Of course, many capitalists try to organise and regiment this process. Ideally, any one of them would 'control' the market for all shirts, worldwide. But they all know it isn't going to happen, and some of them know that a niche market can be more profitable than a large one.

The interesting thing is that, like those performers who dive off a stage into their fans' outstretched arms, none of us is troubled by the amount of trust we daily place in 'the company of strangers'. The true picture of modern life is a world in which the competition is among forces that produce what is a remarkable amount of cooperation. And there are so many instances of cooperation, all around, that we have every reason to suppose that this immense web of human activity will survive almost all disasters that befall it.

It is a commonplace that capitalism is successful because it goes with the grain of human greed and competitiveness. The psychologist Raj Persaud notes, however, that capitalism is based on another human urge: the tendency to trust. We are sophisticated social animals, enjoy placing confidence in others, and are sophisticates in the field. Persaud notes: '[As] we know that deceit is an inevitable part of human affairs, it is our confidence that we can spot deceit in others that leads us to entertain the possibility of giving our trust over, because we feel we can determine when to do so and when not to.' Citing work by Paul Zak of Claremont Graduate University, California, and Steve Knack of the World Bank, Persaud goes on to note that societies in which people don't trust one another are bound to stay poor. That sounds like stating the obvious, until we enrich the mix by suggesting that societies that produce well-being will not merely produce people who are happy because they can take risks, but also because they are surrounded by trusting relationships. Capitalism, it turns out, may be natural because it provides an outlet for trust – which is even more interesting than noting its value in providing outlets for thrill-seekers.[15]

In small matters and large, we live in a world of trust. Shirts will go on being produced. So will food and power and all the other much more crucial things we need. Safety will also be produced. Indeed, even if there weren't health and safety regulations, I would still trust the oil companies to keep me safe, as I daily share the public roads with their potentially explosive tankers. We could scrap regulation and rely on litigation to discipline the unruly, the slack and the wicked. That would be, in a sense, a market approach: the courts would be imposing costs on nuisance.

One could go further and let competition and the market do far more of the good work the world needs doing. Surely that is what must happen in education and health provision? Capitalists do not find it helps their businesses to be unreliable or dangerous. They need to be trusted by their customers, employees, shareholders and investors. Doing any of these down, or doing the dirty on them, is very bad for trade. Capitalists in most industries find that they have so many relationships, with people known and unknown to them, that their private interest turns out to be a much better fit with the public interest than most of us suppose.

The remarkable feat of the Al Qaeda bombers who struck at the Twin Towers was that they made anonymous capitalism and its highest-flyers – the people at the most financial and lofty ends of its relations – suddenly human and individual. Terrorists had declared war on capitalism, and one had either to stand aligned with it and its workers, or be in some much more peculiar position. For the first time, capitalism's beneficiaries – all of us – were invited to consider the personalities of the people who were previously merely conduits of the myriad transactions by which the market works. Barbara Stewart was one of the writers of the *New York Times* 'Portraits of Grief'. These were brief profiles of everyone killed on 9/11. She wrote in the *Guardian*: 'As I wrote the profiles, new windows opened on life in the city and introduced me, so to speak, to many people I would otherwise never have known.' Speaking of the brokers of one famous financial house, she said:

Many of them had graduated from one of the big Catholic universities. Their jobs often paid more than their fathers had earned. The hours were long, the work stressful. The brokers, it seems, tended to be easygoing men who worked hard, felt company loyalty and were saving for a house and family. Many came from big tightly-knit families and wanted nothing more than to have families like that of their own.

These were the 'Masters of the Universe' type, depicted in Hollywood movies and novels as believing that 'greed is good'. Maybe they did believe greed to be good: capitalism certainly puts it to work brilliantly. But it took 9/11 to show the ordinary human quality of their lives, and to remind us that capitalism doesn't dehumanise us. Even terrorism doesn't manage that.[16]

WEALTH CREATION AND THE CREATIVES

'I care more about the music and less about the money than the people in the band': that was the gist of the remark made to me by Miles Copeland, manager of the British super-group The Police in 1979. (He was the brother of the band's drummer, Stewart Copeland.) The remark stuck, because it neatly exploded the myth of the creative person in love with his art, and his managers in love with money. The likely truth of the remark struck swiftly. I had been around rock and reggae musicians for some years, and had watched them from afar for twenty years. Wasn't it obvious that the musicians I knew adored money and amassed it with all the vigour they could muster?

The idea of the artist starving in a garret has such power that it goes largely unchallenged as the norm for artists. The world expects creativity to be noble and glorious, and success to be almost beneath its dignity. And it may be true that many dreamers hope to make a living in the 'creative arts' and fail. And yet we know that creative people have mostly sought affluence, and have done so with a good deal of efficiency.

But let's not overlook the creative person's accountant or his manager. Many of these people admire and envy the creativity of their charges, and perhaps do so more than 'gifted' people admire each other. They certainly demonstrate a good deal of patience, as they handle the tantrums and the egocentricity of their charges.

The relatively functional can also be very important creatively. Take the case of Bob Marley. He was clearly some sort of genius, and quite early in his career was highly rated among reggae musicians. He was advised by Chris Blackwell, a record label manager of great talent, that, if he wanted to gain a wider acceptance, he should make his reggae more recognisable to a white rock-music audience. Marley made the compromise and produced a music that was much more accessible. He became a world super-brand, 'the first Third World Superstar', and left a body of work that will probably last forever, and will transcend all cultures. In so doing, he created 'space' for the purists of reggae to gain acceptance with those white and wider worlds that wanted something more pure. This was paradoxical and very like life: Marley's 'sell-out' led a minority of people to seek out the Ur-reggae he had compromised, and of which the purists would have been oblivious, had it not been for Marley's compromise.[17]

Marley's move was probably in part driven by material considerations: he wanted huge success. He wanted a huge audience for his music, and was happy to be influenced by Blackwell, if popularity was the result. The point in this example is that music, typically of art, is regarded as more likely to be 'pure' if it is unpopular and is an economic failure. It is presumed that there is an inevitable tension between commerce and value. There is something to this: the cognoscenti – the people who know and care and concentrate – are indeed likely to have demanding tastes, which few artists will be able to satisfy and for which there is likely to be a small market. That's a recipe for impecunious artists. But Marley's commercial success, arguably, followed a compromise that enriched the work. As it gained in vulgar success, it gained in quality, too.

He was, perhaps, the first star of the World Music movement. At the 2002 BBC Radio 3 annual awards in this genre ('The sounds of planet earth', in the BBC's mantra) it was remarkable how many of the people introducing the acts wittered on – to great applause – about how their movement confounded capitalism and globalization. They did not seem to spot how blending the musical styles of various rich and poor countries was actually the essence of globalization. Two ethnic musics added together and transcending the parochial are precisely what globalization is about: the local finding a wider – a world – audience. Moreover, the creation of a world market for the genre had lifted musicians out of poverty, as capitalism always does. A musician from Afghanistan said that the passing of Taliban power had liberated him to create music and travel with it. This benign effect of western 'militarism' was overlooked in the festival of the anti-American.

But there is something more, a snobbery about the commercial. Part of the reason why creative people are accepted as being 'better', more interesting, than those who manage their money affairs is that we don't commonly reckon with the creativity of the business world.

This is part and parcel of the way that we rather readily accept that only poetry has poetry: accountancy and entrepreneurship don't. This sort of prejudice sits well with our feeling that architects are creative, but engineers aren't. The architect has the 'vision' and the creativity; by comparison the engineer is mundane.

The architect, after all, works with a pencil and sketchpad, and the engineer does his prosaic stuff with a calculator. The architect waxes lyrical about his 'purpose', while the engineer makes sure the vision doesn't fail its users in technical terms. One is about ideas and the other is about numbers.

To the architect is ascribed a sort of celebrity, but not (at least these days) to the engineer who makes sure the architect's work is not just a dream; nor yet to the accountant, who makes sure the building can actually happen. In *Great Engineers: The art of British engineers, 1837–1987*, Derek Walker and others discuss mournfully the decline in the acclaim accorded engineers.[18] The book was produced for the 150th anniversary of the founding of the Royal College of Art, to remind the world that the place had been set up to promote the design element in engineering.

Curiously, when engineers were most admired, they were also entrepreneurs and artists. The archetype is I K Brunel: his name and fortune were pinned to his vast, named, signature designs. Perhaps that's why we know him: he produced sculpture on an unbelievable scale. And his risks were financial, as well as structural.

The lives of the inventors of the industrial revolution were adventure stories in self-invention, as Joseph Paxton (of Crystal Palace fame) exemplifies: here was social and material advancement of a kind to inspire a Samuel Smiles, with his belief that the Victorian age allowed anyone to get anywhere, socially. But that was the nineteenth century all over. Progress mattered, seriousness mattered, beauty mattered, industry mattered. Profit was likely to be a sign of merit.

We are rather more coy now. The Royal Society for Arts and Industry was intended by its nineteenth-century founders to discuss how artistic ideas and industry could reinforce each other. As the modern RSA, the old institution retains a vestige of that purpose, and yet it is much more a place where liberals who are interested in business, and business people who seek to be liberals, try to soften business's edges, to make it more acceptable to the literati.

It is true that these things were always conflicted and nuanced: for instance, the painter J M W Turner knew and admired scientists and business people alike. 'Turner's curiosity for the sciences was matched by a corresponding practical interest in art among scientists', writes James Hamilton.[19] It is important also to remember that Turner was a businessman (a publican, for instance) and chronicled the drama of industrialisation.

We are in an Enlightenment ideal, and it was inherited from the Renaissance. Constable had sought to understand the chemistry of the paint with which he sought to capture the chemistry of the weather, which, he was also sure, it was a scientific mission to render beautifully. Now Turner saw the 'sublime' (the dangerously beautiful, the pretty rendered splendid by awesomeness) in the engines and fires of the industrial age. His painting *The Fighting Temeraire* sees a glamorous, patriotic, impotent sailing ship of the generation of Nelson (already seen as chivalric compared to the nineteenth century's mundane progressiveness). It is being towed to a scrap yard, on a windless day, by a thrusting, purposeful, nature-defying steam paddle-tug. In *Rain, Steam and Speed – the Great Western Railway* Turner depicts the flaming furnace of a steam engine, as it hauls its carriages out of the mists of the landscape and the past, on the tracks laid on a Brunel bridge across the Thames. A hare is dabbed into the foreground, half-glimpsed, as a real one would have been, seeking sanctuary. These pictures are not just celebrations of progress, and not just festivals of nostalgia, either. One of the glorious features of the nineteenth-century mind was that it saw beauty in function and function in beauty. Important things were being lost and gained, and it was proper to enter into the sense of both. The Romantic flinch from progress was not anything like the universal response of men of sensibility to the age of steam and science, though it is the reaction most inherited by the liberals of our time.

The difference between the 'creatives' and the 'mechanics' has to do with the personal ability to express something unique and uplifting. The mechanic can be replaced, but not the creative.

The trick to respectability, of course, is to seem socialist, artisan, romantic, anti-capitalist and artistic. The visionary wallpaper merchant and medievalist William Morris lived 'A life for our time', as his biographer, Fiona MacCarthy's, subtitle has it.[20] But he was rather more than any single modern character is. He contrived to be the Terence Conran of retailers, the Bob Geldof or Bono of campaigners, the Martha Stewart of good taste, the Dyson of manufacturers, the Anita Roddick of moralising, the Geoffrey Robinson of party funders, the Tony Benn of political radicals. He wished he could have produced gorgeous women's clothing more cheaply: as MacCarthy says, he would have liked to be the Laura Ashley of his day (though the mass production techniques were not sufficiently in place for that).

In fact, it fell to Laura Ashley to understand the commerciality of another aesthetic mission. At Charleston Farm in East Sussex, there is a farmhouse in which stayed, and later lived, various essential Bloomsbury Group artists. Morris-like, they had a firm, Omega, which had the ideal of designing household goods for the discerning. But it was Ashley, forty years later, in the 1970s, who bought the intellectual property in some of the fabric designs they had produced, and turned them out for a world that had adopted Bloomsbury's aesthetics and attitudes en masse.

Craftsmanship still fascinates. In the summer of 2004, Nike surprised the crofters of the Hebrides by placing an astronomically large order for their hand-loomed Harris Tweed. Nike wanted 10,000 metres from a firm used to supplying 100 metres a week. Naturally, the work was farmed out to nearly 50 small firms.[21] For some reason, a swatch-sized scrap of this stuff on a hi-tech trainer conveyed something that Nike wanted to convey. Was this irony? Did some executive note that Nike was famously shoving people into sweatshops and was thus destroying ethnic craftsmanship, and so it decided to boost a dying trade? If so, why revive a trade in the affluent West? Or was it a deeper irony yet? Did Nike note that Harris Tweed had undergone so many evolutions of taste that it would be chic to add another? After all, this was fabric designed to be thorn- and rain-proof: it was a shepherd's delight. It was taken up by the English upper classes as a Saturday homage to the sons of the soil, whence it became the badge of upward mobility for the suburban lower middle classes (and Welsh school teachers in exile from their valleys). Along the way, and slightly refined, it had become the tweed of choice for the Continental upper classes, who thought that the English, though peculiar, had got the gentleman thing down to a T. Long after the English had forgotten how to wear it, foreign exquisites can still do tweed beautifully. Now Nike, a world brand, classless, vulgar, technocratic, spivvily sporty, New Age aspirational, goes with this drizzle-drenched anachronism. It would not be surprising if this were the most sophisticated joke, or a designer's airhead whim (and all the better if it is).

William Morris would have understood, or ought to.

If not quite as rich, he was the inheritor of wealth, in the manner of a Zac Goldsmith. He was selling a high-volume nostalgic dream of Olde England and the Gothic to a middle class that epitomised modern industry and moneymaking. Perhaps his most interesting work was in seeking the right balance (as he saw it) between mass production and craftsmanship. Among his most interesting relationships is one with a dye-works manager, George Wardle, of Leek, Staffordshire. (No brute, says MacCarthy, but religious and paternalist; a recognisable figure of the day, then.) They had a large correspondence, as Morris sought to make his supplier achieve ever greater quality at a decent price. 'You can read his Wardle letters as artist versus industrialist, idealist versus pragmatist. They are also arguments between entrepreneurs', writes MacCarthy. One longs to know more about this side of things: about Morris's profit margins, his cash flow, his use of modern, rather than his preferred ancient, sources of chemicals. Morris is not interesting because he was a socialist or an artist (these are two a penny), but because he was as fully a businessman.

We should not expect logic when people so evidently prefer dreams to the mundane. And yet it is odd how people prefer talk of dreams to talk of cash and materials. Cash measures the flow of life, and accounts are the means by which it is done precisely (as an ecologist seeks to understand a wren's diet to the gram). Numbers are how this can happen.

We should not be at all surprised that people who understand money or numbers or computers often love music. Nor is it right to say that they seek refuge from bleakness of numbers, say, in music. Rather, music is just another form of the pattern-making, the code-making and breaking that thrills the numerate and the risk-taker. Fort Worth famously hosts the Van Cliburn International Piano Competition, and one of the most exhilarating aspects to it is the way that millionaires and billionaires open their sumptuous homes to the often impoverished young musicians who participate. But there is now a fascinating development: since 2000, the Van Cliburn Foundation has held a biennial competition for outstanding amateurs. In June 2004, 74 non-professional pianists competed for this prize. The prize of $2,000 isn't aimed at changing anybody's life. 'It gave me the push to keep music in my life', says the 2002 co-winner, Michael Hawley, director of special projects at the Massachusetts Institute of Technology. Stephen Fierros, information systems adviser for ExxonMobil was emboldened to lose a huge amount of weight, so as to stand a better chance in this year's competition than in his 2002 outing. Viktors Berstis, master inventor, Grid Computing Initiative, for IBM, didn't win but said: 'Programming is just like composing music, but no-one looks at it except the computers. There is real beauty in finding patterns.' John McInerney, a financial communications consultant, said: 'Playing the piano has made me better at my job…you need to be able to tap into people's passion.' Of course, music is a distraction from everyday life, and it can be an escape from it. That can lead to error, though: music's greater value is that it is just another way into the spirit of life, as other forms of maths or risk-taking are.[22]

Architecture – especially the classical architecture of, say, Christopher Wren – enjoys mathematical rules about proportion. Music is, in large part, a matter of patterns that can be expressed in numbers. Architecture, music and maths are closely entwined. The career of Daniel Libeskind, the architect of the winning entry in the competition to re-use the site of the Twin Towers in New York, makes the point, and another besides. He might have been a professional musician (he played with the violinist Itzhak Perlman in Israel) and adores mathematics. 'The language he chooses', writes Tom Dyckhoff, in *The Times*, 'is radically abstract – his musical heroes are Schoenberg and Messiaen – modernist steel, glass and concrete. The core motives they refer to are western and liberal: truth, beauty, reason, order. The aim:…to attack, he says, "globalised marketing and the withered modernism progressively eradicating spiritual life".' Libeskind loves symbolism, as architects always have. Thus, his tower will be 1,776 feet tall, to commemorate the date of the founding of modern America.[23] Here is a man who has been paid £1.4 million for a design, and is claiming another half million for developing it with another architect (the one employed by the site's owner); whose building, like its predecessor, will be largely commercial and which memorialises the deaths of some high-flying capitalists; and who is himself a refugee in a country whose identity is predicated on immigrant economic vigour; and he thinks his new building is a statement against globalization, in effect against the world that took him in and sustains him. Humbug is never far away.

Of course, when dealing with artists of any kind, the important thing is to look at their work, not listen to their opinions. The building that goes up at Ground Zero may be beautiful and come to be loved, and it may be replete in symbolism, but the getting and spending of money will be written in its form as surely as all the witty signals and signs its architect has woven into it. It uses the Statue of Liberty as a shapely motif: it might as well have chosen, and as proudly, the dollar sign.

Why do we feel sure that dealing with numbers as an accountant does is qualitatively less interesting than dealing with them in architecture or music? Well, you say, the accountant is using numbers in a dull way, ploddingly. That is hardly true of the accountant who is conducting guerrilla war with the taxman, or of the accountant who is wrestling with the right options for a young business, as it seeks a way through competing risky options. In his recent film, *Les Confidences Trop Intimes*, Patrice Laconte shows us an accountant who, by mistake, finds he has become a psychiatrist to a mixed-up, sexy woman. He realises his mundane profession equips him rather well for his adopted, exotic trade. Explaining to his 'patient' why this might be so, he notes that an accountant is paid to listen, and to watch the rhythms of birth, struggle and death. For her part, the woman comes to see that he is at least as interesting as she. He has edge, too. The turf accountant or the actuary are dealing with risk, and should be seen as sharing excitement along with the banker. Yet the betting shop is sleazy; the insurance company epitomises tedium; and the bank is the gold standard of respectability. Their similarities are overlooked, while none is taken to have the creative buzz of an artist's studio (however mundane, mercenary or imitative that may be). Part of the wit of the movie *The Secretary* (2002) was that its theme of a sadomasochist lawyer and his masochist secretary touched on the adage of not judging books by their covers. The lawyer (played by James Spader) and his partner in sex (played by Maggie Gyllenhaal) are quiet souls, who are delighted to have found each other. They are dull people in dull professions, if that's how you want to see them. But then, the movie seems to be saying, only fools think the dull are truly dull. And then, of course, there is the delicious implication that political correctness is nearly as bad as dreary old sexism. The PC can only see exploitation where sexism used to see smuttiness. What room is there – in either view – for either proper romance or proper sexuality? Excitement is everywhere, that's the point.

Dealing with money is mostly about assessing risk. Should one be adventurous or safe with this or that parcel of money belonging to this or that person? Similarly, engineering is about risk: it is wrestling with competing forces and exigencies that arise in the physical world. A bridge ought to optimise strength and lightness, it must withstand storms and baking sun. It could, notionally, be designed to be extraordinarily massive and safe (though being massive may not guarantee safety). But that would be boring: the architect and the engineer are thrilled by making the bridge's strength seem improbably delicate, given how soaring and airy they have made its structure seem.

INTELLECTUAL PROPERTY AND CREATIVITY

It was, of course, capitalism that enriched the creative people in its midst. In its primitive form, artistic endeavour was the creature of the economically successful. Creative people were at the whim of patrons until the market developed sufficiently for artists to produce, exhibit and sell works on their own account.

When artists became capitalists, they became free. They picked their own subjects and styles. They took a risk in doing so, but were more creative. Sometimes, their freedom led to an excess of the personal and the hysterical: the Romantics sometimes make one yearn for the patronage of the Classical years, and the disciplines imposed by people more refined than the *farouche* artists they funded. Still, more capitalism equates to artistic freedom.

Capitalism and technology were ever thus. Luther's work – his dissidence – spread fast, as did the Enlightenment's later, because the printing press (privately owned) turned out the disturbing messages quicker than the state could censor them. And the essence of the technology was that it made the messages so cheap that they could be too numerous to scoop up and scrap. Phone and fax are doing the same thing today (and with less state snooping than the Internet seems to be producing).[24]

If musicians are self-promoters when it comes to their fey trade, then it is as much a surprise to find that freethinkers are, too. Erasmus, one of the first public intellectuals, was brilliant at getting his picture out (painted and engraved), just as his modern equivalent gets himself or herself on to the cover of the Sunday supplements. It was the businesslike thing to do.

Why should the process slow down, or worry us? Contrary to the anti-capitalist drift of many music industry observers, have not capitalism and technology combined to make it more, rather than less, likely that a work will get published, released and talked about?[25] It is a commonplace to say that the major music corporations are stifling the less commercial. But the truth is that almost anyone can now get his or her work on to CD and the web.

In pre-capitalist days, people were limited to the market for single works of art. Publication in one form or another made reproduction rights the important milch cow they are now. Being able to print – and protect – one's music made composers rich. In our time, it has been recordings and merchandise that have made it so worthwhile to be, say, a rock musician. Rock concerts and world tours might or might not make money, but they are crucial to the promotion of the latest album, and that is where the money lies. The difference intellectual property makes is that it is usually the composers within a band who need persuading to tour, and the non-royalty owners who long for the road. Royalty cheques incline composers to the studio, and tour sponsorship inclines mere musicians to the stadium.

The rock musicians who now complain that pharmaceutical companies hold on to their intellectual property rights – their patents – in ways that harm the Third World, would probably be perfectly willing to sign up for their industry's condemnation of rip-off CDs. And yet,

Big Pharma arguably does far more creative work with its intellectual property rights, than most rock musicians do with theirs.

A minority of musicians not only dislike the capitalist world, but they believe they eschew it. Some of them set up the sort of micro-firms that capitalism makes it so easy to do. So they have spurned being sub-contractors or suppliers to large firms, and have become entrepreneurs instead – and think of it as rebellion.

Many more musicians affect to dislike the capitalist world they are wedded to and profit from mightily. John Lennon penned 'Imagine' and its wailings about possessions and other worldly ties: but he did so from some of the most expensive property on earth. He had always appeared happy to have enormous sums of money accruing to him, courtesy of the capitalist idea of intellectual property rights.

Classical musicians do not seem to like to talk in these terms, but their careers are about risk and cash and entrepreneurship. Early on, a talented cellist must decide whether to accept orchestral work, or hold out for concert gigs. And then he must decide whether to hold out for difficult repertoire. And then there is deciding on the huge investment in the kind of instrument – worth hundreds of thousands – which will help him make his name. He will probably decide to put aside considerable budget for a press agent, so as to build his 'brand' and prepare a market for himself. He must network: a coterie of similar talents may make a trio or a quartet, and of course the press agent promotes this as a series of decisions made on a creative basis alone. The media and his record label conspire in the assertion of the creative uniqueness of the musician and his choice of collaborators, and there is much in this. But there is also the mutually reinforcing brand value of the collaboration to be con-sidered. The young people will be hitching onto each other's rising stars. There might have been more creative collaborations to be had, but the commercially savvy one is more likely to mature. It is not cynical to point out these things: bums on seats, column inches in papers, prime-time profiles, CDs on motorised trays – these are the ways the world, and the musicians themselves, measure their success. And success is almost as beautiful as a sonata.[26]

1 R H Tawney, *Religion and the Rise of Capitalism*, Pelican, 1937 edition.

2 David Denby, *American Sucker*, Viking, 2004.

3 Terence Blacker, *Sunday Times*, 8 August 2004.

4 www.the-infoshop.com/study/mt16808_work_patterns.html: Mintel, 2003.

5 http://europa.eu.int/comm/public_opinion/archives/eb/eb60/eb60_rapport_standard_en.pdf, page 152.

6 'Never a Dull Moment', *The Economist*, 28 August 2004.

7 As reported in *The Week*, 5 June 2004.

8 Alison Gibson, 'Gap Years for the Grown-ups', *The Times*, 10 July 2004.

9 Faith Glasgow, 'Back to Life, Back to Reality', *Financial Times*, 27/28 December 2003.

10 'Getting Personal: Tracey Emin', *The Times*, 15 July 2004.

11 *The Times*, Saturday Magazine, 3 July 2004.

12 David Mattin, 'Hollywood on a Whim and a Prayer', *The Times*, 30 June 2004.

13 Bruce Caldwell, *F A Hayek: An intellectual biography*, Chicago, 2004.

14 Paul Seabright, *The Company of Strangers: A natural history of economic life*, Princeton University Press, 2004.

15 Raj Persaud, 'The Animal Urge', *FT Magazine*, 28 August 2004.

16 Article reprinted in *The Week*, 11 September 2004.

17 See www.bobmarley.com.

18 Derek Walker, ed, *Great Engineers: The art of British engineers*, 1837–1987, Academy Editions, 1987.

19 James Hamilton, *Turner and the Scientists*, Tate, 1998.

20 Fiona MacCarthy, *William Morris: A life for our time*, Faber and Faber, 1994.

21 See www.harristweed.org/latestnews.asp?id=55.

22 Sue Fox, 'Fortissimo!', *The Times* Magazine, 28 August 2004.

23 Tom Dyckhoff, 'A Man of Ideas: Libeskind faces a crossroads', *The Times*, T2, 7 September 2004.

24 James Gomez discusses Internet censorship at www.jamesgomeznews.com/.

25 I am thinking of Norman Lebrecht's writing in particular, especially his *When the Music Stops: Managers, maestros and the corporate murder of classical music*, Pocket Books, 1997. For a sceptical view of his work, see www.guardian.co.uk/proms2001/story/0,10641,523134,00.html.

26 For some more on this theme, see RDN on Stephen Isserlis at www.richarddnorth.com.

CHAPTER 7

MASS AFFLUENCE AND CORRUPTION

Richard Tomkins noted recently in the *FT* that modern business has been adding to the kind of reputation for scandal that kept him out of the family firm and propelled him toward journalism. He thinks industry's own misdeeds have caused a decline in confidence. 'And if it is now to become synonymous with greed, corruption and sleaze, who will be tempted to enter its ranks apart from the greedy, corrupt and sleazy?'[1] In the ritual struggle between respectability and vigour, business has recently been thought to have swung rather toward vigour. Indeed, the charge is that it has swung toward criminality. This is paradoxical, since business is now required, on all sides, to demonstrate a rather mechanical caring for its employees, customers and the environment. Leave aside the fact that most journalists, even on the *FT*, are inclined to hold their noses when around real business, it will be news to most firms that they are in a cowboy age. Still, fatcat pay, insider dealing and accountancy fiddles have all served to damage the reputation of firms. The point here is that these developments have reinforced the public's perception that big business is corrupting. Its big guns are manipulative, shifty, crafty, and deceptive. They are not above corruptly buying or filching what cannot be got legally. In this view, there is something wrong with the times. Here is Easterbrook on the issue: '...there exists a serious problem of lack of character among American business executives; no class of individuals engaged in legal pursuits has ever revealed itself to have such low standards and lack of character as American top executives at the turn of the twenty-first century.'[2]

ENRON'S CORRUPTION

Old-fashioned frauds, even on a large scale, are, in principle, a commonplace. Enron, though, seemed to be cut from a broader, newer cloth. It was figured as an altogether more gorgeous, more modern piece of skulduggery. The firm and its fraud were vast. Partly it was a case of a delicious nemesis. The firm was famous, even by the standards of a hyped world. It was self-proclaimed as virtuous, even by the standards of corporations that are now committed to public saintliness. It blinded people: it was able to corrupt all and sundry. And yet Enron was a thoroughly recognisable scam in one very important way. It was about selling to the public an empire of nonsense. And probably, like other scams in history, it flowed from its being an innovation, or dealing with an innovation.

Oddly, such scams have often turned out to exemplify what later becomes a new and respectable way of doing business. 'We were doing some very exciting things', Ken Lay, Enron's erstwhile CEO, told the *FT* Magazine.[3]

We were changing markets. We were changing the way people bought and sold a lot of other things. And we were changing the risk management of many different areas, all the way from weather derivatives to ways to hedge oil price or gas prices or coal prices. We were providing cleaner fuel around the world. We were on the cutting edge of really pushing natural gas – the use of natural gas – instead of coal and oil. And we were pushing renewable energy.

Indeed, it has been noted that Enron was lobbying Washington and the Bush White House hard for the Kyoto Treaty: so much for its being in bed with the Administration.

That they were 'cutting edge' was surely true of earlier Bubbles and earlier scam-merchants. It was true of John Law in the eighteenth century, whose understanding of how money worked was also an understanding about how credit and stocks and shares could transform economic life. A biography of him is rightly entitled *Millionaire: The philanderer, gambler, and duelist who invented modern finance.*[4] He was, in effect, France's central banker, as well as the CEO of its biggest Enron. All his life, he was a man who was modernising capitalism, and in this work probably did lasting good: he was working out how public finances and private banking should work, not least when the ideal is an economy that supports investment. For all I know, even his invention of the Mississippi Company – the scam that brought him down – might have worked on the ground, as well as in the public imagination. His trick, as in the best scams, was to have the protection and support of a greedy elite, and to let the punter go mad with greedy desire.

Surely, the Internet Bubble was about a real technology that really was transforming the world, and will make many stockholders very rich. The problem was how to pick the winners when no-one quite knew how anyone – still less, who – would make money in the sector.

Similarly, Jabez Balfour, in nineteenth-century England, was plainly a crook, and not the least important bit of his criminality was his self-promotion as a temperance Evangelical: his bent schemes had the odour of sanctity. His operations in promoting popular investment schemes were almost parochial, but he did represent what would become the norm, and he was something of a pioneer in the form: the idea of assurance companies, in which small investors could gain a toehold on capitalism. His case is also interesting because it is one of the few in which financial journalists (from the *Financial Times* and *The Economist)* were the first to spot the implausibility of a bent offer. Jabez' scams were inventive, and presaged a way of doing business which, in its legal form, would become commonplace. (And still needs watching for folly and worse.)

Enron was the sort of large-scale scam which Edith Wharton (in *The Age of Innocence*, published in 1920 and filmed by Scorsese in 1993) and Anthony Trollope (in *The Way We Live Now*, published in 1875 and televised brilliantly by the BBC in 2001, starring David Suchet) chronicled as the creation of late-Victorian capitalism. Oscar Wilde (in rather sombre mode in *An Ideal Husband*, first played in 1895 and filmed beautifully in 1999, with Rupert Everett) went further and showed how a fantastic scam could suck in politicians and test their probity to the limit. Enron's case – like those the fiction writers latched on to – seemed to contemporary observers to exemplify their time.

Bubbles are about a barely understood new opportunity, which seems so huge a prospect that it would be madness not to have a slice of the action. They are best dreamed up in far-off, magical lands where anything is possible, and where vast profit is at least possible or plausible. They are best if they involve financial mechanisms that are so fresh that they represent the high modern, and that no-one could be quite expected to understand. Enron's scams contained both these elements, as, of course, did the South Sea Bubble and the Mississippi Company, and – replacing the far-off with the virtual – the Internet Bubble.

Presumably, the trading of energy futures – like the trading of greenhouse gas permits (which Enron was also interested in) – will become staples of modern life. Perhaps Enron will prove to have been a pioneer in some aspect of what will become an entirely respectable business in other hands. It was unfamiliarity that made the fantasy possible and alluring.

Anyway, it was a wonderful thing to find that here was a firm that largely made itself up. Like many a good scam, it reeled people in, despite its inherent improbability. It made them suspend judgement, and throw away caution. But the criticism which most sticks is that it corrupted people.

It was natural to blame the Enron bosses: here was wrongdoing of the kind that could only have happened at the instigation, and with the connivance, of the directing intelligences of the firm. But of course, the bosses were merely the most dishonest and badly behaved offenders. The most interesting thing about Enron was that hardly anyone anywhere near the firm behaved well. Some failed in alertness, others in courage. There were hordes of people within the firm who must have known that it was lying. The liberals are tempted to think that the firm corrupted its people. It is as worth saying that the venality of many professionals allowed Enron to erect a deeply corrupted structure and persona. This would be a harsher criticism: it suggests that the inherent cupidity and mild venality of us all can produce criminality.

Regulators either did know, or ought to have known, that something was wrong. Financial journalists ought to have smelled a rat. These people were merely suckered, and ought to feel a bit ashamed that they didn't spot and expose the malfeasance.

The charge of corruption, though, attaches to people whose personal gain made them fail in their public duty. That's true, of course, of the bosses, who had a public duty and neglected it. But it is more interestingly true of the professionals whose job was to be objective. Stock analysts from myriad financial organisations ought to have wondered what was going on: like the journalists and the regulators, they were dazzled. They also often stood to gain by the success of the firm's shares: they were being paid to be honest, and were being rewarded for dishonesty. But the most obviously egregious corruption was in the case of the firm's auditors, who conspicuously failed in their professional duty.

That is to say, they were people who were expected to keep trustworthiness and watchfulness at the forefront of their minds, and to put them at the service of a disinterested independence. The stock analysts had a public duty to be honest, because their work would be published as disinterested. But the accountants were quasi-judicial in the degree to which the public and the state had a right to invest trust in them.

This helps us discern an important continuum. All corruption is the abuse of public trust. The more that trust is enshrined in a person's job description, the more its betrayal matters. Thus, pound for pound, a venal judge is more corrupt than a public regulator, who is more so than an accountant, who is more so than a stock analyst, who is more so than an in-house accountant, who is more so than a finance director. The further we get toward the purely commercial, the less we expect the lofty. But it also matters hugely for the purely commercial to have high standards.

Of course, anyone who is criminally greedy has been corrupted by greed, since everyone ought to balance their private interest against the public interest, and strain to value the latter. But the case is far more interesting when the wrongdoing consists in using a public position to private advantage. And that is, in effect, what Enron's auditors did.

We should not be surprised or worried by Enron. Capitalists are energetic and greedy. We expect that of them. It is hardly credible that such men and women will be less likely to stray or to have a proportion of the unscrupulous among them. Capitalism surprises us by not being a machine of wickedness, and by having powerful vested interests in winkling wickedness out. We will come to that, but for now let's pile on the agony.

SHELL'S CORRUPTION

So we turn to another fascinating energy company. Shell, a firm which, like BP, has gone hand in hand with Empire in its time, seems very different to Enron. This Anglo-Dutch firm was built on geology and engineering. But even this 'heritage' firm from the age of 'Gentleman Capitalism' has virtual elements. Contrary to people's misconceptions of oil companies, about the one thing they don't have much of is oil (or gas, the useful concomitant of oil). They find other people's oil, and undertake to bring it to market. Still, one of the things they need is plenty of available oil in 'their' reserves.

Oil companies are very real. They wrestle with the earth's crust, as well as with the markets and the nation states that mostly own the oil in which they deal.

Shell was found to have overstated its oil reserves, and, at the time of writing (September 2004), the evidence points to a couple of years of cover-up. What's more, the deception is alleged to have originated with a respected professional senior figure: the geologist who was in charge of keeping track of the firm's reserves. And then, when he went on to run the firm, he is supposed to have persisted in the deception, and insisted that others do so. We won't know for some time how wide the conspiracy went: who, within the firm, did or ought to have known, and who ought to have made the firm come clean sooner.

The Shell shock is all the greater because here is a firm whose respectability was its greatest asset. Not a star performer in terms of profits and aggressiveness, it was relied on as the defining Blue Chip. Austere, honest, dull. Ah well, sighed its admirers and critics alike, that's the Dutch (co-owners of the firm) for you. Straightforward and smug, they may be, and not the greatest communicators on earth. But they're not flighty, and you can't have everything in life.

BBC TV's *Money Programme*[5] updated us on the story. Its main insight was that in the late 1990s Sir Phil Watts – the geologist who first inflated the firm's reserves and was now chairman – took Shell into a new phase of US-style aggressiveness. You know the kind of thing that's lurking behind this sort of charge. The firm started to look to the bottom line and the share price hourly and aggressively. Social and environmental concerns began to count for less. The short term came to matter more than the long term. But above all, the firm became unscrupulous and dishonest.

It is a peculiar charge to bring in this case, since Shell's US competitors and partners (presumably well used to US business habits) did not overstate their reserves. Indeed, it was very likely that it was the divergence between the statements of US oil companies and Shell's that put US regulators onto the trail of Shell. Sooner or later Shell would have been exposed, even if it had not realised that the game was up and confessed.

In a nice twist, Shell had, for some years, been earning praise from anti-capitalist campaigners for its newly adopted openness and Corporate Social Responsibility (CSR). After a terrible PR war in the mid 90s, when the firm was under fire from green and human rights campaigners over its proposed disposal of the giant Brent Spar storage facility and, quite separately, its behaviour in Nigeria, Shell had become a pioneer of the 'apologise, cringe and reform' public statement. It seems that, behind the smoke and mirrors of this new 'stakeholder' moralism, the firm had actually been losing its long-held traditions of professionalism and probity. It is possible that managers were taught by campaigners (who already knew these truths as part of their own trade) that spin and flimflam can cover nearly any reality. Certainly, both CSR and lying about reserves seem to have become habitual at the very top of this important company.[6]

Enron and Shell lied to their shareholders. That is probably the most important crime they committed, and it is also the wrongdoing which shows that the firms' failings can best be put right by the market, with as little interference from the law as possible.

Enron was, in part, a non-firm, and so it naturally went bankrupt. Shell is anything but a non-firm, and, at the time of writing, the market has decided it is just as valuable an asset as it was before the news of its deception broke. The feature that most unites the villains in these stories is that they had forgotten how unlikely it was that the truth could, for long, be hidden.

In a desire to stamp out lying, various people's thoughts turned to increasing both the supervision of potential liars and the punishment meted out to those we catch. The critics of capitalism naturally rejoice when their conception – their misconception – of it seems to be reinforced by the malfeasance of capitalists, and they reach for regulation of the beast, because they don't mind if, in taming it, they neuter it, too. We should prefer to remember that, in the end, the facts got out, and that there then followed a natural – market – corrective. Exposure should be the beginning and the end of reform.

In a recent TV gangster series, one of the arch-villains shows off to an associate a particularly wicked and illegal business carve-up. 'That's capitalism', he says.[7] But of course, that's exactly what capitalism isn't. People's greed will often tempt them to be dishonest. But much more importantly, we ought to see that capitalism has a huge interest in integrity. The law crucially reinforces this larger interest against the inevitable backsliding of individuals, just as it defends capitalism against its monopolistic tendencies. But capitalism has powerful in-built defences against dishonesty and monopolies. To exaggerate somewhat, capitalists want and need these defences even more than wider society does. That is why, in the end, capitalists would gang together to fight corruption and monopolies.

Myriad relations in capitalism empower those who have an interest in integrity, and pits them against those who try to cheat. Enron and Shell lied to the state, and that suggests regulation is needed, because it seems that capitalists are crooks. And, yes, firms may indeed be able to keep key employees and even outside analysts onside as they cheat. However, sooner or later, a disaffected or conscience-ridden employee will come clean. The larger point, though, is that absent these mechanisms, the facts would have emerged. These firms lied to shareholders, the whole analyst 'community', and journalists. Sooner or later, these would have twigged what was going on, and would have done so as a function of their own, often capitalist, self-interest. We will talk soon about the wider, more generalised pressures for honesty in capitalist societies. What I want to stress here is the tense, day-to-day pressure toward frankness: the fear of exposure.

The laws that control capitalists ought not to be posited as defending society from capitalism, but as defending capitalism from the proclivities of venal people. As people argue for stronger laws, we need to remind them that new constraints bring new inhibitions and more cautiousness, and that these bring costs. Vigour matters, and needs to be preserved against the nay-sayers who never liked capitalism anyway.

RUSSIA'S CORRUPTION[8]

Capitalism grows because there is a network of interdependency and reliability that brings people together in relationships of trust. Of course, their trustworthiness is reinforced by regulation and law. But what is amazing in capitalism is that the law intrudes rather seldom. One might argue that this is because the law is so feared for its capriciousness and severity that people steer well clear of it. But one might as truly say that, by and large, capitalism exists in societies, and in forms, in which no-one is required to be dishonest, and in which a reputation for dishonesty makes a man or firm a pariah. Capitalism also exists in a goldfish bowl. Almost every statement a capitalist makes will be tested in reality, eventually, and usually quite soon.

The requirement for honesty and legality as building blocks of capitalism is beautifully on display in modern Russia and the rest of the ex-Soviet empire. It is entirely plausible to argue that Russia is now less corrupt than it has been for a thousand years, as Anders Aslund told me in an interview in 2003 (but which did not get broadcast in my BBC series).[9]

The Tsars subcontracted the management of their vast country to corrupt overseers and local authorities, who farmed for themselves the revenues they were supposed to husband for the people. In the seventeenth century, 'justice was openly bought and sold…Taxation was little more than state brigandage.'[10] In the nineteenth century, Gogol's *Government Inspector* satirises this by showing how an entire town assumes that the stranger in its midst must be bribed and accommodated because he is – wrongly – thought to be a government inspector, but is instead a fraudster. Gogol's brilliant device does not charge the government's inspectors, because none are in sight. But the hilarious damage is done, and the villains are seen to be the 'exploited' and the 'victims': the townspeople who fall over themselves in matching the venality of the false inspector.

The Soviet system operated entirely on *blat*, the system of interlocking favours, which people with any power used in lieu of a market economy. There is an argument that this form of corruption had its benign side: given that money didn't work properly, people who wanted to make anything happen – good or bad people, good or bad things – had to use some other recognised currency. Favours were that currency. Corruption was the nearest people could get to the market. In a bad state, it can hardly be a high crime to abuse the state's trust (such as it was). The currency of favours was less tainted than the state-ordained quotas that were supposed to apply.

When communism collapsed, a few thousand very clever people 'bought' the assets of the state, often using a 'loans for shares' system, which meant that the state, in effect, paid for much of the dismemberment of its holdings. In the immediate aftermath of the collapse of communism, Russia seemed to descend into a Mafia Capitalism, which the critics of capitalism almost delighted in, as a sign that socialism might not be all that bad. They believed that we were now seeing capitalism in its true, red in tooth and claw, nastiness.

Half a decade on from the high-Mafia period, and Russia remains a place where speaking freely can attract a very high price. But there is less organised criminality than there used to be. And besides, there is a view, held by knowledgeable people, that 'alternative contract enforcement' (sending heavies in) was indeed necessary for nearly decent business, as well as for crooks. The improvement in the status of the law courts and judges is one of the reasons why there is less recourse to violence. Oddly, one might think, it led for a while to a habit of corrupting judges: the view of some analysts, including Anders, was that this was a sign that the law was becoming valued – a further sign of progress.

The overall result is the system of 'Oligarchs' and their empires, in which elements of the state and of the financial system form a maze of teams, stated and unstated, which own, run or shelter different bits of 'private' enterprise. The Oligarchs – those thirty-somethings – who sit at the centre of these webs, and are notionally worth billions, now find themselves eyed very leerily by the people of their country and by the politicians who run it. And the conundrum facing the politicians is quite peculiar. The deals by which the Oligarchs became absurdly rich were corrupt at their heart, but to interfere with the upshot will undermine confidence among capitalists that the state is going to give up its habit of capriciously interfering in enterprise. Which way lies the most revenue for the state? Where is the real well-being of the people to be found?

The truth of the fast-moving modern history of Russia is that capitalism is working its magic. From a corrupt state system, the economy is evolving toward a mostly legal orderliness. A stable legal framework, overseen by non-partisan and uncorrupt judges (rather than by government diktat), is not an impossible dream in Russia. Indeed it is very likely to arise. At every level, the disciplines of probity are beginning to work. Russian capitalists are desperate for western capital and skills. They know that these partnerships depend almost exclusively on Russia behaving with disciplines that reassure western investors, and the western firms that are their vehicles. Russian energy companies have had to make themselves tolerably respectable partners for potential mergers with western oil interests. But they are merely the tip of a less spectacular iceberg of firms that seek partners overseas. The driving force is western investment and western markets. Sooner rather than later, home-grown investment will be as big a force – perhaps even bigger. Capitalism depends on huge numbers of people trusting it with their savings, and having faith that it will handle these savings honestly and intelligently. It has, of course, quite often failed these investors, but more usually by cock-up than conspiracy or criminality.

This is all very different from the Mafia Capitalism that was certainly to be found in the 1990s, and which the critics of capitalism assumed would linger on, perhaps for ever. They like to believe that gangsterised monopolies are the default position of capitalism, and it was only the years of valiant struggle against these robber barons that have produced the half-tolerable capitalism of the West.

But the game isn't over yet; Enron and Shell prove that it's never over. Besides, capitalism's forms change quite dramatically over time. Countries vary greatly in the degree to which they are responsive democracies, and in the degree to which they believe the state should interfere. Russia has started toward respectability, and while it is very likely that its respectability will increase, its form is not written in stone.

However, capitalism's own demands will provide the greatest discipline for both the Oligarchs and the Kremlin. There is pressure to ensure that journalists can work safely; that the books of a business provide an honest account of its dealing; that the state honours the rule of law – all the underpinnings of a sound, business-friendly society. And all this will come about because the state and the business people figure that this is the only way to make the country rich and to win votes.

There is a critical mass of factors that take societies toward capitalism. Crucially, the interests of the many – of the mass, even – have to matter more than those of the elite. It is generalised well-being that capitalism creates, and this should not come as a surprise, for capitalism can only flourish in societies that take generalised well-being seriously.

Elites can be pretty happy with non-productive *rentier* and gangster societies. *Rentiers* skim the economy legally, and gangsters do it illegally. But neither produces wealth, and neither spreads it very widely. Similarly, elites can be quite fond of corruption: it is a rent on activity that flows criminally upward towards them.

It is only when the vast bulk of the people have to be factored into a nation's policy, when their well-being matters, that we see capitalism doing its benign work. It is then that gangsterism, monopolies and corruption (along with lies and misinformation) become inefficient, as well as immoral. It is then that manufacturing, services and trade matter more than mere possession. It is then that probity becomes an important commodity, valued for its economic worth, as much as for its moral worth. The majority gains when capitalism is at work. The majority of capitalistic players – and that's nearly everyone – have an interest in there being lashings of probity on all sides.

And, of course, it will always be tempting to buck the system. Naturally, too, capitalists and their supporters are inclined to say that its largely self-regulating virtues only need reinforcing by the minimum of regulation. I agree with this latter. But I am very keen, too, on the idea that professionalism and the professions are the best way of reinforcing the essentially individual virtue of honesty.[11]

THIRD WORLD CORRUPTION

In Lesotho in 2003, I pursued a case of corruption, in which an official milked a couple of million dollars out of a handful of international firms that were building an internationally funded dam and water project. It was the biggest construction project in Africa, and the second biggest in the world (after the Chinese Three Gorges project). It looked like a classic case of aid being siphoned off by the elite in a faraway country. Oddly, it seems that the official was working on his own, and the powers that be were happy to bring him to book and trial. He is now in the country's main gaol in the capital city.

There were some weird features to the case. The money involved was a small percentage of the total flow of funds. The 'bribee', the CEO of the Lesotho Highlands Development Authority, was working alone – which is unusual. Though he must have known 'where the bodies were buried' the corrupt official did not cop a plea, and make life easy for himself. Why didn't he shop the shadowy 'representatives' employed by the construction companies to smooth the way? It was peculiar that he had not 'covered his back' by ensuring political support. Perhaps he was unable to: Lesotho may be a place with an honest elite (though it has all the ordinary lesser corruptions of Africa and elsewhere). But the oddest thing of all was that it was hard to see why the bribing firms – and, more to the point, their local fixers – did not call the official's bluff, and shop him to his superiors, rather than pay the bribe. It may have been a case of old habits dying hard: several key players so expected corruption, that they went along with it without noticing that there was no need. Besides, the 'representatives' had a profound interest in maintaining what may have been a fiction: that the construction firms did not need to pay the bribes. Certainly, the firms would not complain in public that they had been bilked by their own agents.

A few years earlier, in 1996, I had explored allegations of Shell's 'corruption' – and worse – in Nigeria's Ogoniland, in the Niger delta. I did so at the time of the anniversary of the execution (after a show trial) of Ken Saro-Wiwa, and with a strong sense that Shell was a good deal more virtuous and valuable a player in Nigeria than its critics in the country and especially in the West supposed. It was plainly very difficult for the firm to have other than corrupt relations with the neighbouring 'community leaders', who were holding it to ransom. Various ruses were at work. One involved making the firm promise to employ local contractors to repair sabotage, and then to profit from the large amount of sabotage that duly followed.

Very recently, there was a report that seemed to have the ring of truth about it. Local campaigners in Nigeria have been complaining that the firm's contractors are making 'inappropriate' payments to local chiefs. These are, the contractor maintains, a good deal lower than the usual 'homage payments' made to local chiefs. And then there are payments made to build or improve local facilities, which may be communal or private according to interpretation.[12] What is certain is that the locals, the region and the country could all be richer if corruption was lessened, and in particular if Shell could do its business in Ogoniland without constant threats of violence. Arguably, it could do more good for the country and region if its community neighbours did not see it as a milch cow with 'Corporate Social Responsibility', and instead as just a law-abiding taxpayer working with decent local and national authorities.[13]

Western firms have reluctantly accepted that doing business in the Third World involves them in corruption. That they have been and are involved is obvious; that this was not to their liking is less so. The fact is that firms respond to legal and moral signals when these are in their interests, or when governments force them to. Naturally, the normal picture is that Third World governments are the source of the corruption on their patch. Rich world governments have only reluctantly, and only recently, become fairly serious in bolstering the determination of their firms to renounce and even denounce corrupt overseas practices. It is likely that it was a sort of critical mass of self-interest that tipped rich world governments from condoning corruption toward condemning it.

In the Third World, it is obvious that the situation is more serious, and causes more serious damage to the weak. What's more, there is more evidence that corruption damages economies. But we need to be careful. Bribes sometimes make good things happen rather more quickly than they would otherwise. Where there are masses of useless laws, for instance, it may be that bribes cut through them to good effect. Some campaigners against corruption argue that it is regulations that are often more the enemy than corruption, and that deregulation is more useful than campaigning for apparent virtue.

RICH WORLD CORRUPTION

We have evidence that corruption continues to thrive in some very rich countries and regions within them. We could point to New Jersey, in the US, or to several European countries, and wonder how it is that corruption is tolerated in some of the strongest democracies on earth. I have been at pains here to pursue a different line: capitalists in sophisticated economies do not need corruption and do not, in general, promote it. If they do, they'll be found out. Meanwhile, the middle classes – and micro-middle classes – want both capitalism and usually an absence of corruption, too. Indeed, it is the triumph of their interests which has done, and is doing, so much to make the world a better place, and not least by beating down arbitrary, self-interested rule by elites, where these grandees simply don't get the point of progress. In sophisticated societies, professions and professionalism are the best bulwark against corruption. In modern economies, capitalists set capital and professionals to work. Entrepreneurs work alongside accountants, engineers, lawyers and technicians of every kind. We have understood well enough that we have to educate these people in the skills of their trade. But we have laid less emphasis on the value they have as people who will not sell everything. A professional has skills, but he or she also has an ethical standard and a brotherhood, which reinforce each other. We need to remember that.

1 Richard Tomkins, 'How Sleaze and Scandal Make for an Ugly Business', *Financial Times*, 2 July 2004.

2 Gregg Easterbrook, *The Progress Paradox*, Random House, 2003.

3 'Lunch With the *FT*,' *FT* Magazine, 7 August 2004.

4 Janet Gleeson, *Millionaire: The philanderer, gambler, and duelist who invented modern finance*, Simon and Schuster, 1999.

5 BBC2, 16 July 2004.

6 CSR has been criticised most tellingly by David Henderson, *Misguided Virtue: False notions of corporate social responsibility*, The Institute of Economic Affairs, 2001 and *The Role of Business in the Modern World*, IEA, 2004.

7 *The Long Firm*, BBC TV, 2004, based on the novel by Jake Arnott.

8 The best historical (but up-to-date) survey of Russia and its historical corruption I know is Rodric Braithwaite, *Across the Moscow River: The world turned upside down*, Yale, 2002. Two good sources for modern developments: David E Hoffman, *The Oligarchs: Wealth and power in the new Russia*, Public Affairs/Perseus, 2002 and Chrystia Freeland, *Sale of the Century: The inside story of the second Russian revolution*, Little, Brown, 2000.

9 Anders Aslund, *Building Capitalism: The transformation of the former Soviet Bloc*, Cambridge University Press, 2002 is a good source on the interrelations between capitalism and corruption.

10 H A L Fisher, *A History of Europe*, various editions since 1935.

11 For RDN work on professions, see www.richarddnorth.com.

12 Michael Peel, 'Shell Unable to Shake Off Troubled Ogoni Legacy as Dispute Over Pipeline Deepens', *Financial Times*, 14 September 2004.

13 For more on this case, my work is at www.richarddnorth.com; Karl Maier's *This House Has Fallen*, Allen Lane, 2000 is pretty good; for a more conventionally liberal account, but not a bad one, try Daniel Litvin's *Empires of Profit*, Texere, 2003.

CHAPTER 8

MASS AFFLUENCE AND SPIRITUALITY

It is often assumed, wrongly of course, that nice people become kindly liberals and nasty people become neo-liberals. We could largely at least agree that the choice is about how kindliness and efficiency work, and may compete. That discussion is about, as it were, 'heart'. This book argues that a certain 'dryness' of approach, a rightward drift, is more morally sustainable than the 'wet' or leftward drift. That is to say: the more you care about other people, the drier you might become – and the less conventionally liberal. Now I want to consider whether people of 'soul' could agree with the drift of this book. I don't mean 'soul' to be synonymous with 'funkiness', but rather with the spiritual.

Suppose someone had that yearning to be thoughtful, to have a still inner centre, to know the true value of things and people. Should they not disdain the world of getting and spending? Should the world of the Mass Affluent dismay them? I say the answer to these questions is 'no'. Rather, we should see that the world of spirituality is not – or ought not to be – a retreat from the world, but rather a progress towards its heart. It'll be peculiar, but it is not life denying, and it does not deny the vigour of the real world.

Rushing about and getting stuff – the supposed scourge of our spirits – is not, in itself, the enemy of spirituality. Indeed, the most irritating thing about supposedly spiritual people is that they 'escape' mundane realities and appetites, and feel themselves to be above them. The best of spiritual people grow out of that sense of superiority, though most remain dreamily leftish in their thinking.[1] We too easily confuse the spiritual quest to see life and ourselves stripped to the essentials, with disdaining the unnecessary. Stripped to our essentials, we as much need ambition (say) as we need solitude.

This matters, because at the heart of centuries of disdain of commercialism there is a muddle about values. Appetites (greediness) have been juxtaposed against aspiration (spirituality). Actually, they can live together much better than the critics of getting and spending – including many capitalists – suppose.

The essence of the spiritual life is that we examine our lives, and life. Thoreau writes of his famous spell of simple living: 'I went to the woods because I wished to live deliberately, to front only the essential facts of life, and see if I could not learn what it had to teach and not, when I came to die, discover that I had not lived.' This sort of feeling took Thomas Merton (the twentieth century's most famous Christian monk) into a monastery. That same feeling takes another man to Las Vegas. In defining the spirituality at work in Thoreau's sojourn in the woods, I focus on its 'deliberate' nature, and when he talks of the essentials, I stress that this may not always mean the minimal by any means. To make sure that one has 'lived', and done so deliberately and with regard to the essentials, one may reach for vigour and extravagance, as well as solitude and quiet.

ASPIRATION, IMAGINATION AND AFFLUENCE

We can begin with the observation that imagination and aspiration are joined with greed in the birth of trade, empire and capitalism. We are familiar with the idea that trade was enabled by, and encouraged, science, not least by turning the heavens from a mystery into a navigation aid. Equipment had to be designed, by which the starry signposts could better be seen, and time better measured. Optics and mechanics prospered. Trade and mathematics did each other favours through the mundane route of accountancy.

It is less obvious that it was fabulous rumour and fantasised Eldorados that made practical, even piratical, people venture far beyond the horizons of their known worlds. It was cost reduction that drove them to discover new worlds, by mistake, as they sought quicker, less taxed routes to old ones. But the Elizabethans were lit up by the drama of their adventure. They were visionaries and romantics, as well as privateers. The goods of the East (and, later, the West), which so quickly came to be greatly desired, could not be imagined until they were obtained. The birth of prosaic capitalism depended on the satisfaction of aspirational wants, not exiguous needs. In the Renaissance 'while Europe predominantly exported bulk goods such as timber, wool, and semi-precious metals, it tended to import luxury and high value goods, whose impact upon the culture and consumption of communities from Venice to London was gradual but profound', says Jerry Brotton in his *From the Silk Road to Michelangelo*.[2] And these wants were not trivial. The European art of the period was, in part, able to produce beauty as it depicted – celebrated – the luxuries brought from the East because of the painting materials brought from there. Brotton notes that the

Bellinis painted eastern silks, using eastern plant extracts. As we watch *Girl With a Pearl Earring* (2003), based on the novel by Tracy Chevalier, we are watching a north European sensibility deploying eastern lapis lazuli.

And then the wealth of the period was folded back into the aspirational: Dora Thornton shows how the Florentine merchant might want to live like a prince, but he wanted to get to heaven and be an intellectual, too. 'By the mid-sixteenth century studies contained a wide variety of objects, many of which had been accumulated with the aim of proving gentility, as well as literacy beyond that required in [a merchant's] work.' A merchant's study was, as well as an office, a room in which he could be private and prove he had an inner life. Naturally, being human, he bragged about it, and could not forebear to show it to his friends. It became a public display – a gallery in which he showed his understanding of the need for private reflection. It required considerable affluence to build a home large enough to provide a private space, as well as to satisfy one's family's demand for public space. (Rather as a middle-aged man's pilgrimage requires sufficient funds to keep the home fires burning, too.) It was a conspicuous and conscious homage to the monastic cell, and especially to the monastic cell of a scholar-saint such as St Jerome, whose image hanging in the study was designed to flatter the clever patron's taste and the room itself.[3]

Wealth creators are like that always. They acquire, and then extravagantly display, whatever it is that shows them to be more than merely productive. Oddly, their imitation of the philosophical or the reflective demonstrates that they do not properly understand their value to the world. They fall into the mistake of their natural enemies – the enemies of progress, often – in despising the world and the means of enrichment it yielded them.

There is, of course, a paradox here. It is irresistible to note that nearly everyone, including the wealth creator, is inclined to see the world of inner being, of the heart and soul, as being at odds with the commercial. Wealth creators seem shy of their success. It is often said that the Englishman has always preferred to be seen as a gentleman than as a creative, industrious or commercial person. The most successful businessmen (and quite a few creative people too) have queued up to be rather indifferent farmers, not at all minding that they might be taken for mud-spattered yeoman farmers (though they may have hoped to be mistaken for squires or even milords). Actually, the desire to be dissociated from trade was a habit right across Europe, and right across the centuries. Social climbing has always consisted in ceasing to be thought merely rich, and to be considered thoughtful or grand as well. Voltaire considered one of the many merits of the English to be their relative absence of snobbery about affluence. But snobbery there certainly was.

Even in America, where to be in business is not stigmatised, the rich soon launder themselves into patrons, connoisseurs or philanthropists. True, some heirs do carry into the second generation the acumen of their forebears, and some manage to combine it with being patrons. Marjorie Merriweather Post (the heir to the health food company that invented Grape Nuts) early saw the value of the Bird's Eye frozen food business, and bought it for her burgeoning General Foods Corporation. She was also energetic as a collector and philanthropist. Her grand residence, Hillwood, in the Washington DC suburbs, remains not so much a piece of swank (it is that) as a public resource of unique artistic value.[4]

The remarkable Teresa Heinz Kerry, a Portuguese woman of parts, is perhaps a more typical sort. She is the heir (by marriage) to the Heinz ketchup millions, and energetically espouses healthy eating while underpinning (and, it is sometimes said, undermining) her second husband's political career: John Kerry was the Democratic candidate for the US presidential elections in November 2004. She presides over about $30 million worth of homes (four in number) and actively manages over $1 billion worth of philanthropic capital. It would be impertinent to speculate whether she disdains the processes by which she has become rich. There are two obvious possibilities. On the one hand, she may see philanthropy as the only way to put right the damage done by the canned and bottled food empire that has enriched her. On the other, her philanthropy may be a fitting tribute to the world that produced the wealth. In a way, of course, it doesn't matter what she thinks. She is just the agent for a social process, which voters could have changed at any point. So the point is, do you and I believe her philanthropy is about making amends in a rather wicked world, or about the natural and rightful unfolding of a relatively benign one? I prefer the latter take.[5]

We seem to have missed something when we counterpoise the worlds of entrepreneurship and management, with those of life-enhancing collecting, creativity or sponsorship or philanthropy.

As trade increased, isn't it remarkable how much of it consisted in trafficking products that were luxuries at first, though they became – with improved plantation systems and slave labour – products for mass consumption? This was the story of tea, tobacco, sugar and coffee. It is mirrored in beef and bread. In time they became staples. And then, of course, some of them became objects of disdain and even horror. Of course, luxuries are extravagances, but that does not at all mean that they are vulgar. Affluent people have sought to express their refinement – their sensibility – in their use of exotic foodstuffs. Only long indulgence, and over-indulgence, turned the civilised and civilising luxuries of some of them into junk food. And we're not done yet, as people increasingly turn away from eating lovely food in a hurry and casually, and demand that the ingredients (the same ingredients, largely) be presented to them with more ritual: the hamburger in a bleak fluorescent waste-land can be reassembled as a spaghetti Bolognese and garlic bread in a candle-lit trattoria.

We are awash in paradoxes. The wealth generated by slavery's brutalities funded the snobbery of the people who oppressed Fanny in Jane Austen's *Mansfield Park*. They wanted to be refined and thought they were being superior, but only succeeded in being unpleasant. Our claim is not that rich people are nice, but that they are rich in opportunities. Signs of the amazing mobility of British society are everywhere. Many of the most gifted aesthetes were of working-class origins: Sir John Soane, one of the very greatest, was the son of a bricklayer; Richard Payne Knight had a housemaid mother.

Payne Knight inherited ironmaster, industrial-revolution money and put it to work for a lofty aestheticism, which included the development of a rather humane view of the landscape and private estate that we would think conservationist now.[6] Other aesthetes of the period depended on plantation wealth earned by the sweat of slaves. Sir Hans Sloane brought to his mass of arcana (which would become the founding collections of the British Museum and the Natural History Museum) plant material from the West Indies, and thought that someone might find a use for the cocoa he found there. It was the kind of discovery and light plunder characterised by the voyage of the *Bounty* (at the direction of Joseph Banks, one of the great collectors). That expedition went in search of breadfruit plants from the Pacific, the better to cheaply feed the slaves in the Caribbean. These voyages may have damaged the Pacific islanders, or may have enhanced their lives. That's a richly disputed story, of course. But we can at least say that the South Sea islanders became – especially once we had contact with them – a staple of our dreams (one that nearly did for Lieutenant Bligh and his unruly crew, and led a few to the gallows). Gauguin was merely the most famous of the people who sought to capture this wonderment on canvas. He had been presaged in the work of Captain Cook's official painter, William Hodges, whose fabulous views of the islands adorned the Enlightenment walls of the Royal Academy in the 1770s.[7] And that voyage could claim astronomy and trade about equally in its multiple motivations.

The luxuries of trade did not happen solely because of man's greed, and nor did the resulting wealth go into mindless display. They went toward building enlightened societies and into aspirational consumption. And even the most outrageous display – the building of a massive house – was not a simple display of power. It was also an expression of culture. The enlightened English gentleman was advised by aesthetes such as Payne Knight and Uvedale Price to meld his house and estate into nature: that was the way to imitate the Roman ideal portrayed by the paintings of the great Claude. And it was, handily, a way of suggesting to his fellow Englishmen that he was not arrogant, and did not deserve the revolution then convulsing France. It was also the birth of the conservation ethic and the Romantic aesthetic.

It is obligatory to say how wrong slavery was. It is suggested that guilt about such exploitation should blight our pleasure in wealth even now. I am inclined to suggest that the people who were slavers, slave-owners and the customers for slave-produced goods were not necessarily particularly wicked, and that I have no doubt that Africans of the day would have enslaved whites as indifferently as whites enslaved them, if they had had the chance. We don't need to argue retrospectively that our slave-owning predecessors ought to have felt guilty: their own contemporaries did that and were better placed to. We can argue, rather, that the modern descendant of slaves ought to be grateful that his forebears paid the high price that got their bloodline out of Africa. Similarly, it is better that modern descendants of the white working class (that's nearly all white people) be grateful that the suffering of factory workers two hundred years ago lifted them, and us, out of squalid rural poverty. Many of the most energetic exploiters were sons of the soil themselves. Many of the exploited swiftly joined the very lucky. Very many of even the exploited had reason – even then – to think their lot better than that of their parents and grandparents.

The path from luxury to household standby can look like vulgar commoditisation. It can look like the path from homely craft to exploitative industrialisation. But it is also the democratisation of good things. Only mass production could satisfy mass markets. The Ironbridge of Shropshire testifies to the use of new metallurgical techniques to solve old problems. But it was iron pots, mass-produced downstream, that were socially revolutionary. People had spanned rivers for aeons; but no-one had found a way of producing cheap cooking pots. And then Turner and Joseph Wright sallied forth and realised that the new industrial scene was as exciting – as fiery and awesome, as 'picturesque' in the language of the day – as the Vesuvius that God had provided. Man had made a wonder of nature.[8]

And, of course, it was inspired, ardent Quakers and other strongly religious dissidents who drove the Industrial Revolution. They were seized of the need to improve the lot of their fellow man, and to do it on earth, now. In the modern age – now – we can find as many peculiarities. Almost all of us use a computer and the Internet, machines and networks designed for business and for the military, and do so as much to fulfil our heart's desire as to make our livings (not that these are always very different). You are as likely to find a website devoted to spirituality (I run one myself: www.thevirtualeden.com) as to bomb-making.

THE DISCARDED AND NEGLECTED

There are other intriguing transmogrifications. Our artists transform trivially mundane but brand new, branded, objects into art; and, of course, since Warhol we have wondered if their stuff is much more than a joke. The point here is that these visual commentaries often delight in being about the manufactured, and enjoy turning a large profit. Are we duped either by the painting of a tin of soup, or by the tin of soup itself? Do we buy soup, or the brand? Was the label artistic, and a suitable subject for art? The age of the mass-produced naturally needs its wry commentary, as every age does. But to be alert to the ironies that can be wrung from soup tins and their labels doesn't stop us going home from the art gallery, late and tired, and glad that there's something simple to open and to pop into the microwave. Warhol was too canny to have a point of view, but his art leads at least this viewer to be glad of mass production. After Warhol's joke, and challenge, we can still enjoy an excellent product.

The Chapman Brothers take plastic toys and rob them of innocence, and we can come up with reasons why the joke may be making a useful point.[9] If they are trying to make us aware of the trashiness of the trash we buy, their attempt may backfire. You can invert and subvert the innocence of a Barbie doll, but you can't make most girls not want weird dolls and mauve ponies. They go on to be feminists all the same, or not.

I am even more impressed by the peculiarity of the artist Joseph Cornell, who wandered the city of New York and was, perhaps, a little pervy round the edges. He could not resist the discarded, and he fetishised it. He wasn't making a point about how much waste we produce, but rather how the unconsidered and the neglected was glorious, even when it had been mass-produced, cheaply bought, and not regretted or mourned as it was thrown away.

His art, like Warhol's, was, in part, about mass consumption. He made something very like art out of his cartons of junk, selected to be conjoined with one another, not exactly by happenstance, nor by the places where they had been used or found. He made small empires of order – categories – out of his own mind and yearnings. His purpose was to create a vision of spiritual order (as the title of one good biography of him suggests).[10] He has one very large message, and it is that value, and even order, are where we find them. He is as moved by plastic dolls as are the Chapmans. He is not mourning the world that produces plastic dolls. Rather he is noting that they have been loved and tossed aside, and that it is up to him to mine them for the love and meaning they once had for someone, and which he wants to memorialise.

Cornell was in a long line of similar obsessives: in the mid seventeenth century Cornelius Gijsbrechts of Antwerp did trompe-l'oeil works of the mundane and spiritual items of a man's life, and now Cornelia Parker mashes up and reassembles miscellanies of objects to squeeze out their meaning. This is like the thirst of the antiquarian (chronicled well by Philipp Blom in *To Have and to Hold*,[11] with its inscription: 'Every passion borders on chaos, that of the collector on the chaos of memory'). From the Ashmolean to the British Museum (via Sir John Soane's house in Lincoln's Inn Fields), and from a taxi driver's dashboard to a woman's handbag, we see the desire for the talismanic, and they are as often made of the haphazard and the serendipitous, as of the formal and the intended.

Shabbiness is very like neglect, and it is treasured. This is because it means that something physical has become drenched with meaning. Nancy Mitford only half understood all this (there wasn't much she only half understood). Towards the end of her life as an aristocratic working woman, sociable loner, populist historian and classless snob, she described how she had been in the sumptuously restored Italian villa of some newly rich Americans: 'It's like a grand hotel. It may sound silly, but I like, especially in houses, a certain amount of shabbiness – couldn't tell you why.' Yet she quoted with enthusiasm a proverb that one is nearer to death in a garden than anywhere else on earth, and she liked her gardens 'cottagey' to the point of wishing they could be a meadow of wild flowers. So she preferred a shabby garden, as she preferred a slightly shabby house.[12]

The reason is surely that shabbiness is a reflection on the liminal, the provisional. The reasons for loving shabbiness are to do with authenticity: that sense that time's crowd has rubbed its shoulders and bums against this object. These old humans have made an impression, but have gone now. They are immortalised in something more enduring than themselves. The worn stone and the sagging sofa both speak of endorsement – just plain use – by our elders and betters who have gone before. We know the past does not contain better people than the present, and yet – like the colours and shapes of nature – we often feel we have no better yardstick of quality. We know that shabbiness speaks of decay, and that a worn-out item is a memento mori (a reminder of death).

Actually, orderliness and progressiveness have their own message about and to death: their cry is of defiance against the entropy we know is the underlying fate of our universe. So sometimes we buy something new, and love it for being ultra-modern, and should perhaps acknowledge (as when we smoke) that we are deliberately defying death, and acknowledging it too. Likewise, when we buy something new and distress it (or buy it ready distressed), or buy something old and do it up so as later to distress it properly, then in all these things we are also acknowledging death. We are surrounding ourselves with stuff that is laden with images and messages – and doing so as truly as a Russian with a religious icon. Rightly, we are sniffy about the over-use of the word 'iconographic', and we are nervous when we hear of the narrative that lurks in every mute object (as we are skittish about the idea that there is a subtext hidden in every remark, and a subterranean agenda in every work of art). But we are the creature whose main distinctiveness lies in seeking and passing on lessons. We interpret everything as best we can, and we see opportunities for interpretation everywhere.

The value of the mass-produced, the discarded and the neglected can be celebrated without rubbishing the crafted, the treasured and the cared for. They can all move and thrill us.

STOP THE WORLD I WANT TO GET OFF

The minimal naturally has particular meaning. Men need a hut. They need a cave to go to the back of, as surely as women need a boudoir and a bathroom of their own. I say need: of course it's not a need. But it is a deep yearning (a yearning that goes deep, and one that has a spiritual dimension). Dylan Thomas had his boathouse at Laugharne, and it seems – in its simplicity – the very model of tranquillity and creative purpose. We read of Thomas Merton, and the hut in which he was allowed to live – itself a great luxury for a Cistercian monk, whose greatest penance is to live in public and in community.[13]

To read *Swiss Family Robinson* or *Robinson Crusoe* is to have the luxury of imagining the simple and the sufficient. We figure that such people have the luxury of scavenging among goods that were once other people's, and they have the exigency of making do. It is a curious mixture. We know it would not really do for us, but also know that it is good for us to think about it. Many of us fantasise about living on a boat, and the more simply the better. The sailing books of Tristan Jones[14] make the point: here was a man even poorer than Joshua Slocum, whose voyages were also done without back-up, in simple boats. And many of us romanticise the life of monks and sailors in identical terms. Here is Adam Nicolson, writing about his voyage up the west coast of Britain in a classic yacht. He has already met monks and been impressed by them. Now he is in harbour and sees a scruffy, battered boat tied up alongside his own:

In the bow was a low decked space, more like a kennel than a home, which served for a cabin. It too was a mess. Through the opening, you could see a little gas cooker in there, a thin mattress and a sleeping bag rumpled and twisted on top of it. All looked as grimy as an anchorite's cell.[15]

It is possible that Nicolson's admiration is a tad sentimental, and certainly he seems, later, to be a little over-ready to hero-worship the loner whose boat he sees (as he had hero-worshipped the monks earlier in the book). Certainly, one has sympathy with those around him who seem rather irritated by his middle-aged, self-absorbed pilgrimage to the edge of Europe (and of himself) – however physically brave this improbable hero proves himself to be. He is, in the end, summoned back to the humdrum cares of his family life.

Nicolson is right, perhaps, that his own classic, restored, simple wooden yacht is a lovelier object than the mass-produced white yachts that most pleasure sailors use. A man offers Nicolson one such. 'His yacht, something called a Bavaria 46, tied up in the marina, was a big fat white empty plastic thing, a bulbous caravan with too many cabins and no soul.' There is no hint that he is aware this instant snobbery is bound to alienate many of the people who will want to read a yachting book. But right there, from page four, one knows the BoHo superiority we will know in the rest of the book. And how it makes one relish the plain, unfussy, go-get-it delight of millions of yachtsmen in their sensible, serviceable white plastic yachts in which they take huge pleasure (and whose bulbous design allows people – especially perhaps wives, not taken on Nicolson's voyage – to be comfortable). The Bavaria owners are mostly people who, unlike Nicolson, do not have a paid skipper to navigate them on their trips.

It's best to avoid the reverse snobbery of sneering at the glossy magazine infatuation with the authentic. Nor is it quite right to mock what any of us might fall prey to, when we are lucky. *Country Living* (the 'Gingham Tendency' as I dubbed it when it was launched years ago) devotes several pages to 'A magical treehouse, nostalgic beach hut and riverside cabin' and we note with delight that, in chintzed-up, styled, 'distressed', faux-lime-washed form, many of them are available for rent or purchase. And why not? The homage affluence pays to the peasant and the workmanlike can never be – it never was – without its paradoxes. True, when it pays homage to the neglected, the rejected, the eccentric, something a bit more peculiar is going on. But it is not so very peculiar.

The £50,000 beach hut is now a standby of British journalism. There are people who will pay £8,000 to have a nineteenth-century shepherd's hut recreated as a sanctuary. It's only corrugated iron (rusty if possible) on a wooden frame on cast iron wheels. Inside one such,

Country Living tells us, there are 'embroidered fabrics from Chelsea Fabrics', and it is a place where one can 'truly relax'.

It seems fair to point out that our forebears were more edgily interesting in their homages to the poor and bereft. The greatest luxury of the mega-rich of the eighteenth century was to have their own hermit, out among the sheep in the wild bit of the estate. The hermit expressed a person's understanding of the anchoretic tradition in religion and art. The hermit was perhaps also the equivalent of the skull a Renaissance gentleman (that newly rich merchant) would keep in his study as a memento mori. And that itself was a reminder that the medieval mind understood that every day, a person of refinement must recall that death would come and level everyone. That was the bit that expressed one's understanding of nature, with its picturesque nod to the Sublime – that place where a person of sensibility artfully allowed enough wildness into his life to have a thrill of the primitive.

It was a tendency that would lead to nineteenth-century Alpine mountaineering by intellectuals and aesthetes; to rambling in the Derbyshire Peaks by working-class radicals; and to women painters heading off for Africa. It would lead to the National Trust and to all those Shell ads. It was a tendency that would be turned into an industry, as Thomas Cook made routine what had been hazardous.

But then, when a thing is commercialised it is also democratised. The early twentieth-century adventures in Antarctica were the last great exploration, the equivalent to heading off westward across the Atlantic half a millennium before. But, true to its being a modern adventure, it was sponsored by consumer brands, seeking to take their image to the greatest tabula rasa left on earth, to leave their spraint there. How different is that, really, to the patronage, patents and monopolies that underpinned the late medieval explorers, as they headed west to seek the gold, which turned out to be much less good for economies than people believed before they got it? And certainly, as Ellen MacArthur leans against the gleaming white blister of BT's satellite tracker on her racing yacht, she expounds on the simplest, most primordial things – on wildness and endurance – courtesy, in several ways, of that telecom company, which seeks to increase the number of its customers, and decrease the resentment they feel when its bills arrive.

The new luxury is not merely minimalist and cool (in the special sense of alienating). The *Financial Times*'s 'How To Spend It' magazine is a fortnightly guide to high spending. But it is the antithesis of vulgar or flashy. Its pages are likely to extol a new Greek resort whose special pitch is that there is easy access to the shores of Mount Athos, the orthodox monastic republic on which no female is supposed to set foot, and which it is not easy even for men to visit. Going one step further, one HTSI featured a pair of luxury hotels in the Himalayan kingdom of Bhutan. These resorts are a homage to nearby Buddhist monasteries. A few pages on, there was a feature on the yoga retreats to be had in Morocco.[16]

Minimalism, expensiveness, spirituality – these go well together. The wittiest proof we have is the case of the Czech Cistercian monks who commissioned John Pawson, the minimalist architect, to design their new monastery. Here was the man who designed Armani's flagship store in New York, at work on a building designed for the order perhaps most devoted to simplicity and poverty. The designer of a modern profit-powerhouse was nonetheless ideal for the job of creating a prayer-powerhouse.[17] My own impression of many monks is that they relish the aesthetic as well as the spiritual: to live in a beautiful building, even if it is bleak and plain and perhaps not warm enough, is part of their pleasure in their vocation. The stylish and the spiritual can go rather well together.

It is easy to detect a whiff of humbug in rich people playing at the monastic. But who's to say such people are not being richly spiritual? Come to that, so may be the youngster in an Ibiza club.

Compared to the rich, the rest of us have very much less colourful opportunities for choice-making in our view of wealth, but they are real for all that. While some ordinarily affluent people opt for high-expenditure pleasures (such as sailing a boat in a wilderness, or flying to grand prix races, or jetting off to swim with dolphins, or to walk pilgrim paths in the Himalayas) others delight in downsizing (taking early retirement in the countryside, or energetically risking all on an organic farm). Some middle-class people trade potential affluence for a more 'meaningful' way of life: they teach, they doctor, they write. In some sense they are choosing poverty over affluence, and it is remarkable how many people make this choice. It is a choice that looks easier in an affluent society, since 'worthwhile' professions can be pretty well paid. Actually, however, it is a bolder choice in rich than in poor countries in at least one sense. In poor countries, 'meaningful' professions are seen as a fast route out of poverty, compared with the hazards of entrepreneurship. Education is prized, not so much as a route to enterprise, as an agreeable alternative to it.

MASS AFFLUENCE AND SPIRITUALITY

Wealth is wonderful in all sorts of ways, but can it be spiritual? Is it at odds with the spiritual?

This is the acid test, since we seem to organise our discussion about the merits of activities according to a continuum that juxtaposes the material and economic with the spiritual. We often seem to posit wealth as the measure of the material (and the venal), and voluntary poverty as the apotheosis of the moral. This is as much as to say that one could not make money and be spiritual: making money is not compatible with the spiritual life. I say 'we': this juxtaposition seems to be common in all cultures, but very prevalent in the Christian, western world.

But not uniquely so. In David Payne's *Confessions of a Dowist on Wall Street*,[18] the protagonist finds strong similarities between the mysteries of the market and the philosophy of the Dow. I agree, and share the hero Sun I's mild dissent from the religious of his monastery in China. They see the market as antithetical to the contemplative and the spiritual. 'The Market' is their expression for the unspiritual world. This is to fail to see the moral value, the poetry and the mysterious quality of the market. It is also to assume that wealth creators are not moral, and could not, therefore, afford the 'examined life'.

Spirituality is not to do with being at peace with oneself, but with insisting that escapism and excuses won't do. Shouldn't one be aiming for 'inner peace' but not at the expense of avoiding life, its rigour and vigour?

I am not sure that my yearning to spend time in monasteries was any more valuable than my yearning (thirty years before) to own a pair of shoes as much like Mick Jagger's as possible. I needed more money than I had (at either time) to achieve either. Each seemed to express my innermost being. Idealism, ambition, love and hope are all bound up with them, and what would life be if we all achieved a stable condition, in which we had enough and wanted no more? Deadly dull.

I don't even think that we can say that yearnings and longings are all right because they are tests, which we are set by life, and in resisting which we pass or fail. Success and failure, alike, are supposed to be impostors. And sure, we need to know what really constitutes success or failure. But lose your appetite for either, and you know that life's race is over for you. Its being over – the storm having passed – is not necessarily spiritual, though it is peaceful.

A HIERARCHY OF ASPIRATIONS

We are bound to want to talk about the difference between trivial happiness and 'deep' happiness. We have the feeling that the fleeting, the thoughtless happiness of swift gratification of 'low' or 'primitive' urges and appetites is somehow not quite the thing. According to taste, people will, perhaps, assume that the hamburger, the SUV, the speedboat, the lap-dancing saloon provide a happiness that is not as grand, as useful, as important, as the better, deeper sort of pleasure to be had in an art gallery or church.

So what might be a deeper sort of satisfaction? When we consider our pleasures, needs and aspirations, we juxtapose the trivial with the important, the easy with the difficult, the light with the serious, the immediate with the delayed, the temporary with the lasting. It's interesting to arrange these things into hierarchies, as Abraham Maslow[19] famously did. His ran something like this (there were different versions):

- Physiology
- Safety
- Love
- Esteem
- Self-actualisation

This seems a rather narrow sort of list: it is composed of what people want for themselves. Here's a rather similar sort of list, but one that supposes people want 'instrumentality' (want to have an effect), as they progress. We might suggest that their hierarchy of desires would run something like this:

- Survival
- Security
- Affluence
- Influence

Suppose we filled that out for a more loftily aspirational sort of person, of the kind I am inclined to think most of us are, or can fairly easily become. A fuller hierarchy for this type might run:

- Food
- Warmth
- Comfort
- Security
- Education
- Travel
- Choice
- Space
- Privacy
- Self-expression
- Influence
- Power
- Spirituality

I do not mean that we can or want to become saints. I mean only that we can conceive of this order as how things work and how they ought to work. It is what we are like, and what we ought to be like. I also mean to imply that, as we secure each rung of the hierarchy, we are within our rights – we are right – to consider the next.

SPIRITUALITY AND PERFECTION

We are inclined to juxtapose the compromised with the perfect, and think spirituality has to do with the latter.

But then, perfection is not spiritual. In *Truck: On rebuilding a worn-out pickup and other post-technological adventures*, by John Jerome, one is reminded that a perfectly restored 1950s pickup truck would be, not only sterile, but frustratingly unattainable. To aim at perfection would be to fail to see the point of restoration, its sufficiency; to aim at perfection would be to court the hopelessly unspiritual misery of frustration. The old wreck that is restored to perfection would have lost most of its authentic nature. The creases in an old truck's seats are its badge of life, as surely as their being left ripped would be the mark of its owner's indifference.

It happens that *Truck* is a hippy-ish affair: it likes the idea of the vehicles of the past that were easily repairable. One might say they needed to be, given how often they broke down. They were polluting, too. And they cost a high proportion of a working person's earnings to own and maintain. Modern motors are more satisfactory in all sorts of ways. Why should they seem less cosy, less rewarding – less spiritual?[20]

These are the balances we all know. If you don't know how to compromise, then you are condemned to suffer, and to waste your time and heart in hopeless yearnings. Barry Schwartz is quite good on this, but too gloomy. He thinks that consumer choice panders to our quest for perfection, and that it is, therefore, very unspiritual, as well as misery making. This would only be true if we made the mistake of imagining that perfection is to be had from shopping. Rather, don't we all know that there are great satisfactions to be had from catalogues and shops, but that balance in this, as in all things, is important to our well-being?

We know that compromise is often wise. Our gardens and older women show these truths every minute. They are works of art worked out of nature. In a garden, too few weeds, and they deny nature; too many and nature has been allowed too much freedom. The older woman's crow's feet are the legacy of her laughter and sorrow: to wish she botoxed them away is to wish her to seem to have had no life; just as surely as to deny her make-up is to refuse her the dignity of being as beautiful as she can be.

Let's not lose touch with reality, or with unexpected spirituality. Our lives are enriched by our unreasonable longings, and to get everything into perspective and behave sensibly is to be half-dead. So, long live the infuriating quest for perfection at the garden centre and the make-up counter! People can get all wise and knowing if they like. I am more likely to be with the unwise and the yearning. They seem more interesting, and they seem more in touch with themselves. Extremists are where most of the action, and a good deal of the spiritual, is to be found. It is a false dichotomy to pitch the spiritual against the vigorous. Indeed, spirituality pops up in the oddest of places.

RESENTMENT AND SPIRITUALITY

There are plenty of people who aspire to the spiritual, along with being busy and successful in the world. Isn't it probable that the successful person is more likely to reach for, and reach, spirituality than the failure? Doesn't failure make one cripplingly bitter, resentful and sour? Sathnam Sanghera, an *FT* writer, went looking for bitterness, and found that many people who seemed likely to have a grudge against life were determined not to be seen as bitter: they were making a sensible decision surely? One of his interviewees, a psychologist working on bitterness, notes a passage in Aristotle's *Nicomachean Ethics*: 'Embittered are those who cannot be reconciled, who keep their rancour; they hold their arousal in themselves, not coming to rest unless revenge has come.'[21] Failure takes courage: the courage of forgiving the world for getting us so wrong. Shouldn't we like success for the liberating enthusiasm and gratitude that ought to be its fruit? Shouldn't we note that spiritual grace consists very largely in refusing to be made bitter by the inevitable disappointments in life? Isn't this what's so profoundly unspiritual in the modern teaching that it is 'the system' that fails us, not us it? When we shunt the blame for misfortune onto the outside world, we are licensing ourselves to fester.

One could go a little further and suggest that the poor should be excused spirituality. Though some show fortitude and resolve – even a saintly refusal to be scarred by envy and resentment – a poor person who did not achieve such a spiritual accommodation could hardly be blamed. The anger of a poor person is a lot more explicable and excusable than that of a rich person. Advantaged people are said to be gracious when they remember to be civil to those they have power over (it's a quality easy to parody). But the grace that most stuns us when we see it is the courage to be decent and calm when one has every right to be angry, despairing or spiteful. One sees it every day in Africa, and almost every time Africans are shown on television. (I don't mean that all Africans have grace. Rather, that it is amazing how many do.) The grace of the starving African shames the Mass Affluent, who notice not merely that they have failed in charity toward the poor. More stinging is the thought that we have not been as graceful in our advantage as they have been in their suffering. Of course Africans are angry – much angrier than westerners can easily judge from watching smiling or suffering people on TV. But some Africans have told me their anger is to do with their own helplessness, and even the wickedness of their leaders strikes some Africans as being the fault of their citizens.

So perhaps we are within our rights to wonder why rich people, who have the opportunity to make spiritual choices, often do not. And yet even here I doubt the utility of the idea that the rich 'ought' to be more spiritual than the poor, or spiritual at all. It is more that rich people have the freedom, and perhaps the obligation, to make good choices, and among those choices is the option to become spiritual. Of course, it isn't required to seek to be spiritual. Being virtuous, useful and amusing – an adornment to life, to be life-enhancing – may all be achieved by the defiantly unspiritual. The 'examined life' is a high ideal, but it is not the only one people may have. And people may do vast good without having very high ideals – let alone this particular one. This has something to do with the deliciously haphazard nature of human life. To want to be spiritual, to have a spiritual dimension, is quite attractive in people. But unspiritual people – people who claim no spirituality, and to whom no one would ascribe it – are often of more value to the rest of us, and perhaps to themselves.

A valuable person (a generous, creative, giving person, say) might be quite unreflective. They may not, in their busy lives, seek 'stillness' or reflection, so much as rest, or relaxation, or recreation of a possibly mindless kind. Similarly, it is possible – perhaps even likely – that a spiritual person might be valueless to those around him. Indeed, one can only be a valuable person if one is of use to others. A spiritual person might be completely alone.

PRAYER AND PROFIT

Henry Ford is supposed to have said that 'Money is just what we use to keep tally.' It measures a certain sort of success. Unless we believe that commercial success is immoral, then we are entitled to believe that success can be maximised. If we believe that firms do good, then their being profitable is good. Profits can be maximised with moral impunity. Or, to be more accurate, they can be optimised: a firm may well forego today's profit on the expectation of future profits. That may be right. But there is something very important in the temporary and the impermanent.

Interestingly, the maximising of profit now is very akin to an understanding that spiritual life can be about carelessness for the future. To be providential, careful, responsible or 'sustainable' (in the over-weening modern word) is the antithesis of what many spiritual guides have thought essential. For one line of spiritual thought, one must remember that the human condition is essentially provisional and liminal. The provisional reminds us that nothing lasts or is meant to. The liminal reminds us that we live in order to change.[22] To think for the future, or to seek permanence, is to deny the needs of the present, but also the spiritual. It is to miss some very handy guides to the purity, the spiritual essence we might aim for. A monk and his monastery should, ideally, have no thought for the future. To worry about building places and financial reserves, to fashion institutions for the future is to be preoccupied with the material, when one should be devoted to prayer. A monk who worries about tomorrow is becoming bogged down and distracted from his spiritual mission. The whole of monastic history is about prayer-driven men seeking to throw away their pasts and their futures. They hurl themselves at the heart of exigency, letting the dead bury the dead. Saints are fed by passing crows. But others join them, and seek guidance, and pretty soon we have – as it were – the medieval accretions of a Cluniac Benedictine monastery (summoned up in fiction by Umberto Eco's *The Name of the Rose*). But this excess, the encrusted ritual and layered hierarchies, will produce a radical reform that again seeks the lean and mean prayerfulness of the hermit.

In this rather important sense, prayer is like profit. Both are the gold standard of what a particular activity is about. The monastery does prayer; the firm does profit. But a certain human vanity and decency makes monks worry about building institutions. They do this because they want to make sure that prayer will happen tomorrow, and they don't want to be a burden on the kindness of others. Like a man who knows it is irresponsible not to be rich enough to look after himself in old age, a monastery sees that its duty is sturdy survival. Tomorrow seems like a sensible thing to think about. But monks can become hopelessly hung up about their kitchen garden or their benefactors, instead of doing prayer. Similarly, a firm can be investing in its future, or its employees, or a cafeteria, and not look after its present profit. A firm may build a future and miss the trick that keeps it alive today. It may be kind, and responsible, and plan and plot for the future. But its intellectual resources may be distracted from making money, and it may thus fail its investors, and its real chance of doing good. Profit is pure, and public purpose is headed for disaster.

The obesity of large firms allows the sprightly to spring up and overtake them. It allows employees to learn their business well, and equips the entrepreneurial among them to leave and do things better or differently, or different things altogether. In doing so, they get back to the entrepreneurial soul of capitalism, to the riskiness of betting on new people and projects. Men and their institutions can't stay pure for long, but the impure creates a new, vigorous desire for purity. Substitute profit or spirituality in that sentence as you please.

Not, of course, that we approve of the monastery that is so into prayer that it goes broke and its monks become a burden on social security. Nor do we admire the firm that makes a fast buck and goes under. Plenty of investors are looking for continuous, long-term profit (just as some benefactors funded monasteries to pray over their souls in perpetuity). Rather, these are conundrums that cannot be made to go away. Monasteries and firms both tend to become bureaucracies, or charities, or institutions. Both need to remember that prayer and profit is what they are there for. Prayer and profit see them at their most pure.

You may say that prayer is obviously spiritual, and that profit obviously is not. I don't agree, but the point here is profitability and spirituality are alike excellent – rather pure – measures of what certain sorts of people very usefully set themselves to achieve. Pursuing either can look brutal, careless – too tough for the ordinary mortal. Pursuing either may lead a person to live fully and usefully, whatever the world at large says. What's more, one can accept that materialism and spirituality are poles apart, and still believe that prayer and profit are alike. To maximise profits is not necessarily at all to be materialistic. It is what a person does to make money – and what is done with the money – that counts.

I am not even sure that, to be spiritual and rich, it is required to spend money in an obviously 'spiritual' way. People can be philanthropic out of guilt, or out of the pleasure they take in exerting power. A collector of paintings may be little more than an obsessive magpie. Conversely, I can imagine that the pleasure a person takes in a Ferrari or a mega-yacht or an SUV may run quite deep. The issue is not whether the object bought is spiritual, but whether the purchaser was pursuing spirituality while making the purchase.

The non-religious can be spiritual, and the religious can fail to be. But there's a bit more to it than that. The religious may be right, and may be doing their duty in seeking and loving God. But I don't think it is at all evident that there is much sign that they are any better at doing spirituality – at being spiritual – than plenty who are not. It seems, then, that when one goes looking for spirituality in people, one wouldn't necessarily begin one's search in monasteries or seminaries.

I have met Greek monks who rise several hours before dawn to meditate and pray in silence for themselves and all humanity until sunrise. But they wouldn't swim in the sparkling Aegean lapping the foot of their monastic fastness, and that fastidiousness seems too life-denying to qualify as an ingredient in a spiritual life. I once came across a bright, successful chemicals industry executive who wore backless driving gloves to steer his hot hatchback into the courtyard of a Cistercian monastery in Burgundy. And then his car spat gravel as he left the next morning, after a night in a sparse cell. His vigorous, world-drenched weekly session of prayer among the monks in the creamy, sunny church struck me as profoundly spiritual. The monks loved him because he made room for the spiritual in his worldly life; and because he brought the tang and zest of the outside world of chemical plants and his family life into the monastery. They had sanctity and quietness in abundance; they appreciated vigour.

DESERT ISLANDS, THE DESERT WITHIN, AND THE CELL

There is a long tradition of devotional thought that suggests the spiritual person should maintain, or identify, a 'desert within'. This is a very handy notion, and it chimes well with the modern usage, in which one 'finds' 'spaces', and goes to 'places' in a purely metaphorical way. The desert within draws on the fourth-century ascetic experience of monks and saints, who sought God away from the corrupting influences of the city. The idea of the desert within can now serve as the 'place' in which one considers one's life, free of whatever it is one chooses to define as clutter.

The absolute reverse of the desert island, is the prison cell. And yet we are struck when we hear a prisoner say that he has discovered freedom in gaol, and then taps his head and says, 'Freedom is in here.' This may happen more in films than in fact. But the point is made: one either achieves peace, and freedom, in one's head – or nowhere. Our civilisation rightly pays a good deal of attention to the idea that somewhere quite else and quite different than the world of getting and spending may be better for us. That's what every Utopia ever written was about, and plenty of people have tried to bring them to real-world fruition. Some have tried to make small communities live out some ideal in a pure way; many more have attempted to nudge society toward an ideal (usually socialism).

The fictional Robinson Crusoe might have been spiritual. Defoe made Crusoe's abandonment on an island into an act of atonement for a sailor's disobedience of his father's injunction to stay at home. Defoe thought atonement could happen on a tropical island, rather as monks have sought the desert. But in real life, Alexander Selkirk, the model for Crusoe – did not enjoy his castaway condition. He thought it a punishment for being disputatious on the ship from which he was marooned. Diana Souhami, in her *Selkirk's Island*[23] says, 'This fate seemed [to him] like a curse. His father had warned him that his temper would cost him his life and opposed his going to sea with the privateers. If he returned to Largo he would make amends, become a tanner, find a wife.' He thought he was a better Christian when on the island, and he prayed often there – to be spared. He claimed later to have been a better man altogether when he was out of the world, but that did not stop him deeply longing to be back in it, if as a reformed character. He had become proficient at surviving (he lived alone for four years and four months). But he was not ennobled: Souhami says that he crippled goats to make them easier to catch for food and sex.

Our point here is that Defoe thought the island a spiritual place (because it was paradisiacal, anchoretic, prelapsarian). Selkirk thought it a hellish purgatory. Selkirk knew how unspiritual this 'paradise' was – at least for him. When he got home, he capitalised on his experience as best he could, for hard cash, and did his best to promote a South Seas trading venture, which might have become its own South Sea Bubble. And of course, bowdlerised and romanticised, he became the model for Defoe.

SPIRITUALITY AND SPENDING

An indebted gambler, a lively party-goer, an ambitious politician, an acquisitive entrepreneur, can, of course, successfully seek a spiritual dimension to their lives, and do so in the heart of what look like noisy, unreflective occupations. Indeed, I have been inclined to think that many people are good around money because they understand its poetry, its mysterious qualities, and find something inspiring in that. That is Payne's point, and it might have been Ford's too.

Even fashion – perhaps especially fashion – is the place to look for spiritual surprises. Emerson remarked: 'I have often observed with admiring submission the women who say there is more tranquillity to be had in being well dressed than in religious observance.' Was this inner peace spiritual, or happy swank? Pleasure in giving pleasure? In making the best of a bad job? Should we not anyway love pride and vanity, if they are self-aware? The man or woman who has no pride is of no interest. Such a person would be too little alive to interest us.

It is never the activity that is or is not spiritual; it is the intention and the success of the individual that may be. After all, Popes aver that they are 'the servant of the servants of the Lord', and cheerfully – literally – pontificate about poverty from the magnificence of the Vatican and the Sistine Chapel. Anti-Catholics dislike the magnificence of the Church, and say that it is immoral and unspiritual. But people who love the Church find very little contradiction there. Indeed, they think the Church's magnificence is a matter of the mortal world putting the best it has to work in worship. The Church can put the material to work both morally and spiritually.

Why should not the faithful believe that worldly magnificence is part of the way they can express their worship of their Creator? Doubtless there are solid gold Buddhas, reminding mortals of the need to see beyond the snares of the mundane world. Arguably, the poor of the world would be better off funding their next little business, rather than credulously donating money to their religious leaders. But that is not, on the whole, an argument that has much appealed to the poor of the world, who have thought that salvation was a worthwhile investment, too, just as rich people believed it to be. They may also believe that it's of spiritual value to donate money toward the Church's opulence, and they may be right to do so.

The very gaudiness of some oriental shrines is spiritual. In Wimbledon every year, there is an open weekend at a Thai Buddhist monastery. From all over the country Thais of every sort arrive, and set up fast-food joints, record stores – an entire market. Englishmen, many of whose wives were probably found by agencies – 'Yellow Pages wives' – are there in force. Money, food, and temples are all mixed up. The temples themselves are decorated in a taste and style that would have been kitsch on a 1970s album cover. The monks offer the usual oxymoronic, gnomic advice to people seated around them. The weekend is not merely life-enhancing, it is spiritual. Fast food, flashiness, fluorescent colours: these are all perfectly compatible with the spiritual.

In Las Vegas, hotel owners have started to amass and display great modern art. This is naturally supposed to be a bizarre idea. Las Vegas is tawdry and materialist. Its delights include tacky recreations of the authentic. Our Post Modern lack of authenticity is supposed to be all about. But what, really, is odd about art being found in a resort full of casinos? Both Munch (rather sadly) and Francis Bacon (much more toughly and successfully) loved gambling at Monte Carlo. Matisse, a man whose work we think of as purity and simplicity itself, loved the Riviera, and not least its worldliness. He produced a dazzling chapel at Vence in the 1950s, just as Jean Cocteau did at Villefranche-sur-Mer a little later.

Kenneth E Silver chronicles these interminglings in his aptly named Making Paradise: Art, modernity and the myth of the French Riviera.24 Its cover photograph is of a 1927 open tourer being driven by the sparkling sea: the picture is by Jacques-Henri Lartigue, a rich man who photographed everything that was happy in his mostly happy life. The effect is not a portrait of the trivial, but a celebration of the positive. Silver quotes Matisse remarking, of his hotel room on the Promenade des Anglais, 'Do you remember the light through the shutters? It came from below as from theatre footlights. Everything was fake, absurd, amazing, delicious.' Diaghilev's Ballets Russes made a dance out of the Blue Train, an ultra-deluxe set of carriages that carried a cargo of only eighty affluent pleasure-seekers south to the ridiculous, inspiring playground.

One of the eeriest products of the French Riviera is the work of

Charlotte Salomon, the daughter of a prosperous German-Jewish couple, the remains of whose family was given sanctuary during the Second World War in a cottage in the Hermitage, a typically prosperous villa in Villefranche. Later, she lived for a while in a hotel in St Jean Cap Ferrat. (It's still there, a modest place.) But it was from the Hermitage that she was taken to Auschwitz, newly married and four months pregnant. Her work, part journal, part comic, is a series of several hundred leaves, now displayed and published as *Life? or Theatre?* Its account of a family of well-to-do doctors, singers, adulterers and neurotics, makes an extraordinary document of religious and psychological turmoil. The few pages set against a Mediterranean backdrop – the indifferent, carefree blue of the shining sea – are a splendid homage to this place, which most represents man's desire to make Eden reappear on earth, and an Eden for real people, not saints.[25]

Many of the greatest modern artists loved and understood money. Picasso's greatest drawings were done for his friend, the dealer Ambroise Vollard (of the eponymous Suite). Much of Picasso's own work was done on the Riviera, whose very existence depended on the world's very rich, many of whom were drawn there by its closely entwined reputations as an artists' Mecca and as a playground. Picasso may or may not have been a spiritual man. The tourist in Las Vegas may or may not be on anything like a spiritual 'pilgrimage' in visiting the desert city. But the tourist standing in front of a Picasso in Las Vegas by day and gambling by night may well be fulfilling the spiritual ambitions of a lifetime.

CONCLUSION

To be spiritual is to believe that we should take the time and effort to examine our lives: to be reflective is crucial to it. The 'examined life' is core to the matter. But even that is not enough. To aspire to be spiritual is to have a notion about value that bears examination. Such examination of one's self and one's moral yardsticks may lead one to charity or wealth creation or prayer or gambling.

The person aiming to be spiritual is aiming to be alive. That granted, we may find spirituality on a fashion catwalk or in a prison cell. It's as likely to be found in a boardroom or an old people's home; at a supermarket till or on a speedboat. If we don't know how to spot it in unlikely places – or don't look – then we're probably not bothering with the spiritual at all.

1 For a good source on these themes, see Monica Furlong, *Merton: A biography*, Collins, 1980.

2 Jerry Brotton, *From the Silk Road to Michelangelo*, Oxford University Press, 2002.

3 Dora Thornton, *The Scholar In His Study: Ownership and experience in Renaissance Italy*, Yale University Press, 1997.

4 Anne Odom and Liana Paredes Arend, *A Taste for Splendor: Russian Imperial and European treasures from the Hillwood Museum*, Art Services International, 1998.

5 Lisa DePaulo, 'The Feisty Lady', *Daily Telegraph* Magazine, 24 July 2004.

6 Stephen Daniels and Charles Watkins, *The Picturesque Landscape: Visions of Georgian Herefordshire*, Dept of Geography, Nottingham University and Hereford City Art Gallery, 1994 and Humphrey Wine, *Claude: The poetic landscape*, National Gallery, 1994.

7 Geoff Quilley and John Bonehill, ed, *William Hodges 1744–1797, The Art of Exploration*, National Maritime Museum, 2004.

8 Stephen Daniels, *Fields of Vision*, Polity, 1993.

9 Jake and Dinos Chapman's work in *Sensation: Young British artists from the Saatchi Collection*, Royal Academy of Arts, 1997.

10 Deborah Solomon, *Utopia Parkway: The life and works of Joseph Cornell*, Noonday, 1997, and Lindsay Blair, *Joseph Cornell's Vision of Spiritual Order*, Reaktion, 1998.

11 Philipp Blom, *To Have and to Hold*, Penguin, 2002.

12 Harold Acton, *Nancy Mitford: A memoir*, Gibson Square Books, 2001.

13 For such men, privacy is a dangerous privilege and having it, Merton soon became one of the typical paradoxes of his order: a well-travelled recluse. See Monica Furlong, *Merton*.

14 Tristan Jones, *The Incredible Voyage* (1978) and *Ice!* (1979) and several others, all published by Bodley Head in the first instance.

15 Adam Nicolson, *Seamanship*, Harper Collins, 2004.

16 *Financial Times*, 'How To Spend It', September 2004.

17 Susan Crewe, 'Cloistered Chic of the Minimalist Monastery', *Daily Telegraph*, 4 September 2004.

18 David Payne, *Confessions of a Dowist on Wall Street*, Ballantine, 1984.

19 www.ship.edu/~cgboeree/maslow.html.

20 John Jerome, *Truck: On rebuilding a worn-out pickup and other post-technological adventures*, Houghton Mifflin, 1977; Bantam, 1978; University Press of New England, 1996; www.breakawaybooks.com/John_Jerome.htm.

21 Sathnam Sanghera, *Financial Times* Magazine, 19 June 2004.

22 Duncan Fisher, *Liminality: The vocation of the church*, Parts I and II, Cistercian Studies, 1989 and 1990.

23 Diana Souhami, *Selkirk's Island*, Phoenix, 2001.

24 Kenneth E Silver, *Making Paradise: Art, modernity and the myth of the French Riviera*, MIT Press, 2001.

25 Charlotte Salomon, *Life? or Theatre?* Joods Historisch Museum, Amsterdam, date unknown, and Charlotte Salomon, *Life? or Theatre?* Royal Academy of Arts, 1998, both published by Waanders Publishers, Zwolle, The Netherlands.

CHAPTER 9

MASS AFFLUENCE AND 'SUSTAINABLE DEVELOPMENT'

What a wonderful creature man is. And how well his planet is managing alongside all his vigour and inventiveness, his greed, enterprise, impatience and risk-taking. But then, he is the first creature on the planet to disinterestedly love the members of species other than his own, and the inanimate world, and all its processes. There are something over six billion people on earth. All but a billion or so have demands never before seen in nature. Over one billion of them constitute the Mass Affluent, with demands no previous generation could have begun to imagine. Yet there is no sign that the planet is turning its back on us. Our trick so far? We have found ways of making the planet live beyond what appeared at first to be its means. In particular, we have found ways of unleashing the energy stored in our dying star. Our future? To find new ways of doing so, and to use even more of the energy pouring out of the sun.

That, broadly, is the message of a long line of 'contrarians', who dispute the comfortable despair of the greens.[1] I say 'comfortable': the greens come from a long line of Romantic 'despairists' who have captured the public imagination. We can see their lineage in the eighteenth-century fashion for Arcadian bliss and we see it in the nineteenth-century poetic loathing of industry.[2]

The worldview of the greens fitted very neatly into the gently leftish, anti-Establishment prejudices of the arts and political science graduates who populate the media and were, until recently, the loudest academics. Challenging the greens on their statement of 'fact', as I have done for 20 years, has been very easy. One had merely to point to the reams of evidence. But to challenge the widespread instinctive, emotional cultural disdain for commerce, trade, industry – that has been a longer and harder haul.

Most of the Mass Affluent live pleasantly in urbanised environments and homes with no sign of pollution. We can eat meat produced by hunters, or in sheds, or from animals grazing in semi-wilderness. We eat vegetables fertilised by animal dung or man-made nitrogen, according to taste. We can wear the product of trappers, of far-flung fields, or of our own countryside. We can get about on horses, or on grand-prix racing bikes, if we choose. More comfortably, there is private or public transport. A few hours' travel takes us to vast vistas of the primordial and the virgin – places in whose wildernesses we escape our workaday world and fantasise about how things might have been if we were alive at the dawn of time, or were savages. At our backdoors, many of us create miniature Arcadias, but most of us can also walk to shared Edens.

The Mass Affluent seem to have pulled off the trick that all nature has longed for. We have defied the entropy by which this galaxy is slowly but surely running down. We are building up vigour and complexity, even as the physical world is weakening and simplifying. We are proving worthy of the stardust that constitutes our being.

Mankind is within a generation or so of being able to use the sun's energy in quite new ways. We are at the very beginning of being able to use atomic power. We have hardly started on what may be the most promising source of energy: converting the day-to-day rays that are largely squandered. We know how to convert salt water into fresh water (with desalination plants). We know how to make good new soil (with composted waste, for instance). We know how to use forest products to make nearly anything from houses to clothes. We know how to make a huge range of materials from oil (let alone from wood). We know how to do all our industrial activity with no serious impact on the quality of air, water or soil. We know how to grow a vast amount of food with agricultural systems that can coexist with lively natural and semi-natural habitats all around. We know how to preserve and even increase biological diversity, even if we can't yet think of any need for it. Technology and skill are constantly being deployed to get 'more from less' from 'eco-design' which is intended to go with the flow of nature.

Of course there are difficulties. We do not know enough about the impact of some of our activities. We certainly don't know how much climate change we are causing, or what form it may take. There are always problems in the management of epidemic diseases, both old and new, which can spring up and surprise us at any time. Some of our chemical and pharmaceutical technologies produce delayed and ubiquitous effects, and there is sometimes a time lag between producing the effect and producing the techniques to measure them. We have been a bit slow to develop the international agreements that would safeguard stocks of free-ranging species such as fish. The poor are still very destructive of their immediate surroundings (their poverty and ignorance combine to make them poor stewards of the hinterlands around their farms). Many rich farmers are lazy about wildlife. But while there is a vast and energetic industry of campaigners that has sought for at least thirty years (arguably for three centuries) to alarm us about these sorts of problems, and others of their own imagining, we can look back on their record and wonder whether they have been a good guide to policy. Like the religious millenarians of the past, they have cried wolf so often that we take their claims and timetables with a pinch of salt.

The poor of the world, often living lives that are 'closer to Nature', do not enjoy many of these benefits. But the richer they become, the more likely it is that the worldwide Mass Affluent will have the benefits so commonplace in the rich world. There is very little sign that this species is short of anything it needs. Its ecological niche seems eminently expandable, the availability of resources all but unlimited. Our ingenuity keeps surprises to a minimum and suggests that we will surmount most of the events the prolonged death throes of this planet and galaxy may chuck at us. If there is a big disaster, whether man-made or natural, it is very likely that a substantial fraction of the humans then alive will dust themselves down and carry on. It is unlikely that their stock of knowledge or capacities will be reversed.

THE ENVIRONMENTAL DILEMMAS OF THE MASS AFFLUENT
Environment issues are either about appetite for risk or about aesthetic taste. If we keep this distinction in mind, we will be wiser and fairer in the way we think about nature and our relations with it. When we are looking at risk, we are usually trying to work out how an action may rebound on us. Will our fossil fuel emissions overheat the planet? Will this chemical plant scupper that nearby river? Sustainable Development, a mantra we look at later, aims to capture this sort of issue. That's to say, SD looks at whether something we want to do now will reduce the future capacity of our environment to support us, or itself.

When we turn to aesthetic issues, we mean to capture the sorts of things that matter to us emotionally. I'm stretching a point here. Under aesthetic issues come airports, roads, housing in the countryside, and nuisances like traffic noise. But you take the point: one might want to reduce the size of car engines on the grounds that emissions damage the planet; and one might want to reduce the numbers of cars on the grounds that building roads for them is wrecking the landscape.

GLOBAL WARMING
Anthropogenic (man-made) Global Warming falls under the first category. When we deal with it, we are assessing risk. It is the perfect ecological issue, but it is not, at first sight, a typical one. Ecology often looks as

though it is about communities of wild plants, or the life of a stream, or of a burrow of animals. However, we get a truer picture if we remember that ecology is about the flow of energy through life systems. It's about how species use energy as they eke out a living on a turbulent planet. How a hunting bird manages, or doesn't, after a volcano sparks a forest fire, which rearranges the cycles of sun-driven plant life, which sustains its prey: that's the kind of relationship that helps us see how global warming is an ecological issue. In this case, we are, as it were, producing our own volcano. We are getting at energy sources – reaching for them and unleashing them – in a way that no other species can. We are affecting our habitat – our ecological niche – much more than any other species could.

All the same, man-made Global Warming does not play well with environmentalists. It is a matter brought to public attention by government-sponsored scientists, and promoted most by politicians of every stamp. European governments have promoted Global Warming as an issue they care about, and industry (not entirely to its credit) has supported that view. Dealing with it (if we decide to) will require some very 'ungreen' developments, and a great deal of public discontent. Dealing with greenhouse emissions will affect the lifestyle of consumers far more than it affects the profits of capitalists. The greens can hardly shout loudly about government indifference when the stumbling block to serious progress is public indifference. It is very likely that most of industry will support government, as the latter makes tentative moves to impose restraints on fossil fuel usage. There will likely be widespread public dissent, and that will slow our response to climate change.

The true test of whether the green campaigners are radical, genuine, and serious is how they will deal with being disliked and unpopular with the very public on which they depend for donations. In short, their populism is about to be challenged.

Naturally, I hope that Global Warming is not a large or largely negative phenomenon. If it is bad, I hope that we can either head it off easily, or respond to its effects easily. I hope these things are the case, because I like our present way of life and think it will be easy to make it even nicer. I can imagine attractive alternatives that are less likely to threaten the climate, but they come with costs in cash and convenience. They'll take time. I am, of course, conflicted. If we hold steady on our present course of very slightly reducing emissions, we are achieving virtually nothing. If we go all out for emissions reductions, we may still achieve very little real change, but do ourselves damage – or just have too little fun. On the other hand, a post-carbon future will be ours one day, and it may well be worth bringing that day forward quite quickly. Luckily, I don't have to decide. Electorates and despots will decide the future for themselves, and what I can do is talk as coolly as I can on the matter. I can discuss the risks and the aesthetics of the issue as best I see them.

I have argued elsewhere that it seems likely that Global Warming – whatever that turns out to be – will, to a large extent, simply unfold. It is a phenomenon that won't go back into its box. However dire its effects for some, there will be plenty of others who will manage very well.[3] We will probably undertake what is cheap and convenient to deal with the 'problem', but there is no sign that mankind will do very much to head off unspecified, uncertain and largely unavoidable risks, to be borne by the as yet unborn, in places not yet identified properly. The pain-for-gain calculus is simply too uncertain, the victims too hypothetical, to appeal to a species that loves its present pleasures, including risk. Only if the dangers of Global Warming are very large, clear and present – and seem avoidable in a cost-effective way – will mankind take very serious action.

There is a case, put very widely by many, but most famously picked up by Bjorn Lomborg, that it will be best to so enrich the world as to make a response to Global Warming's effects the preferred option. That is to say, we need not try to head off Global Warming, but rather learn to live with it. Curiously, this position upsets most of the scientists who espouse the idea that Global Warming is serious, as though it were a denial of their science. And yet it is not. One can accept that Global Warming is a real, large and bad thing, and yet believe that it is cheaper to respond to it than to try to reverse it. What is more, Global Warming is enough to make cowards of us all, but may not reward the cowardly. In other words, it may indeed be very dreadful, but it may not reward a cowardly response.

RESPONDING TO GLOBAL WARMING

If burning fossil fuels is damaging us, or will, should we very quickly reduce our use of all energy? Or should we do so very slightly, and make up the difference with nuclear power? Or invest in very quickly bringing other solar energy sources to fruition? Great strides are being made in solar power, and perhaps especially in the current star option, hydrogen power. Choosing between any of these options involves risks. Even doing the ultra-'safe' thing involves risks, if the people of today or tomorrow must suffer through energy deficiencies, as we impose fines or ration fossil fuels. In Lomborg's logic, doing the 'safe' thing may reduce the capacity of poor people to respond to what none of us can avert.

Global Warming also shows how little appetite for the Precautionary Principle there is. This principle formally supposes that we should take action to avert risks, even in the absence of final proof of danger. It is often taken to mean that we shouldn't do something unless it can be proven to be safe, which is an impossibly high standard. In the case of Global Warming we see a typical but very hard case. We like today's activities, which may lead to Global Warming, and we are very unsure of the risk-avoiding merit of any self-denying ordinance we might go in for. The Precautionary Principle notes that caution may be useful. But it doesn't tell us the only things we need to know: How fearful should we be in any particular case? How risky are the competing alternative courses of action?

Global Warming also usefully exposes the difficulties that lie behind Corporate Social Responsibility. The current consensus of government advice is that all of us should – all other things being equal – reduce greenhouse gases. But the lines of responsibility can easily be misdrawn. It is for the people who drive cars to worry about their emissions, not for the oil companies who supply their fuel. It is for governments to persuade voters to tax fuel (or large engines, or anything else): it is not for firms to make up that kind of policy. If anyone is, say, to ration fuel, it would only be tolerable for democratic governments, not for firms to do it on a whim. Nor is it remotely clear why, say, oil firms should invest in renewable energy systems. Oil firms did not 'cause' global warming, and they have no obligation to 'cure' it. The right people to invest in renewable energy are the people who think they can make money out of it. That will probably be myriad small and inventive outfits doing energetically and cheaply what such small firms do: invent, fail and get rich, according to their talent and good fortune. Their investors will get rich (or not) when larger firms (some of them oil firms, maybe) decide they see a decent bet and snap up the pioneers.

The reason why that process should commend itself to society is that it is the surest and cheapest way to bring developments to the market. Bullying oil companies to get involved must merely mean making them do something they don't want to do, which will usually mean that a politician (or an NGO – Non-Governmental Organisation – campaigner) is insisting on the right to spend shareholders' money.

GLOBAL WARMING AND POOR COUNTRIES
In poor countries, there will be precious little interest in foisting expensive energy sources and technologies on economies that are already straining to stay ahead of increasing populations and their expectations. The West will either have to pay towards such developments, or accept they won't happen.

GLOBAL WARMING AND RICH COUNTRIES

The response of rich countries to the problem is deeply conflicted. The Bush administration has refused to ratify the Kyoto Protocol, which commits countries to reducing greenhouse gas emissions by five per cent from 1990 levels by 2008–12 (some sign up for more and others for less). Meanwhile, individual US states – California, and several on the East Coast – look like taking pretty serious action of their own. Many US corporations are said to be taking the sort of actions they see among European firms: they expect a response to be required sooner rather than later, and might as well be rehearsed. They probably also see the point of the Kyoto Protocol: it is attempting to find cost-effective responses to a serious issue. It would be wise to take Global Warming seriously, whether it is a climatic or a political reality. Most firms probably fancy that a rational, steady and reliable approach to the problem will be easier to live with than a series of ad hoc approaches. What's more, a commercial cynic could argue that Kyoto is a decent smoke-screen: it will keep the greens tolerably quiet, while hardly denting business as usual.

The EU is the greatest fan of the Kyoto process, and has seen emissions fall in recent years, but it is not clear that these trends will be easy to maintain, or will be maintained when they become more difficult. Already, the UK has seen emissions of carbon dioxide rising very slightly between 2002 and 2003, after several years of modest decline. The increase happened not least because it burnt more coal, and imported less nuclear electricity from France.[4] This setback has not reversed the general reduction of UK greenhouse gas emissions, but it does presage the kind of difficulty that will arise when its own nuclear power stations are too elderly to contribute their carbon-free electricity to the grid.

Meanwhile, in the US, per capita emissions are about five times greater than in Europe. The trouble is that total US emissions are rising – driven by population and economic growth, cheapness and indifference to climate change. The EU (led by the UK) had, by 2002, reduced their emissions by three per cent (against 1990 levels), while the US had raised its by 13 per cent. Though it is profligate, the US continues to increase the amount of economic wealth it produces with each unit of energy. The Bush administration committed itself to a reduction of 18 per cent in the Global Warming effect of each unit of economic activity.[5]

Presumably, the US could easily reduce its emissions. As the US Department of Energy notes, 20 years ago there was a period of rapid declining per capita energy use there:

The per capita use of energy has declined 0.8 percent over the last 25 years…In 1978, the per capita use of energy peaked at 365 million Btu – a level not since repeated. Although the population rose 5.5 percent from 1978 to 1983, the energy use per person dropped 14 percent.[6]

GLOBAL WARMING AND TRANSPORT

The most intractable human demand for energy worldwide looks like being in the transport sector. It is possible that the world will find – or will make – moving things and people very much more expensive in the future. We can hardly guess what effect that may have. A *Times* special report, 'Future of Cargo', gives us a sense of the scale of the thing: 'Worldwide seaborne transport of dry cargo traffic has doubled from 1.8 billion tonnes in 1980 to a forecast 3.6 billion this year...World container traffic has been growing at an average annual rate of 9.3 percent [according to Drewry Shipping Consultancy].' The report went on, 'Steve Cuthbert, chairman of the UK Major Ports Group, says: "World trade is growing at roughly double the rate of the growth in GDP so demand, unless there is a world economic downturn or massive national or continental disaster, will continue to grow."'[7]

Responding to Global Warming might make moving mass (people, materials, goods) relatively more expensive, and make moving messages (images, data, whatever) more attractive. We may change the habit of history and abandon the trend toward mass tourism (if we do we will have to disappoint many Chinese people, whose tourism is expected to send 100 million overseas by 2020, up from 24 million now).[8] On the other hand, we may be glad that the international trade in recyclable material has been growing: container ships bringing goods from Shanghai to Europe are returning with 'raw' materials for Chinese industry. The trade, for instance, in second-hand plastic bottles has doubled in value to nearly £8 million in four years.[9] We may electronically outsource our intellectual work, rather than move people to do it. We may favour people staying at home to do their work (whether in our own countries or in their own). But equally, we may find that transport can be made energy efficient, or at least greenhouse gas efficient. It is moot whether we need think too far ahead about these things. The world will adjust to whatever priorities emerge. At this moment, globalization seems replete with so many possibilities and styles that it seems odd to suppose that climate change will affect it very much.

THE MASS AFFLUENT AND ENVIRONMENTAL IMPROVEMENT

Curiously, with our usual lack of gratitude for our good fortune, the Mass Affluent have looked at the environmental advantage and progress, and affect to find a malaise in their midst. Not merely grateful for their health and wealth, people are ungrateful for their ecological situation. Indeed, we affluent affect to believe that it is in our relations with nature that we must pay the price for living so well. Man is, of course, a creature that understands that pride goes before a fall, that guilt can be a decent regulator, and that conscience is an important arbiter. Important figures in his culture are loud, clever and earnest in inviting him to correct his careless, unnatural ways. Prince Charles takes time from his helicopter trips and his collection of top-of-the-range sports cars to tell us to listen to the alarm being sounded by our inner voices about our lifestyles and attitudes. Senator Al Gore writes a misinformed, but passionate, book on environmental policy.[10] Half the rock stars in the world, resting from their worldwide tours, tell us how much they worry about nature. The professional greens continue with their jeremiads.

By the 1990s, the public's environmental anxieties had been pretty well assuaged by the response of mainstream politicians, who managed to find solutions that did not cost taxpayers too much in cash or inconvenience. In the US, as from 1969, environmentalism was brought to the fore by Presidents Nixon and Ford (both Republicans). But it was President Carter, a Democrat, who really gave the cause his imprimatur from his inauguration in 1977.[11]

Republicans were more resistant to the idea, but unwound remarkably little of the environmental and conservation regulation that the country at large seemed to accept. For most EU members, it was obvious that environmental policy was going to be popular, but must be untroubling. In northern Continental Europe there was an appetite for expensive policies on recycling especially, and indeed for 'gesture politics' on the environment in general. In Britain, successive governments – especially from the mid 80s – gave the environment brief to ministers substantial enough to be credible, and yet marginal enough not to be troublesome, as they battled with the Department of Trade and Industry and its desire to avoid burdening industry with new costs. Two recent environment ministers – John Gummer for the Tories and Michael Meacher for New Labour – went thoroughly native, and went on to become indistinguishable from the green campaigners.

The strategy worked. Politically, it was wise to put some talent and effort into the business of countering green claims that much too little was being done. The environment ministers would, on the one hand, argue that their government had improved the country's record, and, on the other, would imply that the environment department was fighting the good fight against other departments. By the very late 1990s the public had lost interest in the greens' case – half-persuaded at last that the environment was in fair shape and aware, too, that to impose much higher standards on industry and households would cost consumers and taxpayers too much. By then, talk of the environment seemed mostly to consist in support for the recycling of domestic waste (a very uncertain way of helping the environment),[12] and a fairly energetic dithering about global warming. Genetic modification of crops was a different matter: the public never could see why one would mess around with nature for so little gain.[13]

THE NURSERYWORLD

As if these triumphantly heaped-up requirements were not enough, there is yet another. Modern people do not accept the adequate, sustainable or attractive environment they can be given. They long for, mourn and demand some totemic perfection in the environment, which they cannot have. I have argued elsewhere that modern people are driven to romanticise nature.[14] They have elevated naturalness – the virgin, the wild, the primitive, the remote – to a sort of paradisiacal Nurseryworld in which the sin of man's activities and exploitations can be forgotten or undone. For modern people, nature is redemptive and sacerdotal.

The clearest and cleverest account of this worldview is in Bill McKibben's *The End of Nature*, which elegantly argued that man's interference with nature had sounded its death knell. Its story is one of alienation and banishment. 'A child born now will never know a natural summer, a natural autumn, winter or spring. Summer is going extinct, replaced by something else which will be called "summer".'[15] He is, of course, right – or he certainly might be. It may be true that man is altering his climate, and quite possibly is doing so in a radical way. This gives us pause for self-reflexive thought, in a Post Modern way. But of course, the moment we consider the artificiality of our situation we find that it isn't really there. If man, a part of nature, has, through his natural skills, thrown up an unparalleled situation, Nature's response (an altered climate) is truly natural. And that's the whole point: Man can only live by Nature's laws. There are no other. It's just that our natural role is to test them, and to find some we do well by, and some that punish us.

In the Nurseryworld view, anything man-made is readily seen as an outrage and an abuse; anything 'natural' as healing. This is an essentially infantile view, but it has to be accommodated by governments and firms as they go about our daily business. Firms must pretend that they can supply everything we want, but without environmental 'harm' (meaning, more accurately, 'change'). Governments suspect that the Mass Affluent will only support Third World development if it comes without any harm to their imagined Eden.

The problem, simply stated, is: how is the planet to sustain perhaps 10 billion people? More immediately, what are we to do about all the important romantics who have a stranglehold on the affection of the media and the public as we discuss these issues?

GREEN MERCANTILISM

Mercantilism was the early medieval doctrine that supposed trade between countries was what we now call a zero sum game, in which one aimed to make money from the flow of wealth, but had no conception that wealth might be increased. Its legacy is the left-winger's sense that there is an economic pie of fixed size, and therefore a game with winners and losers as it is shared out. Ecological mercantilism makes the same assumptions about the natural world's ability to sustain us.

These 'mercantilist' ideas have been around since Malthus supposed that human population would outstrip the world's ability to increase production, which was fixed at a much lower rate of growth. During the 1970s Edward Goldsmith epitomised a confidently doom-laden view that espoused a smaller world population and a halt to economic growth (sometimes called 'Zero Growth', or 'No Growth'). His *Ecologist* magazine was started in 1970, and in that year he co-authored *Blueprint for Survival* with Robert Allen: it was to become a bestseller.[16] In 1972, The Club of Rome (an international group of authors) suggested in *The Limits to Growth* that man's material demands were growing exponentially, while the resources were finite.[17] The American biologist Paul Ehrlich in 1968 created a sensation with his *The Population Bomb*.[18] The biologist Garrett Hardin in 1968 discussed the 'Tragedy of the Commons', which became a very important principle in ecological management, and in 1974 he discussed the earth as a series of 'lifeboats' with such limited space for humanity that it was unwise to use aid to boost the species' numbers: this became notorious.[19] These writers on man's relations with the planet and nature all underpinned the new green politics and campaigns. Interestingly, the campaign groups did not much like the 'anti-human' message of the population doomsters. Even so, the population crisis has been important in the public imagination. Man is routinely figured as a cancer on his planet. He is often talked of as being a brown stain on the pure green and blue we inherited from the pre-human world. Man is a blot on the landscape. His 'footprint' has trampled the primordial.

There are many attempts to tot up the biological resources of the planet, and the degree to which man currently co-opts them.[20] These normally presume that man is at the very top end of the amount of consuming he can do, and that any new people and their lifestyles must be fitted in beneath these ceilings. It is routinely now stated that the western model of development is impossible for the Third World. There are heroically imaginative attempts to suggest how many Planet Earths would be needed to support the unborn billions coming into the world, especially if they were to be given, or to get, Mass Affluence. Sometimes this sort of view concentrates on the proportion of the sunlight arriving on the earth's surface now co-opted to drive man's activities; sometimes it is the rate at which we are converting wild habitat to agriculture or wasteland; sometimes it is the proportion of green-stuff, soil, fish or fresh water that we are supposed to be using up. Sometimes these things are discussed in terms of using up finite resources, such as oil, gas, or minerals.

Another sort of language suggests that we must limit our pollution because the planet has a certain amount of absorptive capacity, and that we have used it up. We have, in the jargon, very little 'headroom' left. And then, naturally, there is the argument that supposes the rich world has been wrong to take all these resources and headroom for itself, and that the rich must scale back their activity to provide 'room' for the poor. On this argument, equity dictates that each of us should only consume his or her fair share of these finite resources and capacities.

The greens believe that ecology says any given habitat or ecosystem has a 'carrying capacity'.[21] And surely, then, the planet is one vast habitat, whose biological 'carrying capacity' is finite. On this view, ecology teaches us that biological life has evolved to survive within natural limits by developing a web of life and a series of balances. So it is natural and not wholly wrong to describe the ecosystem as the editors of the classically green *Ecology For Beginners* did:

'The ecosystem is the complex web linking animals, plants, air, water and every other lifeform in the biosphere. It all hangs together. The system is in a "steady state" of dynamic balance, which means that by altering any one part you affect all the others.'[22]

To be fair to it, this book is not wholly gloomy. It is not 'Deep Green'. Perhaps because it is fairly leftish in its view, it does not disparage man's needs or wants. Still, green cliché predominates. Nature is seen, in effect, as many communities that combine to make one large community, which has a fragile stability. Man is a disruptive, negative force.

These rubrics are seldom applied as primitive absolutes requiring the complete absence of economic growth. Rather, they are used to describe a constrained situation that requires people to share out the available capacity within an assumption of serious scarcity. Like primitive socialists, the greens suppose that there is a finite pie, that the Mass Affluent have hogged it and ought to relinquish some of their share to allow others their chance.

WHAT DOES ECOLOGY REALLY SAY?

It has taken many years for the debate about the role of ecological science, and its transmutation into 'ecologism', to become as richly disputed as it needs to be. It has taken, for instance, the views of a

James Lovelock to show how conflicted the scene is. Lovelock, it will be remembered, believes the earth is, in effect, a single, self-preserving organism. He believes man is ruinously warming his planet.[23] But he believes in nuclear energy as rather a natural solution to man's energy problems, just as he admires the chemical industry's ability to be part of the solution to environmental problems. Similarly, Sir Robert May is a professor of ecological science, a former government Chief Scientist, and president of the Royal Society (one of the world's oldest science institutions). He is guardedly a defender of some of the potential benefits of genetically modified crops. Interestingly, Robert May argues that man's destruction of species is an important threat to biodiversity, but his scientific research says that biodiversity is not a simple or clear guide to the well-being of an ecosystem.[24]

One of the problems faced by the leftish 'limits' view is that sophisticated ecologists understand that opportunism and dynamism are part of the vitality – the strength – of the natural world.[25] They know that the survival of life's communities is richly bound up with the opportunism of organisms, and they understand that natural systems often respond well to the chaotic events that befall them. Volcanoes, forest fires, flood, climate change (of a natural kind): those species are with us that have survived these, and can again. Nature's myriad opportunisms are its strength. Indeed – and this must be galling to the left-minded green – nature shows every sign of being like the free market, in which dynamism and individualism turn out to be the guarantor of survival. That, and a certain insensitivity to the well-being of individuals. Indeed, nature is much more brutal than capitalism, which develops in societies much kinder than the biological world.

It is this latter view of ecology that allows some ecologically minded people to accept that man does not have a fixed and immutable place in the planetary biological system. The biological world around man (and of course he is as much a part of it as the fruit fly) can come to terms with this new, extraordinary kid on the block. The difference is, of course, that man senses his place in the scheme of things and must self-consciously and deliberately work out what he thinks about it, and what he will do about it. He knows that there are biological limits. He believes that nature has laws that cover everything from the flow of energy in the universe to the mathematics of biological communities. But he also knows that (like economic wealth) ecological wealth can, to a very large extent, be invented.

It is not nonsense to carry in one's mind the idea of the planet's carrying capacity. But it is nonsense to assume that we know what it is, or to over-egg the evidence that mankind's progress is blocked by it. Of course, there are natural limits: the facts of the planet and its place in the universe are given. They change, to be sure, but they are given. What is amazing is not how much, but how little, this need limit man.

HOW DO IMPROVEMENTS HAPPEN?

We know from our own experience that the politics of conservation and the environment have proceeded by navigating through a series of pinch-points, as demand for cleaner air, or farmland birds, or whatever, has shoved this or that cause up the agenda, and displaced others. We can see that Brazil, India or China – all growing fast – are facing much the same sorts of demands, and are likely to find their way through them haphazardly, as we did.

In the modern world, even a relatively unresponsive government such as China's is under pressure. Its own elites suffer from pollution, and may well have a degree of environmental ambition along with their obvious desire to run a modern economy. Doubtless, popular opinion filters through to them. And as they seek membership of western clubs, such as the World Trade Organization, they become aware that there is a level of environmental behaviour, below which they may not fall. China's economic growth has already produced what the World Bank reported to be 13 of the world's 20 most polluted cities, and it has produced a patchy, but definite, response. Noting these facts, *The Economist*, a rather green magazine, reported that:

There is no need to be unremittingly gloomy about China's environment, nevertheless. As developing countries get richer, they tend to pollute less. Nationally in China, discharges of chemical oxygen have declined over the past three years, those of industrial dust have stabilised and sulphur-dioxide emissions had been on the downtrend until 2003 when energy shortages increased demand for sulphurous coal. Most east-coast cities are enjoying more sunny days and the pollution load in the rivers is falling. Environmentally, in many places, China may have passed its nadir.[26]

THE 'CONTRARIANS'

Naturally enough, there has always been a spread of opinion ranged against the doomsters. In the US twenty years ago, the Hudson Institute fielded Herman Kahn and Julian Simon, with their *The Resourceful Earth*.[27] In Europe, there was John Maddox, the editor of Britain's premier science magazine, *Nature*, with his *The Doomsday Syndrome* (1972). In the 1990s, Ronald Bailey did battle for optimism from a free-market, conservative US think-tank.[28] So did Gregg Easterbrook with his *A Moment on Earth*.[29] Wilfred Beckerman, an Oxford University economist, argued that present generations should not hope to understand the physical needs of the unborn.[30] I had a go myself, with my 1995 *Life On a Modern Planet: A manifesto for progress*.[31] A few years later, it fell to

Bjorn Lomborg, a charismatic young Danish statistician, to become world famous and hugely influential.[32] Claiming all the authenticity of a Greenpeace member whose heart remained where it always was, he could say that a serious look at the data had converted him to a very different approach.

There was much less writing about Third World development that defended the need for vigorous capitalist growth. Peter Bauer became a rather lonely, if celebrated, cult figure for his understanding that 'resource planning' was very like any other kind of socialist planning: likely to lead to farcical mistakes.[33] Much less noted, there was what I took to calling a 'Literature of Hope'. This was material that used real-world cases of environmental crisis, and showed that often the news was good, not bad, or that the 'damage' we noted was natural rather than caused by humans. Typically of this sort of well-researched writing, Mary Tiffen noted that, contrary to expectation, some 'over-populated' places in Africa responded to the 'pressure' by becoming highly productive.[34]

Given the success of the left-leaning green environmental and development campaigners, it is surprising how long it took for the 'right'-leaning, free-market, pro-capitalism forces to match them. In 2000, Julian Morris (who had been working with the Institute of Economic Affairs) put together the International Policy Network, which draws on Third World pro-development 'contrarian' thinking. The work surfaces in meetings and papers, and achieved stunning success at the latest in the series of UN environment summits, in Johannesburg, in 2002. For the first time the British news media were able to balance the views of conventional campaigners with those of others, arguably more authentic and better informed, from around the tropical world so much under discussion.[35]

THE AESTHETIC PROBLEM

Except for Global Warming, modern rich-world dilemmas are usually not ecological, but aesthetic. They are not about reconciling man's demands with nature's needs. They concern people's competing desires.

To unpick the 'environmental problem' we need to see that we are sometimes using the word 'environment' to capture the attractiveness of the non-human world we would like to coexist with ours, and we are sometimes using it to mean the ability of the world about us to sustain us.

A classic, almost completely overlooked, illustration of this sort of dilemma is provided by the Brent Spar issue. In 1995, Shell sought to dispose of a huge oil storage buoy, the size of a tower block. They had every sort of clearance to dump it in the north Atlantic, where it would do no harm. Greenpeace launched a slow-burn campaign against this ocean dumping. After several weeks, the issue attracted public attention in Germany, and was taken up – belatedly – by the British media. In the ensuing furore, Shell and the UK government ignominiously backed down. Hardly noticed were the opinions of several rather green-minded marine biologists, who suggested that the dumped buoy would have presented no problems and would have been enjoyed as an artificial reef by marine life. They might have pointed out that Greenpeace had approved the same use for the wreck of their own vessel, *Rainbow Warrior*, after it was sunk by the French security services in New Zealand in 1985.[36]

Anyway, in 1999 the Brent Spar was towed to Norway and turned into a quayside. The cost, Shell reported very quietly, was three times the 'dumping' option: £20 million had become £60 million.[37] One interesting feature of the saga was the way the media for the first time questioned its twenty-year relationship with Greenpeace, which was found out in a small piece of misinformation about the toxicity of Brent Spar's contents. Interestingly, even this missed the point: Greenpeace did not build their case on the toxicity of Brent Spar nearly so much as on the principle of dumping.

Here was a case of an aesthetic view triumphing over an ecological one. Greenpeace's aesthetic hates 'dumping', even if it is good for nature, or ecologically sound. The organisation does not seem to mind that Shell must have sold a lot of globally warming oil to pay for the £40 million of extra cost in the 'green' solution.

We want, reasonably enough, to conduct human civilisation (urban, more or less) within an attractive garden (in which farms and wilderness commingle). The West does this to a remarkable degree, but with tensions. We want, also, and quite differently, to so conduct ourselves that we are doing no irremediable harm. But let's look at an interesting collision of these ideas. Many people of a broadly green disposition believe that we should build wind turbines to help wean our civilisation off fossil fuel consumption. Others, equally green, believe these turbines destroy the 'naturalness' of the garden that surrounds our civilisation. One can sympathise with either or neither of these tendencies, while wryly observing that being 'green' is not a simple proposition. It is not a unifying concept, but a tense and conflicted one.

AESTHETIC GREEN ISSUES: PLANNING

The bottom line with aesthetic issues is that they are about reconciling different tastes, different desires.

Some of the most important green problems we face are political and to do with land-use planning. It is likely that this neglected and underrated part of politics will become more and more important. Indeed, the ability to provide decent planning is a crucial blessing of well-governed countries. Discussing the way gypsies are allowed to override local planning laws (presumably because they are persecuted, special people), Roger Scruton notes, '…planning law is a vital part of our social capital, since it underpins the principal savings of our workforce'. He doesn't like to see it 'trumped' by claims to 'human rights'.[38] He might have added that planning law, in its apparently prosaic way, preserves the vital human rights of anonymous persons ('the public', for instance). In poor countries it is among the first needs. In rich countries, we only think the subject is boring until someone tries to build a motorway or bypass near our home.[39]

Planning is about dovetailing competing aspirations. It tends to be a matter of fitting in (or resisting) infrastructure that is needed (or wanted) by one section of society. Sometimes there is a wider public good that locals resist (waste disposal facilities, for instance). Sometimes there is a narrow private desire that locals resist (a mansion on 'public' land). Quite often, the issue is still more tense: existing poor-ish villagers may welcome new social housing; affluent incomers often hate it.

Mass Affluence has robbed the world of some of its tranquillity, quietness, naturalness and simplicity – and it has raised the price one has to pay in order to achieve some of these things. It has reduced the price of rushing around, of loud entertainment, and has made them – some will say – all too available. The Campaign to Protect Rural England (formerly the Council for the Protection of Rural England) was perhaps the first to publish a Tranquillity Map of the UK.[40] It posited that modern roads spread a noise and light blight rather further than was once the case. It is surely true that, during the 60s and 70s, when there was last a large road-building programme, there must have been a large increase in the number of people living within hearing distance of a motorway, with its susurration or roar, depending on the wind direction and one's dislike of the noise. Hypermobility, as many people call it, is supposed to be a modern curse. It often feels unavoidable. Some people drive long distances to the only job available to them, others to visit family members now scattered by divorce, or made numerous by longevity, while others are on the road as part of their work. All and any of these might say that they had not chosen this driving.

But it is, less obviously, pretty easy to avoid the 'Compulsory Consumerism' that is thought to surround us. If they disliked hypermobility, for instance – if it mattered to them – many people could avoid it. Indeed, the stay-at-home person is nowadays better catered to than at any time in history. The Internet plus delivery services – not least from supermarkets – put the world's merchandise at the disposal of a smallholder. Self-sufficiency pure and simple is probably more available to a person now than at any time in modern history.

Where once to live in the countryside a few miles from a city constituted inconvenient rusticity, now one can catapult oneself into the far-distant back-of-beyond and still be in touch if need be.

The impression of a declining tranquillity is unfair in two different ways. Firstly, we are probably more shrill in our demand for peace and quiet now. Modern man has put up with the proximity of railway lines, farmyards, factories and roads for many centuries, and it was accepted that they could be noisy and smelly. Indeed, historically, there were levels of public nuisance – of litter, sewage, mud underfoot, traffic congestion or inconvenience – that are simply unimaginable now. We may not be suffering from an absence of tranquillity, so much as from an inflation of demand for pleasantness. We have all become princesses, worrying about an excess of peas under the mattress. But here, too, help is at hand. We have better insulation, and can combine this with mechanical air circulation: one can be quiet and fresh in very noisy environments. Such developments may often challenge 'naturalness', but our ancestors would have loved to escape stone-age and medieval and early industrial nuisances by such means.

It is quite likely that there is more tranquillity now than ever, and we complain about its absence more. A useful example here is the number of people who have chosen to live in noisy places – and whose house prices have already been discounted to take account of the proximity, say, of an airport – who then campaign against more activity at the airport (even as modern technology ensures it comes with a much less than proportionate increase, or even with a diminution, in noise). We may sympathise with their complaint about increased activity. But we can wonder about a couple of things. These people are not nuisance virgins: they chose to live near an airport. And do we believe that they will suffer serious blight when the new expansion plans come to fruition? We would need to believe that their house would fall in value before we felt much sympathy with their plight. Isn't it as likely to rise? Isn't their complaint a sort of precautionary flinch? Could it be that they prefer to preserve the status quo, rather than risk its being improved or damaged? What we know for sure is that any increase in nuisance will now attract an enormous public protest, which will often successfully delay a project, but hardly ever halt it. The utility of a potential new nuisance has to be tested against a far higher bar of public scrutiny than used to be the case. And yet people do not celebrate the increase in their power to campaign, but only mourn the decline in tranquillity.

It would be an important issue if nuisance were very poorly distributed in society. That is to say, if the rich escaped all nuisance and the poor incurred a vast amount of it: that would worry a fair-minded society. Now, it is of course true that at the sad, poorer end of society, people inflict on each other a great deal of nuisance. Indeed, some of this nuisance flows from the trappings of affluence: they roll home from the pub drunk and noisy, they blast their neighbours with powerful hi-fi. There are neighbours from hell in every social band, but the poor-ish probably suffer more, and more seriously, from the problem. But surely, it is not the presence of money but the absence of manners that makes this nuisance. And it is at least mildly refreshing that the poor are a nuisance to each other more through their mismanagement of what they spend, than because of their poverty.

Obviously, poor people do not enjoy the quality of environment rich people expect. Their 'estates' are not as pleasant as those that are lined with the Bovis Boxes of the middle class, and much less so than those the rich fill with pheasants. But the poor do not suffer disproportionately from the worst of the apparent miseries of Mass Affluence. The Queen and rich residents of Kew and Richmond live under Heathrow's flight path, and there is no evidence that council housing estates have been sited disproportionately close to airports, landfills or motorways.

It would be sad if ordinarily affluent citizens of an affluent state could not visit places rich in quietness and wildlife. Surely it is more true now than it ever was that all but the very poor have the means to hike, ramble, mountaineer, cycle, bird-spot, swim, camp in very attractive places with greater ease than was ever the case?

CONCLUSION

Nature isn't dead. The planet is not doomed. Fitting in 10 billion demanding humans is bound to be a tight fit, at least for a while. We may be in for a roller-coaster ride (or not). If you're nerved up by these anxieties about risk, take a country walk somewhere – there'll be plenty of highly aesthetic possibilities close to most people. If you wanted a safer life, you've picked the wrong species to be a member of.

1 'Contrarians': a soubriquet which got going in the English press when Matt Ridley, Wilfred Beckerman and I all published books within a year of each other, in 1995. We three had not, so far as I know, ever met and only one of us – Matt Ridley – willingly used the word of himself.
2 Tom Stoppard, *Arcadia*, Faber Plays, 1993; John Burrell and John Bull, eds, *The Penguin Book of English Pastoral Verse*, Penguin edition, 1982 (especially the introductory pages); Stephen Daniels, *Fields of Vision*, Polity, 1993; David Mellor, ed, *A Paradise Lost, The Neo-Romantic Imagination in Britain*, 1935–55, Lund Humphries/The Barbican Art Gallery, 1987.
On Britain's counter-industrial culture: Martin Joel Wiener, *English Culture and the Decline of the Industrial Spirit, 1850–1980*, Cambridge University Press, 1981, new edition 1994; Ralf Dahrendorf, *On Britain*, BBC, 1982.

3 RDN Global Warming piece for the *FT*, May 2004 is posted at www.richarddnorth.com.

4 See www.defra.gov.uk/news/2004/040325a.htm.

5 See http://news.bbc.co.uk/1/hi/sci/tech/3143798.stm; http://usinfo.state.gov/gi/Archive/2004/Sep/27-45244.html.

6 Energy Information Administration, *Annual Energy Review 1997*, DOE/EIA-0384(97), Washington, DC, July 1998. See www.eia.doe.gov/emeu/25opec/sld020.htm.

7 'Future of Cargo', *The Times*, 7 September 2004.

8 Alexandra Harney, *Financial Times*, 2 September 2004.

9 'Bin There', *The Economist*, 2 October 2004.

10 Albert Gore, *Earth in the Balance: Ecology and the human spirit*, Houghton Mifflin, 1992.

11 Congress established the Council on Environmental Quality within the Executive Office of the President as part of the National Environmental Policy Act of 1969. Additional responsibilities were provided by the Environmental Quality Improvement Act of 1970.

12 See a paper on waste at www.richarddnorth.com.

13 See a paper at www.richarddnorth.com for the merits of this argument.

14 Richard D North, *Life On a Modern Planet: A manifesto for progress*, Manchester University Press, 1995.

15 Bill McKibben, *The End of Nature*, Viking, 1990.

16 Edward Goldsmith *et al.*, *Blueprint for Survival*, Penguin, 1972.

17 Dennis L Meadows *et al.*, *The Limits to Growth*, Universe Books, 1972.

18 Paul Ehrlich, *The Population Bomb*, Sierra Club-Ballantine Books, NY, 1968.

19 See www.garretthardinsociety.org/articles/art_living_on_a_lifeboat.html.

20 See www.redefiningprogress.org/footprint/.

21 Martin Holdgate, *From Care to Action: Making a sustainable world*, Earthscan, 1996, is a good guide to some of this thinking.

22 Stephen Croall and William Rankin, *Ecology For Beginners*, Writers and Readers Co-operative, 1981.

23 James Lovelock, *Gaia: A new look at life on Earth*, Oxford University Press, 1979.

24 http://education.guardian.co.uk/higher/research/story/0,9865,1092734,00.html; www.learner.org/channel/courses/biology/textbook/biodiv/biodiv_7.html; www.santafe.edu/sfi/publications/Bulletins/bulletinSummer01/features/may.html; http://millennium-debate.org/ind5mar5.htm.

25 Daniel B Botkin, *Discordant Harmonies: A new ecology for the twenty-first century*, Oxford, 1990.

26 'A Great Wall of Waste: China is slowly starting to tackle its huge pollution problems', *The Economist*, 19 August 2004.

27 Herman Kahn and Julian L Simon, *The Resourceful Earth, A Response To Global 2000*, Basil Blackwell, 1984.

28 Ronald Bailey, ed, *The True State of the Planet*, Free Press, 1995 and Ronald Bailey, *Earth Report*, McGraw Hill, 2000.

29 Gregg Easterbrook, *A Moment on Earth*, Penguin, 1995.

30 Wilfred Beckerman, *Small Is Stupid*, Duckworth, 1995.

31 Richard D North, *Life On a Modern Planet*.

32 Bjorn Lomborg, *The Skeptical Environmentalist*, Cambridge University Press, 2001.

33 John Blundell *et al.*, *A Tribute to Peter Bauer*, IEA, 2002. For a complete list of Bauer's work http://cepa.newschool.edu/het/profiles/bauer.htm.]

34 Mary Tiffen, Michael Mortimore, and Francis Gichuki, *More People, Less Erosion: Environmental recovery in Kenya*, Wiley, 1994. See also a booklist in Richard D North, *Life On a Modern Planet*, Manchester University Press, 1995. Post-1995 material of importance would include, as well as Lomborg, James Fairhead and Melissa Leach, *Reframing Deforestation: Global analysis and local realities, studies in West Africa*, Routledge, 1998.

35 UN World Summit on Sustainable Development, Johannesburg, 2002, which followed the Earth Summit held in Rio in 1992.

36 See www.greenpeace.org/international_en/features/details?item_id=485016.

37 Shell UK Exploration and Production, Press Release, Brent Spar Decommissioning Details Given at Close-Out Seminar, undated. The story is told at www.shell.com – look for 'Brent Spar Dossier' and then 'The Story'.

38 Roger Scruton, 'The State Can't Set You Free', *The Spectator*, 16 October 2004.

39 See a paper defending planning at www.richarddnorth.com.

40 See www.cpre.org.uk/campaigns/landscape-and-beauty/tranquil-areas/index. htm.

CHAPTER 10

MASS AFFLUENCE AND THE REAL MODERN MALAISES

Naturally, insofar as I think modern people have any reason to be unhappy, I want to show that it doesn't flow from their affluence. I want to show that it is their own fault, not that of their wallets. Certainly, I don't want it to be the fault of the capitalism that fills their wallets, and stands ready to fill the wallets of the whole world. It would be a bonus if I could show that more misery flows from the sort of mindset shared by the critics of Mass Affluence, than from the affluence they object to. Here goes, then.

The nihilism, rudeness, aimlessness and resentment of many westerners is very irritating. In Britain, we see the pale Chav loitering around the supermarket car park, listlessly smoking and swearing in his Burberry baseball cap. (How extraordinary to see a brand subverted so swiftly, and by its owners, not the Adbusters.) We see middle-class hooligans, whose speech, clothes and behaviour are borrowed from the worst of the working class. We see these aberrations, and wonder: how did they slide into our lives?

Aren't these less awful, though, than the stressed-out, tranquillity-seeking affluent, who pursue their ambitions ruthlessly during the day and yet feel put upon in their free time? At what point in their day do the hyper-successful transmute into victims? Why bother to? Why seek this identity with failure? If it's guilt, then why not expunge the sin, rather than indulge the remedy? When Cherie Blair was found to be spending money and time on a lifestyle guru, she was not scorned. Rather, fleets of successful women journalists came forward to say that they were into colonic irrigation and reflexology, and that they needed these special moments, in which they were the centre of attention. At least these apologists provided a rationale for the otherwise screamingly irrational. Perhaps we can see their habits as no more than a dilute, bottled version of the Pantheism of the tree-worshipping barbarian, or the body-dunking Roman with his multitude of possible gods, or the long traditions of immersion and sulphur-supping, which primitive and civilised man alike have always indulged in. It never made any sense, and yet it sort of worked. It may even be spiritual. At least we may say that candles and pyramids and exotic unguents are preferable to the psychotherapy and psychoanalysis that Freud and Jung and others foisted on a generation or two, when complexes were in vogue rather than stress levels.

THE LEGACY OF THE 1960S

An important part of the ethos of the 60s was to suppose that love would overcome difference. 'Love is all you need.' 'Hang loose.' The young of the 60s proclaimed the arrival of liberalism. At last we all knew what was right, could all 'get it'. The wrong would disappear, and the rest of us could swing merrily along. The stupid would need educating, and we might have to wait for the reactionary to die off, but, for the most part, the way to live had been discovered. Love and relaxation would mulch everything down to a fine tilth.

That record is now under sustained attack. Before he went off to spend his holidays with the ever-youthful Silvio Berlusconi, Tony Blair delivered a remarkable, and really quite cheeky, parting shot. He suggested that what was wrong with modern Britain could be traced to the social revolution of the 1960s. What a long way he seemed to have come from his 'Forces of Conservatism' speech of 2002, in which every old tradition and institution (anything that predated or survived the 60s) was dismissed in favour of New Labour's gleaming modernity: the march of the 1960s continued. This, from a man who only makes sense when seen as a Flower Child in Power. His incoherence of view, his class-denial, his stylistic confusion, all seem likely to stem from the social rot that the social revolution of the 60s gave us. Only his religion – his Anglicanism-cum-Roman Catholicism – seems to fit his moral determination. Maybe he tends toward RC because it is the religion of the oppressed (the Irish working class, for instance), but it – or something we cannot see – provides the moral will and stamina to take the country to war.

Like millions of other middle-aged British males, Tony Blair is Chavistic. We should not be surprised to find someone who has no conception of how to be middle class, elitist and logical. Someone had to be the first Chav Prime Minister. He is not merely socially chippy (which would be weird if it were not becoming routine, even in public schoolboys such as he) but he affects the sleeveless T-shirts of the modern working-class male. As Andrew Pierce, the *Times*'s gossip columnist reported, '"Guys his age should really not be wearing stuff like this", scolded Gareth Scourfield, fashion editor of *Esquire*.[1] It didn't take a fashion editor, or a style guru, to know that Blair, by wearing this sort of kit, demonstrates to the whole world a deep hopelessness. It has mid-life crisis, social insecurity, and desperate infantilism written all over it.

We will, of course, get past this ditheringly hopeless social chaos. We will see that the grandparent generation – the men and women who fought the Second World War – were more right than we youngsters had mostly supposed, as they donned their blazers and cravats, and found Mick Jagger a bit scary. And in particular, did that generation – the people now dying – seem the last generation to be comfortable with adulthood? Do they not now strike one as, well, mature?

The fact is that, for most of my adult lifetime, adults have resisted growing up. We Flower Children of 50-plus have not really known how to acquire maturity or guide others to it. Our children have been given huge freedoms, only to find themselves chartless and insecure. As they become the present generation of parents, busy but childlike themselves, they have produced a generation of children who are both demanding and fragile. What is worse, it is becoming much more difficult to provide public services in a world populated by brats of nearly every age.

One could say that the best working definition of a middle-class person is that they find motorway service stations tiresome places. Here is a classic of the genre. Alan Judd notes in the *Spectator*:

Sartre was right: Hell is other people...we're ugly. My God, we're ugly. The few that aren't are mostly immigrants. It's hard to know which is worse – the drab, shoddy incoherence of our national costume, the wobbling acres of unashamed exposed midriff flab or the closed minds behind those relentlessly closed expressions. Previous generations may have been no better (though they were leaner) but at least there was an awareness that 'better' existed, even if they couldn't afford it...The only poverty on show at any service station is the poverty of aspiration, and its victims are equally unaware of that. They have far more disposable income than their parents – look at their spending, their tenners on lottery tickets, their modern cars, their ludicrously expensive 'trainers', their children with fashion mobiles – but they haven't improved themselves with their wealth, only indulged themselves. Yet they'd be outraged if they had to pay a fiver to see a doctor.[2]

So we see granny at the checkout, wearing a skimpy pink T-shirt with 'Princess' sequined upon it. Her husband will be half-naked, dressed like a teenage sportsman (in the manner of our Prime Minister on his holidays). Their children will be impatiently steaming along, tailgating in their 4x4, he dreaming of football, she of a new beauty treatment. Their grandchildren – the modern eight and ten year olds in the back of the car – will be masters of 'pester power', equipped with mobile phones and fashion mags, their pre-pubescent bodies dolled up as a false prospectus of sexual availability and potency. Grandpa's into bling, dad's got an adolescent crush on sport, mum's dreaming of a boob job, Tracey's a micro-tart and Tyrone's a tyro-gansta in mock camouflage. This isn't working-class culture or Mass Affluence gone wrong, so much as a multi-generational nursery school.

All three generations are, of course, capable of charm and good sense. But all are prone to petulance. They worry very greatly about their self-esteem, and rightly. It is sky high, but prone to plummet. Our three generations have not been required to learn the redeeming features of adulthood. Authority, dignity, self-restraint, a proper pride, and a proper modesty: these are all at a discount. They are hard to discuss, to find, to inculcate. The reason is quite simple: we have been led to believe that growing up is optional.

The 1960s is rightly described as a period when 'youth' was regarded as important. The young had money and many were getting something like a university education. They were interested in 'radical' ideas, most of which supposed that traditions and institutions of every kind were stuffy and backward looking, and that personal intuition and feeling were a more useful guide to inventing the future. Of course, the revolution wasn't new: the combination of nihilism and Romanticism was as old as Goethe and Byron. From E M Forster, people knew that 'Only Connect' was the watchword. Authority was held in low regard. If one wanted to avoid having 'complexes' (the stress equivalent of the day) it was important that one not become repressed. R D Laing and others persuaded people that society was sick and producing sick persons. The Rousseau-esque untutored child had the last chance of nobility, before society crushed him.

In *Century of the Self*, his TV show about Freud and his fall-out, Adam Curtis gave a convincing account of a process which set us up for the institutionalised infantilism that sees no merit in traditional frameworks or in learning to obey them.[3] The result was a fifty-year period in which parents regarded society as a hostile entity that might not give their children their due. This was a reversal of an ancient tradition, by which parents anxiously and diligently prepared their children to be acceptable to society.

As we see from Susan Greenfield, growing up is a matter of developing the more modern parts of the brain, and getting it to assert itself over the undeveloped mind that obtains before civilisation has got to work.[4] Where we see selfish, impulsive, parochial values and behaviours, we are watching undeveloped people at work. We see the primitive structures of the brain being allowed to assert themselves, unmitigated by the broadening, restraining later structures. We are watching people grow old without developing. We are watching the middle-aged become botoxed without becoming civilised. They could not be expected to see that gain flows from pain; that disappointment is inevitable; that life is not fair.

Instead we see child-like behaviour wherever we look:

● Emotional incontinence: Olympic athletes weep at each success or failure.

● Language inflation: Abandoning a race (in the Athens Olympics) or suffering a mudslide (in Boscastle's freak flood) is 'devastating'.

● Short fuses: A small hold-up in traffic or at a checkout produces rage.

● Non-negotiability: People feel 'alienated' from democratic decisions because there have to be compromises.

● Blame culture: Nothing is an accident due to acceptable cock-up. Rather, people are victims of heartless officialdom or greedy capitalists.

● Praise culture: Everyone expects to be told how well they are doing.

● Cult of fairness: Everyone is entitled to whatever they want, and not getting it is 'unfair'. (Diversity is injustice, so down with the 'post code lottery' in health treatment.)

● Only Connect: A person's personal connections (friends and family) matter, but wider society does not.

● Down with the abstract: The parents of a dead soldier are presumed to have a special locus when they question a war.

● Culture of Contempt: Jeremy Paxman and John Humphrys are thought to display independence, as they trash authority figures.

● Bunny-hugging: Animals are treated as soft toys.

● Fantasy worlds: The New Age, hobgoblins, alternative medicine – people are living a fairytale.

INFANTILISM AND POLITICS

Infantilised non-adults cannot govern themselves, and are hard to govern, for two reasons. They will not submit to the wider needs of society, and they do not understand the value of the elitist institutions by which society mediates competing needs. Childlike adults could not be expected to see the merit of representative democracy and stern professions, nor to value compromise. They are bound to be attracted by glamorous campaigners, led by shrill, intemperate and petulant stars (think of Chrissie Hynde, but Geldof and Bono, too). They are drawn to political parties that pretend to be anti-Establishment (think Blair in 'Forces of Conservatism' mode).

So the problem is clear: the 1960s enshrined personal and political doctrines that have infantilised people and politics. We will need to reassert adulthood before we can expect to see the institutions of politics regain their former respect and value. Luckily, these things are largely a matter of fashion. The generation of people now young will relearn dignity and adulthood, because the bill – the real cost – of the 1960s is at last coming home to people. The shifts of fashion will take care of that.

In the meantime, we have a potent source of unhappiness. Our species develops adult ways of thinking and feeling as a way of handling the inevitable complexities and difficulties in life. Our modern pseudo-adults are not happier than previous generations were. Rather, they are condemned to childish upsets without the adult resources with which to deal with them.

Infantilism is a far better explanation of our modern malaise than is Mass Affluence. Our problems with affluence, like our problem in understanding that nature is not perfect or perfectly maintainable, flow from our self-indulgence. We don't need to be poorer, or more risk free. We need merely to grow up.

INFANTILISM AND THE INTELLECTUALS

It is often assumed, especially by the right, that intellectual life has gone to hell in a handcart. We don't teach history, we denigrate the elitist – and so on. There is much in this. And yet we need to be careful whom we blame. Richard Hoggart, we have seen, blames commercial mass media and its pursuit of profit. Frank Furedi comes from a different position. He is a leading figure in the small but influential movement of dissidents (a few of them very public intellectuals) that has grown out of the old Revolutionary Communist Party (which transmuted into Living Marxism and then into Spike Online and the Institute of Ideas). His argument, over several books, has been that society has been numbed and dumbed by the exponents of the Anxiety Society. The fight's gone out of us (our revolutionary ardour, maybe). Now he asks 'Where have all the intellectuals gone?' and bemoans the cult of politically inspired and politically endorsed accessibility, which is making – he seems to believe – our museums and libraries into cultural deserts.[5] A couple of astute critics reply that, actually, insofar as we are now dumbed and numbed, it is because intellectuals embraced multiculturalism in the 1960s, and thus outlawed excellence.[6] Anyway, are we really short of intellectuals? How dumbed down has the audience actually become? Aren't we flocking to intelligent films, art shows, lectures, debates and theatre? Aren't television and radio awash with interesting arguments? Actually, there is a good old-fashioned demand for commercially provided, rather expensive intellectual life. Sure, universities and the arts-sponsorship regime seem to have fallen for dim-witted multiculturalism, but plenty of people are using their wallets to fight back. Certainly, Blair affects a persona, and a politics, that is free of all challenge, bar the instinctually moral ('I only know what I believe', he remarked in

October 2004, in surely the most fatuous utterance of any of his empty party conference speeches). It may even be that he believes in a society as truly stripped of discernment as he clearly wants it stripped of discrimination. But we do not have to believe that our culture is dominated by him. He cannot kill it if we don't want him to.

THE LEGACY OF THE 1980S

The welfare state, as much as the market, contributed to the changes in society that we have witnessed and that we are inclined to mourn. Mrs Thatcher famously said, 'There is no such thing as society.' Her critics suppose her to have meant: 'You're on your own now', free to make and spend as you like, and suffer your failures, without social support. Welcome to the despised individualism which capitalism is supposed to have ushered in. But Mrs Thatcher meant something much more old-fashioned. She meant that society is not a machine, but rather a living human enterprise. In her view society is not automatic. It is something individuals make. Societies owe something to the individuals who make them up; individuals owe much more to society. One should never blame society for one's failings; rather one should ensure one's failings don't damage society.[7]

It is not, actually, clear that the atomised, loner, individualist westerner is as common as myth supposes. Families remain vibrant, if complicated. Networks are flourishing in every facet of social life, even if they are bonds forged between individuals bound by their interests, rather than their geography. The Mass Affluent pay high taxes, with little complaint or fiddling. The users of e-Bay see a strongly social dimension to their trading. Not only does it allow people to find the second-hand, bizarre or rare items that enrich their lives, but they are brought together humanly in the process. Patti Waldmeir wrote in the *FT Magazine* that, 'I hate to shop but I love to eBay – and the bargains are the least of it.' She sees it as the means whereby small-scale producers can supply and meet small-scale consumers, which is not possible in Wal-Mart. That may be a little hard on the shopping mall – but it is at least a useful antidote to the assumption that the modern world is one long descent from cash nexus to computer nerd.[8] These changes are always complicated: it is said that eBay is depriving charity shops of merchandise, as people discover that there is value in things for which they have no further use.[9]

THE MEDIA AND ITS MALAISES

We have been discussing a slew of books and an ocean of commentary that is overtly leftish, and that is, in a way, less tedious than the anti-Establishment populism of a dozen TV sofa-shows and smart-aleck comedy-cum-politics shows (say, BBC TV's *Have I Got News For You*). These are intended as light or middle-brow entertainment. They are intended to amuse. They have no lofty ideal (though satirists sometimes claim to be speaking 'truth to power'), but we might have hoped that they would be mildly life-enhancing. Instead, they depress us, without having a shred of thoughtfulness. The hosts and contributors simply don't realise that they are spreading more gloom, undermining more everyday well-being, than all the exploitive capitalists, the elitist governments, the self-seeking politicians whom they seek to denigrate. These programmes don't spot that it is they, not their targets, that should worry us.

BBC TV proudly runs a series from its comedy section: *Grumpy Old Men* tells us what's wrong with the young. Here are Britain's fifty-somethings bemoaning the mores of the young, just as their parents bemoaned the mores of the young of their day. And what a crew they are. There was the late John Peel, a middle-class public schoolboy who, for decades, affected the flat tones of the Liverpool docks. (Nothing wrong, of course, in being working class: but it's bizarre to reverse centuries of upward mobility by pretending to downward mobility.) Or there's Bob Geldof, whose every other public utterance is foul-mouthed, and whose main claim to political fame is not so much the originality of what he says about Third World poverty, as the bad-tempered intemperance he has adopted. Or consider Will Self, whose demeanour is a cranked-up, professionalised charmlessness, fit to frighten the horses. Or Bill Nighy, whose voice is a calculated sneer. All these men are talented, and good at things which matter to the world: but if society wanted to know how gracelessness became the norm, it could do no better than consider how the style of these heroes and 'role models' has slipped into the mainstream.

This was not the generation, mostly, that drove the 'spirit of the 60s': that cadre is now in its 60s or older. This lot – people of my age, a tad under sixty – are mostly those who were young in that period. We were the followers, rather than the pioneers. We were the early adopters of the 1960s Revolution. Instead of complaining about the unmannerliness of the modern young, we would do better to consider our part in the problem. We have brought up, taught and informed modern society. It grew up on our watch, so we caused its decline in manners and happiness. We inherited a wealth-creating economy and a participatory democracy, but not the good sense with which to turn them into well-being.

I put this strongly. I am trying to get at the way in which such failings as there are in modern society – and they are fewer than is widely advertised – can be blamed on the parents of those who claim distress. If we see forty-somethings, thirty-somethings and twenty-somethings who have problems, we should look to the makers of their childhood and adult worlds for the causes.

'THE CULTURE OF CONTEMPT' AND 'EMBARRASSED LOYALTIES'

Modern society has banished deference and trust, at least as feelings rendered by the majority to the elite minority. Now, indeed, everyone expects 'respect', but few are prepared to give it, and fewer yet are prepared to earn it. We used once instinctively to respect the past: even that has been taken from us now.

At a conference in Rome in 1995, Bishop Donal Murray, Auxiliary Bishop of Dublin, remarked that the Church was suffering from the profound embarrassment people felt about its history of violence (especially in the Irish context). He called this a case of 'Embarrassed Loyalties'. Taking another tack, he went on to say that people were turning from public religion (and, he might have added, public politics) partly because of 'the almost universal perception in modern societies that "agnosticism and sceptical relativism are the philosophy and the basic attitude which correspond to democratic forms of political life"'. He was quoting the luminous *Centesimus Annus* (Paragraph 46),[10] in which Pope John Paul argued that respect for the freedom to hold any opinion should not blind people to the importance of the revealed truth of the gospel and the asserted truth of the Church. (It was an update of Pope Leo XIII's *Rerum Novarum*: the church's discussion of the role of money and politics in spiritual life.)[11] That much is an obvious line for a Roman Catholic Pope to take and insist on, but it has its secular equivalent.

Bishop Murray went on in this more terrestrial vein: 'It is reinforced by what a Church of England Archbishop has called "the culture of contempt" which rejects all institutions and all authority.' And he quoted the then Archbishop of York, John Habgood, as saying:

What we are witnessing is more than a justifiable reaction against abuses of authority, but rather a reaction against the concept of authority itself. It therefore cuts at the root of beliefs and attitudes and institutions which have traditionally held society together. It discounts the accumulated wisdom of past generations. It sees history as no more than a record of human folly and corruption.[12]

These remarks are very valuable. Anyone going through the post-60s educational system was taught scant regard for everything that had been inherited. I have talked a bit in this book about the cultural cringe the West now displays. Not triumphalism is its curse, but constant apology. We now have generations of the educated who flinch at Empire, monarchy, Parliament, the industrial revolution and capitalism. Oddly, only the uneducated are likely to have escaped this mind-laundering, and are seen as unreconstructed reactionaries as they stick with older untutored wisdom.

But note that not merely are all our institutions dismissed as 'embarrassing' and 'authoritarian', but that being anti-authoritarian also now allows – practically demands – that one be positively abusive about the past and about institutions. To be polite about them is to succour them, to allow their sway to continue.

THE MALAISE OF POLITICS

No generation has known a more amazingly responsive government. Modern politicians and officials listen hard to 'The People'. So it is, of course, weird that so many believe they have less power and voice than ever, and that politicians are removed from them.

Tony Blair has almost certainly realised that nearly everything about the politics that brought him to power is absurd or flawed. The chippy, class-ridden resentment politics that he reintroduced to us was, actually, not a response to a modern British problem, but rather the last blast on an ancient trumpet, which had not always worked well even in the past. It was not modern, but antiquated. For two solidly middle-class boys – Tony Blair gushing, Gordon Brown petulant – to bring us a warmed-over 60s revolutionary politics, cleaned up and trimmed for the age of the Argos catalogue, was ripe indeed. Its nadir came towards the middle of Blair's second term, in the 2002 'Forces of Conservatism' speech at the annual Labour party conference: it was an evocation of a long-dead society and its frustrations. The *Observer* told us that it had identified these forces: Old Labour, the Peers, foxhunters, the professions, old-fashioned industry, civil servants.[13] The *Observer* might have added fur-wearers (Blair's backbenchers banned fur-farming in a swipe at them) and the Women's Institute (which took a swipe at Blair). Had he been logical, Blair might have added the monarchy and the traditional Churches (especially the Catholic). And of course, he might have added the Army.

Blair's 'forces of conservatism' were actually the living remnant of some of the most potent forces that had made English history. His modernising mission depended on trampling on them, in the tradition of many teachers. His words were the living embodiment of the phenomenon the churchmen above had noted. This was all the more peculiar, given that Mr Blair bends the knee to Roman Catholicism: he, of all people, should know better than to 'diss' its authority (though he would be hard pressed to take seriously the sermonising of his Anglican Archbishop of Canterbury, whose utterances are Radio 4 at prayer).

What's more, he has very probably come mightily to admire the Queen, and his premiership has given him plenty of opportunity to admire the armed forces.

The Labour Party has been, for all its life, a party of complaint, dissent and reform. It was, as the American academic Samuel Beer pointed out years ago in his *Modern British Politics* (tellingly subtitled: *A study of parties and pressure groups*),[14] a concatenation of pressure groups (as all modern parties were to an extent). In the 1990s, this seemed a very attractive pose for the rising Labour modernisers. They believed in single-issue campaigns, rather than Parliament, they believed in inner truths, rather than institutions. They burned to seem radical. They would try one last fling at making the British bitter about everything their national life was founded on: a long history, a strong rural life, Empire, elitism, aristocracy. Instead of accepting that a lower middle-class grammar school girl, Mrs Thatcher, had burst the nation out of many crippling shibboleths about class, affluence, industry, science and success, the New Labour Project managed the nearly impossible. It contrived to appear modernising, while actually leading the nation back into resentment.

Tony Blair has since led the country into wars, and whether one agrees with the causes (it happens that I strongly do), one imagines he must now realise that the forces of conservatism (the armed services, for instance) have dug deep into their traditions to follow where he has led. And he did lead. He may have surprised himself, but the populist windsniffer had developed into a headstrong unilateralist. The NGOs – Non-Governmental Organisations – on which he had modelled his ethics and approaches were left breathlessly whingeing. His craven backbenchers were left wondering where their will to resist had gone. Tony Blair had changed his spots, and was able to take to war the political and administrative machine he had absent-mindedly crippled. He had wanted a kitchen cabinet, and had created a sofa-borne Kitchener cabinet.

And when the Lords Hutton and Butler examined some of his record in all this, Mr Blair can thank his lucky stars that they seemed to have thought the dignity of his office – of office in general – more important than his personal record (or those of the office-holders around him). Their Lordships gently summoned Mr Blair and those around him back to the last of proper government, but avoided personal criticism. This was seen as a cover-up, but of course it was much more an insistence that process matters more than personalities, and it was a decent old process these people needed to return to.

To be fair, it is worth noting that presidentialism has been nurtured by all modern Prime Ministers. Nor is it all bad: the exercise of leadership cannot be done in committee. But it is reasonable to think that the burden of the super-polite reports by Lords Hutton and Butler in 2004 provided good reason for a return to *primus inter pares* (the rule whereby Premiers are leaders of a team of which they are a member), parliamentary democracy and cabinet responsibility.

This return to tradition is important because of the disconnection from politics the public is supposed now to feel. Modern people are rude because they are angry, and they are angry, so the argument goes, because they feel they can change nothing. One of the most paradoxical features of New Labour's populism is that it has fuelled a sense of impotence in the public. When power is obviously rooted in the privacy of a Georgian house in Whitehall, and Parliament seems a superfluity, we have evidence of aristocratic power rather than parliamentary authority.

But there is something yet more peculiar in modern politics. It emerged clearly in a discussion that Joan Bakewell hosted in a Radio 4 summer season called the *Seven Deadly Sins*. The series had reached Anger, and was discussing an interesting paradox: do modern democracies produce angry people because they promise a degree of empowerment that no-one can really be given, or because those wicked politicians don't 'get' what is needed of them?

The media likes to blame the wickedness of politicians. It pleases the pseudo-dissident to claim politicians are useless, comical or abusive of their power. But how much wiser, surely, to consider the possibility that no democracy can deliver what we now demand? Suppose we have a generation which does not realise that it falls to all of us to contribute to the great choices in public life, and that – by definition – we cannot get all that we want. Political life is about compromise. How could this not be so? The greatest luxury I have in a free society is that others curtail their liberties so I may enjoy mine. One has to return the favour. Get one's mind round that, and one has the reciprocity that makes our lives lovely.

But children find such compromise difficult. They petulantly believe that 'fairness' is the word for their getting their own way. It is a prime feature of our infantilism that we cannot face compromise.

There is a third possibility, and Joan Bakewell herself alluded to it. Being accorded a voice, and getting our way, may prove to be a problem to us. Bakewell wondered if we rage against the very satisfactoriness of our lives. We rage because there is nothing to rage against. We look at this possibility in a moment. It is akin to the problem that some writers have identified in a meritocracy. People now know that whether they are rich, happy or successful is in their hands. Society is now so ordered as to deliver to us what we deserve. Every generation until now could feel that life, class, poverty – whatever – were against them. Now we face the problem that, when we measure our achievements, we measure our worth. We find the conclusion withering.

It turns out, of course, that there is as much conflict as ever between dearly loved liberties and desires. On Joan Bakewell's anger programme, Janet Street-Porter said that people were angry because their town was ringed by supermarkets they had not asked for. This is a typical Radio 4 remark, and is akin to the remark that people are angry that towns get bypasses. The people who use the supermarket and the bypass do indeed choose these facilities; those who hate them are a minority. The minority may be 'right', or not; but the building of the facilities remains the result of one of the most responsive representative democracies in the world. That's to say not merely that this democracy tots up the votes of the winners and losers from a proposed project. It actively, in public and in so many words, also tries to capture enduring values (the environment, conservation, and 'inter-generational equity') that may not be properly captured in demographics or psephology.

The difficulties here are beautifully reviewed and analysed in *Stealth Democracy: Americans' beliefs about how governments should work*, in which John R Hibbing and Elizabeth Theiss-Morse (of the University of Nebraska-Lincoln)[15] explode the myths that membership of single-issue campaigns or involvement in local or any other politics are likely solutions to voter disengagement. They suggest, rather, that most of us do not want to get involved in politics. The authors are anxious to avoid the accusation that they are elitists proposing an elitist politics. But they do urge that 'American politics will not be improved by pretending people are something that they are not; it will be improved by first determining the people's preferences and then initiating the delicate process of moulding democratic processes to suit people's preferences while simultaneously moulding people's preferences to suit realistic democratic processes.'

Contrary to almost all the rhetoric of modern politics, people share the view of one of John Updike's characters that it is a sacred American freedom not to have to think about politics. In that case, they will have to learn to create and trust a professional elite of politicians to do that tiresome work for them. That process will require maturity. One has to find a class of politician and official worth trusting, and then not merely choose between them, but trust them. The modern cult of contempt makes the process tricky.

THE DEMANDING SOCIETY

We do indeed have to account for the rise in anger in society. It seems to be real, and it seems to be explained by people not getting what they are used to getting. This is very different to the diagnosis offered by the Anxiety Status people: that people are angry because they are not getting what they believe they have been promised (by advertising, say), or what someone else has (the envy thing). And of course it is different to being angry about deprivation.

Consider these propositions:

- We are the first generation to expect, even demand, happiness. We are angry when we find how elusive it remains.
- We are the first generation to be ungrateful. We insist that we are worth what we have, rather than are lucky to have it.
- We are the first generation to expect security. We are used to being safe, and are angry when we find life is not safe.
- We are the first generation to suffer the inconvenience of Mass Affluence. The inconvenience of others' affluence angers us.

It is surely true, for instance, that people are less well behaved on the road. But the impatient tailgater is trying to go faster than the legally driven car in front because his car can go fast, and he likes to drive fast, and is angry to find he cannot. Isn't road rage rather well explained by the idea that people, in their satisfactory bubble of self-gratification, seem to be losing the capacity for forbearance of others? They want whatever they want, and they want it now ('I want it all, and I want it now', in Freddy Mercury's fabulous anthem to excess). They are not used to not having what they want. They are spoiled, and the only solution is for them to come to terms with the fact that they cannot always, everywhere, under all circumstances have what they want.

Modern people want a very great deal, and some seem to find it hard to juggle their options. But it is their infantilism that makes it hard, not the existence of choice.

THE DECLINE OF 'COMPULSORY BELONGING'

A further source of misery might be attributed to the decline of status, rather than to its oppressive presence.

People are no longer constrained, disciplined or supported by class, geography, education, religion, rationality or social mores. Compulsion of any kind has been at a discount since the 1960s social revolution. These were all solid, external marker buoys by which we navigated. They didn't shift, and, if we strayed, we could always return to them. Now, we have to make ourselves up, and it is exhilarating when it's going well. When it goes badly, we are at sea.

A striking feature of life until very recently was that people belonged to a structured world. There was a world of 'Compulsory Belonging' (a coining of my own). One used to be rooted in geography (a nation state, and a particular place within it), a faith (in the religious sense), a gender, a social status (a class), a culture (of food, music, and much more), a belief (I mean in the secular sense: capitalist, nationalist, and so on). One was allowed to believe some very comforting things about one's life – indeed, there was a high price to be paid for dissidence, disbelief, disrespect. Mobility of any sort – geographical, social or cultural – often, usually, came at a very high price.

THE LOSS OF RELIGION

Formal old-fashioned religion explained an enormous amount about the world and the unworldly, and it provided a powerful backup to terrestrial ideas about good and evil. Its passing leaves many cultures and individuals very alone. That much is obvious. Less remarked is the irrationality that has flowed from the decline in religion.

The most famous remark in this area was G K Chesterton's, to the effect that once people lose the ability to believe in God they gain the ability to believe anything. He hit on the difficulty that people believe they are freeing themselves from nonsense when they slough off religious faith. But what do we see instead? The faith vacuum is filled by astrology, New Age mysticism, crank medicine and junk science. What is more, and less noticed, is the role of civilised Churches in positively proclaiming that we owe them the faith part of our lives, and that the evidential belongs to science.

Religion tied people to rationality much more securely even than it tied them to faith. The great religions of the West centuries ago came to terms with the gulf between their world and that of science. That delineation became part of the apparatus whereby scientific truth was understood to have very special qualities. The abandonment of faith and these delineations had the paradoxical effect of opening the way for junk science and all kinds of weird nostrums, which now occupy a hinterland between science and religion – a hinterland that faith once kept clear with a cleansing and withering fire. Nature, for instance, became a proxy for religion, and everything human was put at a discount in many people's minds. This has proved corrosive of their well-being.

THE LOSS OF AUTHORITY

Perhaps the most pervasive modern disorientation is in the world of human authority. It is no longer respectable to trust anyone. What once defined respectability, now defines a feeble-mindedness. Institutions are now regarded as inherently oppressive; people who run anything are required to be distrusted; the expert is regarded as a fraud.

THE UNDEMANDING SOCIETY

A further source of misery is the absence of challenge.

Compulsory risk and danger have been taken away from us, and now people find themselves surprised, but seeking them out. However, there is no exigency about voluntary risk, any more than there is about voluntary poverty, or voluntary labour. It is unnerving to be choosing the kind of experiences a previous generation delightedly escaped from. Exigency, necessity – we lack these now. With luck we won't have them back.

Suppose we are obscurely unsettled by the lack of exigency; might that not explain not merely our passion for extreme sports, but also the Rave Culture, drugs and drinking? Half the drinking that goes on now – and much of the drug use – is about using pharmacology to find one's way to the wild, the unrestrained, the desperate. It isn't much, but being sick in a gutter is about as close as modern young people get to the atavistic, the truly primitive. At home and work, there is only pleasantness. Employers bend over backwards to keep them motivated. Canny merchants meet their needs and anticipate their aspirations. Face down in the drizzle, snorkelling a puddle, they know, once a week, what it is to be at rock bottom – at least briefly. Kindly liberalism may have banished initiation rites for young people, so they have invented their own, in imitation of the drinking parties soldiers have always found useful. (It is noted by Anthony Blond that aspiring officers being trained by the British Army were given a 'mess night', which was run by a junior officer on strict orders to get his guests wholly drunk: it was important to know which men got aggressive when drunk. That sort was dangerous.)[16]

Now that danger is a luxury, it comes surrounded by choices and accommodations. Risk, wilderness, tedium, labour: these have all been banished, except as things we volunteer for. But volunteering for them makes them just another luxury, just another choice, a form of consumable. A man without a GPS in the Antarctic is choosing not to be able to tell his rescuers where he is. Is he being irresponsible? Or brave? Is he putting others at risk because he wants to smell risk? In the modern world, people who have adventures have to strike a deal with themselves, their relatives, and those who will come to rescue them. How much risk should be allowed?

As we look about for sources of misery, it is important not to overlook what is perhaps the most obvious. There doesn't seem to be one. Many lives these days are lived without danger, unpleasantness, risk, or drama. It is possible to manage quite a pleasant life without struggle, and there is no requirement for people to put themselves on the line for anything. All around, failure is excused, risk-taking deprecated (or made illegal). The poor once had admirable traits of forbearance and patience: now these are not required and have been abandoned.

A 'good war' would sort that out, of course; or a recession. Even a small disaster does some small-scale 'good' (a train crash, for instance, produces a sudden occurrence of the 'kindness of strangers'), and a large one would do large 'good'. An epidemic might make us buck up our ideas. But we ought to hope that we don't need to lurch from crisis to crisis as the only way to top up on virtue.

Because it is now accepted that we are children, prone to petulance and rudeness, in need of help and nurture, not discipline and danger, we live in a world in which we make excuses for ourselves and for others, and expect the favour to be returned by others. What we don't notice in all this mechanised kindness is that we are building up no reserves of strength. We are like those children who now suffer asthma because they have not been exposed to dirt. We are suffering because too little that is nasty has happened. We crumple, because we are not used to blame.

THE UNAUTHENTIC MODERN

One of the kinder things one can say is that moderns do face a disorienting modernity. It flows from Post Modern anxiety that nothing is authentic any more.

The English have been a wonderful people, with their easeful scruffiness, their haphazardness. They have lived in a world of unreconstructed antiquity (their landscapes and cities are old and not quite tamed). But now, there must be more order. We are driving cars, not carts. Our cleaning is done by chemicals, not soap (or not at all) as in the past. So many of us are tourists now, the countryside must have car parks and signs and lavatories (sorry, toilets). So much of our environment has been refashioned for our convenience that we are forced to see how the authentic – the worn, rubbed, dilapidated – has been eroded.

THE FAMILY MALAISE: MODERN CHILD-REARING

Recent research has accentuated how young women would rather be well off than start a family. The researchers found that couples wanted children, but not yet. Doubtless, part of the effect flowed from women wanting their career to be well under way before putting it on hold. It would be logical enough to want to bank a solid CV before taking time out from reputation-building. They did not want to jeopardise their lifestyle for child-rearing. They delayed child-rearing until they achieved an income that could sustain the addition of children without much denting their lifestyle. This is called 'consumption smoothing'.

The upshot is that women are having children a little later than they did 20 years ago (and probably later than their parents did), and they have fewer children when they do start. That may merely be a small, sensible adjustment. But it may be a sign that young couples have got their priorities in a muddle.

It is very likely that most women (and some men) who have had children would rank that as the single most important work they ever did in their lives. It is true that some work is so compelling that it is worth sacrificing having children, or sacrificing some of the well-being of one's children, to pursue it. It is also true that children don't necessarily suffer when their interests are not always foremost in their parents' minds. Still, something has gone wrong when so many people rank ambition and lifestyle above family. Sure, there's a tension between them all, and, sure, different people will arrive at different balances. But it's probable that quite a lot of people are getting the equation a tad out of kilter. It might be, and one rather hopes it is, the case that delaying child-rearing is thoroughly rational and works out well. There is evidence that couples in their thirties really are better able to 'have it all'.

But read this passage from the report:

Our survey found that people in their thirties without children were likely to be more financially stable and able to support a child but paradoxically appeared to be more concerned with the potential impact of having a child on their income and lifestyle. This desire to minimise the impact of children on quality of life – symbolised by spending and consumption habits – has an impact on those with and without children. It can hold people back from having another child or can mean those without children delay having them.[17]

Doesn't this argue that couples in their thirties risk foregoing the greatest satisfaction in life, for fear of losing material lifestyle? Anyway, none of this is an argument against Mass Affluence. Affluence will make it easier to have a good lifestyle and children, and a career and children. It makes these balances easier, not harder, to get right.

THE SUDDENNESS OF AFFLUENCE

Our modern malaises – rudeness, trash consumption, infantilism – flow in part from the suddenness of affluence, to its coming to people as an explosion of opportunity, unbidden, easily, unmerited even.

The present generation of ex-working class people are the first in their families to know anything like affluence. It is hardly surprising they spend it on 'bad' things like fast food, rather than 'good' things like books. Time will bring the grace that prolonged affluence tended to bring to the middle and upper classes of old.

THE MEDIA

There is a mass of commentary that aspires to seriousness, but is constrained by broadcast regulations to be politically impartial. The effect of this is that the *Today* programme, *Newsnight* (especially when Jeremy Paxman is driving) or Channel 4 *News* (when Jon Snow is in one of his periodic combative moods) speak truth to power 'impartially' by being aggressive. Their target is anyone who has to make society work (business people, officials, politicians), and they pander to anyone who can claim to be a campaigner or a victim.

There was, several years ago, a marvellous moment when the Archbishop of York, John Habgood (quoted above), was being quizzed by Jeremy Paxman on *Newsnight*. The archbishop said there was a dangerous 'culture of contempt' abroad. What did he mean, asked JP? 'Well, people like you, Jeremy. Interviewers.' (I'm quoting his words from memory.) The biter was truly bit. It is, however, only a small minority of the audience that is uneasy: the majority accepts the media's own gloss that its combativeness is proof of its integrity.

So we live in the peculiar circumstance in which those who identify, analyse and assume a malaise in society are actually a large part of it.

1 Andrew Pierce, 'Vest is Never Best For a Man Over 50', *The Times*, August 2004.

2 Alan Judd, 'Chips With Everything', *The Spectator*, 24 July 2004.

3 Adam Curtis, *Century of the Self*, BBC TV, 2002.

4 Susan A Greenfield, *The Private Life of the Brain*, Allen Lane, 2000.

5 Frank Furedi, *Where Have All the Intellectuals Gone?: Confronting 21st century philistinism*, Continuum, 2004.

6 See Noel Malcolm, 'How Highbrows Were Brought Low: Intellectuals largely have themselves to blame for the dumbing down of our society', *Sunday Telegraph*, 3 October 2004.

7 See www.margaretthatcher.org/speeches/displaydocument.asp?docid=106689.

8 Patti Waldmeir, 'Seek and Ye Shall Find', *FT* Magazine, 4 September 2004.

9 Elizabeth Day, 'Charity Shops Lose Out As Secondhand Goods Go to Internet Auctions', *Sunday Telegraph*, 15 August 2004.

10 *Centesimus Annus*, Papal encyclical by Pope John Paul II, Catholic Truth Society/Veritas, undated.

11 *Rerum Novarum*, Encyclical letter of Pope Leo XIII on the condition of the working classes, Catholic Truth Society, 1891 (1991 edition).

12 John Habgood, *Priestland Memorial Lecture*, BBC Radio, 8 October 1995; and Bishop Donal Murray, Auxiliary Bishop of Dublin (Ireland), 'The Culture of the Nation in Christian Perspective', Université Urbanienne, Rome, 30 November 1995; and www.vatican.va/roman_curia/pontifical_councils/cultr/documents/rc_pc_cultr_01031996_doc_i-1996-stu_en.html.

13 'Your Guide to the Forces of Conservatism', *Observer*, 3 October 1999.

14 Samuel Beer, *Modern British Politics: A study of parties and pressure groups*, Faber, 1965.

15 John R Hibbing and Elizabeth Theiss-Morse, *Stealth Democracy: Americans' beliefs about how governments should work*, Cambridge University Press, 2002.

16 Anthony Blond, *Jew Made in England*, Timewell Press, 2004.

17 *Choosing Happiness?*, IPPR/Faberge, 2003.

CHAPTER 11

CONCLUSION

There is a strong and delicious possibility that the solutions to the problems of Mass Affluence will lie quite simply – automatically, even – in the processes of action and reaction that have always made fashions come and go. We do not need to become better, nicer, more wonderful people for the world of the Mass Affluent to become more attractive. We need merely to stop blaming affluence for our woes, and to consider coolly and accurately what we dislike about our lives.

As surely as the Stuart immoralists produced the Interregnum puritans, as 'The Laughing Cavalier' morphed into Cromwell (to put it in stereotypical terms), as the louche Regency produced the upright Victorians, and as the pre-War flappers produced the post-War suburbanites, so the normal reaction will set in. These attitudes and mood swings are normal for a society, and they matter. Manners and morals constantly shift between the libertine and licentious and the polite and pretty. As surely as the flower-power print transmuted into the punk's zipper, the current state of speech and style will witness a backlash.

The normality of these fluxes is a comfort, or ought to be. If they were seriously weird, that would suggest that our times are out of joint in a big way. They are not. We do not have to dignify our little problems by pathologising them. We are not sick; our society is not sick. But whenever was so much success sought and found, and yet fretted over? We have all experienced the young woman tailgating her way to a therapy session. Why not be a little more chilled during the day, and a bit more matter-of-fact at night? When did the British aspire to seem rushed, harassed and impatient? Where did the gentlemanly, 'after you' reflex go? Being considerate was the small luxury even the poor could attain; it was the small largesse demanded of the advantaged as the bare minimum of their social status. We can have it back.

Our problems can be defined as modern, and yet we might as truly say that we are tested with the lovely old array of sins and virtues, and must make good old classical choices. Anger, sloth, gluttony, envy, pride, lust, greed are all there in the bushes, and against them we need the old virtues of fortitude, patience, temperance and justice. How comforting that all we need do is deal with these things as our forebears dealt with them. When we look honestly at our lives, we can see that modernity has not made any of the sins more powerful, nor any of the virtues less necessary.

Great-granny's needlepoint homily is as useful now as ever, and no harder to obey. We just haven't prized the words of wisdom as we should. Indeed, we sneered at them, and the only trades to benefit have been those of the charlatan, the fakir, the pseudo-guru and the false prophet.

We have the first generation of an affluent majority, and we have the first generation to make a mass cult of unhappiness, pressure and stress. But it is not the affluence, or the condition, of society that has led to this, but the misreading of circumstances.

Sure, Mass Affluence is a big new thing, and it takes a bit of getting used to. But that's about the size of it. The squadrons of books that have embarked upon this sea have almost all assumed that the phenomenon is large and threatening, and that modern people may need to unwind some of the 'progress', and shelter from it, rather than take a deep breath and consider if they are failing the world around them.

If the modern world has a malaise, it is rather the absence of grace, respect, boldness and trust, than the presence of money or the overwhelming difficulty it presents.

Modern societies do not take wealth creation to be the only ambition or target one needs. Societies take leisure, redistribution, the environment, and a mass of social indicators into account as they aim to increase wealth. It turns out that rounded societies produce economic growth better than narrow ones. Or rather, we simply have no experience of mean societies doing well. Thus the critics of affluence have their work cut out, since they have to argue that those states that are manifestly already quite socially minded should be yet more so.

The left also face the difficulty that few individuals take wealth creation as their sole aim. And even those that do can be obsessive mavericks only within the bounds of polite societies that outlaw the more obviously brutal approaches to wealth creation. In some very young states – Russia, for instance – wealth creation is possible on a scale not seen since the late nineteenth century in America. But the state-sanctioned purloining of national assets by the 'Oligarchs' will probably soon be unwound: the 'Oligarchs' will presumably end up compensating the state for their sudden accretions. In the rest of the western world, regulation is such that only socially acceptable wealth creation is legal.

When we come to the spending of wealth, it clearly takes many different forms, all of them arguably good for society. Many very rich people, to take an extreme case, are very frugal in their own spending (leaving their wealth in the economy as investment); many others are very socially munificent (doing the redistribution the taxman was cheated out of). It is probable that the open-handed extravagance of spendthrifts is nearly as socially redistributive and beneficial as the taxman's demand. Can one buy a yacht or a country estate – or anything else – without usefully spreading one's wealth?

In any case, many of the most talented people in our society opt for power, influence or creativity over wealth creation. Politicians, journalists and artists of every kind can indeed get rich, and some are very ambitious for wealth, but none of them see the likelihood or the degree of wealth that bankers, lawyers and even entrepreneurs (always a risk-prone subset of the economically active) achieve. The theatre finds its angels, newspapers their backers: the rich seek glamour and influence, and, as they do so, pay for things we all enjoy.

All this is to go toward saying that western societies are not particularly materialist. Nor are the rich the most materialist class, nor are the 'meaningful' unmaterialist.

POLITICS

Nothing will take away the fact of conflict, or all the pain of being overruled. But the acceptance that some people have to lose out when any decision is made is crucial to a happy life in a democracy.

It is very likely that, by misunderstanding the accommodations that liberty requires, we increase the pain and distress we feel. By denigrating the state of democracy, we wilfully inflict a sense that what has been done to us was done arbitrarily. If we insist on underrating our democracy, we volunteer for distress.

The remedy here is to read Isaiah Berlin (or John Stuart Mill), or very nearly any writing on the British Constitution. The 'powerless', 'alienated' British have only to know where their government came from, and what it has been, to understand how strong our democracy is, and how much we should mourn its trivialisation both by those who run it, and by those who comment on it. We cannot hope that the masses will read political philosophy: one day, the journalists who tell them about the world will come to their senses and pass on some elementary, ancient understanding of liberty and government.

We have probably at last emerged at a political consensus that suggests taxation is not a good way of expressing social interdependency. Indeed, the profoundest political change of the recent past will continue to dominate politics for the immediate future. That is, how to get the

Mass Affluent to pay their share of some public goods, while preserving a safety net for the poor?

Paying proper prices and philanthropy will probably emerge as the way to produce both a fair society and a coherent one. I say this as someone who believes that the most difficult problem in modern politics is to provide education and health services that are, so far as possible, shared by everyone. So the trick is: how to get those who can, to pay. And how to enable the poor without making them overly dependent?

Philanthropy will play a role here. It is no use saying that only the rich can afford philanthropy, and they won't cough up. There are now oceans of rich people in the West, and harnessing their goodwill may do them a power of good. Philanthropic giving in the US has more than doubled in real terms since 1963. It runs at getting on for three per cent of GDP in the USA and the UK alike, though volunteering time, rather than money, is a bigger factor in the UK than in the US. (Volunteering cash rather than time is a bigger factor in either country than it is in countries such as Sweden and the Netherlands, which are much more generous, but where voluntary activity is the biggest form of philanthropy.[1]) It may be easier – more practical – to have a mass movement in favour of giving, than to hope to develop a political consensus on raising taxation. It is also plausible to argue that taxation is an economic disincentive, while philanthropy is an economic incentive. Philanthropy may be society's best hope for kindliness, as well as being to the benefit of the person doing it. It is presumed that philanthropy cripples the poor by requiring them to be grateful. We should say, rather, that if philanthropy ennobles the donor, it will do the poor no harm to know that the generosity of a real person has been deployed for their benefit. The graceless 'rights-ism' of the poor is, after all, part of why the middle classes distrust and dislike them, and are disinclined to fund them.

The advantage of taxation is that it is raised on citizens who are shamed into agreeing to pay tax in the heat of elections, and at rates that they might not – would not – volunteer in the quiet of their homes as they fill in their tax returns and await the taxman's demands. That is to say, the state makes us kinder than we would be voluntarily – or rather, holds us to our promises of kindness. What's more, in modern societies there is a great deal of 'churn': people pay high taxes, knowing they do well out of them. A right-winger is free to say that these are mechanisms that numb us to the damage welfarism does.

This is all changing. We have good evidence that politicians of left and right agree now that there is, in each country, a certain level of taxation above which votes will be lost by any party, and that that level is edging downward. Socialism by government does not now seem to be a runner.

The left claims that poverty is getting worse because the last twenty-odd years have seen a rightward drift in economic policy. The case in this book is that poverty has been reduced and eased, and perhaps precisely because of modern economic policy. But it is not part of this book's worldview that we can ignore the misery of poverty, nor that we should necessarily edge away from the kind of policies that, say, the Blair government has introduced with the intention of reducing poverty.

We can reduce poverty by redistributive policy or by economic growth. Probably one is useless without the other. Blair's government can only persuade middle-class people to switch some wealth toward poverty-reduction if they are doing well enough not to notice much.

It is likely that in the future, the poor and rich alike will have to realise that their relationship with each other is essentially voluntary. The state will not interfere nearly as much as it has for half a century.

The same sort of argument may apply to our willingness to take on debt, and our reluctance to buy life insurance. All are cases where we may not have properly thought through the future, and where we may be wise to remember older values than are now prevalent. Part of this is to say that we may not be as rich as we think we are. And part of it is to say that we may overrate material pleasures and misunderstand emotional ones. These failings will probably, in large measure, be put right as time unfolds and the children of the present Mass Affluent decide that this or that fashion or habit needs to be developed or overturned. Again, our being rich will make it easier when we discover, if we do, that we are over-indebted, underinsured or would like to downsize.

PUTTING THINGS RIGHT

Many features of the modern – the Culture of Contempt, Embarrassed Loyalties, the demanding society, the decline of deference, the undemanding society – conspire together to make life difficult, though they appear to make life easier. They are all the result of getting what we hoped for, and were right to hope for. We got things we wanted and are right to want; but they have all come at a cost in unintended consequences. So what else is new?

People of intelligence now sense that there is something at once nihilistic and nannying about modern society, and that this must be addressed.

Luckily, the answer is to embrace challenge. Where once challenges came looking for people, now people have to go and seek them out.

People always did have to opt for challenges. But now that life is so easy, this is more than ever necessary. We have to prove that we have not been enfeebled by good fortune.

A RETURN TO POLITENESS

Politeness was always prized when most people really couldn't get what they wanted. It was understood that only children could be excused for lapses in politeness, and even they were censured for them. Current bad behaviour is seldom more than trivial selfishness. A slight shift in fashion and habit has introduced it: it can as easily be reversed, or turned into a new sense of proper and attractive behaviour.

A RETURN TO ADULTHOOD

The next generation will renounce infantilism: they will refuse to be nannied, and will insist on their duty and right to assert themselves as adults in the public and private sphere.

A RETURN TO DEFERENCE

Similarly, once people fully realise that respecting people of quality is no longer obligatory, but is necessary to a good society, excellence will again be prized. This is important. At the moment, talent gravitates toward monetary reward. But there are many important roles in society that are never likely to attract much money. A judge, nurse, politician or teacher is never likely to be well paid; a volunteer, by definition, isn't. We will need to reclaim respect from its 'gangsta rap' meaning. Respect is what one earns, not what one is owed.

A RETURN TO SERVICE

It is a pity that more people aren't offering to engage in political activity, and that very few indeed are offering to become managers and overseers of the Archipelago State by which modern governments seek to outsource the management of much of the old state. (I am thinking of health and school trusts, for instance.)

While people complain that there is a democratic deficit, and that they feel excluded, actually the modern Archipelago State is holding out thousands of opportunities for people, not merely to influence, but positively to help control the world around them. But they would, for now, rather complain.

All this will deliciously change as we grow into Mass Affluence and discard the culture of blaming others for our miseries and malaises.

1 'Doing Well and Doing Good', *The Economist*, 31 July 2004.

RDN'S PREJUDICES

As you pick up a book, it is best to be clear about its writer's prejudices. Come to that, as one begins to write a book, it is best to be clear about them, too.

It would be nice to say that all my positions are the logical outcome of quiet, rational thought, based on a perfectly large mass of data. But I am a great believer in William James, the American philosopher (or thinker, anyway), who thought that temperament usually underpins what we think. That, and upbringing, I would add, though upbringing works by attraction and reaction in complicated and unpredictable – unchartable – ways. And perhaps awful old Freud is right about some of that. I hope not.

So, here goes. I have been asked to write a book in defence of wealth, and I am thrilled to do so, since it is a theme that has been in my mind for many years. Moreover, it is The Book that remains to be written. By that I mean the world needs such a book. This is not, of course, to say that mine will be a good book. It may do its best by being a bold attempt.

It is also the subject that remains, now that I have rather lost interest in a strongly related area. For after a couple of decades worrying about the environment and environmentalism (they are equally worrying), and about Third World development (why there was less of it than there should have been), the business of affluence seems to me both key and poorly discussed.

I should also say that the 'problem' of affluence is the problem that brought me into environmentalism – into greenery – in the first place. It is the heart of much of what my sort of environmentalism was about.

It is also by far the greatest difficulty that environmentalists address. To outsiders, the environment seemed like a technical matter – a matter of drains and smokestacks. And maybe of the conservation of forest and species, too. To its real fans, it was much more than that. And – I am pretty sure – its adherents were most wrong when they addressed this inner heart of their subject. In short, they were more wrong about the aesthetics, the morality, the point of wealth, than they were about the ecology of its production and consumption; more wrong about the spiritual matters that lurked in the heart of their concern, even than they were about the terrestrial matters that they ostensibly drew our attention to. I should perhaps celebrate their seriousness, but instead I find myself a little repelled by their negativity. (They say, of course, that I am cynical and in denial, while they are standing on a high headland, watching the dawn and willing a better future out of it.)

I am tolerably clear about what I think about the environment, and I am fairly clear about Third World development, as globalization used to be called. I have become pretty clear about capitalism. That's to say: I think the Third World could do with the kind of liberties that underpin western society, and I think capitalism is a very remarkable wealth-creating machine, which flows from these liberties, as night follows day. In short, I am content with the Western Project and the Enlightenment. The important features of civilisation have been understood for a couple of thousand years. They have proved themselves in the western world (which has slighted them too much) and are badly needed in the Third World (where they are slighted and hungered after in about equal measure).

So much you might expect to hear from a fairly ordinary supporter of a free-market think tank such as the Institute of Economic Affairs (whose media fellow it has been my great pleasure to be) and of the Social Affairs Unit (whose broadly conservative agenda I am rather a fan of and which commissioned this book).

I am, of course, a conflicted free-marketer; but that's fine too, since I find very few of those who share that persuasion are other than conflicted. We are all of us fascinated by the degree to which good government is essential to the project of the market. We differ in the amount of government interference we support; but I think we all agree both that there should be some, and that there should be as little as possible. This is not mealy-mouthed. Even loving and caring about government as much as I do (which is more than many free-market people), I loathe 'the left' and its passion for regulation. Even more than its longing to shackle the vigour of the market, I dislike its premise that 'The People' are systematically put at threat by those who run the firms that provide everything upon which life depends, and by the wealth that capitalism cheerfully allows to spread rather widely.

The left exists to complain, and to encourage others to complain. I am instinctively on the side of those who are the subject of all this moaning. When I watch consumer programmes, I instinctively side with the scam-merchants who are beset by a rising tide of self-righteousness from parasitic campaigners and journalists. The fact is, right or wrong, I am on the side of the 'do-ers' against the 'do-gooders'. Nothing very remarkable here: a taste for the underdog makes one identify with whoever is being hounded by the press, and whoever is in handcuffs.

Now we are in the interesting territory I want to address in this note on my prejudices. I fear some autobiography is in order.

I am self-taught. That's to say, though I attended (fee-paying) 'preparatory' and 'public' secondary schools, I failed the latter's exams, and then went to what we used to call 'Tech' – a further education college, where I think I passed an exam (in British Constitution, 'A' level). Much later, I went, aged 25, to university (Cambridge) to study philosophy, I didn't last very long there, and left early without sitting exams.

I am not exactly a wolf-child, however. In the ordinary way of a public school boy in the 50s and 60s, and perhaps more than some, I read history and English literature willingly, if wilfully. By willingly, I mean that I read more than the curriculum demanded; by wilfully, I mean that I didn't study all that the curriculum demanded. Indeed, I think I read intensely for pleasure, and not studiously for examination purposes.

I do not want to over-egg the effect of this informality of learning, but I think it means that I am suspicious of orthodoxies and am an outsider. I speak like a middle-class person, and am rather more than ordinarily snobbish, yet I have a visceral dislike of middle-class smugness and middle-class certainties. Since the middle class is notable for its affluence, security and left-leaning views – none of which I share – I would say that my peculiar position is to be in a kind of awkward squad.

I should, perhaps, add a rider here: though I sound like an educated middle-class person, I do not think like one. Indeed, in some respects I have more sympathy with the uneducated new middle-class modern Mass Affluence has created. I like vulgarity, excess and extravagance. I understand bling. But then, I like the picaresque almost as much as the picturesque. And I usually opt for the greasy spoon over the Starbucks, and the roadside snack caravan over McDonald's. But not always. I go to Starbucks when I want only to be among fairly well-behaved and clean young people; and I go to McDonald's when I suddenly want a hamburger (a thing one wants very much from time to time).

But I do not want to exaggerate my disaffection and peculiarity. I am pretty happy with almost everything I read in the *Telegraph*, which is the middle-brow, middle-class paper bought by a million people a day, and whose general tenor must be shared by many more. I am a natural *Spectator* reader (though of late it has peppered its Toryism with rather too much of the adjectivally picaresque; I feel tweedy when I read the *Spectator*, and it has just got into ripped jeans). Of course, I draw the line at the *Daily Mail*, a paper that is strident and disloyal (one day inveighing against what it next day stoutly defends). But then, I prefer the patrician to the populist. I believe in unpopularity. I think 'The People' and the mob are almost always wrong.

I do, however, believe in the value of the basic hooliganism of the Anglo-Saxon. The British hate orthodoxy: they dislike its uniformity, its bossiness, its absence of nuance. We do not like the inescapably logical, and the counter-intuitive will always exert an appeal. The British are inclined to behave badly, but not so it matters. (In contrast, one feels, to the Continentals who behave terribly well until the consequences of so much passivity cause the outbreak of street rebellion, riot and revolution.) The middle class, if it has a failing, believes in repression. To that extent, there is something in the view, expressed by Lord Randolph Churchill, that: 'The aristocracy and the working classes will always unite against the middle classes in their love of sport and immorality.'[1]

And yet I recoil from the mechanical and joyless libertinism of recent social revolutions. Hedonism never whinged so much as in the social revolution of the 1960s.

I am a natural conservative of the reactionary school, in that I think 1960s liberalism has spoiled much more than it has enhanced. In other words, I think my own generation has been a wrecking generation. Yes, I know that this is what any generation in its middle age is inclined to believe; and yes, much has improved; and, yes, I was in the vanguard of some of the changes. But the fact is, when Swinging London and the Sunday Supplement social revolutionaries were trumpeting change – even back then – I was not a part of the movement.

Jill Tweedie and Bel Mooney were never my idea of clever and interesting.

I thought the middle classes were comical, when they espoused the aesthetic of the Provencal kitchen while avoiding any of the reality that underpinned its real attractiveness. They were pernickety, when their ideal was earthy. Contrariwise, I had not read Zola, but I knew we were doing something odd when we flinched at the appearance of peasanthood, even as we finally abandoned anything of its morality (or bigotry, more like).

It never seemed likely to me that women 'could have it all', or that they were much oppressed in recent history. Feminism produced very few insights of value, and it mostly demonstrated the opposite of the case it sought to put. The rows between feminists showed how little being female provided a coherent or valuable vantage place from which to view matters.

I was becoming a dissident – but not against The Establishment or the Powers That Be. I was a dissident against what I took to be a liberal hegemony. Perhaps I wanted to be the outsider's outsider; but not from any sense that I would profit from this vantage point. I did not feel my position was contrived, and it did me no good. I could not show off my position to anyone, or parlay it into anything. It was the place (as we say now) that my prejudices and experience took me.

I can describe some of these positions quite easily. I had very much enjoyed reading nineteenth and twentieth-century writing on the British Constitution: I thought British parliamentary government, and its Whitehall administration, one of the loveliest things made by man. I was a patriot. By that I mean I was inclined to celebrate the things Britain had done, and the bits of its present that reflected its past. Military pageant in London, royal funerals and marriages, British Empire, British trade and industry – these were all things I was inclined to admire. I did not like to see them fail (which they sometimes did, both morally and technically) and I did not like to see them criticised (which they often were). I might feel shame at the state of British management and manufacturing (the executive who thought management was best done on the golf course or the British Leyland car that could not go out in the rain), but I did not enjoy listening to those who enjoyed criticising these failings as 'typical' of 'this country'.

Someone said that the liberal loves every country more than his own, and it is a trenchant criticism.

I could, and did, claim – still do – that the generation that fought two world wars deserved better than this. They had died defending better values than these. And yet, of course, the young who went to war in these wars – and especially in the second – were often cynical and anti-Establishment themselves. The wars did not turn them into reactionaries such as I was: the wars took in working-class and middle-class conservatives, and turned many of them into middle-of-the-road socialists. Their new enthusiasm explains the 1945 election victory for Labour. Arguably, it took them until the late 70s to work out fully that socialism was grim and useless.

The left and the social revolutionaries struck me as mildly – trivially, but irritatingly – traitorous, or treacherous, in their dislike of Britishness.

I have flirted with the right, of course. More or less a neo-liberal in economic terms, I read the *Spectator*, mostly with pleasure. Something of a reactionary, I don't give money to beggars and think prison should be hard work. But I don't worry about the decline of British society in quite the way that is habitual with, say, Roger Scruton, Digby Anderson or Anthony O'Hear. They seem to relish the decadence of Britain as though it were real, deserved and permanent. Having abandoned some-thing big – like tradition, the classics, or whatever – our sorry plight (as they see it) is merited. I would rather see the British condition as being a patchy relapse into a part of Britishness that is always there. Our scruffy philistinism, our cultivated yobbishness, our unreflective multicultural-ism – these are all dreary, limited and surmountable.

I was and am a snob. This takes the form of a dislike of lower middle-class uptightness (now largely banished, and more easily mourn-ed in its absence). I am patronising about the working class (except when they are fighting British wars or bravely upholding British values, in the police or fire services, for instance, or fixing something I can't, or looking after the infirm) and admiring of the upper classes (except when they are excessively chinless or arrogant). I regard Royalty as wholly admirable as a general principle. The Queen strikes me as A Very Good Thing, and never more so than when she resisted the hysteria surrounding Diana's death, at least for the crucial few days when she kept 'The Boys' away from the maelstrom.

Among other effects, my snobbery produced a dislike of Margaret Thatcher: the elocution class showed too clearly. Of course, I was interested in her ambition to have the country run like a lower middle-class suburb, when her true effect was to release the lower middle class from their niche, at once subservient and superior. They became indebt-ed and inebriated, just as the upper and lower orders had always been. Always squeezed and unhappy, they abandoned their unpopular fight for respectability, and went down to Alicante, the pub, and the mall. I am afraid I enjoyed her comeuppance, as her natural supporters took the money and ran. At least she had freed us all from the tyranny of unions run like gangs.

Oddly, perverse to the last, I found one of the last outposts of the lower middle class – the campaign for public decency – very attractive. Mary Whitehouse's permed assault on television's pornographers was far more right than wrong, though the violence was more reprehensible than the sex. Doubtless, she will one day be celebrated as prescient. In an age – ours – in which Norman Tebbit has become a national treas-ure, can her rehabilitation be far behind? I am, of course, a cheerful con-sumer of soft pornography: how absurd for anyone to claim to be immune to its charms. And can't *Pulp Fiction* or *LA Confidential* or *Seven* all claim to be among the great creations of our time?

I was and am a snob, knowing how absurd snobbery always was, but also wondering what it would become. Britain's class system was always markedly porous (as was remarked upon by most foreign observers with eyes in their heads, and especially Voltaire).[2] And it never defined people (as is clear from, say, the David Lean/Noel Coward 1944 film *This Happy Breed*). We do not need the old stratifications back, but we do badly need to reassert the merit of the class with which I identify: the middle class with bohemian overtones.

At this rate, I will have you see me as a very old-fashioned type, and I am not. I fell, indeed, for one of the fashions of the 70s: environmentalism. (No, two: I was a confirmed ligger at London's rock and reggae scene.) I can claim, at least, to have done this a little differently to most.

In the early 70s I read, and thought profound, the works of Ivan Illich. His Big Idea was that industrialisation and institutionalisation had produced the effect that our needs and wants were now being provided by means that were manufactured or professionalised. I was hugely drawn to this sort of view, and duly proposed that children should be taught at home and that the private car was anathema. I went, though, with neither: my young family went to school and we acquired a car. I might as well confess it: I was a domestic tyrant – more or less forcing cycling, the lack of a TV and veganism on my young family, at least until I got bored with it all.

But I do not think that as a 'green' radical in the 70s, I was other than a reactionary, too. I don't subscribe to the view that the green movement is next door to a fascist one, or anything like it. But in those years, I was intensely nostalgic for bits of the British past. Throughout my late twenties and thirties, I was romantically attached to the industrial architecture of Britain, even while – from my thirtieth birthday – I was writing about show business and especially about rock music and reggae.

I took my bike with me on the train to Cannes, to hang out with The Who for an *Observer* piece about their 1979 movie of *Quadrophenia* (I hated its celebration of violence). I declined to fly Concorde (or any other plane) to hang out with my great hero, Bob Marley, in Jamaica (as offered by his record company). Marley was, by the way, one of the few people I have ever met who seemed to me a sort of saint. I spent a little time with him in July 1980: I dogged his footsteps as he prepared in Brighton in July 1980 for what would be among the last handful of gigs he ever performed. He was gentle and gentlemanly, and – I am pretty sure – no more a believer in Rastafarianism than I was myself. He must have known that he was very ill. He was certainly a very peculiar sallow colour.

I wrote a piece in *The Times* wondering – as Illich had taught me – whether man, like a gramophone record, had a proper speed. Wasn't it perhaps the speed of a bike? Or maybe around 50 mph, the speed at which cars and trains can optimise speed and fuel efficiency?

To my attachment to Illich, I had added an interest in William

Cobbett and Tom Paine. No-one can fail to be moved by English radicalism, even when Tony Benn is its main contemporary exponent. Its charm will even survive its being espoused by George Monbiot. Its courage and vigour are entrancing. But my attachment to it was romantic and sentimental, not much analysed. I soon found it a moving curiosity, rather than a guiding principle. Besides, Cobbett was as much a reactionary, which makes him easier to bear. (Just as Thoreau's 'contrarianism' makes him more likeable than he at first seems.)

Similarly, I haunted pump houses and beam engines and East End warehouses and docklands and ancient railway stations. As a boy, I rummaged in any ruined houses or boats I could find. Later, I rummaged in abandoned farmyards in France and vehicle scrap yards in England. Even now, my favourite television shows are set in junkyards and among cranky restorers.

But then – and this is the least explicable of my influences – I have always been passionately attached to the 'Swiss Family Robinson' fantasy. The heart of it is this: one is given a random selection of the goods of one's civilisation and one takes them to a paradisiacally warm place to recreate a civilisation.

This is the aesthetics and spirituality of the neglected and the discarded.

I believe in the power of our imaginations. This is very Jamesian. The excitement of the entrepreneurial is not its virtue and its good sense: it is the passionate desire to buck trends, to overcome the odds. Entrepreneurship is courage and passion. It is making the real world make one's dream come true. It is willing the world to move over and make room for this new business. It is often about little more than charisma bending lesser people to its will. We would do it an enormous disservice – rob it of its human excitement and reality – if we were to stress its value and usefulness over its being – like art – a triumph of the imagination.

In my thirties, I was working as a Welsh shepherd (seasonally, at lambing time), part-time French peasant (and wine-maker) and part-time London bike-mender. From these experiences I was able to condescend to the self-sufficiency movement, which was then at its (not very great) height.

There never were many people who wanted to live on smallholdings. But then, the aspiration to do so was vaguely radical. Nowadays, of course, there are television series about such things, and an even greater disjunction between those who more or less do them, and those who merely read, watch and admire from afar. But even then there was a small publishing industry based on those that did. They either did not notice, or did not care, that real peasants are too busy and too tired to write books and articles about their experiences, or to proselytise them. I knew people who dragged their families off to Welsh hillsides, and only those who had brilliant entrepreneurial and marketing skills made a go of it. In short, their abandonment of the modern and the large scale was wholly false. Often it was Post Modern: the smallholder made mainstream showbiz success out of his pseudo-peasantry. Hadn't Thoreau done the same when he built a public reputation on a flirtation with abandonment in a hut in the woods? Didn't Thomas Merton, when he seemed to retreat deeper into his Cistercian monasticism in his hut away from the monastery, but was actually using it as a springboard to the world stage? The latter is one of many monks whose politics were conventionally Hampstead Liberal. (Evelyn Waugh admired Merton's early writing and his spirituality; it fell to Evelyn's son Auberon to point out, much later, his tedious leftiness.)[3]

I had none of the strength, skills or courage required to be other than a part-time peasant.

In the late 1970s, I wrote for the *Observer* (as a legman for the Pendennis column, written by the lyrical and wily Tom Davies), the *Listener* (as a TV critic and profile writer) and the *Guardian* (very briefly and sporadically as a colour-writing reporter). My second home was Richard Boston's pioneer green magazine *Vole* (which I briefly edited in its last year) for which I wrote a column about cycling as a metaphor for everything about life I admired, and later what I think may be the world's first regular column about rubbish disposal.

By the mid 70s, I was becoming some sort of 'green', and an enemy of the European Common Market's Common Agriculture Policy. It took me longer to realise how bad its environment policies were. By the mid 80s I had decided unilaterally that I would never promote the view (a standby of the writers of the time) that Britain was 'the dirty man of Europe'. I developed a distaste for the lectures Continental northern Europeans delivered to us. I didn't believe in the superiority of their expensive, anally retentive environmentalism, with its empty gestures. I rather liked British scepticism, our taste for scruffiness, and our wary acceptance that something – as little as possible – ought to be done. Our environmental science was more right than theirs, too.

My *Vole* work made me a fan of the British waste disposal industry, because landfill sites and incinerators are interesting, and because at every level of the waste trade there were things and people to delight. How could one not warm to the piratical spirit of the bin men on their lorries, or to the ex-quarrymen, gypsies and carters who were transmogrifying into technocratic waste disposal entrepreneurs, milking the regulations and the planning system as best they could?

In any case, I was never a green in the sense of supporting any of the campaigns or the Ecology – now the Green – Party, almost all of which I thought tiresome and simplistic. Greenpeace seemed like an advertising agency with a brave marine spearhead. Friends of the Earth seemed woebegone. I have never had any friends among the greens. I never thought the greens very interesting. One or two were nice enough – but none seemed stimulating. Worst, the most serious of them seemed desperately negative, and that was too dreary to bear. I make an exception for Andrew Lees, an obsessive Friends of the Earth campaigner who died young, while campaigning in Madagascar.

I was, in short, rashly determined to reconcile very various influences.

From the mid 60s on, I met a wide range of people and read a yet wider range of material. I came across literary and media people – film makers, actors, writers of various sorts. There were homosexuals of every sort, including dramatic queens, pederasts, pretty boys. I knew commercially successful Jews, and intellectual Jews, and – the bigger surprise to a British goy, who did not know such things could be combined at all – Jews who were both. Americans, chancers, Indian immigrants and many other types and characters I met all populated my mind and set me free – or adrift – from comfortable verities. I knew business people of all sorts, and admired them. I met actresses, pop stars and novelists, and their success – their wealth and fame – seemed very attractive. I learned to dislike only those who affected a disdain for their good fortune. Poor socialists were wrong in their prescription for lessening the misery of poverty. But rich socialists seemed really absurd, if not actually despicable.

All my life, I have read widely, but not voraciously. (Certainly not the many hours a day Isaiah Berlin insists an intellectual needs. I would rather be sailing or watching *Lovejoy*.) Among those who have appealed to me are Teilhard de Chardin, Konrad Lorenz, Bruno Bettelheim, Peter Kropotkin, and Michel Foucault. Some of those embarrass me now, but so be it. Among the people I met or read in the 70s and whom I admired, I'd place Norman McRae, General Sir John Hackett (not in his green mode, though), Barbara Ward, Gerald Leach, Peter Bauer, Herman Kahn, Julian Simon.[4] Some of these were anti-green, and their pro-growth optimism stunned me. I was not wholly persuaded – indeed I was almost chilled – by (say) Kahn and Simon. I met Simon much later, and thought he was all the more interesting for having been unhinged by depression, until he discovered the redeeming power of an optimistic thought. In short, he was an optimist because the imitation of optimism had saved his life.

This is very Jamesian. Which comes first: the desire for optimism or the evidence for it? I have often been accused of being Panglossian.

Certainly, I am predisposed to think things will turn out all right. I am a glass-half-full person (at least until I get frightened, when cowardice will make me pretty wobbly). I don't think people are very good, or very bad. Almost everything I espouse or deprecate is predicated on the belief that one must go with the flow – go with the grain – of people's being not awful and not divine. Socialism would work, if only we were a little bit nicer. Conservatism deals with the realities of our natures better.

I would have been wiser and braver if I had poured scorn on green thinking, in the way that John (later Sir John) Maddox, editor of *Nature*, did in his *The Doomsday Syndrome* (1972). In fact, I did not know about his book until the early 1990s. I should have responded more positively to the work of Herman Kahn and Julian Simon in the late 1970s. I knew it was giddily exciting. I can say that I did not have a firm enough grip on the issues, and was too isolated, to become useful to such ideas. They were too extraordinarily in conflict with the Illichian ideas I was still wrestling with. Anyway, to my shame, I went with puffing the Club of Rome. I have to accept that I wasted perhaps 10 years. This was cowardice, but not of the worst sort. It was tolerably brave then to try to do journalism on the environment and Third World development. It would have been all but suicidal to try to do so from the point of view of knocking this new area. No – not suicidal. But bolder than I could afford to be, or knew how to be. I did not know there was a think-tank world (and there wasn't much of one in the UK then) that might have informed, or even funded, more interesting work.

Being an outsider didn't help: I did not have the confidence to strike out on my own.

On the other hand, my amateur and underfunded researches into British conservation issues, into Third World development matters, and into the waste industry did produce *The Real Cost* (Collins, 1984) and it wasn't the worst book in the world, though it should have been more gung-ho for capitalism and development, and instead dithered on the sidelines. All these turmoils matured into something of merit when I finally worked as environment correspondent for the Independent (1986–90) and the *Sunday Times* (1990–92) and as author of *Life On a Modern Planet: A manifesto for progress*.[5] With this last book, I thought I was at last putting mature and informed reflection onto the page, and that it was so timely that I would also become a best-selling celebrity, or at least have steady sales to universities. The book got a great deal of publicity and sold 2,000 copies over the next five years.

By the mid 80s, I had become a committed voice against green extremism, and if my critics decried my efforts as those of a turncoat, for my part I thought my remarks were those of a case-hardened and experienced observer. Even now, when I hear the anti-green fundamentalists inveighing against the campaigners, and in favour of unbridled capitalism, I am inclined to notice that they have a rather primitive enthusiasm, and I rather prefer my own conflicted variety. But those battles over the environment are almost old history now. We seem to have reached a point that is closer to my concerns in the mid 70s. We can have Mass Affluence without a degraded environment, even if this remains a fraught proposition in the Third World. We can perhaps say now that the problem with Mass Affluence is not ecological, but aesthetic; and emotional and moral, not material. The greatest problem with Mass Affluence is whether it can be sustained spiritually. Not the soil or stuff, but our souls may be the limit to wealth.

Spirituality is a problem. Is it just a pretence, an affectation? Is it the word we use for lofty selfishness? I am unclear, and have addressed it in this book because it is so important to the critics of Mass Affluence. In the early 80s, I visited many monasteries, and stayed in several. I was drawn to them, and remain so. The result was *Fools For God*.[6] It is a great pleasure to enter a monastery for a few days, and almost as great a pleasure to come out into the world of cafes and nightclubs afterward. Every issue of importance is to be found in monastic history. How to build a society that explores the extremes of spirituality (of anything at all) while preserving men's sanity? How to construct an extreme way of life that will repel the crazy and sustain the sensible? How to build institutions while recalling always the valuable impermanence of everything human? How to be busy but still? How to live for today and tomorrow – and the hereafter – all at once? How to forget the world when the world keeps wanting to know your secret? Monasticism is, of course, very high on the food chain of civilisation. It can be done on a shoestring, by the self-sufficient. That is, indeed, its dream. But its delicious value is that rich men and rich societies admire monasteries, and have always founded and sometimes funded them. A good monk knows how much his virtuous retreat from the world depends on the engaged worldliness of others.

A monk knows he will be visited by all and sundry. Monastic cells in the desert were perhaps the first real examples of tourism, as men of the world sought solace among men who had left the world. Affluence is forever paying homage to poverty: tourism, fashion, food, and furnishing all play this game. Spirituality and affluence are not at odds. That is the very heart of this book.

Living with monks, and being deeply drawn to them, taught me to love the world of economic vigour almost as much as living and working with peasants had. This is why I am glad that I have always read *The Economist*, always admired wealth creators, and enjoyed having had money periodically. I am pleased that I have driven Rolls-Royces and sports cars, eaten in the Savoy, stayed in the best hotels on paradise islands, flown sometimes in first class and routinely in business, crossed the Atlantic first class in QE2 and so on. I have known and liked rich people, and been among their number. I have dined in boardrooms and been schmoozed by senior politicians.

I have known and adored applause.

While speaking in public I have often wondered if I have overdone it. Was I too dramatic? Too noisy? A little too rude about my 'enemies'? Twice, in very different circumstances, a worldly Spaniard (a different one in each case) has come up to me and said, in effect, that I had a certain spirit and must not alter it at all. They seemed to have no more idea than I what this thing is, but they bothered to say that I shouldn't worry about it, mess with it, diminish it. They came unbidden. Each showed every sign of being thoroughly Establishment, conventional and all that. What had worried me in my style was that it alienates such 'types' and that it betrayed a certain chaos of being. I would risk saying that those men were spiritual, and they had rightly reckoned I was trying to be. I have felt warmly about the Spanish ever since, though I know sentimentalising an entire nation is hardly wise. A pair of random, but coincidental, incidents is hardly a rationale.

Rich or poor, we are dependent on the kindness of strangers. Whether I was well off or hard pressed, people who were often very much poorer than I looked out for me as I mined their societies for amusement and insight. While I was being ditzy and diverted, they put aside their daily struggle with survival and handed me back the stuffed wallet that had fallen at their feet. What's more, while I dare to question whether Islam is the most useful religion on earth, it is the Muslim understanding and use of the idea of the 'human' (as in, 'it's the human thing to do') that makes being an infidel in Islamic countries often a very soothing thing to be.

When I first left school at 17, I embarked on a mixed bag of jobs in retail (books and clothes) for a few years, and could have become very good at those trades. Instead, I dropped out and became a van driver in London. I did that for five years, between 1965 and 1970. Then, for a year, I was a chauffeur to Leonard Cheshire, VC. (He was an extraordinary man, and probably would have loved to be a saint; but for all his courage and compassion, his egocentricity, a sort of childishness, would probably have debarred him.) During the van-driving years, I was pretty broke, not least because I was not properly working class. This meant that I didn't have a council flat, as most of my co-workers did. I worked among, and knew well, men and women of the London working class. They were very unlike the modern less well off. They were intensely respectable. They were the last Britons to have a sense that people were born to a certain place in society. They were the last generation of the last class in Britain (apart, perhaps, from the first-born of aristocrats) to believe in class, in the important respect of believing that one inherited a social position and was condemned to stay there. They were wholly unambitious. I didn't sentimentalise them, though there were mean and fine, agreeable and disagreeable among them, of course.

Being broke did not set one adrift. Everyone I met knew I was an educated middle-class person, and a recognisable bohemian type. I wasn't even a hippy, and people knew that too.

I enjoy knowing that I can look back now on half a century of alert observation, which has taken me from the top to the bottom of this society, and several others. I have been drunk and sober, rich and poor, smart and scruffy, in much of England and plenty of other countries.

The prejudices I maintained throughout this time did not much vary, and nor indeed did my tastes. When I was a vegan (very early 80s) I didn't forget how much I like rare roast beef (as indeed I did not during the BSE crises in the late 80s and the mid 90s). Now that I don't smoke or drink (not since 1995), I don't forget the pleasure I derived, off and on, for thirty-odd years, from the first early cigarette and red wine of the day. Tastes are deeply embedded. In my 40s I discovered marijuana and found it suited me excellently. I could not recommend any substance more highly, but only in occasional small doses. Consumed often, or in big doses, it seems rather dangerous stuff. To be very mildly stoned while watching new young bands play Glastonbury (on TV nowadays) seems to me a great luxury.

In my late 50s, quite a lot seems settled. But plenty of conundrums remain. The biggest is: why am I not on the side of the angels? My greatest hero is probably Erasmus, who sought a humanistic reform of Catholicism. He was a great man, but a compromiser. I find I cannot warm to a Wilberforce, or a Wesley, or a Pankhurst, or a Martin Luther King. Certainly, they were all on the side of right, and assuredly I do not like, say, racism. And yet I find I want to debunk the easy verities that sprinkle white guilt about slavery, or masculine guilt about women. Similarly, the horrors of the industrial revolution seem to me probably to have been preferable to village life, and in any case they swiftly led to modern society, with its hygiene and longevity and mass education.

I am emotionally on the side of those who resist morally driven reform. I sympathise with those who love the old order and fear the new. I am drawn more to those who resisted democracy than to those who pushed for it. I like the Royalists more than the Puritans. I love to read how Lord Melbourne, the arch-Whig, despaired of egalitarianism of any kind. His cynicism is funny, of course, but it was also wise.

He thought mass education might be a folly. 'It will do the working class no good, and may do us a lot of harm.' Seeing, as we do, a yobbish society that despises any sort of educated elite, who is to say that he was very wide of the mark? And yet I admire progress, especially if it is technological.

I settle these internal disputes by seeing in British history (if I am pushed, in human history) a sort of divine working-out. The tensions between classes, between interests, between radicals and conservatives produce real progress. Neither side is dishonourable, and one may belong to either honourably. But you see the difficulty. Conservative as I am, I like progress. I do not believe in the perfectibility of man or his society, and I am nostalgic; but I do believe that our human developments are all exciting.

Let me play this game a little longer. I admire Noel Coward and Terence Rattigan more than John Osborne; and Tom Stoppard more than David Hare. The playwrights I more admire, then, are those that are less worthy and less angry (or who discipline, rather than milk, their ire). I wish the Conservative Party well (though I think it vulgar). I prefer the Stuarts to Cromwell (though the Stuarts were silly and Cromwell wasn't philistine). I prefer corporations to campaigners. I thought we were right to go to war in Iraq, and I expect that things will get a good bit worse before they get better. If I was offered a weekend in New York, I'd take it if the ticket were business class, and refuse if the ticket were tourist (even though I believe that more space equals more global warming, mile for mile). If Abramovich offered me a cruise in his huge yacht, I'd accept, even though I criticise Prince Charles for lecturing me about global warming while borrowing large private yachts for his holidays. But then, it is not Charles's cruising I dislike, but his humbug in lecturing me about my pale imitation of it. And I have learned that I would take these opportunities for the pleasure they bring. I would not go as an observer, to sneak about the wrongness of such things later. '"Take what you want", says God, "And pay for it."' That's an admirable Spanish aphorism, and though it's a little bold for me – a little courageous – I nonetheless note that most of us are only radical when we're on the losing end of progress. Even socialists, as someone remarked, always live in the biggest house they can afford.

I am inclined to think that the poor in the rich world are either stupid or lazy or both, and may soon constitute an embarrassing and troubling underclass. Luckily, the world always produces a need for the caring and security services, neither requiring great skill, and that may keep the problem at bay. I wish that modern societies had not decided to use their new social freedom to imitate the worst of the mores of the yob working class. I wish sport was not sponsored, though it doesn't much matter to me, since I hardly bother with sport. I dislike the way Mass Affluence has perversely produced the effect that so many people now dress, speak and behave as only the worst sort of poor person once did. Aristocrats, showgirls, actresses and provincial shop girls are all indistinguishable in their semi-nakedness. Noting that a minor aristocrat has his family crest on his arse and that Emma Parker Bowles has a kitten on hers, India Knight opines that 'Prole-chic is everywhere.'[7] Mass fashion seems nastier and nastier. The mass availability of 'exclusive' brands has led to a sort of label pollution. The media, even the 'posh' media, is full of gossip, and not even of the interesting 'exclusive' gossip of the old *Daily Mail*. On a bad day, people seem 'needy' and whining and self-pitying. On a worse day still, I am these things myself.

Especially on ferries or in airports, I am often afflicted with an intense dislike of my fellow man. Sprawling, raucous, mewling and semi-naked as they are, I find them terribly low. At such moments, I yearn very deeply for the First Class lounge, or to be at home. Perhaps I have had too much 'Access All Areas' privilege. Skipping past crowds and lines of fans at gigs became second nature during my ligging years. I have been a visitor to places of some grace: African villages, London's gentlemen's clubs, monasteries, billionaires' homes in Fort Worth: they planted a standard in my mind which spoils other, lesser, places for me. The memory of moments of intense yearning (and some fairly shameless begging for upgrades, too) reminds me that I have longed to be distinguished from the herd, to be treated better than the Average Joe. I hate to be left out of almost anything I have even half an interest in. Luckily, this very ordinary human trait has seemed to apply only to going to gigs or into Club and First Class, and not often and not so it mattered much. Spurned, I haven't shrivelled and mourned, but instead pretended that I didn't want what I couldn't have, and was actually too fine a fellow to want such silly things anyway. A pathetic ploy, you may say: but it works.

Enough self-help manual-ism. But I would not have you think I was immune from yearning. I have longed, in my time, for particular cars and computers and cameras and coats and Chelsea boots. I still do a fair bit of yearning and longing for the goods and services of the world. But I do not think I have yearned for these things much more or less than anyone else, and I do think the yearning is terribly unseemly. Luckily, my dreams of contentment are bound up with earning or having relatively small sums of money, and I have very little desire for grandness of any kind. So, in the scale of things, I am not hugely interested in wealth – at least not as it is understood in the West.

1 Quoted in *The Week*, 15 May 2004, quoting the *Daily Telegraph*.

2 Cited in Tom G Palmer, *Globalization and Culture: Homogeneity, diversity, identity, liberty*, Liberales Institut, Potsdam, 2004. www.libinst.de.

3 Monica Furlong, *Merton: A biography*, Collins, 1980.

4 Herman Kahn and Julian Simon, *The Resourceful Earth*, Blackwell, 1984; and Julian Simon, *The Ultimate Resource*, Princeton University Press, 1983 and *The Ultimate Resource 2*, Princeton University Press, 1996.

5 Richard D North, *Life On a Modern Planet: A manifesto for progress*, Manchester University Press, 1995, available as a free download at www.richarddnorth.com.

6 Richard D North, *Fools For God*, Collins, 1984, available as a free download from www.richarddnorth.com.

7 India Knight, 'Keeping Up With the Chavs', *Sunday Times*, 15 August 2004.

RDN'S SPECIAL HEROES

My special heroes appear below, together with a sense of how they helped me get where I now find myself. These are not so much the major influences of my life, but rather the oddities that make it peculiar. (See Appendix I for a note on my prejudices.)

TEILHARD DE CHARDIN (1881–1955)
By the time I was fourteen or so, I was naturally awash in that sea of hormones and intellectual development that makes one aware of the interconnectedness of things. Nowadays, writers like Susan Greenfield can explain pharmacologically why certain drugs, both artificial and natural, induce this effect, and we are aware of how our thoughts and our emotions are strongly interlinked.[1] In the nineteenth century, American thought discussed such matters (see below) as it were theoretically. But then, in the late 50s, I lived the 'unbearable immanence of being' of a blossoming spring day in a suburban road (Orchard Rise, as it might well have been). Every star and petal, every iceberg and molecule was known to me. I knew that I was a part of the universe, but caught sudden shattering glimpses of the way that it had a spirit and that I – or at any rate, humanity – represented the best of it. This is big, crazy stuff, and if you have never sensed it when young then I probably can't help you see how significant it can be to people.

Matter becoming self-aware was and is of course a peculiar idea.

I was perhaps 16 (say in 1962) when I first came across Teilhard de Chardin on my mother's bookshelves. The effect was powerful. His argument in books such as *Le Milieu Divin* (1960 in English edition), *The Phenomenon of Man* (1965 in English edition), *The Hymn of the Universe* (1965 in English edition), and the *Future of Man* (1964 in English edition) was essentially that the universe – and particularly this planet – was the scene of an extraordinary emergence of consciousness. 'Throughout my whole life', he wrote, during every moment I have lived, the world has gradually been taking on light and fire for me, until it has come to envelop me in one mass of luminosity, glowing from within...The purple flush of matter fading imperceptibly into the gold of spirit, to be lost finally in the incandescence of a personal universe.

You can either take that sort of writing, or not. I confess that I can. (And on the contrary, I found I could not stomach the leaden good sense of a Fritz Schumacher. And I am allergic to most guru-ism.) Teilhard was a palaeontologist (now regarded as suspect, I am pretty sure, by the profession) and sought to explain the emergence of biological life and the subsequent development of intelligence. To match the 'biosphere' of life, he proposed 'the Noosphere' of consciousness. Because he was a Catholic priest and Jesuit (and a French one at that), he sought to see not merely the way that intelligence was spreading, but that some sort of spirituality was spreading, too. God had created matter, and out of it he was summoning forth a spirit worthy of himself: the process was both natural (evolutionary) and religious (God directed). Teilhard's work was to wrestle with this contradiction.

At the time, one was aware that television, satellite communication, global media, and space travel were all greatly increasing the communication between people. At the same time, a liberal culture was also becoming globalized. I was struck that liberalism made it all but impossible not to insist that people empathise with one another. The Enlightenment Liberal is merely someone who senses that the seventeenth-century philosophers had got to grips with this in a form that, for the first time, looks thoroughly modern, for all that it has ancient roots. (Political correctness is merely that process formalised, and – one might say – rendered mechanical and unattractive.) To make another person 'The Other' was becoming impossible. This was a matter of the globalization of a particular ethic. It was mightily empowered by television. In previous centuries, one empathised with the few people one knew or bonded with, or rationalised as being within one's moral sphere. Now, it became vividly obvious that 'The Other' was no such thing. The person who was supposed to comprise 'The Other' had become all too vivid, so say nothing of the notion's being an affront to biology.

I believed then, and am inclined to believe now, that these 'evolutions' – technical and then moral – make up the most interesting of the underlying stories of human life by which we explain ourselves. I do not suggest I have much of an idea whether it will turn out to predominate; nor can I picture what a world that hosts enormous amounts of empathy will look like.

Moreover, though Teilhard's poetics may be hard to take (I find them invigorating) and his science flaky (I can barely judge and couldn't care less), his Noosphere is a highly expressive way of thinking about the human spirit and globalization, and a very positive one.

MICHEL FOUCAULT (1926–1984)

In the mid 1960s my worldview was dramatically influenced by Michel Foucault's assertion that a dominant story about nearly any aspect of human life can drown out some other, alternative view. He was arguing that elites invent, circulate and make compulsory various 'narratives' that make it easier to control society. I didn't buy that, but I was nonetheless struck by the way that crime and punishment, and madness and treatment, have been figured and dealt with. His *Madness and Civilization* (1961) hit me at about the same time that Cream released their first album and the Beach Boys brought us 'Good Vibrations' – that is, around 1966. Should a criminal be reformed? Was he mad or bad? How should he be reformed (alone or in company)? These were the years of Bruno Bettelheim and R D Laing: was it mad people who were mad, or was it the society that made them? One did not have to abandon the commonsensical (I did not) to see that narratives matter. All this would degenerate into the awful structuralist years (whose legacy many academics still flounder in): but that's another story. The devastating account of Foucault – whether as historian of ideas or historian of fact, or philosopher, or political philosopher – given by Jose Merquior now seems wonderfully wise.[2] Roy Porter, whose accounts of the Enlightenment are among the best we have, writes well (and rather sympathetically) about Foucault's excesses. Porter's *Madness: A brief history* would be worth reading for these passages alone (though every page is a delight).[3]

IVAN ILLICH (1926–2002)

Ivan Illich's *Deschooling Society* and *The Celebration of Awareness* were first published in the UK in 1971.[4] Illich was a bombshell for me and for many others at the time. I was moving in decidedly unintellectual circles then, and his words burned in me pretty much without challenge. His argument in *Deschooling Society* was that schools did not educate people, but stultified their investigative originality. Yet schools were made not merely convenient, but compulsory and costly. His *Celebration of Awareness* claimed, among much else, that aid to the Third World could only imprint redundant and destructive western habits on the poor. And he believed that if priests were sent to the poor of the Third World, it did them – everyone involved – irreparable harm.

The excitement of Illich was partly his giddy inversion of the normal, kindly liberal, way of thought. But also that he wanted change: get rid of schools, stop aid, cease missionary work. This was properly radical.

I do remember that he was championed by A H Halsey, the sociologist, who (I am almost sure) did an interview with him on BBC Radio 3 in 1970 or 1971. In time, further books appeared, with titles such as *Energy and Equity* ('Beyond a critical speed, no-one can gain time without forcing another to lose it...Beyond a certain speed, motorised vehicles create remoteness which they alone can shrink.') It supposed that modern industrial and institutional society was a machine for robbing people of the ability to be healthy, to feed themselves, to travel, to learn (and much else) outside of the vast apparatus it had constructed. Crucially, the structure imposed 'Radical Monopoly'. This is easily imagined when one reckons that the car imposes distance and speed. Shops are sited a long way from people's homes: one must move long distances quickly if one is to eat. Almost everything one wants – take health as a good case – involves certificated professionals, and it becomes impossible and illegal to look after one's own health. The alternative was a 'convivial' society (described in his 'Tools for Conviviality', 1973) in which society made decisions about technology based on whether the tools and structures (absence of structure, often) we need for living are kept in our own hands.

There was great excitement (among rather a small number of people) when Illich came to give a series of lectures at the Architectural Association (a radical hang-out for intellectual architects, which appealed, not least, because its degrees did not confer the right to sign off architectural work). I had never heard fluency like his: it came with very great charm, vast experience of the world of which he spoke, and prodigious reading. He wrote and talked in aphorisms – a style infuriating to many, but very dear to me.

I never did buy all he said, but it was a very powerful vision. It was a 'parallel universe', a mirror image of the modern world. It was, if you like, a narrative with the power of a Foucault inversion of the normal.

For a long time, I wrestled with the two questions it posed: what were the limits we should be imposing on ourselves, and how could they be agreed upon. For a while, I wouldn't own a car or fly in an airplane. I remember arguing that people's right to own land should be limited. I thought that energy might need to be rationed in some way, along with speed and distance. I was not a hippy. Indeed, I was more drawn to the thinking of men like William Cobbett (the nineteenth-century radical conservative, if that beast can be imagined). Illich struck me as attractively like a Peter Kropotkin, in believing that the logic of a 'chosen simplicity', and even a 'voluntary poverty', might appeal to people. There are socialist moments in Illich, when he talks of the need for state imposition of limits; but he avoids talk of the compulsion that would be needed to bring his world into being.

Early on, I was amused that Illich travelled the world by air, rather than use modern communication techniques to send images rather than his person. When we met – I profiled him for *The Times* in the early 1980s – I was tickled that his chosen rendezvous was Les Deux Magots or maybe the Café De Flore in St Germain des Prés. Whichever, it was closed and we went somewhere pretty sprauncy round the corner. (A similar surprise awaited me when I took Wilfred Thesiger to lunch in London, and that legendary ascetic walloped down good wine in quantity, while regaling me on the materialism of the fallen desert Arabs, rendered degenerate by modernity and affluence.)

Bit by bit, I gave up. I came to the conclusion that this deeply attractive vision of the world did not touch the ambitions, the vision, the vigour of real people. An imposed dictatorship might achieve an Illichian world, but it would not be chosen by anyone. It was a pretty standard Utopia, though it brilliantly discussed modern patterns of consumption, whether of goods or services. Even now, I can imagine that something like a Convivial Society might emerge. It may be the postgrowth world in which people decide that 'enough is enough'. But I cannot see that this would be worthwhile, unless it is a voluntary and chosen way of life, or a way of life that is accepted because the realities of life make it necessary.

JULIAN SIMON (1932–1998)

By the early 80s, I was aware that there was a mirror image to Illich's thinking. It was pioneered by the Americans, Julian Simon and Herman Kahn, of whom the former was the more luminously clear. His idea was that human inventiveness – the vigorous pursuit of our excitement in new ideas, our delight in risk – had made the triumphs of the modern world, and would continue to solve the rather small difficulties that it threw up as the human adventure rolled on. In particular, he argued that every new birth was an opportunity. He asserted that population pressure had produced innovation in the past, and that the process shows us that each new birth is an opportunity, not a cost. This was doubly so because, while every new mouth produces pressure on the rest of us, any new mind might prove to be the intellect that solves the problem of the pressure. What is useful here – lovely, really – is the idea that, instead of bemoaning the large number of young people there are in the world, it is wiser – truer – to see that any one of them might be the source of our rescue. Isn't this the profound thing? We can disparage or celebrate the human life about us. We are bound to dislike much of it, but the effort of will which celebrates it finds life easier to bear; is more likely to be conducive to people flourishing; is more likely to make the thing go well.

It is true that much green and leftish thinking simply asserts that the positive is to be found in restraint. For my part, I argue that the fullness of the lives around me seems to consist in a chosen life, not an imposed one. Nor is it good enough to suggest that, in an ideal world, people will choose restraint: they will choose vigour, too, I hope. Simon had been a depressive, and he believed that it was the optimism of his thought that cured him.[5] One might argue that his ideas were therapeutic, rather than logical: that Simon's wish was father to the thought that was father to Simon's well-being. But one sees in the work of Raymond Tallis the view that it really is the well-being which flows from good ideas, and the misery which flows from bad, that is part of how we may judge ideas. Tallis castigates the 'Enemies of Hope' because they make us impotent to develop, even before we start.[6]

WILLIAM JAMES (1842–1910)

As I wrestled with Simon's ideas, I realised that I was trying to find a way of talking about the spirit of the human enterprise. I could see the force of Illich. I was drawn also to the values of many Christian, and especially monastic, writers as they discussed the 'desert within': the human hunger for sufficiency. I wrote a book about that.[7] I am hopelessly nostalgic and romantic about the neglected and the discarded, in objects and people. I was as prone as the next person to want the world to stop, so that I could get off.

But I was much more drawn, in practice, to the triumphantly active, adventurous and aggressive. Competition, risk, excess, extravagance and vigour strike me as being vital. A society that does not understand, accept, encourage and accommodate the vigour of its people is dead, boring, repressive and set to explode. It happens that I am not brave and not particularly strong: when I espouse the vigour in life, it's done with admiring submission (as Emerson said in a different context, as you'll see if you read on).

The conservative political tradition is all about the tension between allowing the vigour (even the evil) in people the rein it needs. This is because, harnessed, they are a force for good; wholly repressed, they are a recipe for disaster. Expression and restraint: in manners and morals, these are the twin necessities and the twin antagonists.

The American nineteenth-century thinker William James deals with these themes. He was watching the modern world develop in his country, and he was appalled and thrilled by it. He was temperamentally wholly split between activity and inactivity. He was constitutionally unable to commit to a woman or a profession. He was drawn to the theoretical and the intellectual. But it was the sheer vigour of life (what his brother Henry called the 'elemental blur')[8] that thrilled him.

In notes that went toward one of his essays ('What Makes a Life Significant', 1899), William describes his experience of returning to the big bad Eastern US after a sojourn in a much more ideal, small-town community:

Ouf! What a relief. Now for something primordial and savage…to set the balance straight again. I soon recognised that it was the element that gives to the wicked outer world all its moral style, expressiveness and picturesqueness, – the element of precipitousness, so to call it, of strength and strenuousness, intensity and danger. What excites and interests the looker-on at life, what the romances and the statues celebrate and the grim civic monuments remind us of, is the everlasting battle of the powers of light with those of darkness; with heroism, reduced to its bare chance, yet ever and anon snatching victory from the jaws of death.

He thought the perfect embodiment of (what his brilliant biographer calls) his 'risk-taking ideal' 'the sight of a workman doing something on the dizzy edge of a sky-scraping iron construction'.[9]

James goes to battle on the big themes. The result is a large paradox: knowing that free will is an illogical idea, our first act of free will should be to assume we have it. Then he goes on to even bolder ideas. What a free people choose is as near to right as we can find. The nearest we get to truth is what the real world doesn't contradict. The point of life is to enter into it, fully.

This seems to be in the American Transcendentalist tradition, which flourished just before William's time and is represented by Ralph Waldo Emerson, as he describes the 'lords of life: surface, illusion, temperament, succession, surprise and reality'. We are what we are, and must enter into it fully. We are not given the whole picture, and have to get on with the glimpses we have. The present, the moment, the active: these matter. Emerson is another intellectual, it seems, who realises that intellectuals don't get the essence of life: that it must be entered into, surfed, got on with. It must be both penetrated and skimmed.

These men were about 'the considered life', but having done a lot of considering, they end up with a respect for the vigour and good sense of people rather more animal than they. They do not propose a recipe of action over thought, of the gung-ho over the cautious. It is rather that they come to see that consciousness is not just about the study or the monastic cell. It is about the market, the skyscraper, battle and dynamism too. So the problem in philosophy and politics alike is how to be rational and yet vital.

The power of the visionary individual, the vigour of the spirit of an age, these are essential themes in nineteenth-century thought, and they produced the nastiest bits of history we have ever known.

So do not imagine that I underestimate the value of the cool, rational, pragmatic, epigrammatic sceptic as he or she hoists unbelief as a trusty shield against dangerous enthusiasms.

1 Susan A Greenfield, *The Private Life of the Brain*, Allen Lane, 2000.

2 J G Merquior, *Foucault*, Modern Master series, Fontana, 1985.

3 Roy Porter, *Madness: A brief history*, Oxford University Press, 2002.

4 All Ivan Illich's titles were published by Calder and Boyars, or by Marion Boyars, of London, though some have appeared from other imprints as well.

5 I regret that I can't find the reference for this: his more obviously available accounts of his depression don't talk in quite these terms. See my obituary of JS at www.richarddnorth.com.

6 Raymond Tallis, *The Enemies of Hope: A critique of contemporary pessimism, irrationalism, anti-humanism and the counter-enlightenment*, Palgrave Macmillan, 1996.

7 Richard D North, *Fools for God*, Collins, 1986, available as a free download at www.richarddnorth.com.

8 Henry James thus described the horror of the First World War, which both thrilled and appalled him. The remark was made in a letter to the journalist Filson Young, the second husband of my grandmother Vera Bax. See www.richarddnorth.com for more on either.

9 R W B Lewis, *The Jameses: A family narrative*, Andre Deutsch, 1991.

APPENDIX III

A NOTE ON SPIRITUALITY

Are the 'examined life' and 'inner peace' the result of philosophical thought? Is to be 'philosophical' code for being spiritual? Well, clearly not in a technical sense. Philosophy can be a mathematical or logical matter that has inner peace or examined life neither as its purpose nor its outcome. However, moral philosophers at least do often turn their minds to considering the means of measuring good. They often find themselves wondering whether 'conscience' may not be a better guide to goodness than some abstract calculus. And when they do, they are considering one sort of inner peace. They are certainly then aware that people's examination of their own lives is a large part of what makes people good. 'Being philosophical' can be about becoming reconciled to the facts of one's life; and it can be about working out what needs to be done to achieve that accommodation with one's 'inner voices'.

There is another popular sense of 'philosophical', in which people have 'toga moments' when the sweet balm of reasonableness overcomes the gnawing anxiety and the stomping anger with which we might have approached some matter or other. Very lofty, very calm – that's what your philosopher is supposed to be.

But none of these quite gets to the distinction we make when we suggest that there is a quality that we can call spiritual. When we come to this really big stuff, we seem to be opposing the worldly with the spiritual. It is perhaps nonsense to do so, when we consider, as many modern people do, that there is nothing that is non-worldly. The other-worldly is not for them: it is a non-place. For the non-religious, the idea of a life and a 'Life-giver' beyond the worldly is not real. For this sort of modern – I am one – there is nothing 'transcendental' to be reached for.

But I am inclined to persevere with looking for, even aiming at, the spiritual. It would be a grim world in which there was no use for the word 'spirituality', and grimmer still to fancy it has meaning and to feel barred from aspiring to it.

One decent analogy is with the word 'soul'. Those for whom the transcendental has no meaning may also find the idea that man has 'a spark of the divine' to be nonsense. And yet, in ordinary use, we still find the word very useful. The essence and the value of a person can still usefully be described as 'soul', even for people who do not believe the essence and value flow from God. In short, we would not trust a society or person that did not treat people as having a soul, even when its origin has changed – and with that, its meaning.

To face God – to believe one faces God – is to address spiritual matters. But spirituality is not exclusive to the religious. Nor is spirituality anything like the whole of godliness. Some people serve God in self-denying, constant activity on behalf of others – they are very different from those who do so in contemplative, 'useless' seclusion. The former may not be reflective, the latter are little else. The former might not think themselves spiritual, and may not be.

I am inclined not to follow convention in believing that spirituality attaches solely to the transcendental. That's to say, I don't think that one needs to posit God, and God-given 'soul', to construct what is happening with spirituality. It's traditional and handy, but not necessary. I have met people I thought spiritual who were not religious. I have met religious people I thought were spiritual, and a good few I thought the antithesis. Indeed, by making a profession (in the senses both of a living and a proclamation) of spirituality, religious people are even more likely to be seen to fail than those who hardly try. Perhaps what is attractive about them is that they take the huge risk of advertising that spirituality is what they are after (and to be open to failure at the task).

So let's flesh out a little what we are looking for when we are on the hunt for spirituality. People would variously ascribe this sort of quality – or ambition – to walking, thinking, gardening, reading, listening to music, visiting an art gallery – and of course much religious activity. One would obviously include meditation, whether it was secular or religious. We somehow assume that the natural, the quiet, the still, are all qualities of the spiritual. Oddly, visiting an old person in a nursing home probably would not figure in a list of spiritual experiences: the smells, the anxieties, the decline in such places are too irritating or disturbing to make them quite do the trick. And yet, that's odd isn't it? Isn't spirituality to do with facing death, and doing so with equanimity?

Spirituality isn't, surely, to do with niceness, fragrance, the surface of things? A 'peaceful place' isn't spiritual. Maybe 'inner peace' does better. But outer peace can merely be dullness, and noisiness – or the smell of an old people's home – certainly doesn't preclude inner quiet.

We also reserve the word for a variety of modesty. The braggart is not spiritual. Nor is the man whose self-assessment is that he merits any advantage he has. But gratitude won't quite capture it either: one may be all too grovelling in one's gratitude. Dignity comes into it, but especially dignity under fire. The older religious world admired a quality that was ascribed to being 'favoured by God': the idea of grace. It works well in the secular world, too.

This is very difficult terrain. Spirituality, like virtue, is something we are inclined to believe is best observed in others than ascribed to ourselves. Anyone who says he is virtuous practically excludes himself from serious consideration as being virtuous. His virtuousness is blown out of the water by his arrogance, or his smugness. Similarly, self-declared spirituality is not likely to survive the charge of arrogance or self-centredness. Indeed, one of the hardest things about spirituality is to spot the moment when the 'centred' becomes the self-centred; when the consideration of one's spirit becomes solipsistic.

Nothing is more spiritual than the ascetic, anchoretic – nothing, either, is more prone to the charge of neurotic self-absorption. We are inclined, aren't we, to suppose that much New Age spirituality is a code for pandering to oneself? Monks have had centuries of thought about the 'sin' of self-absorption. It is a little like ennui, but is rather especially reserved for those who profess spirituality.

Altruism is far from defining spirituality. Doing good has very little to do with being spiritual, at least not directly. A busily altruistic person may be valuable and valued, and may even feel good, and feel it deeply, without being spiritual. Indeed, a spiritual person might well feel that doing good, and the virtuous warmth to be had from doing good, are the antithesis of being spiritual.

Even being moral is no guarantee of spirituality. The apparent conundrum is bound up with the way that being moral has to do with public outcomes, and being spiritual has to do with private aspirations. To be moral is to want there to be more good in the world, and to do something about it. To be spiritual is to want to stand up to a certain sort of self-examination. That will include the moral, for sure, but not end there. One might, for instance, believe that one had worked hard and successfully for a better world, and yet have failed spiritually.

So what is spirituality? I follow convention in opposing it to materialism. But only if materialism is taken as a creed. I don't at all think that the rich can't be spiritual, or that the poor are more likely to be.

IVAN ILLICH'S RADICAL MONOPOLY

RADICAL MONOPOLY

This is part of what Ivan Illich discussed in the late 60s and early 70s. He argued that modern life made complicated and costly what once had been simple. It industrialised and institutionalised a range of goods and services, especially health, education and transport. The advent of the car, for instance, made distance costly, and imposed distance on people. With its arrival, one could shop at a supermarket miles away with a car, but one could not shop locally on foot. A wonderful benefit had been conferred, but an important one had been taken away.

He described some of these mechanisms as Radical Monopoly, by which he meant to expand on the idea of a firm acquiring domination of a market. A Radical Monopoly was acquired by a technology, or method, rather than by a firm. It is a valuable idea: if it is true that cars have created and co-opted distance, then that is a phenomenon indeed. Oddly, it produces an argument for public transport. If the car has co-opted distance, then those without a car will need alternative provision. This is because the car's Radical Monopoly has, in a sense, privatised distance, and the poor will – in justice – have to be given access to it.

Note that it is wealth that has produced this new potential poverty. It was wealth that produced the new technology, and Mass Affluence that made it nearly ubiquitous. It is wealth that creates the necessity of considering those without wealth.

There are other extensions of the idea that are valuable. Some rights might be thought to pre-exist others. That's to say: might one not argue that walking has a prior right over motoring? Or that silence has a prior right over noise? This latter is part of what we mean by nuisance. We take it that people have a right to quiet enjoyment of their street, of a swimming pool, or their home. Thus, traffic in a street, muzak in a swimming pool, or a neighbour's hi-fi are, in some sense, radically monopolising the soundscape. The simple is being abused by the complex; the prior (the right to quiet) by the secondary (the right to do as one likes).

Let's take the case of a car. Primitive critics suggest that ads make us want a car when we don't need one, and – or – then make us yearn for a particular brand. Ivan Illich is not cited by Klein, but 30 years before her offering, he notes the Radical Monopoly by which the existence of the car renders car ownership compulsory.

Klein suggests that the car will be designed not merely to appeal to our personality, but to help us create one. The ad and the item conspire together to make us into particular sorts of yearning creatures. And worse, capitalists know that if one of them doesn't shape us into perfect consumers, then another will. We can choose from quite a wide range of personality-shaping items of consumption, but not escape the personality-shaping function of consuming.

ERICH FROMM ON IVAN ILLICH[1]

Dr. Illich's papers deal precisely with such examples as the usefulness of compulsory schooling, or of the present function of priests. Many more could be added, some of which are implied in the author's papers. I want to mention only a few like the modern concept of 'progress', which means the principle of ever-increasing production, consumption, timesaving, maximal efficiency and profit, and calculability of economic activities without regard to their effect on the quality of living and the unfolding of man; or the dogma that increasing consumption makes man happy, that the management of large-scale enterprises must necessarily be bureaucratic and alienated; that the aim of life is having (and using), not being; that reason resides in the intellect and is split from the affective life; that the newer is always better than the older; that radicalism is the negation of tradition; that the opposite of 'law and order' is lack of structure. In short, that the ideas and categories that have arisen during the development of modern science and industrialism are superior to those of all former cultures and indispensable for the progress of the human race.

[1] From Erich Fromm's Introduction to Illich's *Celebration of Awareness*, Penguin, 1971.

INDEX

Page numbers in **bold** refer to footnotes in the text

Abramovich, Roman 123, 281
accountants 174–5, 179–80, 187
Ad Mass 36
Adbusters 53, 58–9, 242
Addison, Joseph (1672–1719) 85–6
advantage 42–3, 48–50, 57, 261
advertising 43, 51–5, 55–61, 60, 207
aesthetics 26, 48, 61, 235–9, 268, 294
Affluenza 22–3, **34**, 42, 96
affordable payments 29
Afghanistan 174
Africa 32, 94–5, **106**, 194–5, 212–13
    and grace 2, 212–13, 282
    poorer 84, 102–3
    potential 207, 235, **241**
aggression 155, 189, 289
Al Qaeda 173
Allen, Robert 231, **240**
'alternative contract enforcement' 192
alternativists 49–50
ambition 29–30, 49, 110–14, 126–30, 234
America 17, 82, 89
American Moment 118
Anderson, Digby 22, 26, **34**, 271–2, 297
anger 212–13, 253–5, 262
Anglosphere 16, 23, 65, 68–82, 161
    taxation 45–6, 65, 68–82
animal studies 115–16
Antarctic exploration 207
anthropology, working-class 130–4
anti-democratic teaching 42
anti-Establishment 14, 42, 221, 241, 246, 271
anti-globalization 19, **33**, 55–60, 174
    Seattle 17–18, 22, **34**
anti-heroes 42–3
anxiety 40, 115, **153**, 257
    see also status
Anxiety Industry 14, 247, 260
architecture 175, 179, 196, 208, 273
Ardizzone, Sir Edward (1900–79) 54
Argentina 99

Argos 122, 251
aristocrats 47–50, 51, 96, 148–9, 151, 252
    formation of 13, 24–5, 112, **153**
Aristotle (384–322 BC) 212
Armenians 86
Army, British 210–12, 252, 257, **260**
Ashley, Laura (1925–85) 54, 176
Asia 17, 84, 103, **107**
Aslund, Anders 191–2, **196**
aspiration 59–60, 117, 136, 244
    to stimulation 46, 198–203
aspirations
    competing 237–9
    deflected by brands 58–9, 138, 143–4
    spiritual 198–210
attitude, to wealth 42–3, 141
Auschwitz 219
Austen, Jane (1775–1817) 124, 135, 141–2, 201, 210
Australia 79, 81, 99
authenticity 258
authority, disrespect for 250–1

Bacon, Francis, Viscount St. Albans (1561–1626) 92, **101**
Bailey, Ronald 234, **240**
Bakewell, Joan 253–4
balance 128, 259, **260**
Balfour, Jabez 185–6
Bangalore 98
Bangladeshis 70
Banks, Iain 147
Banks, Joseph 201
Barbed Wire Elite 31, 95–8
Bartlett, Bruce 72–3, **83**
Bauer, Peter 235, **241**, 245, 276
BBC see British Broadcasting Corporation
Beckerman, Wilfred 234, **240**
Beckham, Victoria 123, 142
Beckham, David 31, 122, 142
Beer, Samuel 252, **260**

Belgium 81–2, 92
Benn, (A.) Tony (1925–) 19, 177, 274
Berlin, Sir Isaiah (1909–97) 12, 263, 276
Berlusconi, Silvio 243
Bernays, Edward (1891–1995) 52–5, **63**
Bettelheim, Bruno 276, 286
biodiversity 233, **240**
bitterness 212, **220**, 252
black, anti-social 91, **106**
Blacker, Terence 158, **183**
Blackwell, Chris 173, **183**
Blair, (A.) Tony, Chav P.M. 16–17, 28–9, 55, 68
   infantilism 243–8, 251–2
Blair, (Booth) Cherie 242
blat 191
Blofeld, Henry 151
Blom, Philipp 204, **220**
Blond, Anthony 257, **260**
Blundell, John 100, **107**
Blyth, Myrna 163–4
Body Shop 58
Boeing 58
bohemians 51
BoHo lifestyle 121, 206
Boscastle 246
Bossy Middle Class 31, 94–8
Boston, Richard 275
Botton, Alain de 19–20, 33, 115, 126, 141–2
bourgeois 138, 145
BP 54, **106**
Bragg, Melvyn (1939–) 135
Brains Trust 135
brands 14, 55, 57, 88–9, 182, 207
   and art 53–4, **63**, 200, 203–4, **220**
   consumers 50–63, 120–4, 130–1, 166–7, 296
   false 121–2, 130–1
   Third World 122
Branson, Richard 57–8, 60
Brazil 97, 99, 122, **153**, 234
Brent Spar 188–9, 235–6, **241**
British Broadcasting Corporation 139–40
British Constitution 263, 269–70
Brittan, Sir Samuel (1933–) 65

Brody, Hugh 134, **154**
Brotton, Jerry 198–9, **220**
Brown, Gordon (1951–) 251
Brunel, I. K. (1806–59) 175–6, **183**
BT 54
Bubble, Internet 185–6
Bucket, Mrs 125, 143, **153**
bulk-buying 62–3
Bunting, Madeline 16, 21–2, **34**, 164
Burama, Ian **153**
Burberry and chavs **34**
Burger King 160
Bush, George H. W. (1924–) 119
Bush, George W. (1946–) 68, 72–4, 83, 119, 227
Butler, Lord, of Brockwell 252–3
Butler, Samuel (1835–1902) 132
Byron, Lord (1788–1824) 14, 42, 245

Cabinet government 252–3
Camel 56
Campaign to Protect Rural England 22–3, 237, **241**
Canada 46, 74–5, **83**, 134, **154**
Canterbury, Archbishop of 13–14, **33**, 251
Capitalism
   and good 11–12, 16–22, 141
   voluntary 59–63, 159, 250–1
Capp, Andy 145, **154**
cargo 228, **240**
Caribbean 70, 91, 201
Carlyle, Thomas (1794–1881) 132
Carney, Ray 117, **153**
'carrying capacity' 232–5, **240**
cars 56–7, 60–1, 130, 145, 161, 271, 278–9, 296
   '4x4' 27, 36, 40–1, 209, 244
Carter, James E. (1924–) 229, **240**
caveat emptor 50–1
CBI *see* Confederation of British Industry
Center for Global Development 101, **107**
Centre for Economic Performance 44
challenges 48, 117, 128, 257, 265
Chapman, Jake *and* Dinos 203, **220**
Chardin, Teilhard de (1881–1955) 276, 284–6

charities 149, 152, **154**, 215, 248
Chav P.M., Blair, Tony 28–9, 55, 243–4, 247–8, 251–2
chavs 27, **34**, 142, 168, 242, 266–7
Cheshire, Lord, G. Leonard, V.C. (1917–92) 279
Chesterton, G. K. (1874–1936) 256
children 36, 245, 249–50, 258–9, **260**
China 3, 31, 91, 101, 103, **107**, 139, 194, 228, 234, **240**
choices 49, 59, 81–2, 163–5, 177
  for aristocrats 47–50, 148, 151
  individual 24–9, 48, 204–9
  and neo-liberalism 19–23, **33**, 40
  and pleasures 49–50, 61–2, 198–200
Chomsky, Avril Noam (1928–) 52, 59, **63**
Christianity 42, 47, 101
Churchill, Lord Randolph (1849–95) 270, **283**
Clark, Alan 121
Classical era 181
Clifford, Max 151
Cline, William 101, **107**
Clinton administration 17, 68–9, 72
Clinton, William (1946–) 16, 29, 118–19
Clover, Charles 54, **63**
Club Petrovich 136
Club of Rome 231, **240**, 277
Cobbett, William (1763–1835) 85, 273–4, 287
Coca-Cola 14, 57, 86
Cohen, Pete 35
Coke, Sir Edward (1552–1634) 92
Collins, Michael 131–4, **154**
Columbia 99
Common Agricultural Policy 275
competition 29–30, 157, 169, 172, 289–**91**
complaints 15, 23, 36, 114, 226, 252–5, 268–9
compromises 174, 211, 246, 253–4
Confederation of British Industry 16
Congressional Budget Office study 72
consensus 134, 263
Conservative 26, 230, 281, 289
Constable, John (1776–1837) 176

consumer 16, 50–63, 167–8, 269
Consumer Society 51
consumerism 21, **33**, 52, 237
consumption smoothing 258–9, **260**
contentment 37–9, 265–8, 292–4
Continental 20, 40–2, 139, 229, 270, 275
  capitalism 16–17, 68, 76–7, 79–82
Continental Consensus 44, 68
contracts 44, 168
contrarians 221, 234–5, **239**, **241**, 273
Cook, Captain James (1728–79) 201
Cooke, Alistair (1908–2004) 120, **153**
cooperation 168–72
Cornell, Joseph 203, **220**
corporate business 18–19, **33**, 155–7
Corporate Social Responsibility 54, 188–9, 194–5, **196**, 226
corruption 39, 52, 96, 98–100, **107**, 184–**96**
counter-culture 168, **183**
counter-Freudians 53
counter-snobbery 108–9
courage 24–5, 212
craft-work 59–60, 159–60, 177
Crass Affluence 27
creativity 156–9, 173–**83**, 198–203, 263, 278
Crosse and Blackwell Pot Noodle 57
culture 19–22, **33**, 81–2, 94–5
Culture of Contempt 246, 249–50, 260, **260**, 265
Curtis, Adam 52–3, 245, **260**
Cusack, John 41
customer 15–16, 44, 56–7
  understanding 52–4, 166–8, 171–2, **183**

Dalyell, Sir Thomas of the Binns, Bt. M.P. (1932–) 133
Das, Gurcharan 99, **107**
debt 113, 265
deference 245–6, 249–50, 265–6
Defoe, Daniel (1660–1731) 216–17, **220**
democracy 32–**3**, 66, 90–4, **106**, 263
  and business 18, **33**, 254, **260**
Democratic policies 17–18, 29, 47, 229

Denby, David 157, **183**
Denmark 23, 29, 46, 79, 86, 100, 116
Department of Trade and Industry 140
dereliction 275
deserving and undeserving poor 67
designers 176–7
developing countries 101–2, 230, 234
diasporas 91
dignity 44, 68, 245, 261, 294
disadvantage 110, 114–17
display 199–203, 207–9, 217–19
dissent 152–3, 181, 224, 270–1
dissidence of left 42, 152
Dollar, David 102, **107**
downsizing 45–6, 49, 61–2, 70, 208, 265, 287
downspeak 37, 139, 143, 282
dreams for sale 53–60, 178
Dyckhoff, Tom 179, **183**
Dylan, Bob (R. A. Zimmerman) (1941–) 14, 42
dynamism 114, 233, 290

Easterbrook, Gregg 22, 40–4, 48, **63**, 184, **196**, 234, **240**
eBay 248, **260**
ecology 223–5, 228, 268, 276, 278
economic arguments, happiness 17–19
economic growth 84–94, 262, 265
    lack of 37, 39, 262
    resources 32–3, 80, 104, 222–3, 226–7, 232
education
    investment 110–14, 137, 144
    and poverty 109, 135, 208, 222
    Third World 86, 98–9, 104, **107**, 280
efficiency, economics 86, 156, **183**, 296
Ehrlich, Paul 231, **240**
Elizabeth, H.M. The Queen 239, 252, 272
Embarrassed Loyalties 250, 251, 265
Emerson, Ralph Waldo (1803–82) **63**, 118, 217, 289–90
Emin, Tracey 167–8, **183**
emotion 21, 265, 276, 285

Empire 90–4, **106**, 120, 149, 270–1, 280
    attitude against 151–2, 250–2
engineers 175–6, 180, 196
Enlightenment 86, 153, 176, 181, 201, 268
Enlightenment liberal 10, 285
Enron 156, 184–90, 193, **196**
entrepreneurs 95–100, 104–7, 196
    and creativity 157–8, 163–4, 176–82, 202, 214, 263, 274–5
    and happiness 76, 80
    risk 113, 140–1, 160
environmental dilemmas 223–32, 262, 277–8
environmentalism 55, 267–8, 275–8
environmentalists 143–5, 267–8
Erasmus, Desiderius (c1466–1536) 12, 14, 280
Esso 54, **63**
Establishment, The 42, 149, 270, 279
Ethiopia 100
Eurobarometer 37–9, 44–5, **65**, 163, **183**
European model 95–8, 227
European 'poverty league' 75–6, **83**
Eurosclerosis 44, 76–7
    see also Continental, France, Germany
Exclusively for Everyone 52–3
existential depression 20
expectations 20, **33**, 44
expenditure 30, 198, 269
ExxonMobil 89, **106**

failure and success 126–30
false consciousness 15, **33**, 46
fashion 14, 121, 167–8, **183**, 217–19, 273
    lifestyle sales 19, **33**, 37–9, 57–8
    in mores 135, 137–9, 150–1
    in politics 246–7, 265
fecklessness 51, 65, 134
Ferguson, Niall 94, **106**, 135
films 97, 147, 150, 180, 186, 199
    and Frontier 116–20, **153**
    and patriotism 138, 272–3
    US 117–20, **143**, 146–9, 157–8

Finland 109
fish 222, 232
Fisher, H. A. L. (1865–1940) 12
Flew, Antony 12
flower power 52, 60, **63**, 243–4, 261
focus groups 55, 252, 254, **260**
food marketing 139
Foot, Paul (1937–2004) 133, **154**
football hooligans 36–7, **63**, 134–5
forbearance 24, 257
Forces of Conservatism 245, 246, 251,
   260
Ford, Gerald R. (1913–) 229
Ford, Henry (1863–1947) 117, 213,
   217
Forster, E. M. (1879–1970) 245
Fort Worth 282
Foucault, Michel (1926–84) 52, 276,
   286, **291**
France 46, 86, 96, 114, 126, 185, **196**,
   284
Frank, Thomas 18, **63**
fraud 13, 184–96
free trade 25, 100, **107**, 268
Freud, Sigmund (1856–1939) 52–3,
   135, 243
Fromm, Erich (1900–80) **296**
Furedi, Frank 247, **260**

G8 101
gas emissions 41, 226–34, **240**
Gates Foundation 89
Gates, William 30
Geldof, Bob 246, 249
generosity 24, 84, 95, 264
genetically modified organisms 230,
   232, **240**
gentleman 118, 130, 188, 199, 207,
   261, 282
George, M. D. 151–2, **154**
George V (1865–1936) 150–1, **154**
German 10, 52, 76, 126
Germany 23, 44, 46, 81–2, 114,
   235–6
getting and spending 24, 47–50, 59,
   197, 262
   globalization 85, **106**
Gibbon, Edward (1737–94) 12
Gingham Tendency 206–7

Glasgow, Faith 165, **183**
glass ceilings 108–14, **153**
Glastonbury Festival 121, **153**
GlaxoSmithKline 89, **106**
global warming 223–8, 235, **240**, 281
globalization
   diatribes against 13–14, 52–6,
      85–9, 174
   history of 23, 90–4, **106**, 285–6
   and Mass Affluence 84–**107**, 165,
      173–5, 268
Goebbels, Joseph (1897–1945) 52
Goethe, J. W. von (1749–1832) 245
Gogol, Nikolai V. (1809–52) 191
golden-ageism 37, **63**
Goldsmith, Edward (1928–) 231, **240**
Goldsmith, Zac 178
Good Housekeeping Happiness survey
   35–6, **65**
Gore, Al, Senator 229, **240**
Gove, Michael 22
government 104, 167
grace 13, 23, 25, 43–4, 212, 259, 282,
   294
   lost 37, 41, 249, 261
Grant, Duncan (1885–1978) 54
Granville Barker, Harley
   (1877–1946) 133
gratification, deferred 61–2
gratitude 12, 23, 43–4, 80, 212, 292
   withheld 41, 228–9, 264
Gray, John 17, **33**
'Great Backlash' 18
Greeks 25, 38, **65**
'green' evidence-led optimism 40
Greenfield, Susan 245–6, **260**, 284,
   291
Greenpeace 235–6, 275–6
greens 25–6, 80, 224, 227, 230–**41**
   brands 59, 272
   romantic 273, 277–8, **283**
Gress, David 93, **106**
Griffith, Mickey *and* Alison 165, **183**
Grossman, Lloyd 124
Guatemala 53
Guevara, Ernesto Che (de la Serna)
   (1928–67) 14–15
Gummer, John M.P. 229

Habitat 137–9
Hackett, General Sir John (1910–97) 276
Haiti 99
Halsey, A.H. 287
Hamilton, Clive 16, 21, **34**, 115
Hammond, J. L. *and* Barbara 152, **154**
Hapgood, Rt. Rev. Dr John *see* York
happiness 35–63, 127–31, 262
  and materialism 35–6, 47–50, 79
  measuring 37–9
  relative 17–22, 45, 66, 78–9
  see also Eurobarometer
Hardin, Garrett 231, **240**
Harper, T. N. 90, **106**
Hasan, Sheeraz 171, **183**
Hayek, F. H. 171, **183**
Heals 137
Hearst, W. R. (1863–1951) 117
Heath, Sir Edward R. G. (1916–) 78
Heffer, Simon 78, **83**
Henderson, David 103, **107**, 190–3, **196**
heritability 14, 112
heroes 284–9
Hertz, Noreena 19, **33**, 87–8, **106**
Heseltine, Michael R. D., Lord (1933–) 121
Hiaasen, Carl 147
Hibbing, John R. 254, **260**
Hill, Christopher (1912–2003) 92–3, **106**, 155
Hispania 92, 94
Hodges, William 201, **220**
Hodgson, Godfrey 18, **33**, 40, 42
Hoggart, Richard (1918–) 23, 132–5, **154**, 247
Hollywood 41, 116, 129, 146–9
  see also films
Holt, Douglas B. 89, **106**
hooligans 36–7, **63**, 134–5, 149–51, 270
hormones 116
horses, symbolic purity 119–20
'How To Spend It' magazine 207, **220**
Human Development Index 81, **83**
human faults 28
Humphrys, John 246

Hutton, Lord (1931–) 252–3
Hutton, Will 16–18, **33**, 40–3, 71, 87
  social mobility 109, 126
  hypermobility 237–8, **241**

IBM 161
IKEA 121–2, 136–9
Illich, Ivan (1926–2002) 273, 286–8, 291, 295–6
  tools for conviviality 128, 160, 287
IMF *see* International Monetary Fund
immigration 70–1, 78, 91, 111
Indian 86, 97, 99, 103, **107**, 234
  immigrant 70, 139
individuality 52–5
Indonesia 99
industrial development 96, 104, 112, **153**, 202, 250–2
Industrial Revolution 152, **154**, 156, 169, 201–2, 202, 280
inequality 31–3, 46, 64, 81, 84, 147
  extreme 13, 32, 94–5
  and Mass Affluence 50–5, 64–**83**
  rates 64–8, 71–7, **83**, 101–3, **107**, 110, **153**
infantilism 130, 134, 243–9, 251–3, 253, **260**, 266
'inner flake' 58
inner peace 11, 211–12, 288, 292–4
innovation 85, 91–4, 157, 161
Institute of Directors 79, **83**
Institute of Economic Affairs 268
Institute for International Economics 101, **107**
Institute for Public Policy Research **63**, 64–5, 259, **260**
intellectual capital 88, 91–92, 95, 105, 247–8
intellectual property 181–3
International Monetary Fund 17–18, **33**, 86, 101
International Policy Network 235, **241**
Inuit 134
IPPR *see* Institute for Public Policy Research
Iraq 55
Ireland 75, **83**
Ironbridge 202, **220**

Islam 46, 279
Isserlis, Stephen 182–3
Italy 38, **63**, 73, 79, **83**

Jacques, Martin 16–17, **33**
James, Henry (1843–1916) 118, 150, 289, **291**
James, Oliver 20, **33**, 116, 125–9, 143, **153**
James, William (1842–1910) 63, 118, 267, 275–6, 280, 289–**91**
Japan 79, 81, 86, 93
Jerome, John 211, **220**
job insecurity 46, 159–61
John, Elton (1947–) 121–2
John Paul, Pope 250, **260**
Johnson, Frank 79, **83**
Johnson, Paul 12
Jones, Eric 93, 103, **106–7**
Jones, Tristan 205, **220**
Jopling, Michael M.P. 121
Jordan, W. K. 149, **154**
Joseph Rowntree Trust 75–6, **83**
Judaism 47, 52, 91, 276
Judd, Alan **154**, 244, **260**
Jung, Carl G. (1875–1961) 53, 243

Kahn, Herman (1922–83) 234, **240**, 276–7, **283**
Kennedy, John F. (1917–63) 18, 72, 118–19
Kerry, John, US Senator 119, 200
Kerry, Teresa Heinz 200, **220**
Kew 239
kindness 70, 264, 279, 287–9
Klein, Naomi 14, 19–20, **33**
   brands 55–60, 115, 166–7, 296
kleptocracy 95–6, 104–5, **106**
Knack, Steve 172
Knight, India 282, **283**
Knight, Richard Payne (1750–1824) 201–2, **220**
Koon, Jeff 122
Kronenberger, Louis 117, **153**
Kropotkin, Prince Peter (1842–1921) 160, 276, 287
Kuper, Simon 134–5, **154**
Kyoto Protocol 185, 227

Laing, R. D. (1927–89) 52, 245, 286
Landes, David 92, **106**
Latin America 84, 89, 97
law 90–100, **106–7**, 168–9, 192–3, 196
   and market 181–3, 188–90, 237–9, 262
Law, John (1671–1729) 185–6, **196**
lawyers 196, 263
Lay, Ken 185, **196**
Layard, Professor Lord Richard 19, 44–7, **63**
Leach, Gerald 276
Learned
   Helplessness 126, 163
   Optimism 126
Lees, Andrew 276
Lennon, John (1940–80) 182
Leonard, Elmore 147
Lesotho Highlands Development Authority 194–5, **196**
Less Developed Countries 101, **107**
Levellers 42
Lever Brothers 57
liberal
   definition 10, 197
   elite, last class 137–8
   response inequality 104, 147
liberalism 41, 176, 243, 257, 297
libertarian 14, 19, 26–7, 104, 270
liberties 268
Libeskind, Daniel 179, **183**
Liddle, Rod 29, **34**
Lipstick Radical 55
Litvin, David **196**
Llewelyn-Bowen, Laurence 138–9
Lomborg, Bjorn 55, 225, 234–5, **241**
London 151, 152, **154**
London School of Economics 44
longevity 128–30, **153**, 237, 280
Lorenz, Konrad 115–16, 276
Lovelock, James 232–3, **240**
'low-taxes' liberal definition 10
luck, grace, gratitude 23, 30, 36, 43, 140
lung cancer 53, 62
Luther, Martin (1483–1546) 181
luxuries now staple use 200–3
Lyons Teashops 54

Mabey, Richard 11
MacArthur, Ellen 207
MacCarthy, Fiona 176–7, **183**
McDonald's 31, 54, 59, 139, 160, 269
McJobs 128, 160
McKibben, Bill 230, **240**
McRae, Norman 276
Maddison, Angus **107**
Maddox, Sir John 234, 277
Madonna (singer) 14–15
Mafia Capitalism 191–3
Magna Carta (1215) 93, **106**
Maier, Karl **196**
malaise, modern 25, 40–4, 242–60
Malaysia 94, 100
Malone, Thomas W. 128, **153**
Malthus, Rev. T. R. (1766–1834) 169, 231
manifesto, personal 11–12, 267–**83**
manners 13, 22, **34**, 131–5, **154**
  and happiness 36–7, 39, 249–52, 289–**91**
market 15–16, 51–5, 123
  and free people 27, 92–4, 168, 171–3, **183**, 289–90
  and moral qualities 44, 155, 189–**96**, 208–10, 268
Marks and Spencer Ltd., Exclusively 52–3
Marley, Bob (1945–81) 174, **183**, 273, 274
Maslow, Abraham 210, **220**
Mass Affluence
  class and disapproval of 14–23
  and corruption 184–**96**
  and globalization 84–**107**
  and happiness 35–63
  and inequality 64–**83**
  and modern malaise 242–60
  and society 155–83
  and spirituality 197–220
  and status 108–54
  and sustainable development 221–41
materialism 11, 114–15, 141–2, 296
  crass 31–2, 117
  and happiness 35–6, 282
May, Henry F. 86, **106**

May, Sir Robert 233, **240**
Meacher, Michael M.P. 229
meanness, healthy 62–3
media misery 41–2, 247–9, 270, 282
mega-yacht 31, 123, 215, 281
Melbourne, William Lamb (1779–1848) 12, 280–1
mental health, as radicalism 52
mercantilism 80, 231
Merquior, Jose 286, **291**
Merton, Thomas (1915–68) 198, 205–9, **220**, 275, **283**
Mexico 79, 97, **106–7**
Micro-Middle class 98–100, **106**
middle class
  mores 39, 61–2, 149, 269
  rise 94–100, 195–6
  see also Barbed Wire, Bossy, Micro-Middle class *and* mockney
migration 23, 90–1, 105, **106**
Mill, John Stuart (1806–73) 263
mindshare, tyranny of 20, **33**
minimum wage 42, 68, 77–8, 105
Mississippi Company 185–6, **196**
Mitford, Hon. Nancy F. (1904–73) 51, 124, 148, **153**, 204, **220**
mockney middle classes 37, 266
monasteries 11, 198, 205–7, 214–17, **220**, 278, **283**
Monbiot, George 15, 18–19, **33**, 274
money 36, 50–1, 173–83
monks 190, 205–9, 214–16, **220**, 275, 282, 290, 292
Mooney, Bel 137–8, **154**, 270
Moore, Michael 18
moral 13, 17–19, 23, **33**
  challenges 24–8, 79
  choices 42–3, 155–6, 193–6
  failure 24, 41–2, 184–92
  happiness 36–7, 39
  and poor 42–3, 47–8, 76–82, 95–8
  qualities 44, 142
mores, fashionable 138
Morris, Julian 235, **241**
Morris, William (1834–96) 176–8, **183**
mortality 71, 152, 169
Mount Athos 207

Mount, Peggy (1918–2001) 131–2, **154**
mousetraps, better 170–1
multiculturalism 247, **260**, 272
multinationals 54–9, 88–9
municipal policies 95–6, 152
Muniratnama 98, **107**
Murray, Bishop Donal 251, **260**
museums 91, 94, **106**, 200–4, 247, **260**
music 133, 173–5, 178–9, 181–2, 273
and gloom 244, 246, 249, 255

Nash, John 54
National Theatre 135
National Trust 124, 141, 207
Native American 134
'nature' 222–3, 230–5, 237–9, **239–41**, 256–7
needs 19, 49–55
negative externality 45
neglected 203–6, 274
Nehru, Jawaharlal 99
Nelson, Horatio, Viscount (1758–1805) 143, 152
Nemli, Melih 103, **107**
neo-liberalism 15–17, 19–22, **33**, 42–4
definition 10
and inequality 64–5
mindset 16–17, 197
Netherlands 86, 93, 116
New Jersey 195
new rich, options 48
New York 85, 208
New Zealand 79, 236, **241**
Newfoundland 92, **106**
NGO *see* Non-Governmental Organisation
Nicolson, Adam 205–6, **220**
Nigeria 88, 104–7, **106**, 188–9, 194–5, **196**
Nighy, Bill 249
nihilism 41–2, 61, 146, 242, 246
Nike 58, 60, 89, **106**, 168, 177
Nixon, Richard M. (1913–94) 229
Noblesse oblige 24, 43
Nokia 58
Non-European cooperation 90–1

Non-Governmental Organisation 89, 97, 101, 165, 166–7, 226, 252
see also PR Project
Noosphere 285–6
North, Richard D.
personal 6, 267–83
references 33–4, 63, 88, **106**, 153–4, **183**, **196**, 234–5, **240–1**, 292–4
Norwegian 76, 87
nostalgia 136
nuisance 238–9
numbers 179–80, 198, 233

obligations 25, 42–3, 47, 76–82, 95–8
officials 98–100, 117, 126, 215
O'Hear, Anthony 271–2, 297
oil 31, 53–4
oil firms 63, 89, **106**, 172, 192, 226
Oligarchs 192–3, **196**, 262
Only Connect 245–6
opportunities 27, 44, 47–50, 263, 266, 288–9
opposites in advertising brands 52–4
options, new rich 48, 165
Orientals 70
O'Rourke, P. J. 18
Osbournes, Kelly *and* Ozzie 142
Oscar Effect 129
outsourcing 18–19, 29, 128, 266
Oxfam-chic 121

Packard, Vance 51–2, 115–17, 120, **153**
Paine, Thomas (1737–1809) 42, 273–4
painting 54, 118, 157, 174, 198–9, 203, 207, 218–19
Pakistanis 70
Palmer, Tom G. 85–6, **106**, 250
Panagariya, Arvind 101, **107**
Panel Study of Income Dynamics 71–2, **83**, 110, **153**
paradoxes 155, 184, 199–201
Parker, Cornelia 204
Parnell, Val 133
patience 24, 174, 257, 261
patriotism 138, 271–2
patronage 200

Pawson, John 208, **220**
Paxman, Jeremy 246, 259–60
Paxton, Sir Joseph (1801–65) 17, **183**
Payne, David 209, 217, **220**
Pearson, Geoffrey 37, **63**, 151, **154**
peasants 59–60, **63**, 101, 16
    and romantics 39, 158–60, 274–5
People, The 13, 28, 124, 130,
    268, 270
Persaud, Raj 172, **183**
pharmaceuticals 89, **106**, 181–2, 222,
    257
philanthropy 30, 44, 48, 89, 151–2,
    154
    and spirituality 200–3, 213–14,
    264–6
picaresque 134, 269–70
picturesque 207, 269
Pierce, Andrew 243–4, **260**
planning 236–9, **241**
plays and playwrights 272–3, 282
pleasures 49–50, 198–202, 208, 262,
    265
    material 19–20, **33**, 120–4, 130–1,
    281–2
Plumb, J. H. 149–51, **154**
politeness 147, 266
politics of the environment 229
poor 36, 62, 64–70, 92–105, 264
    countries 94–104, 222–3, 226
    left view 16–17, 25–6, 28, **33**
    and status 82, 108–14, 121
    young 50, 71, 108, 114, **153**
population 103, 169, 227–8, 230–1,
    288
    and income 84, 111
Porter, Roy 12, 286, **291**
Portugal 28, 38, **63**, 75, 83, 134–5
positive thinking 40–3, 48
Post, Marjorie Merriweather 200, **220**
Post Modern 61, 166–7, 218, 258,
    275
    structuralists 53
post-scarcity society 20
poverty 21, 47, 106–9, 149, **153**, 222
    Canada 74, **83**
    comparative 69–79, 114–16, 278
    decrease of 13, 67–76, 102–4,
    110–14, 264–5

relief of 149, 151–2, **154**, 212, 265,
    276
    severe 70–1, 74–6, **83**, 101–4, 114,
    212, 239
    and the spiritual 21, 30, 208–10
PR Project 53
prayer 213–16, **220**
Precautionary Principle 225–6
Price, Uvedale 202
Priestly, John Boynton (1894–1984)
    133
Prochaska, F. K. 152, **154**
Procter and Gamble 89, 99, **107**
productivity 154–5, **183**
professionalism 97, 104, 163, 193–6,
    208, 246
prole-chic 282, **283**
propaganda 52
proper-ganda 53
Protestant values 118, 146, 147, 149,
    155–7
PSID see Panel Study of Income
    Dynamics
psycho-engineering 53–63
psychology 19–22, **33**, 53
psyops 51
Public Relations 51–5
Putnam, Robert 120

quite-rich, moaning 36

Raban, Jonathan (1942–) 54
radical monopoly 295
radicalism, 52, 274, 281, 286–7,
    295–6
Raleigh, Sir Walter (1552–1618)
    92–3, **106**
Rasmussen, Steen Eiler 152, **154**
Reagan, Ronald W. (1911–2004)
    78–9, 119
Reaganomics 67–8, 72–4, **83**
recession poverty 51, 71–4, 81, **83**,
    109
reclusion 205–9, 216–17, 275, 278,
    284
recycling
    as art 203–5, 217–19, **220**
    waste 228–30, **240**, 275, 277
redistribution 65

reflectives 11–12, 198, 206–17, 213, 219
regulations 98–9, **107**, 126, 186–7, 268
    or discipline 39, 172
    and outsourcing 19
    and trade 19, **33**, 93, 99, 262, 268
    see also corruption, officials
Reich, Robert (1946–) 16, **33**
Reich, William 52
Reid, Dr John M.P. (1947–) 62
relationships, stable 127
reliability 170
religion 243, 256, 286
    and spirituality 292–4
Renaissance 176, 198, 207
Republican policies 18, 29, 147, 229
resources and economic growth 32–3, 80
restraint 288–9
Richmond 239
Rio Tinto 166
risk 125–30, 140, 152, 156–9, 170–2, 179–80, 239, 263
    environmental 222–5
    search for 46–7, 256–7, 288–9
Roberts, Andrew 135
Robinson Crusoe 205, 216–17, **220**
role models 142–3
Roman Catholicism 217, 243, 251–2, 280, 285
Romans 25, 203, 242
Romantics 39, 42, 176, 181, 198, 202, 221, 230, 245
    and planet 222–8
Rome, Club of 277
Rousseau, Jean Jacques (1712–78) 42, 245
Royal College of Art 175, **183**
Royal Shakespeare Company 135
Royal Society for Arts and Industry 176
RTZ *see* Rio Tinto
Rubin, Robert E. 68
Rubinomics 68, **83**
Russia 86, 96, 101, 136, 204, 262
    corruption 10, 190–3, **196**, 262
    economic crises 17

Saatchi and Saatchi 41
Sacco, Amy 170, **183**
safety net 44, 264
Salomon, Charlotte 219, **220**
Salon.com 53, **63**
Sanghera, Sathnam, 212, **220**
Sao Paolo 99
Sapolsky, Robert M. 116, **153**
satire 144–5
satisfaction 38
Scandinavia 16, 44, 76–7, 79, 81–2
Schadenfreude 31
Schumacher, Fritz (1911–1977) 285
Schwartz, Barry 20, **33**, 40, 48, 157, 163, 211
Scott, Robert Falcon (1868–1912) 152
Scourfield, Gareth 243–4, **260**
Scruton, Roger 22–3, 26–7, 237, **241**, 271–2
Seabright, Paul 171–2, **183**
Seattle demonstration 17–18, 22, **33**
Self, Will (1961–) 249
self-discipline 111, 140–1, 245
self-employment 161–3
self-enfeebled 36, 265
self-help 282
self-improvement 140–4, 148
self-interest 43, 46, 190, 195–6
self-sufficiency 48–9, 60, 157, 274–5, 278
    at public expense 50
Seligman, Professor Martin 48, **63**, 126, 163
semiology 53
Sennett, Richard 16, 22, **34**
sentiment 134, 203–5
serotonin 116, 127–9, **153**
Shaftesbury, Lord (1801–85) 152, **154**
Shanghai 225
Shell 166, 188–9, **196**, 235–6, **241**
    associations 53–4, **63**, 207
    Nigeria 88, **106**, 188–9, 194–5, **196**
Sierra Leone 99–100
Silver, Kenneth E. 218, **220**
Simon, Julian (1932–98) 43, **63**, 103, 234, **240**
    influence of 276–7, **284**, 288–9, 291

Singapore 94
sins 11, 261–2
skills 160–5, 181–2
slavery 91–2, 201–2, 280
Sloane, Sir Hans (1660–1753) 201
Slocum, Joshua (1844–c1910) 205
small-town life 40, 117–19, 290
small-town values 149
Smiles, Samuel (1812–1904) 175, **183**
Smith, Adam (1723–90) 30, 93, **106**, 171
smoking 53, 62
snobbery 22, 88, 121, 137, 143–5, 150
  of author 269, 272, 282
  commercial 175, 200, 206–8
Snow, Jon 259
Soane, Sir John (1753–1837) 201, 204
Social Affairs Unit 269, 297
social exclusion 50–63, 68–70
social institutions 41, 124–6
social mobility 70–2, 108–14, 124–30, 131–45, 160
  lifestyle 199–200, 248, 256, 272, **283**
social reformers 152, **154**, 280, 286–8
socialism
  abandoned 16, 45–6, 52, 76, 101, 264
  economic failure 169, 235, 264, 271, 276–7
  old, complaints 15
society 41, 265
  agreeable 39, 46, 92–4, 104, **106**
  open 31–2, 147, 156, 255
  ordered 27, 124–5, 280–1
solar energy 222, 225, 232
Sony 56
Soto, Hernando de 98, **106**
Souhami, Diana 216–17, **220**
South Africa 79, 100, **107**
South Korea 94
Spanish 38, **63**, 75, 92, **106**, **183**, 279, 281
Spear, Ruskin 54
Spectator 29, 85–6, 244, 269–71
spelling 9
spending 198–208, 217–20, 263
spiritual poverty 21, 30, 291

spirituality 12–13, 30, 157, 171, 197–220, 278–9, 284
  and religion 292–4
Starbucks 22, 54, 269
State Take 29, 39, 64, 76–7, **83**, 96
  inefficient spending 44
  and voters 39, 42–4, 68, 72–4, 76–82
  'stationary state' 20
status 19–20, **33**, 82, 108–54, 199
Status Anxiety 19–20, 31, **33**, 69, 123–5, **153**
  reduction 130–1, 141–2, 247, 254–5
Status Anxiety Industry 14
Stewart, Barbara 173, **183**
Stiglitz, Joseph 17–18, **33**, 87
Stoppard, Tom (Thomas Straussler) (1937–) 12, **239**, 282
Street-Porter, Janet 254
stress 116, 125–7, 159, 162–4, 173, 242, 262
'stuff' and spirituality 12–13, 197–200
success 126–30, 140–1, 181–3, 212, 216–17, 261
succession 213–16
sustainability 213, 221–41
Sweden 46, 79, 81–2, 86
swing, of pendulum 243, 261
swinging Britain 137, 243, 270
Swiss Family Robinson 205, 275
Switzerland 85, 109
System, The 13, 15, 28

talent 111, 113
Tallis, Raymond 289, **291**
taste and habits 27, 36–7, 148, 270, 280
Tawney, R. H. (1880–1962) 155–7, **183**
tax
  acceptable 43–6, 65, 67, 263–4
  churn 76–7, 264
  consumers 68, 77, **83**
  farming 193
  progressive 45, 68, 72–4, 248, 264
  rises 42–5, 67–8, 115
  take 73–4, 76–7, 79–83, 96, 263
  yield 45, 68, 73–4, **83**

Taylor, A. J. P. (1906–90) 12, 135
Taylor, Matthew 13, **33**
Teasdale, Eric 163, **183**
Tebbit, Lord Norman B. (1931–) 272
technicians 196
technology 96, 98, 105, 128, 130,
   136, **153**, 165, **183**, 237–8
   censorship 181, **183**
   and spirituality 163, 202
Telegraph 269
television 22, 27, 31, 158, 248–9
   aggressive 22, 259–60
   position 123, 133, 135, 139–45,
   154
   US 124, 148
Thackeray, W. M. (1811–63) 149
Thatcher, (Lady) Margaret (1925–)
   63, 78–9, 127, 248
Thatcher, Sir Dennis Bt 78
Thatcherism 67–8, 252, **260**, 272
Theiss-Morse, Elizabeth 254, **260**
Thesiger, Wilfred 288
Third Way 16–18
Third World 96, 98, 188–9, 194–6,
   196
   development 92–100, 230–5,
   267–8, 277–8, 286, **291**
   education 86, 98–9, 104, **107**, 280
   production 100–1, **107**, 166–7
   relief 111, 122, **153**, 165, 168,
   181–2, 249
Thomas, Dylan Marlais (1914–53)
   204
Thoreau, Henry D. (1817–62) 198,
   274–5
Thornton, Dora 199, **220**
Thurley, Simon 124, **153**
Tiffen, Mary 235, **241**
Tocqueville, A. C. H. C. de (1805–59)
   120, **153**
Tompkins, Richard 184, **196**
trade 42, 80, 85, 149–50, 167,
   198–203, 248
   and cargo 228, **240**
   as Empire builder 90–4
   and trust 155–7, **183**
traditionalists 25–7
Tranquillity Map 237–9, **241**, 242

Trash Affluence 15, 59
Trollope, Anthony (1815–82) 186
Trump, Donald 31
trust 155–7, 168–73, **183**, 187–8,
   192–3, 256
Turner, Adair 16
Turner, Janice 163–4, **183**
Turner, J. M. W. (1775–1851) 176,
   183, 202
Twin Towers 173, 179
tyranny of consumerism 21
tyranny of mindshare 20

Uganda Asians 70
UK 16, 76–81, 130–1
underclass 111, **153**, 281
undercutting 105
unearned wealth 31, 157–8
Unilever 57, 89
Updike, John 254
Urban Institute 109, **153**
US 40–1, 71–4, 264
   and Continental economies 44,
   81–2
   frontiers and movies 116–20, **153**
   social mobility 71–2, 109–10, **153**
   wealth compared 85, 109, 130–1,
   145–9, **154**
   and welfare state 16–17, **33**, 40–4,
   68, 79, 254, **260**

value to customer 56–8, 246–7
values 145, 203–5, 213, 265, 290
   see also Protestant values
vigour 11–12, 28, 184, 190, 222–3,
   289–**91**
Virgin products 57–8
Virtual Empire 85–6
Virtual Firms 58, 166–8
virtue and expenditure 30, 32
virtues 156, 261–2, 295
Voltaire, F. M. A. (1694–1778) 112,
   150, **154**, 199, 272, **283**
volunteering 22, 28, 44, 127, 257,
   264, 266
voters and State Take 42–3
vulgarity 12, 25, 130–5, **154**, 269

Waldmeir, Patti 248, **260**
Wales, H.R.H. Prince of, Charles P. A. G.
   (1948–) 229, 281
Walker, Derek 175, **183**
wants and work 49–50
Ward, Barbara 276
Wardle, George 178, **183**
Washington 85, 96
waste 275, 277
Waterstone's 54
Watts, Sir Phillip 188, **196**
Waugh, Evelyn (1903–66) *and*
   Auberon (1939–2001) 275
Wax, Ruby 140, 158
wealth 13, 31, 108–24, 122–4, 155
   creation of 4–5, 45, 80, 155–68,
      192, 199
websites 9
wedge issues 18
Welfare State, state of 67–8, 248
West, fortunate 41–4
Western Project 268
Wharton, Edith N. (1861–1937) 150,
   186
Whitehouse, Mary (1910–2001) 272
Wilde, Oscar (1854–1900) 186
wilderness 222, 230, 239, **240**, 257
Williams, Rt. Rev. Rowan *see*
   Canterbury
Wilson, Baron (J.) Harold (1916–95)
   76, 78
Wilson, Harriette (1786–1855) 151,
   154
Winner, David 135
Wolf, Martin 105, **107**
Women's Institute 251
work
   benefit 50, 75–8, **83**, 111, 166–7
   enjoyment 38, 147, 158–65, **185**
   and women 54, 161–2, 470
workers, overworked 16, 22, **34**
working class 130–4, **154**, 279–80
   definition 135–6
   life abandoned 23, 62, 112, 133–4
World Bank 17–18, 33, 86, 99–102,
   107, 234, **240**
world economies 84–5, **106**

World Trade Organization 17–18, **33**,
   86, 101, 234, **240**
World Wars 51
worship of lesser gods 246
Wren, Sir Christopher (1632–1723)
   179
Wright, Joseph (1734–97) 202, **220**
WTO *see* World Trade Organization

yobbery 22, **33**, 131, 135, 246–8,
   281–2
York, Archbishop of 250, 260, **260**
young poor 50, 71, 108–10, 114, **153**
'youth' 245

Zak, Paul 172
Zeigler, Philip 12
Zimbabwe 100, **107**
Zola, Emile (1840–92) 270

THE SOCIAL AFFAIRS UNIT

THE TIMES **WRITES**
'The Social Affairs Unit is famous for driving its coach and horses through the liberal consensus, scattering intellectual picket lines as it goes. It is equally famous for raising questions which strike most people most of the time as too dangerous or too difficult to think about.'

THE SOCIAL AFFAIRS UNIT
Morley House, Regent Street, London W1B 5SA

www.socialaffairsunit.org.uk